Arthur Herbert Dyke Acland

A handbook in outline of the political history of England to 1890

Arthur Herbert Dyke Acland

A handbook in outline of the political history of England to 1890

ISBN/EAN: 9783337132125

Printed in Europe, USA, Canada, Australia, Japan

Cover: Foto ©ninafisch / pixelio.de

More available books at **www.hansebooks.com**

A HANDBOOK IN OUTLINE

OF THE

POLITICAL HISTORY OF ENGLAND

TO 1890

Chronologically arranged

BY

ARTHUR H. DYKE ACLAND, M.P.

HON. FELLOW OF BALLIOL COLLEGE, OXFORD

AND

CYRIL RANSOME, M.A.

MERTON COLLEGE, OXFORD; PROFESSOR OF MODERN HISTORY AND ENGLISH LITERATURE
YORKSHIRE COLLEGE, VICTORIA UNIVERSITY

FIFTH EDITION

LONDON
LONGMANS, GREEN, AND CO.
AND NEW YORK: 15 EAST 16TH STREET
1891

CONTENTS.

	PAGE
Explanations	xv
List of Genealogies	xvi

PART I. GENERAL OUTLINE.

	PAGE			PAGE
Roman Empire and Early English History to Egbert	3	Henry III.,	1216	33
		Edward I.,	1272	39
Egbert,	802 . . 5	Edward II.,	1307	43
Ethelwulf,	839 . . 5	Edward III.,	1327	45
Ethelbald,	858 . . 7	Richard II.,	1377	49
Ethelbert,	860 . . 7	Henry IV.,	1399	53
Ethelred I.,	866 . . 7	Henry V.,	1413	55
Alfred,	871 . . 7	Henry VI.,	1422	57
Edward the Elder,	901 . . 7	Edward IV.,	1461	65
Athelstan,	925 . . 9	Edward V.,	1483	67
Edmund,	940 . . 9	Richard III.,	1483	67
Edred,	946 . . 9	Henry VII.,	1485	69
Edwy,	955 . . 9	Henry VIII.,	1509	71
Edgar,	959 . . 11	Edward VI.,	1547	77
Edward,	975 . . 11	Mary,	1553	79
Ethelred II.,	979 . . 11	Elizabeth,	1558	79
Edmund,	1016 . . 13	James I.,	1603	85
Canute,	1017 . . 13	Charles I.,	1625	87
Harold I.,	1035 . . 13	The Commonwealth,	1649	101
Hardi Canute,	1040 . . 15	Charles II.,	1660	107
Edward the Confessor,	1042 . . 15	James II.,	1685	115
Harold II.,	1066 . . 15	William and Mary,	1689	119
William I.,	1066 . . 17	Anne,	1702	125
William II.,	1087 . . 19	George I.,	1714	129
Henry I.,	1100 . . 19	George II.,	1727	133
Stephen,	1135 . . 21	George III.,	1760	139
Henry II.,	1154 . . 23	George IV.,	1820	171
Richard I.,	1189 . . 27	William IV.,	1830	177
John,	1199 . . 29	Victoria,	1837	187

PART II. SUMMARIES.

SECTION A. SUMMARIES WHICH EXTEND MORE OR LESS OVER THE WHOLE COURSE OF THE HISTORY.

			PAGE
Parliament, Part	I. (Preliminary) to 1295		233
,,	,, II. 1295-1430		233
,,	,, III. 1430-1689		235
,,	,, IV. 1689-1832		237
,,	,, V. 1832-1881		238

CONTENTS.

		PAGE
Ecclesiastical, Part I. to 1070		239
,, ,, II. 1070-1527		239
,, ,, III. 1527-1559.	The Reformation	241
,, ,, IV. 1559-1661.	Section A, Church; Section B, Nonconformists	243
,, ,, V. 1661-1881.	Section A, Church; Section B, Nonconformists	244
Wales, 577-1543		246
Scotland, Part I. To 1290		247
,, ,, II. 1290-1603		248
,, ,, III. 1603-1707		250
,, ,, IV. 1707-1881		252
Ireland, ,, I. To 1494		252
,, ,, II. 1494-1801		253
,, ,, III. 1801-1882		254
Law Courts, 1107-1881		256
Army, 1073-1881		257

SECTION B. SUMMARIES WHICH BELONG TO SPECIAL PERIODS.

Gradual Union of England into one Kingdom, 449-827	259
The Northmen in England, (1) 787-897; (2) 907-937; (3) 980-1017	259
The Union of Normandy and England, 1002-1071	261
Struggle between the Kings and the Feudal Nobility, 1074-1174	262
Laws, Codes, and Charters up to the time of the Great Charter, c. 600-1215	262
The Hundred Years' War between England and France, 1338-1453	262
York and Lancaster, 1385-1563	264
The Council to 1641	266
American War of Independence, 1764-1783	266
Jacobites, 1691-1807	267
French War, 1793-1815	268
Catholic Relief, 1778-1829	270
Corn Laws, 1815-1846	272
India, 1600-1881	273
Reform, 1745-1881	275

APPENDICES.

I. List of some of the Chief Officials in Church and State to the beginning of Queen Anne's reign	279
II. Table of the Members of the House of Lords at various times	284
III. Table of the number of Members of the House of Commons, and their distribution, at various times	285

INDEX	289

PREFACE.

It is hoped that this little book may be found useful to those who are interested in English Politics, and to the general reader of English History and Political Biography. It may tend to give clearness and exactness of outline where, for those who have not unusually good memories, there may be an occasional haziness. As a companion to larger books, it may supply in a small space information which is not always readily at hand. We believe, also, that those who are specially interested in the politics of the last half century, may find here, within moderate limits, an adequate statement of the more important facts.

The method of arrangement alone can be called original. The facts are the common property of all who read or write about history. To verify these facts, however, a good deal of trouble has been taken, and in the very many cases where historians differ as to their account of an event, or as to the date given for it, we have tried, by going to the sources of history, to ascertain the truth. Except where we have through inadvertence made absolute mistakes, it may be assumed that both the form of expression used and the date assigned have been chosen after some careful study, though in a work of this kind it has not been possible to explain the reasons of our choice.

The right-hand page alone of Part I. contains the continuous outline of events arranged in chronological order. On the left is a selection of foreign and colonial events, as well as various notes and quotations, to the number of which the reader may add considerably, in the blank spaces, by notes and observations of his own. The Summaries which are contained in Part II. are collections of events arranged for clearness' sake, in their own connection, under various selected heads, such as

PREFACE.

"Parliament," "Ireland," "The Corn Laws." With a few exceptions these events have been already mentioned in the General Outline.

Many may differ from us at various points about our selection or omission of events. Our general principle has been to keep clearly in view, as our main object, the development of the political history of England, and especially the growth of the English Constitution. We have omitted therefore, with reluctance, but for clearness' sake, many social, literary, and other facts of great importance in their bearing upon the general growth of the nation.

We have been led also to believe, from the encouragement given us by various teachers, and from use made in teaching of part of the work privately printed, that the book may be found useful as a kind of syllabus, or outline for building upon, in lecturing and class-teaching. It would appear that of late oral teaching by means of simple lectures has gained ground, as a method of instruction, in our Public Schools and High Schools, in preference to the method of only asking questions upon a previously prepared portion of a text-book.

For many reasons it might be desired that the course of history-teaching in higher schools should be wider than it is at present, that it should be more European, less insular, and that ancient, mediæval, and modern history should be taught as parts of one continuous whole. The outlines of "world history" may be taught very early in the course of a child's education, first in their simplest form, conveying perhaps little more than an idea of the distance of events from one another. As time goes on these outlines may be more and more filled in. That the value of such a system is considerable, the results of much of the higher school teaching in France and Germany show.

But in any case it would seem that the method of teaching the whole outline from the beginning, and steadily and systematically filling in that outline in its various parts, is to be preferred as a method to that of stimulating interest in various isolated portions of the history, without being first sure that the general outline of the "before and after" has been grasped.

While a multitude of histories of persons and periods, excellently written, are put into the hands of young people, the dry bones of history are rather at a discount. The old unintelligent schoolroom drill, which involved learning strings of dates, had, with many disadvantages, at least some advantages. And a boy or girl may be better prepared to take an intelligent interest in history in the future if they know, so that they will never forget them, the dates of the Kings of England, of some leading events, and of the Prime Ministers from Walpole to the present time, than if they have been prematurely interested in the detail of special periods, to the exclusion of a knowledge of the general outlines. If the outlines have been insisted on and intelligently taught, the interest in private reading of history, for its own sake, will be increased rather than lessened.

At present English history is the only part of modern history which is largely taught in schools. One of the main advantages for teaching purposes of English history is its continuity. If this continuity is lost sight of it is a great disadvantage to the learner. The *grammar*, or continuous outline of English history, may be taught while the memory is fresh and strong, and on this foundation the knowledge of the whole constitutional and political history may be gradually built up. Our aim, however inadequately carried out, has been to keep this principle of continuity in view; not to encourage "cram," except so far as this sometimes misused word may include accurate and well-arranged knowledge.

The present book, of course, could only be used by the higher forms in schools. Should it be thought desirable, an abridged form, on exactly the same method, would be published, and a third form simpler still. In this way, the same plan being preserved, the pupil would advance from the simplest outline, not to a new book, but merely to one containing additional facts surrounding the old facts, and thus confusion of ideas would be avoided.

PREFACE.

It may be said that all abstracts of history should be made by pupils themselves, but the use of a book like this, by way of grammar or for reference, in no way precludes the pupil from making abstracts of his text-book or of larger books, which, when independently done, will often be of more use than any ready-made analysis.

At the risk of apparent presumption, it has seemed well to explain as clearly as we could the way in which, as it appeared to us, this book might be made useful in the teaching of history.

We have to acknowledge the useful criticisms of Mr. Watson, Fellow of B.N.C., Oxford, and Mr. York Powell of Christ Church, Oxford, and also the help of Mr. Beaven of Preston, Lancashire, who has generously placed at our disposal many of the results of his learned studies in English political history, but who is in no way responsible for any errors that we may have made.

We shall be grateful to any one who will take the trouble to call our attention to any mistakes which may, notwithstanding a good deal of care, have crept into the book.

September 1881.

PREFACE TO THIRD EDITION.

In bringing out a New Edition of this work, we have carried the Chronological Table down to the close of the year 1887, and have, where needful, brought forward the Summaries to the same date. With a view to making reference more easy we have added an Index, in which we have attempted to make amends for the necessary brevity of the titles given in the text, by supplying the full name, initials, or rank needful for the identification of the individuals mentioned. Our thanks must again be given to many friends who have aided us with advice or corrections.

March 1888.

EXPLANATIONS.

PART I. GENERAL OUTLINE.

RIGHT-HAND PAGE.
1. A *second column* has been introduced into this page for Prime Ministers at the year 1721.
2. *Differences of type.* Many of the more important events and the names of leading persons, especially at their first appearance, are in darker type. A very few events of great importance are in large capitals. Events which are specially connected with Constitutional History are in *italics* when not already in larger type.
3. Reference, when it seemed useful, has been occasionally made in the course of the Outline to the *Summaries*, generally at the point where a Summary or a section of a Summary ends.

LEFT-HAND PAGE.
1. The "*Foreign*" column (which becomes "*Foreign and Colonial*" after 1600) contains a selection of foreign events which have a special connection with English History, together with a few general foreign events of leading importance. The arrangement of Irish and Scotch events has presented some difficulty. It has been thought best to consider, as a general rule, purely Scotch events foreign up to 1707, and purely Irish events foreign up to 1800. [Those more important events abroad which form an integral part of the general course of English History are to be found on the right-hand page.]
2. The "*Notes*" column. Various notes have been added, and space has been left for the addition of more notes at various points. From 1721 lists of the *Ministries* have been added in the Notes. These lists do not pretend to be exhaustive, nor are they restricted to the members of Cabinets only. The names of the leading Ministers have been given, and subordinate Ministers whose names afterwards became well known are often mentioned. Members of Cabinets in the Ministries of the last quarter of a century are indicated by an asterisk.

Several blank pages are left at the end of the General Outline for the insertion of such current events as the reader may think of sufficient importance to be entered.

PART II. SUMMARIES.

A complete list of Summaries will be found in the Table of Contents, and also at the beginning of Part II. As a rule, the facts mentioned in the Summaries have already appeared in the General Outline. Where there are exceptions to this rule, this is usually indicated either by a special note or by the use of brackets. Space is left by the side of the Summaries for various additions.

LIST OF GENEALOGIES GIVEN IN THE NOTES TO PART I.

	PAGE
Genealogy of the Early English Kings	4
,, Danish Kings	12
,, Norman Dukes	14
,, Norman Kings	16
,, Kings of the Scots to Alexander III.	18
,, Kings of France to Philip IV.	20
,, Counts of Anjou	22
,, English Kings from Henry II. to Henry III.	22
,, English Kings from Henry III. to Henry IV.	34
Claims of Balliol and Bruce	40
Genealogy of Kings of Scotland from 1306	42
,, English Kings from Edward III.	44
,, French Kings from Philip VI.	46
Claim of Edward III.	46
Genealogy of John de Montfort	46
The Yorkist Line	50
Genealogy of the Warrennes and Arundels	52
The Lancastrian Line	52
Genealogy of the Dukes of Burgundy	58
,, the Beauforts	60
,, the Woodvilles	64
,, the Staffords	66
,, the De la Poles	68
,, Charles V.	70
,, the Tudors	70
,, the Poles	74
,, the Howards	76
,, the Dudleys and the Sydneys	76
,, the Suffolks	76
,, the Guises	78
,, French Kings from Henry II. to Henry IV.	80
,, Darnley	80
,, Henry IV.	80
,, William III. of England	82
,, the Russells	114
,, the Stuarts	116
,, the Churchills and Godolphins	120
Pedigree to illustrate the War of the Spanish Succession	124
Genealogy of the Carterets and Granvilles	134
,, the Fox Family	136
,, the Grenvilles and Pitts	144
,, the House of Hanover	158
,, the Bentincks and Cannings	164
,, the Napiers	198

PART I.

GENERAL OUTLINE.

[Notes.]

FOREIGN.

c. 450. St. Patrick converts the Irish.

c. 500. The Scots invade Caledonia, and expel the Picts from the west.

529. Benedict founds his monastery at Monte Cassino.

590. Gregory the Great becomes Pope.

632. Mohammed (born 571) dies.

ROMAN EMPIRE.

B.C.	
55.	Cæsar's first invasion of Britain.
54.	Cæsar's second invasion of Britain.
30.	Augustus becomes Emperor of Rome.

A.D.	
43.	Claudius begins the conquest of Britain.
50.	Defeat of Caractacus.
61.	Conquest of the Druids of Mona by Suetonius Paullinus. Death of Boadicea.
78-84.	Rule of Agricola, and complete conquest of Britain.
81.	Building of Agricola's line of forts between the Firths of Clyde and Forth.
121.	Building of Hadrian's Walls between the mouth of the Tyne and the Solway Firth.
211.	Death of the Emperor Severus at York.
306.	Constantine is proclaimed Emperor in Britain.
401.	The Roman legions are withdrawn from Britain.
410.	Rome is sacked by the Goths. Honorius releases the Britons from their allegiance.

[400—655] ENGLISH.

c. 400.	The English begin to settle in Britain.
449.	The kingdom of **Kent** is begun.
477.	The kingdom of **Sussex** is begun by Elle and his son Cissa.
495.	The kingdom of **Wessex** is begun by Cerdic and his son Cynric.
520.	Arthur defeats the English at Badbury in Dorset (Mons Badonicus).
547.	The kingdom of **Northumbria** is begun.
577.	Battle of Dyrham. The West Saxons divide the West Welsh from the North Welsh by taking Bath, Gloucester, and Cirencester.
597.	**Conversion of Ethelbert, King of Kent, by Augustine.**
c. 600.	*Ethelbert issues the first English laws that have come down to us.*
	Supremacy of Northumbria.
603.	Defeat of the Scots by Ethelfrith, King of the Northumbrians, at Dagsastan.
607.	Battle of Chester. The Northumbrians divide the North Welsh from the Strathclyde Welsh.
617.	Edwin, King of Northumbria, subdues all England except Kent.
627.	**Conversion of Edwin by Paullinus.**
633.	Battle of Hatfield. Edwin is defeated and killed by Penda, King of Mercia. Flight of Paullinus.
634.	Aidan, from Iona, reintroduces Christianity at Lindisfarne, under King Oswald.
635.	Birinus begins the **conversion of Wessex.**
642.	Battle of Maserfield. Oswald is killed by Penda.
655.	Battle of Winwidfield. Penda is killed by Oswy.

[Notes.]   FOREIGN.

718-755. Boniface, the English "Apostle of the Germans," follows up the earlier work of Irish missionaries in Germany.

(a) GENEALOGY OF THE EARLY ENGLISH KINGS.

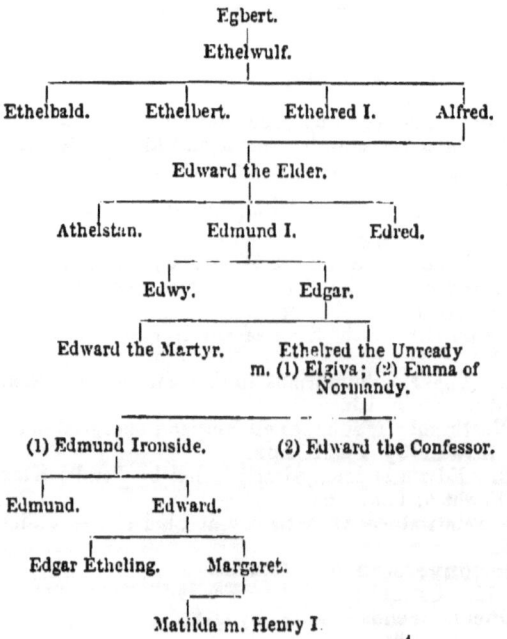

782. Alcuin, the Englishman, joins the court of Charles the Great.

795. Invasion of Ireland by the Northmen.

800. Charles the Great is crowned emperor.

843. Union of Picts and Scots under Kenneth II.

661.	Wulfhere, King of Mercia, ravages Wessex.
664.	Conference of Welsh and Roman priests at the Synod of Whitby. The Roman ritual and time for keeping Easter are adopted.
668.	Arrival of **Theodore** of Tarsus, Archbishop of Canterbury, who organizes the National Church.
681.	**Wilfrid**, driven from the bishopric of York, **converts the South Saxons.**
685.	Egfrith, King of Northumbria, is defeated and killed by the Picts.

End of the Supremacy of Northumbria.

687.	Death of Cuthbert, Bishop of Lindisfarne.
688.	*Ine* becomes King of the West Saxons, and *publishes his laws.*
728.	Ine dies at Rome.
731.	The Venerable Bede finishes his History; and dies, 735.
737.	Ethelbald of Mercia ravages Northumbria.
752.	Cuthred, King of the West Saxons, defeats Ethelbald at Burford.
755.	*Sigebert, King of Wessex, is deprived of his throne by the Witan.*

Supremacy of Mercia.

757.	Offa becomes King of Mercia.
774.	Offa defeats the men of Kent at Otford.
777.	Offa defeats Cynewulf of Wessex at Bensington.
779.	Offa makes his dyke, from the Dee to the Wye, to protect Shrewsbury and his other conquests from the Welsh.
786.	Egbert, heir to the throne of Wessex, driven into exile by Brithric, takes refuge with Charles the Great.
787.	Lichfield is made an archbishopric with the leave of Pope Hadrian. **First Invasion of the Northmen.**
796.	Death of Offa.

EGBERT, 802—839 (37 Years) (a).

802.	Egbert becomes King of the West Saxons.
825.	Egbert defeats the Mercians at Ellandun.

Supremacy of Wessex.

826.	The men of Kent, Sussex, Essex, and East Anglia submit to Egbert.
827.	Egbert conquers the Mercians, and the Northumbrians submit to him. [See *Summary: Gradual Union of England into One Kingdom,* p. 259.]
836.	Egbert defeats the Northmen and West Welsh at Hengest's Down, on the Cornish side of the Tamar.
837.	Egbert is succeeded by his sons, Ethelwulf in Wessex as overlord, Ethelstan as underking of Kent, Sussex, and Essex.
839.	Egbert dies, and is succeeded by his son Ethelwulf.

ETHELWULF, 839—858 (19 Years).

847.	Ealstan, Bishop of Sherborne, and Osric defeat the Northmen at the mouth of the Parret.
851.	Ethelwulf defeats the Northmen at the battle of Ockley in Surrey.

[Notes.]

FOREIGN.

872. The Northmen come from Ireland and ravage Scotland.
876. Rollo, the Northman, overruns Normandy.

(a) *Peace of Wedmore.*—The boundary was to be, according to the Peace, "up on the Thames and then up on the Lea, and along the Lea unto its source, then right to Bedford, then up on the Ouse unto Watling Street."

855.	The Northmen for the first time remain over the winter in Sheppey.
856.	Ethelwulf on his return from Rome marries Judith, daughter of Charles the Bald, King of the Franks.
858.	Ethelwulf is succeeded by his son, Ethelbald.

ETHELBALD, ETHELBERT, AND ETHELRED I., 858—871 (13 Years).

860.	Ethelbald is succeeded by his brother Ethelbert. The Northmen sack Winchester.
865.	The Northmen ravage Kent.
866.	Ethelbert is succeeded by his brother Ethelred.
867.	The Northmen passing from East Anglia take York.
868.	The Northmen take Nottingham.
870.	The Northmen defeat and kill Edmund, King of East Anglia.
871.	The Northmen invade Wessex. Battle of Englefield, Northmen defeated. ,, Reading, ,, victorious. ,, Ashdown, ,, defeated. ,, Basing, ,, victorious. ,, Merton, ,, victorious. Ethelred is succeeded by his brother Alfred.

ALFRED, 871—901 (30 Years).

	Battle of Wilton, Northmen victorious. Peace between the Northmen and the West Saxons.
872.	Peace between the Northmen and the Mercians.
875.	Halfdene, the Northman, ravages Northumbria.
876.	**The Northmen apportion Northumbria.**
877.	**The Northmen apportion Mercia.**
878.	The Northmen under Guthrum invade Wessex. Alfred retreats to Athelney. Battle of Ethandun, English victorious.
879.	Peace of Chippenham (or Wedmore) (*a*). England north of Watling Street is ceded to the Danes.
880.	**The Northmen apportion East Anglia.**
c. 890.	*Alfred issues his laws.*
893.	The Northmen defeated at Louvain, passing from Boulogne, ravage England again, assisted by the new Northmen settlers. [Much fighting all over England for four years.]
897.	Alfred builds a new fleet and stops the invasions.
901.	Alfred is succeeded by his son Edward the Elder.

EDWARD THE ELDER, 901—925 (24 Years).

	Ethelwald, son of Ethelred I., rebels, and flies to the Northmen of Northumbria.
905.	Ethelwald is killed in battle with the Kentishmen.

[Notes.]

(a) This was the district often known as that of the Five Burghs (Leicester, Lincoln, Nottingham, Stamford, and Derby).

(b) Athelstan, through the marriages of his sisters, is brother-in-law to Charles the Simple, King of the West Franks, Lewis, King of the Lower Burgundy, Hugh, the Great Duke of the French, and the Emperor Otto the Great.

FOREIGN.

913. Rollo is recognised by Charles the Simple as Duke of Normandy. He and his people become Christian.
918. The Northmen's host from Gaul tries to invade the west of England, but is driven off and goes to Ireland.

907.	Ethelfleda, the Lady of the Mercians, sister of Edward, fortifies Chester.
910.	War with the Northmen renewed.
912.	Edward recaptures London.
913.	Edward fortifies Hertford and Witham. Ethelfleda fortifies Tamworth and Stafford.
914.	,, fortifies Warwick.
916.	,, defeats the Welsh.
917.	,, captures Derby.
918.	Leicester surrenders to Ethelfleda, and the men of York make a treaty with her. She dies at Tamworth. Mercia is annexed to Wessex.
919.	Edward captures Bedford.
921.	East Anglia and Essex submit to Edward.
922.	Edward captures Stamford. The district south of the Humber submits (a). The North Welsh seek Edward for lord.
923.	Edward advances into Northumbria and captures Manchester.
924.	Edward fortifies Nottingham. The Scots, Northumbrians, and Strathclyde Welsh choose Edward for father and lord.
925.	Edward is succeeded by Athelstan.

ATHELSTAN, 925—940 (15 Years).

926.	The Cornishmen, Scots, South Welsh, and Northumbrians swear faithfulness to Athelstan at Earnot.
937.	Anlaf, with Northmen from Ireland, joined by Constantine, King of Scots, and by the Strathclyde Welsh, is defeated at Brunanburh by Athelstan.
940.	Athelstan (b) is succeeded by his half-brother Edmund.

EDMUND, 940—946 (6 Years).

945.	Edmund conquers Cumberland and gives it to Malcolm, king of Scots, on military tenure.
946.	Edmund is succeeded by his brother Edred. Rise of **Dunstan.**

EDRED, 946—955 (9 Years).

955.	Edred is succeeded by Edwy (son of Edmund), whose younger brother Edgar is underking in Mercia.

EDWY, 955—959 (4 Years).

956.	Dunstan is banished.
957.	All England north of Thames revolts and chooses Edgar to be king in his own right, who recalls Dunstan.

[Notes.] FOREIGN.

962. Otto the Great, King of Germany, is crowned Emperor at Rome.

975. The Danes, now separated from the other Northmen of Norway and Sweden, have to do homage to the Emperor Otto II.

984. Brian Boru becomes supreme king in Ireland.

1014. The Northmen are defeated at the battle of Clontarf, the turning-point of their conquests in Ireland, but the death of Brian Boru plunges the country into anarchy.

EDGAR, 959—975 (16 YEARS).

959.	Edwy dies, and Edgar is chosen king of all the English.
960.	**Dunstan, Edgar's Prime Minister, becomes Archbishop of Canterbury.** He assists the monastic revival.
	Pacification of England by Edgar.
966.	Edgar divides Northumbria, and grants Lothian to Kenneth, King of Scots, to be held by him as his man.
973.	The triumph of Edgar at Chester.
	[*Edgar's Ordinance of the Hundred and other Laws, 959—975.*]
975.	Edgar is succeeded by his son Edward.

EDWARD, 975—979 (4 YEARS).

	[Struggle of the secular clergy and the feudal lords of the south of England against the monks and the yeomen of the north.]
979.	Edward is murdered. Ethelred, his half-brother, is chosen king at the age of ten.

ETHELRED II., 979—1016 (37 YEARS).

980.	**The invasions of the Northmen begin again, and continue for thirty-six years.**
988.	**Dunstan dies.**
991.	Battle of Maldon. Northmen victorious, *Danegeld paid (ten thousand pounds) by decree of the Witan, for the first time.*
994.	Sweyn, King of the Danes, and Anlaf, King of the Norwegians, attack London, receive money (sixteen thousand pounds) and food, and pass the winter at Southampton. Anlaf returns to his own country.
1000.	Ethelred ravages Cumberland.
1002.	Ethelred marries as his second wife Emma, daughter of Richard I., Duke of Normandy.
	Tribute (twenty-four thousand pounds) is paid to the Danes.
	Massacre of Danes on St. Brice's Day.
1003.	Sweyn in revenge invades England again.
1007.	Edric Streona is made alderman of Mercia. Tribute (thirty-six thousand pounds) is paid again.
1008.	Money is collected to provide a fleet.
1011.	Tribute (forty-eight thousand pounds) is paid again.
1012.	**Murder of Archbishop Alphege by the Danes.**
1013.	Sweyn harries England. Ethelred flies to Normandy, and Sweyn is acknowledged as king.
1014.	Sweyn dies. The Danes choose Sweyn's son Canute, the English Ethelred, for king. Ethelred drives out Canute.
1015.	Canute attacks Wessex. Edric Streona goes over to him with forty ships, and Wessex submits to Canute.
1016.	Canute marches through Mercia to York.
	Ethelred dies.

[Notes.]   FOREIGN.

(a) GENEALOGY OF DANISH KINGS.

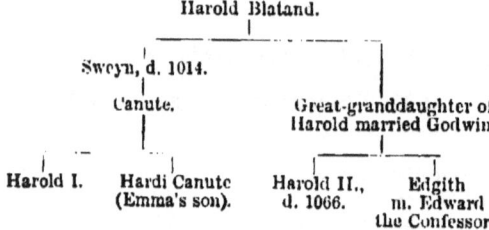

1028. Canute conquers Norway.

1035. William the Conqueror becomes Duke of Normandy.

EDMUND, 1016 (7 Months).

1016.   The people of London choose Edmund, the rest choose **Canute** for king.
Edmund leaves London, which is besieged by the Danes.
Edmund collects an army.
Battle of Pen Selwood.   Danes defeated.
Battle of Shirestone.   Danes defeated.
(Edmund relieves London.)
Battle of Brentford.   Danes defeated.
(Edric Streona joins Edmund.)
Battle of Assandun.   Edmund defeated by the treachery of Edric Streona.
Partition of England.   Edmund has Wessex, Essex, and East Anglia; Canute, Mercia and Northumbria.
Edmund, having reigned seven months, is murdered.

CANUTE, 1017—1035 (18 Years) (a).

1017.   Canute is chosen king.   [See *Summary: The Northmen in England,* p. 259.]
Canute divides England into four parts, retains Wessex, sets Edric Streona over Mercia, Thurkill over East Anglia, and Eric over Northumbria.
Canute marries Emma, widow of Ethelred.
Edric Streona is put to death.
Leofric becomes Earl of the Mercians.
1018.   *A Witan is held and Edgar's law renewed.*
1019.   Canute goes to his kingdom of Denmark.
1020.   **Godwin is made Earl of Wessex.**
1027.   Canute makes a pilgrimage to Rome, and is present at the coronation of the Emperor Conrad.
1029.   Canute returns to England.
1031.   Canute goes to Scotland, and Malcolm submits to him as his overlord.
[Malcolm had obtained possession of Lothian, which had been apparently lost by the Scots since Edgar's reign, and he did homage for it now as an English earldom.]
1035.   Canute dies.
[His dominions are divided between his three sons.   Sweyn has Norway; Hardi Canute has Denmark.   England is divided; north of the Thames it acknowledges Harold Harefoot, south of the Thames Hardi Canute, who is represented by Earl Godwin and his mother, Emma.]

HAROLD I., 1035—1040 (5 Years).

1036.   Edward and Alfred, sons of Ethelred and Emma, come over from Normandy to Wessex.   Alfred is blinded, and dies.   Edward returns.

[Notes.] | FOREIGN.

(a) GENEALOGY OF NORMAN DUKES.

Rollo.
|
William Longsword.
|
Richard I.
|
┌─────────┴─────────┐
Richard II.   Emma (wife of Ethelred
| and Canute).
|
Richard III.   Robert the Devil.
                   |
               William the Conqueror.

1056. Malcolm Canmore becomes King of Scotland.
1060. Philip I. becomes King of France.

1037.	Harold Harefoot is chosen king of all England, and Emma is driven out.
1040.	Harold Harefoot dies.

HARDI CANUTE, 1040—1042 (2 YEARS).

1041.	Hardi Canute sends to Normandy for his half-brother Edward.
1042.	Hardi Canute dies.

EDWARD THE CONFESSOR, 1042—1066
(24 YEARS).

	Edward the Confessor is chosen king.
1044.	Robert of Jumièges (the first Norman bishop in England) is appointed Bishop of London. Other foreigners obtain influence in the kingdom.
1045.	Edward marries Edgith, daughter of Godwin.
1051.	Robert of Jumièges is made Archbishop of Canterbury.
	Eustace of Boulogne, on a visit to Edward, quarrels with the men of Dover. Godwin refuses to punish them. The king calls on Siward of Northumbria and Leofric of Mercia for aid. Godwin leaves the kingdom.
	William of Normandy (a) visits Edward.
1052.	Godwin and his family return, and the foreigners are outlawed and take to flight. Stigand is made Archbishop of Canterbury.
1053.	Godwin dies. Harold his son becomes Earl of Wessex.
1054.	Earl Siward, in the interest of Malcolm, defeats Macbeth.
1055.	Earl Siward dies, and Tostig, son of Godwin, becomes Earl of Northumbria.
	Expedition of Harold against the Welsh.
1057.	Edward, the son of King Edmund, returns to England. Leofric, Earl of Mercia, dies, and is succeeded by Alfgar, his son.
1063.	Harold again invades Wales with Tostig. Griffith the king is soon afterwards slain by his own men.
1065.	Tostig is expelled by the Northumbrians, and Morcar, son of Alfgar and grandson of Leofric, made earl.
1066.	Jan. 5. Death of Edward the Confessor.

HAROLD II., 1066 (10 MONTHS).

Harold is crowned king at Westminster.
William of Normandy sends to claim the crown, and is refused.
Harold collects an army, and fortifies the southern coast.
Sept. 20. Tostig and Harold Hardrada, King of Norway, land in Yorkshire, and defeat Morcar and his brother Edwin, Earl of Mercia, at Fulford.
Sept. 25. Tostig and Harold Hardrada are defeated and killed by Harold at Stamford Bridge.

[Notes.] | FOREIGN.

(a) GENEALOGY OF NORMAN KINGS.

```
                    William the Conqueror.
      ┌──────────────┬──────────────┬──────────┐
Robert of Normandy.  William II.  Henry I.   Adela.
      │                           m. Matilda.
      │              ┌─────────────┬──────────┐
Robert of Gloucester.  William,   Matilda    Stephen.
                      d. 1120.   m. (1) Emperor
                                    Henry V.
                                 (2) Geoffrey
                                    of Anjou.
                                      │
                                    Henry II.
```

(b) *English Bishoprics existing at the Conquest* (see also note (d), p. 72)—

    Canterbury
    London
    Rochester
    York
    Winchester   } Founded before Egbert.
    Dorchester
    Hereford
    Lichfield
    Worcester
    Wells.
    Durham.
    Thetford, afterwards Norwich.

Bishoprics which became extinct before or during the reign of William I.—

    Dunwich.
    Lindisfarne.
    Elmham, afterwards Thetford.
    Lindsey.
    Hexham.
    Leicester.
    Whithern.
    Selsey, afterwards Chichester.
    Sherborne, } afterwards Salisbury.
    Ramsbury }
    Crediton, afterwards Exeter.

(c) *William also laid down certain rules for the Church*—
1. That no Pope or Papal Letters or Papal Legate should be received in England without his leave.
2. That no synod should be called or enact anything without his leave.
3. That no baron or servant of his should be excommunicated without his leave.

1070. Malcolm of Scotland marries Margaret, sister of Edgar Etheling.

1073. Gregory VII. (Hildebrand) becomes Pope (to 1085).

1066.	*Sept.* 28. William of Normandy lands at Pevensey. *Oct.* 14. **BATTLE OF HASTINGS. DEATH OF HAROLD.** **Edgar Etheling**, grandson of King Edmund, is chosen king by the Witan in London. William marches to Berkhampstead to cut off London from the north. Edgar Etheling, Edwin and Morcar, and the men of London submit to William.

WILLIAM I., 1066—1087 (21 Years) (*a*).

Born 1027; Married, 1053, Matilda of Flanders.

	Dec. 25. William is crowned at Westminster.
1067.	William visits Normandy, leaving Odo, Bishop of Bayeux, and William Fitz-Osbern in England. Rebellions in Kent and Hereford. Edgar Etheling takes refuge in Scotland.
1068.	William subdues Exeter, and the insurrection in the west. The people of Northumberland rebel and call in Edgar Etheling; they are subdued by William. Harold's sons ravage Bristol and Wales, but have to retire to Ireland. Malcolm of Scotland makes peace, and does homage for Cumberland.
1069.	**Great rising of the north**, with the assistance of the Danes and of Edgar Etheling. William retakes York, and ravages the country between the Humber and the Tees.
1070.	Stigand is deposed, and **Lanfranc is made Archbishop of Canterbury.** Several bishoprics and many abbeys are filled up (*b*). [See *Summary: Ecclesiastical, Part I.*, p. 239.] *The laws of the English are declared by twelve men elected from each shire.* [At the end of this year only two bishoprics remain in native hands.]
1071.	**Last struggle for independence.** Edwin is killed. Morcar joins Hereward, who is defeated by William. [See *Summary: Union of Normandy and England*, p. 257.]
1072.	William invades Scotland, and Malcolm "becomes his man."
1073.	William leads an English army into Maine, and conquers it.
1074.	**Conspiracy of the Norman earls.** Ralf Guader and Roger of Breteuil rise in arms. Waltheof, the son of Earl Siward, refuses to join them.
1076.	Execution of Waltheof. William refuses the demand of fealty, made through a legate, by Gregory VII. (*c*).
1078.	**Rebellion of William's son Robert**, supported by Robert of Bellême, Robert Mowbray, and others.
1079.	William besieges Robert at Gerberoi; Robert submits.
1082.	Bishop Odo, Earl of Kent, is apprehended, and his possessions seized by William.
1084.	*William renews the Danegeld* (which Edward the Confessor had abolished), *demanding* 6*s.* *per hide instead of* 2*s.*

[Notes.]

FOREIGN.

(a) GENEALOGY OF KINGS OF THE SCOTS TO ALEXANDER III.

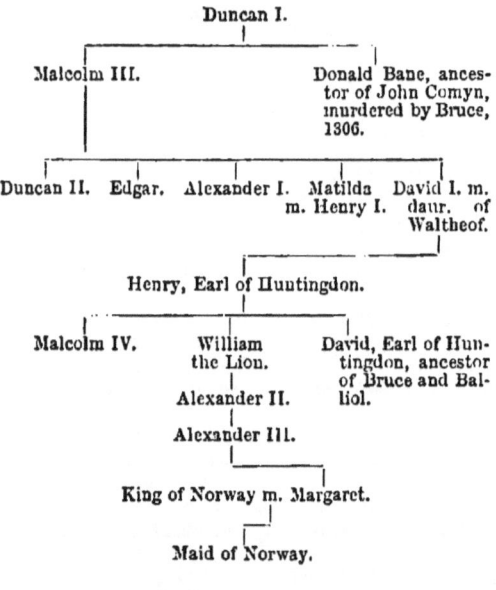

(b) *Charter of Henry I.*

1. The Church is to be free, and all bad customs are to be abolished. The king will not take advantage of the vacancy of sees and benefices.
2. Reliefs and amercements are to be just and lawful. The heiresses and widows to tenants-in-chief are not to be given in marriage against their will. Tenants-in-chief are to be guided by the same rules in reference to the mesne tenants. Personal property may be disposed of by will.
3. The forests are to remain in the king's hands.
4. Lands held by knight-service are to be free from other imposts.
5. The laws of Edward the Confessor are to be retained, with William the Conqueror's improvements.

1089. Robert of Normandy quarrels with his brother Henry, and imprisons him.

1093. Malcolm Caumore killed, and is succeeded by Donald Bane.

1096. Robert of Normandy goes on the first crusade.
1097. Donald Bane is deposed, and Edgar is established on the throne of Scotland by his uncle, Edgar Etheling.
1099. Jerusalem is taken by the Crusaders. A Christian kingdom is founded there.

1085.	A general survey of England is ordered by William. *It is taken by inquest. Each hundred and township appears by representative jurors.*
1086.	**Domesday Book,** *the result of the survey, is produced. At William's great court at Salisbury all the landholders of England swear allegiance to him.*
1087.	William makes war upon Philip, King of France, and burns Mantes. William dies. Robert succeeds to Normandy. [By an undated charter of this reign *spiritual jurisdiction is separated from the secular courts of law, and assigned to separate spiritual courts.*]

WILLIAM II., 1087—1100 (13 Years).
Born c. 1060.

	William hastens to England, and is elected king by the influence of Lanfranc.
1088.	Rebellion of Normans, headed by Odo of Bayeux and Roger, Earl of Shrewsbury. William appeals to the English, and suppresses it.
1089.	**Lanfranc** dies. The see of Canterbury is vacant four years.
1090.	William makes war on Robert in Normandy. William grants land in Wales to any one who will take it, and in consequence a war of conquest goes on for many years.
1091.	Treaty between William and Robert arranged by the barons. Malcolm of Scotland, in alliance with Edgar Etheling, invades England (*a*). William compels him to do homage.
1092.	William takes possession of Cumberland, and settles peasants from Hampshire at Carlisle.
1093.	**Anselm becomes Archbishop of Canterbury.**
1094.	**Ranulf Flambard becomes justiciar,** and helps William in his work of systematic extortion. William refuses to give Anselm the temporalities of his see. William, fighting with Robert, sends for 20,000 men. Flambard collects them at Hastings, deprives them of their journey money, dismisses them, and sends the money to the king.
1095.	The rebellion of Robert Mowbray, Earl of Northumberland, and Norman nobles is crushed.
1096.	Robert pledges his duchy to William for money to go on a crusade.
1097.	Anselm, unable to bear the wickedness of William, retires to Rome.
1100.	William is killed in the New Forest.

HENRY I., 1100—1135 (35 Years).
Born 1068; Married { 1100, Matilda of Scotland. { 1121, Adela of Louvain.

Henry is chosen king, and crowned. He grants a charter (*b*). Ranulf Flambard is arrested.

[Notes.] | FOREIGN.

(a) The election of bishops is to be in the hands of the Chapters, but held at the King's Court; the consecration in the hands of the archbishop and bishops; and the temporal estates are to be conferred by the king.

(b) GENEALOGY OF KINGS OF FRANCE TO PHILIP IV.

Hugh Capet.
|
Robert.
|
Henry I.
|
Philip I.
|
Louis VI.
|
Louis VII.
|
┌─────────────────┴─────────────────┐
Margaret m. Henry, son of   Philip (II.) Augustus.
Henry II. of England. |
                                  Louis VIII.
                                    |
                                  Louis IX.
                                    |
          ┌─────────────────────────┴─────────────────┐
        Philip III.   Robert, Duke of Clermont, ancestor of the Bourbons.
          |
        Philip IV.   Charles, Count of Valois, ancestor of the house of Valois.

(c) *Stephen's Charter.*
All the good laws and customs of Henry I. and Edward the Confessor are to be observed, and the breakers of them are to be punished.

1107. Edgar of Scotland dies, and is succeeded by Alexander.
1108. Philip of France dies, and is succeeded by Louis VI. (the Fat) (b).

1122. The Concordat of Worms between Pope Calixtus II. and the Emperor Henry V.
1124. Alexander of Scotland dies, and is succeeded by his brother David.

1137. Louis VI. dies, and is succeeded by Louis VII.
1138. Defeat of David I. of Scotland (1124-1153), who administers the northern counties till the end of his reign, his son Henry having received the earldom of Northumberland from Stephen.

1100.	Anselm is recalled. **Henry marries Matilda, daughter of Malcolm of Scotland.**
1101.	Robert comes to England and claims the crown, but the English support Henry. A treaty is made, and Robert withdraws.
1102.	**Robert of Belléme rebels,** and is expelled from England.
1103.	Anselm differs with Henry about investiture, and leaves England.
1104.	Robert of Belléme having been received in Normandy, war breaks out.
1105.	Henry settles Flemings in Pembrokeshire.
1106.	Battle of Tenchebrai. Robert is captured, and Henry subdues the whole of Normandy.
1107.	**Anselm and Henry agree on terms** (*a*). **Roger of Salisbury becomes justiciar.** He organizes the Curia Regis and founds the Court of Exchequer.
1109.	**Anselm dies.**
1114.	Henry's daughter, Matilda, marries the Emperor Henry V.
1116.	Great council at Salisbury. Homage is done to William, son of Henry, by the Normans.
1117.	Henry goes to Normandy for the war with France, Anjou, and Flanders, and remains three years.
1118.	Henry defeats at Brenville his rebellious barons and Louis of France, who with Robert of Flanders and Fulk of Anjou has supported William, the son of Robert.
1120.	Peace is made, and Henry returns to England. **His son William is drowned.**
1121.	Henry marries Adela of Louvain.
1123.	Rebellion in Normandy in favour of William, son of Robert, led by Count Waleran.
1125.	Henry, the emperor, husband of Matilda, dies.
1126.	The council of the realm swear to receive Matilda as their future sovereign.
1128.	Matilda marries Geoffrey of Anjou. William, son of Robert, in asserting his claims to Flanders, is killed at Alost.
1131.	Fealty is again sworn to Matilda.
1133.	A son (afterwards Henry II.) is born to Matilda, and fealty again sworn to her.
1135.	Robert of Normandy dies in prison. Henry dies.

STEPHEN, 1135—1154 (19 YEARS).

Born c. 1094; Married, 1124, Matilda of Boulogne.

1136.	Stephen is received as king in England and accepted in Normandy. Stephen grants a charter (*c*).
1138.	Robert, Earl of Gloucester, natural son of Henry I., throws off his fealty to Stephen. David of Scotland, uncle of Matilda, defeated at the battle of the Standard, near Northallerton.

[Notes.] FOREIGN.

(a) Roger, Bishop of Salisbury, Chaplain and Treasurer to Henry I., and after his accession Justiciar, had been Henry's right-hand man, and his family had in their hands the whole organization of the Curia Regis and Exchequer Court.

(b) GENEALOGY OF COUNTS OF ANJOU.

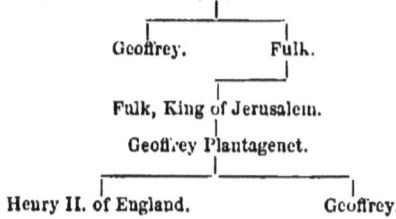

Ermengard, heiress of Anjou, m. the Count of Gâtinais.
— Geoffrey. Fulk.
— Fulk, King of Jerusalem.
— Geoffrey Plantagenet.
— Henry II. of England. Geoffrey.

(c). *Foreign Dominions of Henry II.*

Normandy and Maine, *from his mother.*
Anjou and Touraine, *from his father.*
Poitou,
Saintonge,
Limousin,   } *from his wife.*
Guienne,
Gascony,

(d) GENEALOGY OF ENGLISH KINGS FROM HENRY II. TO HENRY III.

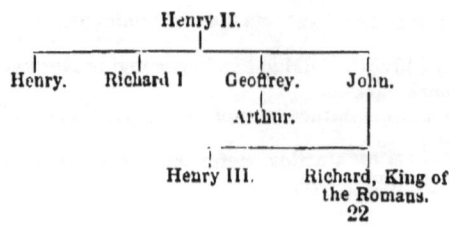

Henry II.
— Henry. Richard I. Geoffrey. John.
— Arthur.
— Henry III.   Richard, King of the Romans.

1147. Second crusade preached by St. Bernard.
1151. The Irish Church is organized by a bull of Pope Eugenius III.
1152. Frederic Barbarossa becomes Emperor (to 1190).
1153. David of Scotland dies, and is succeeded by Malcolm IV.

Adrian IV., Nicholas Breakspear, Pope, 1154-1159.
1154. Adrian IV. bestows Ireland upon Henry II. by the bull *Laudabiliter.*

1159. Double election to the Papacy, Alexander III. and Victor IV.

1139.	Stephen arrests the **Bishop of Salisbury** (the justiciar) (*a*), his son (the chancellor), and his nephew (the Bishop of Lincoln). The Bishop of Ely, another nephew, is banished.
	Matilda and her brother, Robert of Gloucester, land at Portsmouth. Civil war begins.
1141.	Stephen is captured at Lincoln.
	Henry, Bishop of Winchester, papal legate, brother of Stephen, vexed by his conduct to the bishops, joins Matilda.
	Matilda is acknowledged as queen, but soon estranges her supporters. Routs of London and Winchester.
	Robert of Gloucester is captured and exchanged for Stephen.
1142.	Matilda is besieged at Oxford, and escapes. She leaves England.
1147.	Death of Robert of Gloucester. Many warriors join the crusade.
1151.	Henry, son of Matilda, becomes Duke of Normandy and Count of Anjou.
1152.	**Henry marries Eleanor of Guienne, divorced wife of Louis VII.**, and acquires her provinces.
	The bishops refuse to associate Eustace, the son of Stephen, with him in the kingdom.
1153.	Henry invades England, and renews the war. Eustace dies, and by the **Treaty of Wallingford** Henry is made heir to the throne.
1154.	*Oct.* Stephen dies.

HENRY II., 1154—1189 (35 Years) (*b*).

Born 1133; Married, 1152, Eleanor of Guienne (*c*).

Dec. Henry (*d*) lands in England, is crowned, and issues his charter.

Thomas Becket becomes chancellor.

1155.	Henry resumes the royal demesnes, and destroys many of the newly built castles.
1156.	Henry, on the Continent, drives his brother Geoffrey out of Anjou.
1157.	Henry causes Malcolm, King of Scots, to give up the northern counties and do homage for the earldom of Huntingdon, which David had held in right of his marriage with the daughter of Waltheof.
	Henry's first expedition against Wales.
1158.	Henry goes to France for five years. The queen and the young Prince Henry represent him in England. Henry negotiates a marriage for his son Henry with the daughter of Louis.
1159.	Henry claims Toulouse in right of his wife, and, accompanied by the King of Scots, makes war on the Count of Toulouse. Henry remains on the Continent till 1163, partly engaged in a quarrel with the King of France.
	Scutage (a payment in money instead of military service) *is first regularly instituted.*
1162.	**Thomas Becket is elected Archbishop of Canterbury.** He resigns the chancellorship.
1163.	On *Henry's return a quarrel ensues between him and Becket on a matter of taxation* (probably the exaction of Danegeld).

[Notes.]   FOREIGN.

(a) THE CONSTITUTIONS OF CLARENDON.

1. Disputes about advowsons and presentations to be tried by the King's Court.
2. Criminous clerks to be tried by the king's courts, unless the justice sends the case to the ecclesiastical courts, and clerks thus convicted are to be punished as laymen.
3. No clergyman to quit the realm without the consent of the king.
4. Appeals from ecclesiastical courts to go to the king, and unless he consents that they shall go further, the disputes are to be terminated by his order in the court of the archbishop.
5. No tenant-in-chief or minister of the king to be excommunicated without the consent of the king.
6. Clergy to hold their lands as tenants-in-chief, and to perform all duties and attend the King's Court with the other tenants-in-chief.
7. Elections of archbishops, bishops, and abbots to take place by order of the king in the King's Chapel, and the man elected to do homage for his lands before he is consecrated.
8. Sons of villeins not to be consecrated without the consent of their lords.

1165. Malcolm of Scotland killed, and is succeeded by William the Lion.

1166. Henry's son Geoffrey marries Constance, heiress of Brittany.

1169-70. The Normans, under Robert Fitz-Stephen and Richard Fitz-Gilbert, surnamed Strongbow, and Maurice Fitz-Gerald, at the invitation of Dermot, gain a footing in Ireland for the first time.

(b) List of Earldoms of England in 1174.

Arundel.	Huntingdon.
Chester.	Leicester.
Cornwall.	Norfolk.
Derby.	Northampton.
Devon.	Oxford.
Essex.	Pembroke.
Gloucester	Salisbury.
Hertford.	Warwick.

1163.	Three months later a quarrel arises about the jurisdiction over criminous clerks.
1164.	**THE CONSTITUTIONS OF CLARENDON** (a). Becket accepts them. The quarrel is renewed at the Council of Northampton. Becket's enemies intrigue against him. Becket leaves the kingdom. The struggle continues for six years.
1165.	Expedition against Wales.
1166.	*The Assize of Clarendon.* It rearranges the provincial administration *of justice.* *A jury of presentment is ordered in criminal cases.* *General visitation of England by two justices.* Henry is absent from England for four years. Frederic Barbarossa proposes to Henry to support the anti-pope. Henry arranges his daughter's marriage with Henry the Lion of Germany.
1167.	Louis VII. of France, who supports Pope Alexander III., gives shelter to Becket.
1169.	Peace is concluded between Louis and Henry.
1170.	Henry returns to England. All the sheriffs are removed (officers of the Exchequer being substituted), and an inquiry made into their accounts. Henry, the king's son, is crowned in England by Roger, Archbishop of York. Becket and Louis VII. are indignant. Henry hastens to be reconciled with Becket, who returns to England and excommunicates Roger and the other opposing bishops. **Becket is murdered at Canterbury.**
1171.	Henry goes over to Ireland, and his supremacy is acknowledged by the chiefs.
1172.	Henry leaves Ireland for Normandy, and there submits to the representative of Pope Alexander III., clearing himself of the death of Becket.
1173.	Henry the younger flies to the court of Louis of France. Queen Eleanor tries to join him, but is taken and imprisoned during the rest of the king's life. **General league against Henry** by the king's sons (Henry, Richard, and Geoffrey), Louis of France, the Count of Flanders, the King of Scotland, the Norman barons, and others. Henry defeats the French and Bretons in Normandy. Richard de Lucy and William Mandeville defeat the insurgent barons in England. The Scots invade England.
1174.	The king comes to England, and does penance at Becket's tomb. The English and Welsh remain faithful. William the Lion, King of Scotland, is captured at Alnwick, and the insurgent barons in Norfolk are put down. Hugh Bigod and other rebels submit (b). [See *Summary: Struggle between Kings and Feudal Nobility*, 1074-1174, p. 202.] Peace is made, and Henry returns to the Continent. William the Lion is set free on condition of doing homage for the kingdom of Scotland, and the castles of Lothian are placed in English hands (by the Treaty of Falaise).

[Notes.] | FOREIGN.

(*a*) "Their work was to hear all suits that were brought before the king, not only criminal but civil; . . . all the business, in fact, which came at a later period before the Courts of King's Bench, Exchequer, and Common Pleas" (*Stubbs*).
Exchequer business had already existed as a special department since Henry I.

1180. Louis VII. of France dies, and is succeeded by Philip Augustus.

1187. Jerusalem taken by the Saracens.
1189. Third Crusade.

(*b*) *List of Crusades.*

First Crusade, 1095-1099.
Second Crusade, 1147-1149.
Third Crusade, 1189-1192.
Fourth Crusade, 1204.
Fifth Crusade, 1216-1220.
Frederic II. goes to Jerusalem, 1228.
Sixth Crusade, 1248-1254.
Seventh Crusade, 1270.

Albigensian Crusade, 1208-1229.

1190. Henry VI. Emperor (to 1197).

(*c*) "The establishment of the corporate character of the city under a mayor marks the victory of the communal principle over the more ancient shire organization. . . . It also marks the triumph of the mercantile over the aristocratic element" (*Stubbs*).

1175.	Henry returns to England, and remains two whole years.
1176.	*The Assize of Northampton.* *It gives instructions to itinerant justices, which are carried out by six detachments of justices sent on circuits.* The marriage of Henry's daughter with the King of Sicily is arranged.
1177.	John, son of Henry, is nominated Lord of Ireland. Henry arbitrates between Castile and Navarre.
1178.	*A selection of five judges (a) is made from the Curia Regis, out of which are afterwards developed the Courts of King's Bench and Common Pleas. The highest appellate jurisdiction is reserved to the king in the Ordinary Council.*
1179.	**Richard de Lucy** (who has been justiciar for twenty-five years) retires, and is succeeded by **Ranulf de Glanvill**.
1180.	Henry goes to Normandy, and of the remaining nine years of his reign spends only two and a half in England in four different visits.
1181.	The Assize of Arms is issued to regulate the national fyrd (or militia).
1183.	War between Henry's sons. Their revolt against him. Henry, eldest son of the king, dies.
1184.	*Assize of the Forest, to regulate the management of the royal forests.*
1186.	Geoffrey, the king's son, dies.
1188.	*Saladin tithe. First tax upon personal property.*
1189.	Henry is expelled from Touraine by his son Richard and Philip of France, who are abetted by John. Henry dies. [*By the Great Assize established in this reign recognition by jury in civil cases is allowed (as a substitute for trial by battle).*]

RICHARD I., 1189—1199 (10 Years).

Born 1157 ; Married, 1191, Berengaria of Navarre.

Richard receives investiture of Normandy, and comes over to England, where he is crowned.
He persecutes the Jews, raises money for the crusade (*b*), and releases William the Lion from his engagement with Henry II.
He leaves England only to return once for two months in 1194.

1190.	**William Longchamp**, the chancellor, becomes justiciar and papal legate. John, brother of Richard, receives a large grant of land. *Sept. 14.* Richard, going on the third crusade, reaches Messina. Glanvill and Baldwin, the archbishop, die in the Holy Land.
1191.	Queen Eleanor leaves England for Sicily, and takes Berengaria of Navarre, whom Richard marries in Cyprus. Richard arrives at Acre. *July 12.* Acre is taken. Geoffrey, Archbishop of York, and John combine with the barons against Longchamp, who is expelled, and retires to Normandy, and is succeeded in the government as justiciar by Walter of Coutances, Archbishop of Rouen. The communa (or corporation) of London is first legally recognised (*c*).
1192.	*Oct. 9.* Richard sails from Acre, and on his way home is seized

[Notes.] | FOREIGN.

(a) *Richard I.'s Ransom.*

1. Aid 20s. on the knights' fee.
2. Tallage on towns and demesne lands of the Crown.
3. Hidenge } Taxes on land, taking the place of
4. Carucage } Danegeld.
5. A quarter of the movables of every person in the realm.

(b) *Growth of the Towns.*

"If these are the predecessors of the twenty-five aldermen of the wards, the year 1200 may be regarded as the date at which the communal constitution of London was completed" (*Stubbs*).

"The two limits of municipal change between the reign of Henry III. and that of Henry VII. may be simply stated.

"In 1216 the most advanced among the English towns had succeeded in obtaining, by their respective charters and with local differences, the right of holding and taking the profits of their own courts under their elected officers, the exclusion of the sheriff from judicial work within their boundaries, the right of collecting and compounding for their own payments to the crown, the right of electing their own bailiffs, and in some instances of electing a mayor; and the recognition of their merchant guilds by charter, and of their craft guilds by charter or fine. The combination of the several elements thus denoted was not complete. . . .

"At the close of the period (the reign of Henry VII.) the typical constitution of a town is a close corporation of mayor, aldermen, and council, with precisely defined numbers and organization, not indeed uniform, but of the same general conformation; possessing a new character denoted by the name of corporation in its definite legal sense; with powers varying in the different communities which have been modified by the change, and in practice susceptible of wide variations" (*Stubbs*).

(c) COUNTS OF BRITTANY.

Allan Fergant.
|
Conan III.
|
Bertha.
|
Conan IV.
|
Geoffrey m. Constance.
of England. |
Arthur

1197. Philip of Suabia (to 1208) and Otto IV. (to 1215) become rival Kings of Germany.

1198. Innocent III. becomes Pope (to 1216).

1204. Fourth Crusade.

	by Leopold, Duke of Austria, and handed over to the Emperor Henry VI.
1193.	John does homage to Philip of France for Normandy.
	Richard's ransom is raised by five different kinds of taxes (a).
	Hubert Walter, Archbishop of Canterbury, Glanvill's nephew, succeeds Walter of Coutances as justiciar.
1194.	Richard is set at liberty.
	He comes back to England, and raises more money by sales and extortion. He is crowned a second time.
	He goes to Normandy in May, and is reconciled to John, and does not return to England again.
	He engages in a series of wars with Philip of France till his death.
1195.	Hubert Walter by his heavy exactions excites the discontent of the poorer citizens of London, led by William Fitz-Osbert.
1197.	Richard builds Château Gaillard on the Seine above Rouen.
1198.	*Hugh of Avalon, Bishop of Lincoln, refuses to pay money to support the war in France, considering himself bound to render military service in England only.*
	Geoffrey Fitz-Peter succeeds Archbishop Hubert as justiciar.
	A carucage is assessed before knights elected in behalf of the shire.
1199.	Richard is mortally wounded at Chaluz, and dies.

JOHN, 1199—1216 (17 Years).

Born 1167; Married { 1189, Hadwisa of Gloucester.
{ 1200, Isabella of Angoulême.

	John is acknowledged in Normandy, and receives the surrender of Anjou and Maine, while Eleanor secures for him Poitou and Guienne.
	Arthur, son of Geoffrey and Constance, takes refuge at the court of Philip.
	Archbishop Hubert, William Marshall, and Geoffrey Fitz-Peter, at Nottingham, secure the election of John as King of England.
	Archbishop Hubert becomes chancellor.
1200.	Philip makes peace with John, and acknowledges him as king.
	John divorces his wife Hadwisa, and marries Isabella of Angoulême, the betrothed of Hugh, Count de la Marche.
	Twenty-five citizens are chosen to help the mayor in the care of the city of London (*b*).
1202.	Philip summons John for oppressing the barons of Poitou.
	John refuses to appear, and Philip and Arthur attack his dominions.
1203.	Arthur having been captured by John, disappears (*c*).
	Philip summons John to answer for Arthur's death, and in default of John's appearance attacks Normandy.
1204.	Queen Eleanor dies.
	Philip takes Normandy, Maine, Anjou, and Touraine.
1205.	**Archbishop Hubert Walter dies.**
	The younger monks of Canterbury elect their sub-prior, Reginald; the elder, the king's nominee, John de Grey, Bishop of Norwich. The suffragan bishops put in a claim, and all three parties appeal to Rome.

[Notes.]

(a) "To the first representative assembly on record is submitted the first draught of the reforms afterwards embodied in the Charter" (*Stubbs*).

(b) PROVISIONS OF THE GREAT CHARTER.

1. *Church.*

General statement of its freedom, especially in election of bishops.

2. *Feudalism.*

a. Remedy of feudal abuses in reliefs, wardships, marriage, and collection of debts.
b. No aids or scutages to be collected by the king from the tenants-in-chief, except the regular three (to ransom the lord's body, for the knighting of his eldest son, and for the marriage, once, of his eldest daughter).
c. Mesne (or under) tenants to have the same advantages from their lords.

3. *Constitutional.*

Any other aids or scutages are to be voted by a council of prelates and greater barons summoned separately, and of lesser barons and tenants-in-chief summoned by writ addressed to the sheriff in the county court.

4. *Justice.*

a. Common Pleas shall not follow the King's Curia, but be held in one fixed place (Westminster).
b. Recognition of *novel disseisin* (recent eviction), *mort d'ancester* (inheritance of real property), *darrein presentment* (last presentation to a living), to be tried by a jury at the county court, before the king's judges and four knights of the shire chosen by the shire, every quarter; and amercements are not to be ruinous, but fixed by a jury of equals of the condemned.
c. No sheriff, coroner, constable, or bailiff of the king is to try pleas of the Crown (*i.e.* criminal prosecutions carried on in the name of the Crown).
d. No man is to be imprisoned, outlawed, punished, or molested but by the judgment of his equals, or by the law of the land.
e. The sheriffs and officers are to know the law of the land.

5. *General.*

a. The writ "præcipe" (*i.e.* for calling cases into the King's Court) is not to be used.
b. Goods of those who die without a will are to go to their heirs.
c. Ferms (fixed taxes) of the shires are not to be increased.
d. All goods seized by the king's purveyors to be paid for.
e. All are to have their choice of payment or labour in person, if work is to be done for the king.
Merchants are to come in and out of the kingdom freely.

6. *Forests and Rivers.*

a. All forests made in the last reign are to be disforested, and all rivers opened for navigation.
b. The forest abuses are to be inquired into by twelve sworn knights.
c. Forest law is only to apply to those who live in forests.

7. *Temporary.*

a. The king will give back all charters to their owners.
b. Foreign mercenaries and officers are to be dismissed.
c. Justice is to be done to the Welsh, and to the King of Scots.
d. The charter is to be carried out by twenty-five barons, of whom the Mayor of London is one.

FOREIGN.

1214. William the Lion of Scotland dies, and is succeeded by Alexander II.

1215. Lateran Council. Trial by ordeal abolished. This causes the substitution in England of trial by a petty jury in criminal cases.
Frederic II. (Emperor) is crowned King of Germany at Aix-la-Chapelle (dies 1250).

1206.	Innocent III. causes the monks of Canterbury at Rome to elect **Stephen Langton**.
1207.	Innocent consecrates the new archbishop.
1208.	John refusing to receive him, **England is placed under an interdict**.
1209.	John marches to the north, and receives homage (which he had received also in 1200) from the King of Scotland, such homage as was received before the Treaty of Falaise. John is excommunicated by Innocent, and in revenge seizes the property of the bishops.
1210.	John goes to Ireland.
1211.	Innocent threatens to depose John, and to employ Philip to do the work. Wales, taking advantage of the threat, makes war on John.
1213.	**John** is reconciled to the Church, receives Langton, and **does homage for his kingdom to the Pope**, binding himself to an annual payment of 1000 marks. English victory over the French fleet at Damme. John proposes to invade France, but the barons refuse to follow him because he is excommunicated. Archbishop Langton absolves him, but the barons again refuse because their tenures forbid them. *Aug.* 4. *First united representation of townships on the royal demesne; four men and the reeve are summoned from each township to the assembly at St. Albans called to estimate the damage due to the bishops, and for other business* (a). *Aug.* 25. At a council at St. Paul's the charter of Henry I., which had been mentioned by the justiciar at St. Albans, is produced by Stephen Langton. **Geoffrey Fitz-Peter** dies, and **Peter des Roches**, Bishop of Winchester, becomes justiciar. *Nov.* 7. *Each sheriff is directed to send four discreet men of the shire to consult with the king at Oxford.*
1214.	The battle of **Bouvines**. Otto the Emperor, the Count of Flanders, and the Earl of Salisbury, John's half-brother, are defeated by Philip of France. John, being in Poitou, and hearing of the battle, makes peace, and returns to England.
1215.	John grants to the Church freedom of election to episcopal sees and religious houses, demands an oath of allegiance throughout England, and takes the cross for the crusades. The barons collect an army, and are received in London. *June* 15. John is forced to sign **THE GREAT CHARTER** at Runnymede. [(b) and *Summary: Laws, Codes, and Charters up to* 1215, p. 262.] John collects mercenaries under Falkes de Breauté. Pandulf, the papal legate, excommunicates the chief leaders of the barons. Archbishop Langton goes to Rome. Innocent disallows the Great Charter, excommunicates John's enemies, and suspends Langton. The barons offer the crown to Louis, son of Philip of France. [The first preserved national record in French belongs to this year.]

[Notes.]

a) From this time the Archbishops of Canterbury on appointment always become "legati nati," but this does not preclude the sending of legates "a latere" from Rome.

FOREIGN.

1216. Fifth Crusade.
July. Death of Innocent III.
Confirmation of the Order of Dominican Friars (1216) and Franciscans (1223) by the Pope.

1221. Joan, sister of Henry III., marries Alexander II. of Scotland.
1223. Philip Augustus dies, and is succeeded by Louis VIII.
1226. Louis VIII. dies, and is succeeded by Louis IX.
1227. Gregory IX. Pope (to 1241).

1216.	John marches as far as Berwick, and subdues the northern barons. *May* 21. **Louis himself lands in England,** and captures Winchester. Almost all the barons desert John. The King of Scots comes to Dover to do homage to Louis. John marches north to cut off his retreat, and dies at Newark, October 19.

HENRY III., 1216—1272 (56 Years).
Born 1207; Married, 1236, Eleanor of Provence.

	Henry is crowned at Gloucester, and does homage to the legate. [*The permanent continual Council (whence arose later the Privy Council) attending the king dates its importance from this time.*] **William Marshall,** Earl of Pembroke, is elected regent. The Great Charter is republished, with the omission of the clauses about taxation and the national Council. Louis maintains himself in the eastern counties.
1217.	*May.* Battle of Lincoln. The king's party victorious. *Aug.* **Hubert de Burgh** destroys the French fleet. Treaty of Lambeth. The departure of Louis is arranged. *The Charter of Forests deals with the abuses of the forest-land.*
1219.	**Death of William Marshall the regent.** **Peter des Roches, Pandulf,** and **Hubert de Burgh** act as the king's guardians.
1221.	Resistance to the king's guardians. Pandulf resigns his commission. William of Aumale is brought to submission. Langton obtains a promise from the Pope, that as long as he lives no other papal legate shall be sent (*a*).
1224.	Falkes de Breauté, at this time sheriff of six counties, falls, and with him the influence of foreigners brought in by John.
1225.	Expedition to France. Gascony is secured to the English.
1226.	The Pope's demand for the revenue of a prebend in every cathedral, and an equal contribution in every monastery, is rejected.
1227.	Henry declares himself of age to govern, and continues Hubert de Burgh as justiciar, who administers for five years. Peter des Roches goes to the crusade, and stays away four years.
1228.	One of the series of petty wars against the Welsh, who throughout this reign support the opposition barons. **Death of Archbishop Langton.**
1229.	*The Pope, Gregory IX., levies a tenth of all property, which the barons resist, but the clergy have to grant.*
1230.	Henry goes to France, marches to Poitou and Gascony, where he receives homage.
1231.	Return of Peter des Roches.
1232.	**Fall of Hubert de Burgh, the last great justiciar.** [**Twenty-six years of bad government under Henry follow.**] Peter des Roches obtains influence, and **the Poitevins** begin to receive offices. Opposition formed, headed by **Richard Marshall,** second son of the late regent.

[Notes.]

FOREIGN.

1235. Henry III.'s sister marries the Emperor Frederic II.

(a) GENEALOGY OF ENGLISH KINGS FROM HENRY III. TO HENRY IV.

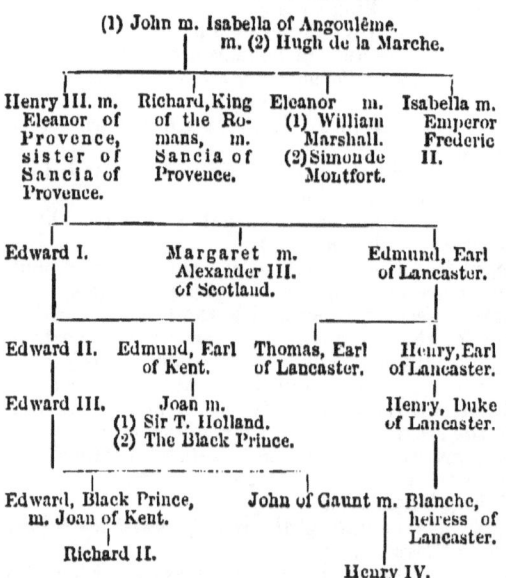

1241. Defeat of the Mongols at Liegnitz.

1243. Innocent IV. Pope (to 1254).
1245. Council of Lyons.

1248. Sixth Crusade.
1249. Alexander II. of Scotland dies, and is succeeded by Alexander III.
1251. Alexander III. marries Margaret, daughter of Henry III.
1254. Alexander IV. Pope (to 1261).
Death of Conrad IV.

1233.	Richard Marshall is declared a traitor. Peter des Roches denies his right to be tried by his peers. Richard takes refuge in Wales, is joined by Hubert de Burgh, and defeats the king and the Poitevins.
1234.	Richard Marshall is killed by treachery in Ireland. **Edmund Rich**, Archbishop of Canterbury, insists upon the dismissal of Peter des Roches.
1236.	The king marries Eleanor of Provence. Her uncle, William of Valence, with the **Provençals**, obtains great influence in England.
1237.	The king's extravagance forces him to ask for a large grant. *A grant of a thirtieth of movables is made.* Cardinal Otho arrives as papal legate, and continues the papal exactions, which cause great irritation among clergy and people.
1238.	Henry marries his sister Eleanor (widow of William, eldest son of William Marshall, the late regent) to **Simon de Montfort** (a).
1240.	Simon de Montfort, in disgrace with the king, leaves England for two years.
1241.	**Boniface of Savoy**, the queen's uncle, **is chosen Archbishop of Canterbury**, and consecrated 1245. Peter of Savoy, another uncle, is made Earl of Richmond. Loss of Poitou.
1242.	Expensive expedition of Henry to Gascony in support of his stepfather. Indecisive battles of Taillebourg and Saintes.
1243.	Henry returns, followed by a new band of **Poitevins**.
1244.	*The earls, barons, and bishops, including Cornwall, de Montfort, Grossetête (Bishop of Lincoln), and Cantilupe (Bishop of Worcester), meet in parliament, and demand control over the appointment of ministers.* Similar demands and complaints are made by parliaments in following years.
1246.	At the Council of Lyons the English complain that 60,000 marks a year go into the hands of the Pope and the foreigners.
1247.	Henry's half-brothers, including another William of Valence, and Ethelmer (made Bishop of Winchester) arrive in England.
1248.	Simon de Montfort assumes the government of Gascony.
1250.	Henry takes the cross, and the Pope allows him to exact money from the clergy.
1252.	*A writ is issued for the enforcing of Watch and Ward and the Assize of Arms.*
1253.	In return for a grant Henry confirms the charters for the sixth time.
1254.	*First summons to Parliament by royal writ of two knights of the shire.* **The crown of Sicily** having been refused by Richard, the king's brother, **is accepted from the Pope** by Edmund, the king's son, then nine years old. The Pope, with Henry's name and credit, makes war in Sicily.
1255.	*Parliament again demands the appointment of ministers, but is refused.*
1256.	*All persons owning property of £20 a year are forced to receive knighthood.* The claim to "annates" is first made in England by Pope Alexander IV. for five years.

[Notes.]

(a) "The king was helplessly in debt; when he returned from Gascony he had spent 350,000 marks, now 140,000 more were gone, and it was calculated that since his wasteful days began he had thrown away 950,000 marks" (*Stubbs*).

(b) *Provisions of Oxford.*
1. A temporary committee of twenty-four is appointed to reform grievances in Church and State.
2. A permanent body of fifteen is to act as council to the king.
3. The fifteen are to hold three annual parliaments and to communicate with a body of twelve representing the barons.
4. Another body of twenty-four is to negotiate financial aids.

(c) *Provisions of Westminster.*
These embody the grievances of the barons stated at Oxford, and mainly concern the administration of justice and local government by the sheriffs.

(d) Mise=misa=a capitulation or arbitration.

(e) By this new arrangement the council of nine replaced the council of fifteen, and also took into their hands the appointment to all offices of State which had formerly been in the king's hands.

(f) *The Dictum of Kenilworth.*
1. Re-established Henry in his full authority.
2. Proclaimed an amnesty for the rebels on payment of a fine.
3. Annulled the Provisions of Oxford, and the conditions recently forced on the king.
4. Provided that the king should keep the charter which he had freely sworn to.

FOREIGN.

1257. Richard, Henry's brother, is chosen King of the Romans.

1268. Death of Conradin and end of the Hohenstaufen.
1270. Seventh and last Crusade. Louis IX. dies, and is succeeded by Philip III.

1257.	The king tells the Parliament that his debts to the Pope amount to 135,000 marks (a). The clergy grant 52,000 marks. **Simon de Montfort** quarrels with William of Valence, the king's half-brother, and **assumes the leadership of the Opposition.**
1258.	The Mad Parliament meets at Oxford and presents its grievances. A committee of twenty-four is chosen to reorganize the government. It draws up the **PROVISIONS OF OXFORD** (b). Many foreigners leave England. Henry and his son Edward (aged nineteen) swear to accept the Provisions. In accordance with the Provisions of Oxford, *the four knights of each shire present their complaints against the sheriffs.*
1259.	The slowness of the council of fifteen in proceeding with reforms causes a quarrel between Simon de Montfort and Richard of Clare, Earl of Gloucester, head of the barons. The provisional government makes a treaty of its own with France. The Provisions of Westminster are agreed to by the king (c).
1261.	Henry receives from the Pope absolution from his oath to accept the Provisions.
1262.	The Earl of Gloucester dies, and his son Gilbert (aged nineteen), the new earl, takes the side of de Montfort.
1263.	Henry refuses to confirm the Provisions, and the quarrel is referred to St. Louis of France.
1264.	By the Mise of Amiens (d) St. Louis sets aside the Provisions. War breaks out. **Battle of Lewes.** The barons are victorious, and the king and Prince Edward give themselves up by the Mise of Lewes. De Montfort, Gloucester, and Stephen Berksted, Bishop of Chichester, are elected to appoint a council of nine to manage the government (e).
1265.	*A parliament meets, to which are summoned two knights from each county, and for the first time representatives from cities and boroughs.* **Quarrel between de Montfort and Gloucester.** Prince Edward escapes, and defeats de Montfort's son at Kenilworth. **Battle of Evesham, Simon de Montfort is defeated and killed.**
1266.	**The Dictum of Kenilworth** (f) restores the government to the king.
1267.	In the Parliament of Marlborough the Provisions of Westminster are renewed by the king and re-enacted as a statute.
1268.	Prince Edward takes the Cross and goes on the Crusade in 1270.
1271.	Death of Richard, King of the Romans.
1272.	Death of Henry. [*By the end of this reign the staff of Curia Regis judges is broken up into three distinct bodies for the Courts of Exchequer, King's Bench and Common Pleas.*]

[Notes.] | FOREIGN.

(a) *Statute of Westminster I.*
1. Regulated the freedom of elections.
2. Fixed the occasions and the rates of aids and reliefs.
3. Regulated the law of wreckage and other matters.

(b) Mortmain means the holding of land "*in mortua manu,*" i.e. by a corporation.

1282. The Sicilian Vespers.

1284. The Maid of Norway, granddaughter of Alexander III., is declared heiress to the Scottish throne.
1285. Philip III. dies, and is succeeded by Philip IV. (Le Bel.)
1286. Death of Alexander III. of Scotland.

EDWARD I., 1272—1307 (35 Years).

Born 1239; Married { 1254, Eleanor of Castile. 1299, Margaret of France.

1272.	Edward is proclaimed king in his absence. The Archbishop of York carries on the government with Walter de Merton as chancellor. The barons in person, and the counties through their representatives, swear allegiance to Edward.
1273.	Edward on his return from the Holy Land reduces Gascony. Robert Burnell (**the first great chancellor**) is appointed chancellor.
1274.	Edward settles a commercial dispute with Margaret, Countess of Flanders, and returns to England.
1275.	*The Statute of Westminster I. (a) is passed.*
1277.	Llewelyn having refused to swear allegiance to Edward, and having planned a marriage with the daughter of Simon de Montfort, with a view to continuing the disturbances of the last reign, war breaks out. The Welsh are defeated. Llewelyn keeps only Anglesea and the district of Snowdon.
1278.	Alexander III. of Scotland does homage to Edward for his English fiefs alone, and not for his kingdom. Writs of "quo warranto" are issued to inquire into titles to land. *A writ of distraint of knighthood is issued, by which all possessors of £20 worth of land are compelled to be knighted.*
1279.	*Statute of Mortmain (b) (or de religiosis)* to check the bestowal of estates on religious foundations.
1282.	The Welsh war breaks out again. Llewelyn goes to the south. His brother David, who has been on the English side and has deserted it, raises the north. *The king's treasurer is sent round to negotiate separately with the counties and boroughs for a subsidy.* Llewellyn is killed on the Wye.
1283.	*Two provincial councils, containing representatives from both clergy and laity, meet at York and Northampton, and make various grants.* David is captured, condemned by the assembly of Shrewsbury, and executed.
1284.	The Statute of Wales settles the administration of the country.
1285.	*The Statute of Westminster II. is passed, containing the clause " De Donis," which founded entails, and other important clauses. The Statute of Winchester re-enacts the Assize of Arms, and regulates the militia.*
1286.	Edward goes to Gascony for three years. Edward mediates between France and Aragon.
1289.	Edward returns to England, and banishes and fines the judges for corruption of justice.
1290.	All Jews are ordered to leave England. *The Statute of " Quia Emptores " is passed to prevent subinfeudation.*

[Notes.]

(a) CLAIMS OF BALLIOL AND BRUCE.

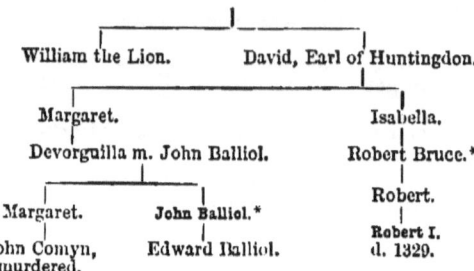

* Competitors for the crown in 1292.

(b) 1. *Barons and Prelates.*—In the writ to the prelates it is said, "As the most righteous law, established by the provident circumspection of the sacred princes, exhorts and ordains that *that which touches all shall be approved by all,* it is very evident that common dangers must be met by measures concerted in common."
2. *Inferior Clergy.*—The bishops are premonished (by the *præmunientes* clause) to bring the heads of the chapters, the archdeacons, one proctor for the clergy of each cathedral, and two for the clergy of each diocese.*
3. *Commons.*—Writs are issued to the sheriff, ordering the election and return of two knights from each shire, two citizens from each city, and two burgesses from each borough.

[From 1295 onwards judges and other members of the ordinary (or permanent) Council have been summoned to Parliament (the Commune Concilium of the Three Estates), not as members of Parliament, but as assistants and advisers.]

* It is found very difficult to induce the clergy to attend as an Estate in Parliament; and from the middle of the fourteenth century their grants are made, as a rule, in Convocation.

(c) *Confirmatio Cartarum.*

1. The charters of liberty and of the forest are confirmed, and all judgments against them are to be void.
2. The recent exactions are not to be made precedents.
3. No aids, tasks, or prizes are to be taken but by the common assent of the realm, and for the common profit thereof, *saving the ancient aids and prizes due and accustomed.**
4. The maletote of wool, a toll of 40s. a sack, is to be discontinued

* In the "De tallagio non concedendo," probably an unauthorized abstract of the Confirmatio Cartarum, this reservation is omitted.

FOREIGN.

1290. Death of Margaret of Scotland.

1294. First alliance between Scotland and France against England.

1295. Members for counties are sent to the Irish Parliament.

1296. Boniface VIII. publishes "Clericis Laicos," which forbids the clergy to pay taxes to the secular power. Balliol's kingdom is treated as a forfeited fief, and John, Earl of Warrenne, appointed by Edward guardian of the kingdom, with Cressingham treasurer and Ormsby justiciar.
1297. Rising of Wallace, who on his victory acts as guardian for Balliol.

1290.	Death of Queen Eleanor. The Scots consent to the marriage between Margaret of Norway, now of Scotland, and Edward, Prince of Wales. [See *Summary, Scotland, Part I.*, p. 247.]
1291.	**Meeting at Norham with the Scots, who acknowledge Edward's claim to decide the question of the succession as overlord** (a).
1292.	Decision in favour of John Balliol, who accepts the kingdom as vassal of England.
1293.	Appeals against Balliol are made to the English law courts. Balliol is summoned to London to answer them. Battle between English and French merchant fleets, the French defeated. Edward summoned to Paris, declines to appear.
1294.	Philip retains the castles of Gascony, which Edward had put into his hands during the negotiations. Extensive seizure of wool by the king. A parliament is assembled in October. *The clergy are forced to grant one-half, the barons and knights of the shire grant one-tenth. By a separate negotiation one-sixth is collected from the towns.*
1295.	**FIRST COMPLETE AND MODEL PARLIAMENT OF THE THREE ESTATES** (b). [See *Summaries, Representation to 1295; and Taxation to 1295,* p. 233.] Invasion of Scotland. Rebellion of Madoc in Wales suppressed.
1296.	Battle of Dunbar. Scots defeated. Surrender of Balliol, who is dispossessed. *Archbishop Winchelsey and the clergy, in accordance with the bull "Clericis Laicos," refuse to grant supplies.* Edward outlaws them.
1297.	Parliament at Salisbury. Edward proposes to go himself to Flanders, while **the Constable, Earl Bohun of Hereford, and the Marshal, Earl Bigod of Norfolk,** are to go with an army to Guienne. They, encouraged by the example of the clergy, *refuse on the ground that they need only follow the king in person.* Edward seizes the wool of the merchants. A military levy of the whole kingdom is called. The two earls still refuse to go, and demand a confirmation of the charters. Edward gets the chief men who had come to the military levy to grant him an aid. The clergy enter into a compromise. Edward goes to Flanders. The two earls forbid the collection of the aid. Battle of Cambuskenneth. Wallace is victorious, and acts as guardian for Balliol. *Parliament summoned. The Prince of Wales confirms the charters, with seven additional articles, which forbid the collection of any taxes without the consent of Parliament.* The **CONFIRMATIO CARTARUM** (c) *is signed by Edward at Ghent.*
1298.	Truce with France. Invasion of Scotland. Defeat of Wallace at Falkirk. Edward attempts the constitutional union of England and Scotland.

41

[Notes.]

(a) Guienne is confirmed to Edward, who marries Margaret, Philip's sister, while Edward, Prince of Wales, is betrothed to Isabella, Philip's daughter.

(b) "The Royal Chancery was now regarded as a resource for equitable remedy against the hardships of the Courts of Westminster, as the Courts of Westminster had been a remedy against the inequalities of the shire-moot" (*Stubbs*).

(c) *Example.*—"In the 29th Edward I. John Lawrence was indicted for the murder of Galfred Doudal. He came and admitted that he had killed him, but said that the said Galfred was a mere Irishman, and not of free blood. The jury found that Galfred was an Englishman, upon which verdict John Lawrence was convicted and hanged" (*Richey*).

(d) KINGS OF SCOTLAND FROM 1306.

Robert I.
|
David II.
|
Margaret m. Walter Stuart.
|
Robert II.
|
———————————————
| |
Robert III.   Robert, Duke of Albany.
| |
| Murdoch, Duke of Albany.
|
———————
| |
David, Duke of   James I.
Rothsay. |
                 James II.
                 |
                 James III.
                 |
                 James IV.

(e) *Ordinances of the Lords Ordainers.*

1. Provision was made for the maintenance of peace and the privileges of the Church, and for the observance of the charters.
2. No gifts were to be made by the king without the consent of the Ordainers.
3. The customs were to be collected by Englishmen and paid into the Exchequer, and the foreign collectors were to give an account of their receipts.

Besides these, Parliament drew up thirty-five articles of reform, stating old grievances and restraining the royal power, especially in the appointment of the great officers of state.

FOREIGN.

1299. Boniface VIII. claims Scotland as a fief of the Papacy.

1301. At this time it is counted no offence in the king's courts to kill an Irishman (c).

1306. Accession of Robert Bruce.

1309. Pope Clement V. goes to live at Avignon. Beginning of "the Babylonish captivity" (1309-1377).

1311. The castle of Linlithgow is taken by the Scots.

1312. Perth surprised by Robert Bruce.

1313. Roxburgh and Edinburgh are taken by the Scots. Stirling is besieged by the Scots under Robert Bruce.

1299.	Comyn is placed by the Scots at the head of a regency for Balliol. Treaty of Chartres (a).
1300.	By the Articuli super Cartas *the Chancery and King's Bench are still to follow the king; and the Exchequer is to remain with the Court of Common Pleas at Westminster* (b).
1301.	Parliament of Lincoln. Final confirmation of the charters. The barons disallow the Pope's claim to Scotland as a fief of Rome.
1303.	The Scots under the Regent Comyn defeat the English. Invasion of Scotland. Edward reduces the country. Wallace is caught and executed, 1305.
1304.	Comyn makes a treaty with Edward.
1305.	Edward gets from the Pope absolution from his engagements of 1297.
1306.	Robert Bruce murders Comyn and rebels. Bruce is crowned at Scone by Wishart (d). Invasion of Scotland. Bruce is defeated, and many of his adherents executed. Edward prosecutes Winchelsey at Rome, who is suspended.
1307.	*The Parliament of Carlisle asks for legislation against provisors, firstfruits, and other exactions of the Papacy.* Edward banishes Gaveston. Edward dies near Carlisle on his road to invade Scotland.

EDWARD II., 1307—1327 (20 Years).

Born 1284; Married, 1308, Isabella of France.

	Piers Gaveston is recalled, made Earl of Cornwall, and enriched. Edward goes to France to do homage, and to be married, leaving Gaveston as governor.
1308.	The Knights Templars are arrested, and their lands seized throughout England. The barons, headed by **Thomas of Lancaster**, demand in council the dismissal of Gaveston. Edward consents, and appoints Gaveston Lord Deputy of Ireland.
1309.	Gaveston returns by agreement of the Baronage at Stamford. Lancaster and others refuse to meet Gaveston in council.
1310.	Gaveston leaves the court. A council meets at Westminster. **Twenty-one bishops and peers are appointed to regulate the king's household, under the name of Lords Ordainers.** Edward and Gaveston invade Scotland.
1311.	Parliament meets and ratifies the ordinances of the Lords Ordainers and banishes Gaveston (e).
1312.	Gaveston is recalled, and excommunicated by Winchelsey. **Thomas of Lancaster**, at the head of the barons, takes up arms and seizes Gaveston. Gaveston is seized by the Earl of Warwick, and executed. The king is forced to promise pardon to the barons.
1313.	Parliament meets and grants the pardons. The king prepares to invade Scotland. **Winchelsey** dies.

[Notes.]

FOREIGN.

1314. Philip le Bel dies, and is succeeded by Louis X.

1315. Edward Bruce invades Ireland, obtains great successes over the colonists, and is joined (1316) by his brother, Robert Bruce.
Louis X. dies, and is succeeded by Philip V.
1317. Robert Bruce returns to Scotland.
1318. Edward Bruce is defeated and killed in Ireland near Dundalk, but great anarchy follows the invasion.
1322. Philip V. of France dies, and is succeeded by Charles V.

(a) A series of six articles were drawn up stating the king's incompetence, his rejection of good counsel, his injustice to the nation and to the Church, and his loss of Scotland, Ireland, and Gascony.

(b) GENEALOGY OF ENGLISH KINGS FROM EDWARD III.

```
                        Edward III.
    |            |              |            |
Edward,      Lionel, Duke of  John of    Edmund, Duke
Black        Clarence,        Gaunt.     of York,
Prince.      ancestor of                 ancestor of
    |        Edward IV.          |       Edward IV.
Richard II.                   Henry IV.
    |                             |
  Henry V.   Thomas,    John,    Humphrey,
    |        Duke of    Duke of  Duke of
 Henry VI.   Clarence.  Bedford. Gloucester.
```

44

[1314—1327]   *ENGLISH.*

1314.	Edward invades Scotland. **Battle of Bannockburn.** The English are totally defeated. Edward is obliged to dismiss his chief officers, and their places are filled up by the nominees of **Thomas of Lancaster, who now obtains the first place in the government.**
1315.	A year of great famine. The Scots ravage Northumberland.
1316.	The Welsh rebel, but are quickly suppressed. A fresh invasion of Scotland is proposed.
1317.	John XXII., now Pope, "reserves" the appointment of eighteen episcopal sees in England in the next seventeen years, in many cases playing into the hands of the king.
1318.	Robert Bruce retakes Berwick and ravages Yorkshire. Lancaster refuses help against Scotland.
1320.	**Hugh Despenser and his son come into power.**
1321.	Parliament at Westminster banishes the Despensers. The queen is refused admission to Leeds Castle, in Kent. This causes a reaction in favour of Edward. War breaks out.
1322.	Edward defeats the Mortimers, recalls the Despensers, defeats Lancaster at Boroughbridge. **Lancaster is executed at Pontefract.** Roger Mortimer is imprisoned. Parliament at York with representatives from Wales, the only time except once before Henry VIII. The Ordinances are revoked. *The principle that what concerns the whole realm must be treated by a complete Parliament is stated.* [*The Commons now finally gain a share in legislation.*] *The wages of members of the House of Commons are fixed at 4s. a day for a knight, and 2s. for a citizen or burgher.*
1323.	Truce of thirteen years with Scotland.
1324.	Roger Mortimer escapes to France.
1325.	The queen being in France about the affairs of Gascony, meets Roger Mortimer. Edward, Prince of Wales, goes to France to swear allegiance for the foreign dominions.
1326.	**The queen, Mortimer, and Edward, Prince of Wales, land in Suffolk.** The elder Despenser is taken, and hanged at Bristol. The king endeavours to escape, but fails; he is captured with the younger Despenser. Despenser is hanged.
1327.	*Jan.* 7. Parliament meets at Westminster. Bishop Orlton asks whether they will have father or son for king. They declare for the son (*a*). The allegiance of Parliament is withdrawn from the king. This is notified to Edward at Kenilworth, who accepts it.

EDWARD III., 1327—1377 (50 YEARS) (*b*).

Born 1312; Married, 1328, Phillippa of Hainault.

Edward is proclaimed king.
[The government is in the hands of Queen Isabella and Roger

[Notes.]

FOREIGN.

(a) GENEALOGY OF FRENCH KINGS FROM PHILIP VI.

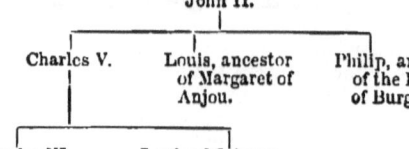

Charles, Count of Valois.
Philip VI., 1328.
John II.

- Charles V.
  - Charles VI.
  - Charles VII.
  - Louis XI.
  - Charles VIII.
- Louis, ancestor of Margaret of Anjou.
  - Louis of Orleans, ancestor of Louis XII. and Francis I.
- Philip, ancestor of the Dukes of Burgundy.

(b) CLAIM OF EDWARD III.

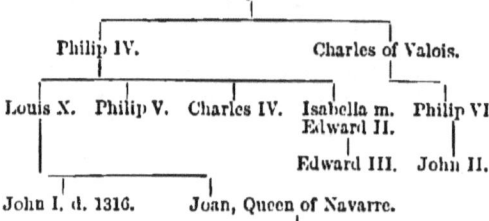

Philip III.
- Philip IV.
  - Louis X.
    - John I, d. 1316.
  - Philip V.
  - Charles IV.
  - Isabella m. Edward II.
    - Edward III.
- Charles of Valois.
  - Philip VI.
    - John II.
  - Joan, Queen of Navarre.
    - Charles the Bad.

(c) These concessions were—
1. That the accounts should be audited by auditors elected in Parliament.
2. That ministers are to be appointed by consultation between the king and his lords, and that when named they are to be sworn before the Parliament to keep the law.
3. That at the beginning of each parliament ministers are to resign their offices into the king's hands and be compelled to answer their complaints.

The proceedings of the Parliament of 1341 are of very great significance; . . . they very distinctly mark the acquisition by the Third Estate of its full share of parliamentary power " (*Stubbs*).

(d) (1) Marie of Limoges m. Arthur, m. (2) Yoland of Dreux, Duke of Brittany. Countess of Montfort.

- John III., Duke of Brittany, d. 1341.
- Guy.
- John, Count of Montfort.

Jeanne m. Charles of Blois.

1328. Charles IV. of France dies, and is succeeded by Philip VI. (a).
1329. Robert Bruce dies, and is succeeded by David Bruce, aged seven.
1331-1338. English and Irish in Ireland are ordered to submit to the same law, and only English officials are to be appointed.
1332. Battle of Duplin. Victory of Edward Balliol, who is crowned king, but has immediately to fly from Scotland.

1341. Burgesses appear sitting in the Irish Parliament.
1343. The Ottoman Turks begin to form settlements in Europe.
1345. Jacob van Arteveldt killed at Ghent.

1327.	Mortimer.] Henry, Earl of Lancaster, holds the first place in the standing council appointed for the king. *Sept.* 21. **Murder of King Edward II.**
1328.	Peace concluded with Scotland at Northampton. The complete independence of Scotland is recognised. Edward marries Phillippa of Hainault.
1329.	Edward does homage for his lands in France.
1330.	Execution of the Earl of Kent for a supposed plot against the government. Edward, supported by Henry of Lancaster, arrests Mortimer. His fall and execution.
1331.	Edward again goes to France to do homage.
1332.	*The knights of the shire are first definitely recorded as deliberating apart from the lords and the prelates, and in the next year as sitting with the citizens and burgesses.* *An order for the collection of a tallage on the royal demesne is issued, probably for the last time, the power of levying it being once more and finally abolished in* 1340.
1333.	Invasion of the Scots. Siege of Berwick and battle of Halidon Hill. Victory of the English. Balliol is reinstated.
1334.	Balliol's second expulsion from Scotland.
1335.	Edward and Balliol invade Scotland.
1336.	Philip promises help to the Scots, and invades Gascony.
1337.	**Edward takes the title of King of France** (*b*).
1338.	**Beginning of the war with France.** The French attack Portsmouth (*June*) and Southampton (*October*). Edward embarks for Flanders. [Edward is in alliance with the states on the north-east of France.]
1339.	Edward invades France unsuccessfully.
1340.	Edward returns to England. Heavy taxation. *June.* Edward defeats the French fleet at Sluys. Truce for a year. *Nov.* Sudden return of Edward to England. Dismissal of Robert Stratford, chancellor, and other state officers. Robert Bourchier, the first lay chancellor, is appointed.
1341.	The king having accused **John Stratford, Archbishop of Canterbury,** of wasting his money, orders him to answer in the Court of Exchequer. *The Lords insist that a peer must be judged in full Parliament and before his peers.* Edward consents, and concedes the further demands of Parliament (*c*), but in October repudiates the concessions. Edward supports the claims of John de Montfort to the duchy of Brittany (*d*).
1346.	*July.* Edward invades Normandy and advances to Paris. He crosses the Seine and retreats toward Calais. *Aug.* 26. **Victory of Crecy.** *Oct.* 17. Defeat of the Scots at Nevill's Cross. Capture of David II.
1347.	**Surrender of Calais.**
1348.	*The separate equitable jurisdiction of the Chancellor in the Court of Chancery is from this time definitely recognised.*

[Notes.]

(a) This statute, which attempts to fix the amount of wages and forbids the giving of alms to sturdy beggars, was confirmed or amended by enactments in 1351, 1362, 1368, and other years.

(b) *Statute of Provisors.*—All persons receiving papal provisions are to be liable to imprisonment, and all the preferments to which the Pope nominates are to be forfeited for that turn to the king.

(c) *Statute of Treasons.*—Its object was to prevent—
1. The compassing of the death of the king, queen, or their eldest son.
2. Uncertainty as to the legitimacy of the royal family.
3. Levying war against the king, or assisting his enemies.
4. Mutilation of the coin, or murdering the king's high officials in the discharge of their duty.

(d) *Statute of Præmunire.*—The name "Præmunire" is taken from the opening word in the sheriff's writ of summons to the delinquent. This statute, which condemns to forfeiture and imprisonment those who unlawfully prosecute suits in foreign courts, does not mention the court of Rome by name. This is done, however, in the strongest terms by the great Præmunire Statute of 1393.

(e) *Peace of Bretigny.*—Edward gave up all claim to the crown of France, and to the hereditary domains of William the Conqueror and the house of Anjou. He retained the dominions of Queen Eleanor of Guienne, the dowry of Queen Isabella, and the districts of Calais and Guisnes.

(f) This statute has to be renewed in 1371. "The wearisome contest so long continued for the maintenance of this branch of the prerogative comes thus to an end" (*Stubbs*).

(g) *The Statute of Kilkenny* forbade—
1. Marriages or intercourse between the English colonists and the Irish.
2. The use by Englishmen of the Irish language.
3. The adoption by Englishmen of Irish laws, customs, or manners.

(h) *The Stuarts.*—The family name of the dynasty was Allan or Fitzallan, but they got their other name from their hereditary office of High Steward.

(i) From this time tonnage and poundage becomes a regular parliamentary grant, and ultimately the recognised provision for the safeguard of the sea.

(j) The king was to remain under the care of his mother. The government was to be carried on by a council, from which the king's uncles were excluded, elected by the magnates.

FOREIGN.

1350. Philip VI. of France dies, and is succeeded by John II.

1356. The "Golden Bull" issued by the Emperor Charles IV.
1358. Meeting of the Estates General.
The Jacquerie in France.
1361. Lionel, Edward's son, who had married the heiress of William deBurgh, Earl of Ulster, goes to Ireland as Lieutenant.
1364. John II. of France dies, and is succeeded by Charles V.
1366. Statute of Kilkenny (g).
1371. David II. of Scotland dies, succeeded by his brother-in-law, Robert Stuart (the Steward) (h).

1377. Gregory XI. returns to Rome from Avignon. On his death begins "the Great Schism."
1378. Urban VI. Pope in Rome. Clement VII. at Avignon.

1380. Charles V. of France dies, and is succeeded by Charles VI.

1349.	**The Black Death.**
	The first Statute of Labourers (*a*).
1351.	*The first Statute of Provisors,* to prevent encroachments by the Pope on patronage (*b*). [In this year begin a series of petitions against the usurped jurisdiction of the Privy Council.]
1352.	*The first Statute of Treasons* (*c*).
1353.	*The first Statute of Præmunire,* to prevent usurpations of jurisdiction by the Pope (*d*).
1356.	The Black Prince marches from Bordeaux to Berri. *Sept.* 19. **Victory of Poitiers,** and capture of John II.
1360.	Edward besieges Paris. Peace of Bretigny (*e*).
1362.	*Enactment that no subsidy should be set on wool by the merchants or any other body without consent of Parliament* (*f*).
	The English language is ordered to be used in the law courts.
1364.	John II. of France dies at the Savoy.
1367.	Expedition of the Black Prince to help Pedro of Castile.
1369.	The Black Prince is summoned to Paris on account of his heavy taxation of the Gascons. Queen Philippa dies.
	Renewal of the war.
1370.	Invasion of Gascony by the French. Massacre by the English at Limoges.
1372.	Defeat of the English off Roebelle by the Spaniards.
1373.	John of Gaunt's disastrous expedition from Calais to Bordeaux.
	Tonnage and poundage is formally granted by Parliament for two years (*i*).
1374.	Loss of all French dominions, except Calais, Bordeaux, and Bayonne.
1376.	John of Gaunt is at the head of the administration.
	The Good Parliament, *supported by the Black Prince and William of Wykeham, impeaches Lords Latimer and Neville, Alice Perrers, and others.* [*This is the first instance of an impeachment.*]
	June. **The Black Prince dies.**
	John of Gaunt returns to power. *He throws into prison Peter de la Mare, the Speaker of the Good Parliament.*
1377.	**Wickliffe** is cited to appear at St. Paul's.
	June 21. Death of Edward III.

RICHARD II., 1377—1399 (22 Years).

Born 1366; Married { 1381, Anne of Bohemia.
1395, Isabella of France.

	The French ravage the south coast.
	Peter de la Mare is released from prison, and elected Speaker of Richard's first parliament.
	Appointment of provisional government (*j*).
	Walworth and Philipot are appointed treasurers of the parliamentary grant.
1379.	A graduated poll-tax is imposed.
1380.	An additional poll-tax is imposed.

[Notes.]

FOREIGN.

(a) THE YORKIST LINE.

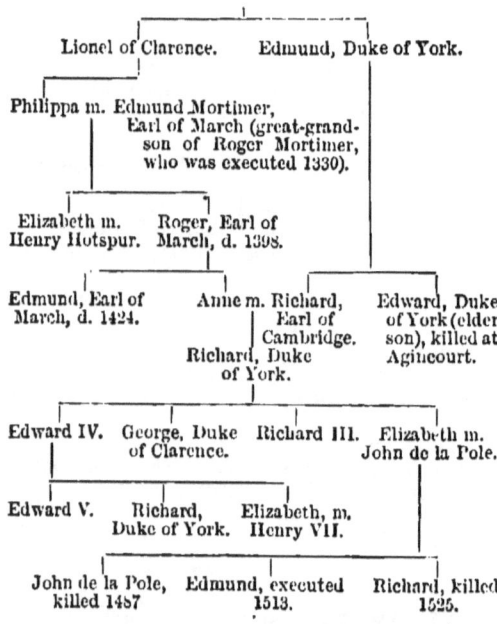

(b) "In our land of Ireland," wrote Richard II., "there are three kinds of people—wild Irish (our enemies), Irish rebels, and obedient English. To us and our council it appears that the Irish rebels have rebelled in consequence of the injustice and grievances practised toward them, for which they have been afforded no redress; and that if not wisely treated, and given hope of grace, they will most likely ally themselves with our enemies" (*Richey*).

(c) Haxey had introduced a bill reflecting censure on the king and court. On the demand of the king the Commons gave up his name, and he was imprisoned.

1390. Robert II. of Scotland dies, and is succeeded by Robert III.

1396. Sigismund and many French and other knights are utterly defeated by the Turks at Nicopolis.

1381.	**Rising of the Commons** (in Kent, Essex, and elsewhere) under **Wat Tyler and Jack Straw**. Murder of Simon of Sudbury, Archbishop of Canterbury. Richard meets the rioters at Mile-end and Smithfield. Dispersion of the insurgents. [Virtual end of villenage.]
1382.	Continued influence of John of Gaunt. A statute is passed against heretic preachers, which is repealed in the next Parliament.
1384.	**Death of Wickliffe.**
1385.	Richard ravages Scotland, which had received help from France. *A scutage due for this war is remitted.* [*After this time scutage hardly ever appears again.*] Death of the Princess of Wales. Roger, Earl of March, is declared heir to the throne (*a*).
1386.	John of Gaunt goes to Spain for three years. [*The first records of the Privy Council appear in this year.*] Parliament demands the dismissal of ministers. Richard refuses. *Impeachment of Suffolk* (Michael de la Pole), Richard's Chancellor. **A Council of Eleven is appointed** as a commission to sit for a year, and to regulate the royal household and the kingdom.
1387.	The judges appealed to by Richard decide that the council is illegal. The Lords Appellant (the Duke of Gloucester, the Earls of Arundel, Derby, Nottingham, and Warwick) take up arms. Battle of Radcot Bridge. De Vere, Duke of Ireland, is defeated. Fall of the court party.
1388.	**Meeting of the "Merciless" Parliament.** *Impeachment of the king's favourites, De Vere, Suffolk, Neville, Archbishop of York, Sir Simon Burley, and others.* Battle of Otterburn. The Scots are victorious, but Douglas is slain.
1389.	**Richard takes the government into his own hands**; he rules apparently well for eight years. Reconciliation of the Lords Appellant to the king. Return of John of Gaunt to England. *The Commons pray that the Chancellor and the Council may not after the close of Parliament make any ordinance contrary to the common law.*
1390.	*Statute of Provisors* [re-enacting statutes of 1351 and 1362].
1391.	*Statute of Mortmain* is re-enacted (see 1279), and evasions of ecclesiastical lawyers are finally stopped.
1393.	*The great Statute of Præmunire.* (See 1353, note.)
1394.	Death of the queen. Richard goes to Ireland for nine months (*b*).
1395.	The Lollards present a remonstrance to Parliament against the power of the clergy and abuses in the Church.
1396.	Richard marries Isabella of France at Calais, and a truce for twenty-five years is made.
1397.	Parliament confirms the Act by which Richard makes the children of Katharine Swynford (the Beauforts) legitimate. Haxey's case. *Interference by the king with the Commons' freedom of debate* (*c*).

[Notes.]
(a) GENEALOGY OF THE WARRENNES AND ARUNDELS.

William de Warrenne, m. Gundred, daur. of William the Conqueror.
created Earl of Surrey.
|
William, Earl of Warrenne and Surrey, d. 1135.
|
— William, Earl of Warrenne and Surrey, d. in Second Crusade.
— Adeline m. Henry of Scotland.
   |
   William the Lion, King of Scotland.
|
Isabel m. Hameline Plantagenet, natural son of Geoffrey of Anjou, and brother of Henry II.
|
William, Earl of Warrenne and Surrey, d. 1240.
|
John, Earl of Warrenne and Surrey, d. 1304, commanded against Scots, *temp.* Edward I.
|
William, d. 1285.
|
— Edmund Fitz-Alan, m. Alice. 8th Earl of Arundel.
   |
   Richard, Earl of Arundel and Surrey, d. 1376.
— John, Earl of Warrenne and Surrey, d. 1347. Fights against Gaveston, *temp.* Edward II.
|
— Richard, Earl of Arundel and Surrey, beheaded 1397.
— Thomas, Archbishop of Canterbury and Chancellor, *temp.* Henry IV.
|
— Thomas, Earl of Arundel and Surrey, d. 1415.
— Elizabeth m. Thomas Mowbray, Duke of Norfolk.
|
Margaret m. Sir Robert Howard.
(Ancestors of the Dukes of Norfolk.)

(b) THE LANCASTRIAN LINE.

Blanche m. John of Gaunt m. Katharine Swynford.
of Lancaster
|
— Henry IV.
— John, Earl of Somerset.
— Cardinal Beaufort.
|
— (1) Henry V. m. Katharine m. (2) Owen Tudor.
   of France.
— John, Duke of Somerset.
|
— Henry VI.
— Edmund Tudor, m. Margaret, Earl of Richmond.
   |
   Henry VII.

FOREIGN.

1400. The Emperor Wenceslaus, brother-in-law of Richard II. is deposed.

1402. Timour defeats the Ottoman Turks at Angora.

1397.	**Richard attacks the Lords Appellant in Parliament.** Gloucester dies in custody. Arundel is beheaded, and his brother, Archbishop of Canterbury, banished (*a*). Warwick is imprisoned for life.
1398.	**Parliament of Shrewsbury.** (1) Annuls the Acts of the Merciless Parliament. (2) *Grants customs to the king for life.* (3) *Delegates its authority to eighteen of its members.* Richard, virtually absolute, rules arbitrarily. Quarrel between Hereford (formerly Earl of Derby) and Norfolk (formerly Earl of Nottingham). They are banished by Richard.
1399.	*Feb.* 2. **Death of John of Gaunt.** His estates are seized by Richard. *May.* Richard goes to Ireland. *July.* **Hereford, now Duke of Lancaster, lands at Ravenspur,** is supported by the Percies, and joined by the Duke of York (the regent) and the mass of the people. Richard returns from Ireland and surrenders. *Sept.* 29. **Richard,** a prisoner in the Tower, **resigns the crown.** *Sept.* 30. Parliament meets, accepts the resignation, and after hearing the articles of accusation, deposes the king.

HENRY IV., 1399—1413 (14 YEARS) (*b*).

Born 1366; Married { 1380, Mary de Bohun.
{ 1403, Joan of Navarre.

	The Acts of Richard's last parliament are annulled. The Acts of the Merciless Parliament are re-established. Richard is put in prison.
1400.	Rebellion of the Earls of Rutland, Huntingdon, Kent, and Salisbury; betrayed by Rutland and easily suppressed. Many persons involved are executed. **Richard II. disappears, and his funeral is celebrated.** Glendower rebels in Wales, and maintains himself in Wales during the whole reign, in spite of a series of expeditions undertaken by the king and the Prince of Wales. Invasion of Scotland, and burning of Leith. Manuel Palæologus, Emperor at Constantinople, visits Henry, seeking help against the Turks.
1401.	**The Act "De Heretico comburendo" is passed by the Lords and clergy at the prompting of Archbishop Arundel.** Execution of William Sawtre by royal writ [the first execution for Lollard heresy in England].
1402.	The Scots invade England, and are defeated at **Homildon Hill** by the Percies.
1403.	The king makes **Henry Beaufort,** his half-brother, chancellor.

FOREIGN.

1404. Philip of Burgundy dies. His son John begins to quarrel with his cousin of Orleans for the Regency of France.

1406. Robert III. of Scotland dies, and James I. (then a prisoner in England) succeeds.

1407. Murder of Louis, Duke of Orleans, at the instigation of the Duke of Burgundy.

1409. Council of Pisa fails to end the "Great Schism."

1403.	**Conspiracy of the Percies, Mortimers, and Glendower, assisted by Douglas** (caused by the poverty of Henry, who is unable to pay them his debts). Battle of **Shrewsbury.** Victory of Henry; death of Hotspur. The Bretons land in Wales and burn towns on the coast, in this and the next year.
1404.	The French king makes a treaty with Glendower. *Henry, at the special request of the Commons, names six bishops, nine lords, and seven commoners to be his "great and continual council."* [In 1406 and 1410 a similar request is made.]
1405.	James, heir to the Scotch crown, is captured by the English. Conspiracy of Mowbray and Archbishop Scrope in favour of the Earl of March. They are captured and executed. Unsuccessful expedition of Henry against Glendower.
1406.	*Regulations are enacted on the petition of the Commons concerning the elections to Parliament in the county court with a view of preventing the sheriff from making a false return.* *The Commons insist upon a proper audit of the accounts of their grants.* [From this time onwards this right is never contested by the Lancastrian kings.]
1407.	*The king has to concede the right of the Commons only to originate money grants, and of perfect freedom of deliberation on such grants between both Houses.* Archbishop Arundel becomes chancellor for the fourth time.
1408.	The Earl of Northumberland again rebels, is defeated at Bramham Moor, and killed.
1409.	Sir Thomas Beaufort becomes chancellor.
1410.	**The knights of the shire now [as well as in 1404] propose to confiscate the property of the Church for military purposes.**
1411.	Henry sends troops to help the Duke of Burgundy. Retainers are prohibited by Parliament for the third time in this reign.
1412.	Arundel becomes chancellor again, instead of Thomas Beaufort, and Prince Henry is removed from the Council. Henry, changing sides, sends an army to help Orleans under his second son, Clarence, who ravages Normandy and Guienne.
1413.	Death of Henry.

HENRY V., 1413—1422 (9 Years).

Born 1388; Married, 1420, Katharine of France.

Henry Beaufort, Bishop of Winchester, becomes chancellor instead of Arundel, Archbishop of Canterbury.
Arundel urges Henry to persecute the Lollards. Sir John Oldcastle, a leading Lollard, is convicted, and escapes from the Tower.

1414.	Meeting of disaffected Lollards summoned at St. Giles' Fields. new statute is passed against the Lollards.

[Notes.]

(a) The "Great Council" (Magnum Concilium regis et regni), a form of the national General Assembly which had survived from the time before the inferior clergy and the Commons were summoned, may be considered either as a sort of enlarged Privy Council, or as the House of Lords (or magnates) sitting out of Parliament.

It was not unfrequently summoned by the Plantagenet kings after 1295, for purposes of deliberation and advice.

FOREIGN.

1414-1418. Council of Constance ends the "Great Schism." Pope Martin V. unanimously elected (nominated by the Bishop of London). Condemnation and burning of Huss.

1418. Massacre of the Orleanists in Paris.
1419. Assassination of John, Duke of Burgundy, by the party of the Dauphin.
Philip the Good succeeds him.

1414.	*It is agreed by Parliament and the king that statutes shall be made without alteration of the petitions on which they are based.* The property of priories belonging to foreigners is confiscated to the Crown by Parliament. Chichele succeeds Arundel as Archbishop of Canterbury.
1415.	Henry claims the French crown. A "Great Council" (*a*) is summoned, and resolves that war shall begin. Meeting of the troops at Southampton. **A conspiracy to place Edmund Mortimer, Earl of March, on the throne is discovered.** The Earl of Cambridge, father of Richard, afterwards Duke of York, and brother-in-law of Mortimer, is executed with others. Henry lands at Le Havre, Bedford, his brother, acting for him in England. *Sept.* Capture of Harfleur by siege. *Oct.* 2. Henry sets out on his march towards Calais. *Oct.* 25. **Battle of Agincourt. English victorious.** Death of Edward, Duke of York, and capture of Charles, Duke of Orleans. *Nov.* Henry returns to England.
1416.	**Sigismund, King of the Romans, visits England** to mediate between England and France, and to heal the "Great Schism." Henry allies himself with John, Duke of Burgundy.
1417.	Henry (now in alliance with towns on the east and north-east of France) returns to France, and captures many towns in Normandy. The Scots invade England. Sir John Oldcastle is captured and executed. [Martin V. becomes Pope at Council of Constance and ends the schism. During his papacy he "provided" as many as thirteen bishops in England in two years.]
1418.	Henry continues his captures in Normandy. Rouen is taken (1419).
1419.	Henry allies himself with Philip, Duke of Burgundy.
1420.	**Treaty of Troyes;** Henry to be regent during Charles VI., his father-in-law's life, and king after his death.
1421.	Henry returns to England with his new queen, Katharine. The Duke of Clarence, his brother, is defeated and slain at Beaugé by the French with the help of the Scottish contingent. Henry returns to France, and captures Dreux.
1422.	Henry captures Meaux, falls ill, and dies.

HENRY VI., 1422—[DETHRONED] 1461 (39 YEARS), [DIED] 1471.

Born 1421; Married, 1446, Margaret of Anjou.

The Council authorize Gloucester to summon a parliament.
Henry V.'s will is set aside by Parliament, as without binding force.

[Notes.]

FOREIGN.

1422. Charles VI. dies, and is succeeded by Charles VII.

(a) GENEALOGY OF THE DUKES OF BURGUNDY.

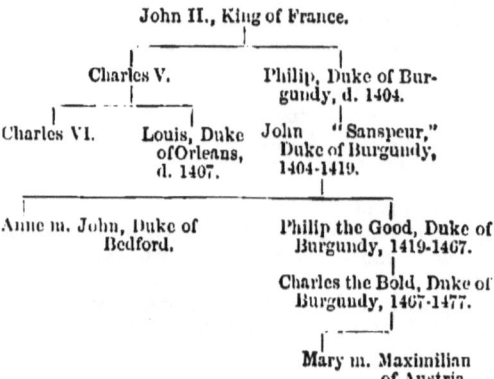

John II., King of France.
— Charles V. → Charles VI. → Louis, Duke of Orleans, d. 1407. → Anne m. John, Duke of Bedford.
— Philip, Duke of Burgundy, d. 1404. → John "Sanspeur," Duke of Burgundy, 1404-1419. → Philip the Good, Duke of Burgundy, 1419-1467. → Charles the Bold, Duke of Burgundy, 1467-1477. → Mary m. Maximilian of Austria.

1424. Humphrey of Gloucester irritates the Duke of Burgundy by trying to get possession of the property of his wife, Jacqueline of Hainault.

James I. returns to Scotland.

1429. *July.* Charles VII. is crowned at Rheims, but fails to enter Paris.

(b) The French offered to give up Normandy and Guienne if the English king would renounce the title of King of France.

1422.	John, Duke of Bedford, uncle of the king, is made Protector of the realm. Humphrey of Gloucester, uncle of the king, in Bedford's absence is to be Protector, and the king's chief councillor. [*The Privy Council acts as a real council of regency nominated by a regular Act of Parliament.*]
1423.	*March.* Gloucester marries Jacqueline of Hainault, and then quarrels with Burgundy about her inheritance. *April.* Bedford, who has been made Regent in France, marries Anne, sister of Philip the Good, Duke of Burgundy (*a*); Arthur of Richemont, brother of the Duke of Brittany, marries her sister Margaret. Battle of Crevant (secures the communication between the English and Burgundy).
1424.	Peace is made with Scotland. James I. of Scotland is released. Henry Beaufort, Bishop of Winchester, is again made chancellor. Battle of Verneuil (secures the communication between the English and Brittany).
1425. 1426.	**Gloucester quarrels openly with his uncle, Henry Beaufort.** A Privy Council (summoned to prepare business for Parliament) tries to effect the reconciliation of Gloucester and Beaufort. Bedford, who has been recalled, arbitrates between them on the meeting of Parliament. Bedford goes to France for seven years, and Beaufort is absent from England for two years. Beaufort is made a cardinal. The Pope tries to suspend Archbishop Chichele from his legatine office because he will not procure the repeal of the Statutes of Provisors. Chichele protests, and the bulls of suspension are seized by royal order.
1428.	The siege of Orleans is begun. [In England there is a continuous struggle between Beaufort and Gloucester for some years.]
1429.	Battle of the Herrings. French defeated by Sir John Fastolf. *April.* **The siege of Orleans is raised by Jeanne Darc. The English retire.** The French capture the Earl of Suffolk and defeat Sir John Talbot. *Nov.* Henry is crowned at Westminster, and the Protectorate ceases.
1430.	*The election of the knights of the shire is regulated, the vote being restricted to persons possessing freeholds worth 40s. a year.* [See *Summary: Parliament, Part II.,* p. 233.] Truce with Scotland renewed.
1431.	Jeanne Darc is burned at Rouen. Henry is crowned at Paris by Beaufort.
1432.	Beaufort is secured by statute against all risks of suffering the penalties of "præmunire" for being cardinal. Bedford's wife dies.
1433.	Bedford marries Jacquetta of Luxemburg, sister of the Count of St. Pol (afterwards mother of Elizabeth Woodville), which displeases Burgundy. He visits England for a year.
1435.	The **Congress of Arras** meets. The English refuse conditions of peace (*b*).

[Notes.]

FOREIGN.

1436. James I. of Scotland murdered, and is succeeded by his son, James II. (six years old).

1440. Discovery of the art of printing by moveable types made by Gutenberg.

(a) GENEALOGY OF THE BEAUFORTS.

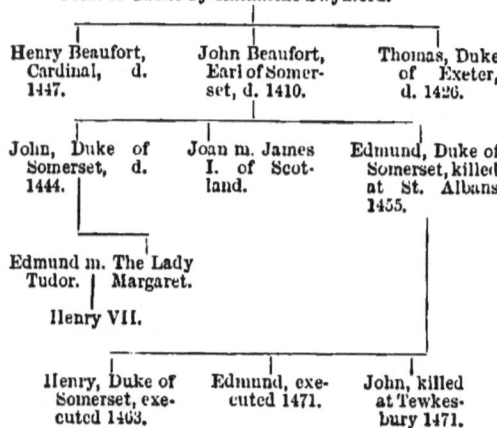

1447. *July.* The Duke of York is appointed Lieutenant in Ireland.

(b) Practically, however, both at this time and onwards, Convocation usually follows the example of the Commons in money grants until the time of Charles II. (See 1663.)

[1435—1450] ENGLISH.

1435.	*Sept.* 14. **Bedford dies, and is succeeded by Richard, Duke of York, as regent of France.** The Duke of Burgundy joins France, renouncing the English alliance. War goes on, with the gradual loss of Guienne and Normandy, till 1444, when a truce is made.
1436.	Paris is taken by the French. The Burgundians besiege Calais, but have to retire.
1437.	The king begins to nominate his own council absolutely. [*From this time the Privy Council loses connection with the Parliament, and becomes " a mere instrument in the hands of the king or the court."*] Queen Katharine dies.
1440.	The Duke of Orleans (kept in prison since the battle of Agincourt) is set at liberty by the influence of the peace party in spite of the opposition of Gloucester.
1442.	Henry comes of age.
1443.	John Beaufort (Duke of Somerset, August) leads an expedition to France.
1444.	**John Beaufort** (*a*) **dies, leaving a daughter, Margaret (mother of Henry VII.).** Edmund, his brother, becomes the representative of the family. A truce is concluded with France, negotiated by William de la Pole, Earl of Suffolk. [*See Genealogy,* p. 68.]
1445.	Henry marries Margaret of Anjou. It is agreed that Anjou and Maine shall be given up to René, her father. **Suffolk (now marquis)** is thanked for his negotiations by both Houses of Parliament. **He takes the lead in the Council**, and devotes himself to the service of the young queen.
1447.	*Feb.* Parliament at Bury St. Edmunds. **Gloucester** is arrested and charged with high treason, February 18. **He is found dead, February 23. This leaves Richard of York heir apparent.** *April.* **Cardinal Beaufort dies.** *Sept.* Edmund Beaufort (Duke of Somerset, 1448) is appointed Lieutenant in France.
1448.	Anjou and Maine being given up, the garrisons which are set free ravage Brittany and capture Fougères.
1449.	The French consider the truce broken, and invade and conquer Normandy. [**At the end of this year the English hold in the north only Honfleur, Bayeux, Caen, and Cherbourg.**] War breaks out with Scotland, and a truce is made. *The Commons attempt to tax the clergy, but the king refers their proposal through the Lords Spiritual to Convocation* (*b*). Unpopularity of Suffolk and his ministers, Moleyns, Bishop of Chichester, Ascough, Bishop of Salisbury, and Lord Say.
1450.	*Jan.* Murder of Moleyns at Portsmouth. *Feb.* **Suffolk is impeached, puts himself on the king's mercy. He is banished for five years, but is overtaken and beheaded, May 2.** *May.* Rebellion of Cade. *June.* Ascough is murdered in Wiltshire.

[Notes.]

FOREIGN.

1453. Conquest of Constantinople by the Ottoman Turks.

1459. The Irish Parliament declares Ireland to be independent of English legislation.
1460. James II. of Scotland dies, succeeded by James III.

1461. Charles VII. of France dies, succeeded by Louis XI.

[1450—1461] *ENGLISH.*

1450.	*July.* Cade enters London and beheads Lord Say. Fight on London Bridge. The insurgents are driven out, terms are accepted by them, but Cade, continuing the insurrection, is killed. The Duke of York returns from Ireland to England. The Duke of Somerset returns from Normandy to England.
1451.	A proposal is made in the House of Commons to declare York heir to the throne. Loss of Bordeaux and Bayonne.
1452.	York collects an army, and demands the dismissal of Somerset. Somerset and the king force York to swear allegiance.
1453.	**Defeat and death of Talbot at Châtillon. Final loss of France except Calais.** [*See Summary: The Hundred Years' War between England and France,* p. 262.] The Duke of York arrests Thorpe, the Speaker of the Commons. In the next parliament they assert their privilege in his behalf, but he remains in prison. Henry falls ill, and becomes unable to govern. *Oct.* Birth of Prince Edward. *Dec.* **Somerset is imprisoned.**
1454.	**Richard, Duke of York, is appointed by the Lords to a limited protectorate of the realm** without prejudice to the rights of the Prince of Wales. He makes his brother-in-law, Salisbury, chancellor.
1455.	Henry recovers. **York is dismissed.** Somerset is released, and with his friends **returns to power.** The Duke of York, Salisbury, and his son Warwick take up arms to protect the king, really against Somerset. First battle of **St. Albans. Death of Somerset. Capture of Henry.**
1456.	The king recovers from another short illness. The queen and the Lancastrians intrigue with Scotland and France.
1458.	Reconciliation between the two parties at St. Paul's.
1459.	The queen's attempt to arrest the Earl of Salisbury brings on the battle of **Bloreheath.** Yorkists victorious. Panic at Ludlow. Flight of the Yorkists. In the Parliament at Coventry York and his friends are attainted.
1460.	*July.* The three Yorkist earls, March, Salisbury, and Warwick, cross from Calais and win the battle of **Northampton.** The king is taken. The queen flies. York claims the throne and is made heir to Henry by Parliament. The queen raises forces. *Dec.* Battle of **Wakefield.** Lancastrians victorious and **York killed.** Salisbury is taken and is executed at Pomfret.
1461.	*Feb.* 3. **Edward, Earl of March,** fights against Pembroke at **Mortimer's Cross.** Yorkists victorious. *Feb.* 17. The queen fights against Warwick at the second battle of St. Albans, and sets the king free, who retires to the north. Lancastrians victorious. **Edward comes to London and is declared king.**

[Notes.]

(a) GENEALOGY OF THE WOODVILLES.

John, Duke of m. Jacquetta of m. Richard Woodvil.
Bedford.   Luxemburg.

ony, Lord   John, exe-   Elizabeth m. Edward IV.
vers, exe-   cuted 1469.
ted 1483.

ard V.   Elizabeth.   Katharine m. Sir W. Courtenay.

Henry Courtenay, Marquis of Exeter,
executed 1539.

Edward Courtenay, proposed as husband
for Queen Elizabeth, d. 1566.

FOREIGN.

1465. Law is so far in abeyance in Ireland that the Irish Parliament declares it lawful for any free man to kill a thief, or suspected thief, and deliver his head to the government.

1467. Charles the Bold succeeds his father, Philip the Good, as duke of Burgundy.

[1475-1484]   *ENGLISH.*

1475 Edward lands at Calais. Treaty of Pecquigny between him and
       Louis XI. Edward receives a pension and returns to England.
1478 Clarence, disowned by his brother, is attainted and executed.
1482 Richard, Duke of Gloucester, on behalf of his brother the king,
       helps the Duke of Albany in Scotland against James III.
       Edinburgh and Berwick are captured.
1483 Louis XI. breaks off the marriage contract he had made with
       Edward, who prepares for war.
       April 9. Edward dies.

EDWARD V., 1483 (2 Months, April—June).

Born 1470.

The Council and the queen dispute for the guardianship. The
  Council send for the young Edward, who advances to London
  from Ludlow.
Gloucester and Buckingham (4) meet him at Stony Stratford, and
  send his escort, Lord Rivers his uncle and Sir Richard Grey
  his half-brother, prisoners to the north.
May 4. The king and the dukes enter London. Gloucester is
  proclaimed Protector of the kingdom by the Council,
  with the support of Hastings.
Gloucester and Buckingham plot together and cause Hastings to
  be beheaded.
Jun. 16. The king's younger brother Richard joins him in the
  Tower.
Jun. 25. The Crown is offered to Gloucester by a body of
  lords and others, and he declares himself king.
Rivers and Grey are executed at Pontefract.

RICHARD III., 1483-1485 (2 Years).

Born 1450; Married, 1473, Anne Neville.

Richard makes a progress through the country and is well
  received.
**Disappearance of the young Edward V. and his brother
  Richard.**
Buckingham, Henry Tudor, Earl of Richmond (afterwards
  Henry VII.), Morton, Bishop of Ely, and the Woodvilles plot
  a conspiracy against Richard.
The rebellion of Buckingham in Wales is a failure. He is
  brought to the king at Salisbury and beheaded. Henry of
  Richmond reaches Plymouth but returns.
1484 A parliament is held and a statute passed abolishing the illegal
       practice of exacting benevolences.

[Notes.]

FOREIGN.

(a) GENEALOGY OF THE WOODVILLES.

John, Duke of m. Jacquetta of m. Richard Woodville.
Bedford.   Luxembourg.

Antony, Lord   John, exe-   Elizabeth m. Edward IV.
Rivers, exe-   cuted 1469.
cuted 1483.

Edward V.   Elizabeth.   Katharine m. Sir W. Courtenay.

Henry Courtenay, Marquis of Exeter,
executed 1539.

Edward Courtenay, proposed as husband
for Queen Elizabeth, d. 1566.

1465. Law is so far abeyance in Irelai that the Irish Parli ment declares it lawf for any free man to k a thief, or suspect thief, and deliver t head to the gover ment.

1467. Charles the Bo succeeds his fathe Philip the Good, duke of Burgundy.

[1475—1484] ENGLISH.

1475.	Edward lands at Calais. Treaty of Pecquigny between him and Louis XI. Edward receives a pension and returns to England.
1478.	Clarence, distrusted by his brother, is attainted and executed.
1482.	**Richard, Duke of Gloucester**, on behalf of his brother the king, helps the Duke of Albany in Scotland against James III. Edinburgh and Berwick are captured.
1483.	Louis XI. breaks off the marriage contract he had made with Edward, who prepares for war. *April* 9. Edward dies.

EDWARD V., 1483 (2 Months, April—June).
Born 1470.

The Council and the queen dispute for the guardianship. The Council send for the young Edward, who advances to London from Ludlow.

Gloucester and Buckingham (*a*) meet him at Stony Stratford, and send his escort, Lord Rivers (his uncle) and Sir Richard Grey (his half-brother), prisoners to the north.

May 4. The king and the dukes enter London. **Gloucester is proclaimed Protector of the kingdom** by the Council, with the support of Hastings.

Gloucester and Buckingham plot together and cause Hastings to be beheaded.

June 16. The king's younger brother Richard joins him in the Tower.

June 25. **The Crown is offered to Gloucester by a body of lords and others, and he declares himself king.**

Rivers and Grey are executed at Pontefract.

RICHARD III., 1483-1485 (2 Years).
Born 1450; Married, 1473, Anne Neville.

Richard makes a progress through the country and is well received.

Disappearance of the young Edward V. and his brother Richard.

Buckingham, Henry Tudor, Earl of Richmond (*b*) (afterwards Henry VII.), Morton, Bishop of Ely, and the Woodvilles plot a conspiracy against Richard.

The rebellion of Buckingham in Wales is a failure. He is brought to the king at Salisbury and beheaded. Henry of Richmond reaches Plymouth, but retires.

1484.	*A parliament is held and a statute passed abolishing the illegal practice of exacting benevolences.*

[Notes.]

(a) GENEALOGY OF THE DE LA POLES.

William de la Pole, of Kingston-upon-Hull.
|
Michael de la Pole, Earl of Suffolk, minister of Richard II., d. 1388.
|
Michael, restored to his earldom in 1399, d. at Harfleur 1415.
|
┌─────────────────────┬─────────────────────┐
Michael, 3rd Earl, killed at Agincourt 1415.
William, Duke of Suffolk, minister of Henry VI., impeached and murdered 1450.
|
John de la Pole, m. Elizabeth, Duke of Suffolk, sister of d. 1491. Edward IV.
|
┌──────────────┬──────────────┬──────────────┐
John, Earl of Lincoln, killed at Stoke 1487.
Edmund, Duke of Suffolk, surrendered title of Duke for that of Earl 1493, executed 1513.
Richard, d. at Pavia 1525.

(b) Henry is assisted in his extortions by Morton (Archbishop of Canterbury, 1486 ; Chancellor, 1487), Empson, and Edmund Dudley (see Genealogy, note (b), p. 76). Empson was Speaker of the House of Commons in 1491, Dudley in 1504.

(c) At this time the colony was in such danger that orders were given to build a rampart or ditch to defend the counties of Kildare, Dublin, Meath, and Louth against the Irish.

FOREIGN.

1488. James III. of Scotland dies, succeeded by James IV.

1492. The conquest of Granada from the Moors is completed. Discovery of Hispaniola by Columbus.

1494. Poynings' law prohibits the Irish Parliament from passing any law which has not received the sanction of the English Council (c). Charles VIII. makes his great expedition to Italy and captures Naples ; but finds it necessary to retire to France, winning on his way the battle of Fornovo.

[1484—1496] ENGLISH.

1484.	**Death of Richard's son, Edward, Prince of Wales.** John de la Pole (*a*), Earl of Lincoln, declared heir to the throne.
1485.	Death of the queen. Richard proposes to marry his niece, the Lady Elizabeth.
	Aug. 7. **Henry, Earl of Richmond**, having sailed from Harfleur, lands at **Milford Haven**.
	Aug. 22. Battle of **Bosworth**. **Richard is defeated and killed.**

HENRY VII., 1485—1509 (24 Years).

Born 1456; Married, 1486, Elizabeth of York.

	Henry goes to London and is crowned. Parliament entails the crown on him and his heirs.
	The son of Clarence, Edward Plantagenet, afterwards Earl of Warwick, is imprisoned in the Tower.
1486.	**The king marries Elizabeth of York.**
	Unsuccessful rebellion of Lord Lovel.
1487.	Lambert Simnel (calling himself the Earl of Warwick, son of Clarence), and John, Earl of Lincoln (*a*), land in Ireland and then in Lancashire. They are defeated at Stoke, and Lincoln killed.
	The queen is crowned.
	A new court is established for the trial of powerful offenders, which is afterwards merged into the Star Chamber Court, and revives and extends the old criminal jurisdiction of the Ordinary Council.
1488.	Resistance in the north of England to the subsidy granted against France for the help of Brittany.
1489.	Henry's troops which he has been compelled to send to the help of Brittany remain inactive, and Brittany is united to France by the marriage of Charles VIII. and Anne of Brittany (1491).
1492.	**Perkin Warbeck** (calling himself Richard, Duke of York, son of Edward IV.) lands in Ireland, and is afterwards invited to the court of France. Money is raised by benevolences (*b*).
	Henry goes to France and besieges Boulogne.
	Treaty of Etaples. Henry receives a pension and returns.
1493.	Warbeck goes to Flanders, where Margaret, Duchess of Burgundy, receives him as her nephew.
1494.	Poynings' law is passed in Ireland. [See *Summary: Ireland*, Part I. p. 252.]
1495.	Sir William Stanley is executed for conspiracy with Warbeck.
	Warbeck makes a descent on Kent, but fails. He goes to Ireland and thence to Scotland, where he is received.
	A statute is passed giving security to the subject who obeys the king on the throne for the time being.
1496.	The Great Intercourse, a commercial treaty, is made with Philip, Duke of Burgundy, and provides that Warbeck shall not be received in Flanders.
	Warbeck advances with James, King of Scotland, into England, but returns, after ravaging the country.

[Notes.]

(a) GENEALOGY OF CHARLES V.

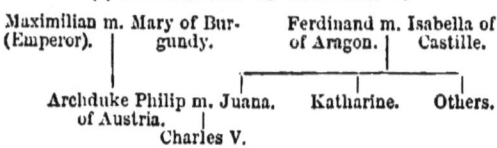

(b) See Genealogy of the De la Poles, p. 68.

(c) GENEALOGY OF THE TUDORS.

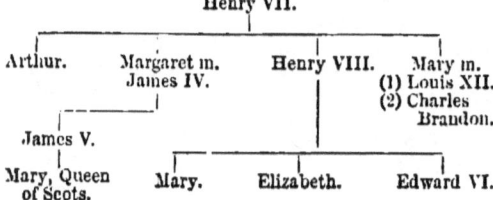

FOREIGN.

1497. Discovery of mainland of America by John Cabot.
1498. Charles VIII. of France dies, succeeded by Louis XII.
Vasco de Gama discovers the sea-route to India.

1513. James IV. of Scotland dies, succeeded by James V. (2 years old). Maximilian the emperor joins the league against France.

1515. Louis XII. dies, and is succeeded by his son-in-law, Francis I.
1517? Luther publishes his theses at Wittenberg.
1519. Maximilian dies, *Jan.* 12.
Charles V. becomes emperor, *June* 28.

1522. The Turks take Rhodes.

1497.	Cornish rebels, resisting the subsidy for the Scotch war, are defeated at Blackheath.
	Warbeck, coming from Ireland, lands in Cornwall, fails to revive the insurrection, and is captured.
1499.	**Warbeck,** having escaped and been recaptured, **is executed with the Earl of Warwick.**
1501.	**Arthur, Prince of Wales, marries Katharine** (*a*) **of Aragon.**
1502.	Arthur dies, and **Katharine is contracted to Prince Henry, then eleven years old.**
	The Princess Margaret marries James of Scotland.
1503.	The queen dies.
1506.	The Archduke Philip (*a*), wrecked in England, has to agree to deliver up the Earl of Suffolk (*b*), nephew of Edward IV.
1509.	Henry dies.

HENRY VIII., 1509—1547 (38 Years) (*c*).

Born 1491; Married
- Katharine of Aragon, 1509.
- Anne Boleyn, 1532.
- Jane Seymour, 1536.
- Anne of Cleves, 1540.
- Katharine Howard, 1540.
- Katharine Parr, 1543.

	Henry marries Katharine of Aragon.
1510.	Empson and Dudley having been pronounced guilty of high treason, are executed.
1511.	Henry joins the Holy League against France.
1512.	A useless expedition is made to the south of France.
1513.	Suffolk is executed after seven years' imprisonment.
	Aug. Henry goes over to the north-east of France, and the French are defeated at the battle of Spurs.
	Sept. **Battle of Flodden Field.** Defeat of the Scots and death of James IV.
1514.	Peace is made with France and Scotland, and Mary, Henry's sister, marries Louis XII. (who dies three months later, and she afterwards marries Charles Brandon, Duke of Suffolk).
1515.	**Wolsey is created Cardinal, and becomes Lord Chancellor.**
1516.	Birth of the Princess Mary.
1517.	**Wolsey is made papal legate,** with special licence from the king to accept the commission.
1519.	Henry becomes a candidate for the empire.
1520.	**Charles V.** (*a*) **visits Henry at Canterbury.** Henry goes to France and visits Francis on the Field of the Cloth of Gold, and on his way to England again meets Charles V. at Gravelines.
1521.	Edward, third Duke of Buckingham, is charged with treason and executed.
	Henry receives from the Pope the title of Defender of the Faith for having written a work against Luther.
1522.	Charles V. again comes to England, and Henry sends an army against France.

[Notes.]   FOREIGN.

(a) Hitherto no Parliament, or almost none, had ever been held for more than one year, and there was therefore a fresh election for each year. Annual Parliaments had been the general rule till the Wars of the Roses began.

(b) In the last paragraph of the petition occur the following words: "And in case the Pope would make any process against this realm for the attaining those annates, ... that it may please the king's most noble grace to ordain in this present Parliament that the obedience of him and the people be withdrawn from the See of Rome."

(c) A *congé d'élire* is a licence to the dean and chapter of a cathedral, giving them leave to hold an election to fill the office of bishop, and is accompanied by a *letter missive* naming the person whom they are to choose, which they must do within twenty days, or incur the penalties of præmunire.

(d) *List of Bishoprics* (see also note (b), p. 16)—
1. Sees created about the time of the Norman Conquest—
   Ely.
   Lincoln.
   Salisbury (to New Sarum in 1218).
   Bath.
   Exeter.
   Norwich.
   Chichester
   Carlisle
2. Sees created at the Reformation—
   Westminster (1540 to 1550 only).
   Oxford, 1545 (Osney from 1542).
   Peterborough, 1541.
   Chester, 1541.
   Gloucester, 1541, ⎫ joined
   Bristol, 1542,   ⎬ 1836.
   Sodor and Man (an old see annexed to Province of York, 1542).
3. Sees created since the Reformation—
   Ripon, 1836.
   Manchester, 1848
   Truro, 1876.
   St. Albans, 1877.
   Liverpool, 1880.

1525. Peasants' war in Germany.
Battle of Pavia. Francis made prisoner by Charles V.
1526. Great victory of the Turks at Mohacs.
1527. Rome is sacked and Pope Clement VII. imprisoned by the Imperialists.

1530. The Diet of Augsburg is held. The Confession of that name is published at this time.
League of Schmalkald formed.

1534. Insurrection of the Kildares. From this time a policy of forfeiture and colonization was steadily carried out.

1523.	The House of Commons (*of which Sir T. More is Speaker*) refuses to grant the whole of a grant of money claimed by *Wolsey* in person. [No Parliament had been called since 1515, or was called again till 1528.] Wolsey begins a visitation of the monasteries. Wolsey fails a second time to obtain the Papacy.
1525.	**Henry changes his policy, and makes a treaty with France.** Henry's attempt to levy forced loans being resisted, is withdrawn.
1527.	Wolsey goes to France, and the treaty is renewed, with a proposal for the marriage of the Princess Mary. **Henry having doubts about the legality of his marriage with the queen, submits the case to the Pope.**
1528.	A commission to Cardinals Wolsey and Campeggio to try the question of the king's marriage is granted by the Pope.
1529.	. Katharine appeals to the Pope, and the cause is finally avocated to Rome. **Fall of Wolsey.** Sir T. More becomes chancellor. *Nov.* 3. **The Seven Years' Parliament, which carries out the severance from Rome, now meets for the first time** (*a*). [See *Summary: Ecclesiastical, Part II.,* p. 239.] Parliament regulates fees paid to the clergy and forbids pluralities.
1530.	**Cranmer** carries the opinions favourable to the divorce which had been received from the universities to the Pope. Wolsey is arrested for high treason, and dies at Leicester.
1531.	**The clergy** incurring the penalty of præmunire, and being fined for acknowledging Wolsey as papal legate, address **Henry, after much protest, as "Head of the Church and Clergy so far as the law of Christ will allow."** Convocation makes the first proposal to limit the Pope's power by petitioning the king and Parliament to abolish the payment of annates to the Pope (*b*).
1532.	Parliament reforms the spiritual courts, and strengthens the mortmain statutes.
1533.	**An Act for restraining all appeals to Rome is passed.** *Nov.* Henry marries Anne Boleyn. Cranmer is consecrated Archbishop of Canterbury, and declares Henry's marriage with Katharine void and that with Anne Boleyn legal. *Sept.* Princess Elizabeth is born.
1534.	**An Act forbidding the payment of annates to Rome is passed,** and the election of bishops by *congé d'élire* (*c*) (*d*) finally arranged. The clergy are forbidden to make laws binding on themselves in Convocation without the king's consent. [The legislative power of Convocation is thus practically suppressed.] The succession to the throne is settled on the children of Anne Boleyn by Act of Parliament. *April.* For refusing to accept this Act, Sir T. More and Fisher, Bishop of Rochester, are sent to the Tower. *May.* Execution of the Nun of Kent. **An Act abolishing the authority of the Pope in England is passed.** The Convocations of Canterbury and York declare that "the Bishop of Rome has no greater jurisdiction con-

[Notes.] | FOREIGN.

(a) A statute on the subject was passed also in 1531, and this statute was confirmed in 1541. Benefit of clergy continued to be used as a legal fiction for the purpose of mitigating the punishment of death for certain felonies which were called clergyable felonies. It was finally abolished in 1827.

1536. John Calvin publishes the "Institutio Christianæ Religionis." The Anabaptists at Münster are crushed. The Act of Supremacy is passed by the Irish Parliament.

(b) See note (a), p. 64.

1538. James V. of Scotland marries Mary of Guise.

(c) Asserted (1) truth of Transubstantiation; (2) that communion in both kinds was not necessary; (3) that priests might not marry; (4) that vows of chastity ought to be observed; (5) that private masses ought to be continued; (6) that auricular confession must be retained. The penalty for denying the first was death; for the rest forfeiture of property for first offence, death for the second.

1540. Confirmation of the Order of Jesuits by the Pope.

1541. John Calvin returns to Geneva and obtains great influence (dies 1564).
1542. *Dec.* Death of James V. of Scotland, succeeded by Mary, Queen of Scots, aged one week.

(d) GENEALOGY OF THE POLES.

George, Duke of Clarence.
|
Margaret, Countess m. Sir Richard of Salisbury, executed 1541. | Pole.   Edward, Earl of Warwick, executed 1499.
|
Henry Pole, executed 1539.   Sir Geoffrey Pole.   Reginald, Archbishop of Canterbury, d. 1558.
                              |
                         Arthur. Edmund.

1535.	ferred on him by God in the Kingdom of England than any other foreign bishop." **HENRY TAKES THE TITLE OF "SUPREME HEAD OF THE CHURCH OF ENGLAND,"** by the *Act of Supremacy*. Fisher and More are executed, practically for refusing to swear to the Acts of Succession (1534) and Supremacy. Thomas Cromwell is appointed vicar-general.
1536.	Katharine of Aragon dies. Benefit of clergy is now restricted by Act of Parliament, and henceforth in the matter of jurisdiction clergy and laymen are on an equality (*a*). The union in matters of law, etc., between England and Wales is finally completed. [See *Summary: Wales*, p. 246.] The smaller monasteries and nunneries are dissolved, and their property transferred to the crown. *May* 19. Anne Boleyn is executed on a charge of adultery. *May* 20. Henry marries Jane Seymour. An English translation of the Bible is set up in the churches. An insurrection breaks out in Lincolnshire and in Yorkshire (called in Yorkshire "**The Pilgrimage of Grace**").
1537.	The insurrections continue, and many executions follow. The "Council of the North" is instituted to keep order. *Oct.* 12. Edward, Prince of Wales, born. *Oct.* 24. The queen dies.
1538.	The Countess of Salisbury, mother of Cardinal Pole, is imprisoned. The Marquis of Exeter (*b*) and others are executed for treason.
1539.	*The king's proclamations are declared by Parliament to be as valid as Acts of Parliament.* **All monasteries are now dissolved and their property granted to the king.** (The Order of the Hospitallers is dissolved, 1540.) **The Act of the Six Articles** (*c*), with severe penalties for disobedience, is passed.
1540.	*Jan.* 6. Henry marries Anne of Cleves. *July* 24. The king's marriage is abrogated by Parliament. **Fall and execution of Thomas Cromwell** (*July* 28) *by bill of attainder without being heard in his own defence.* *July* 28. Henry marries Katharine Howard.
1541. 1542.	The Countess of Salisbury (*d*) is executed. The king takes the title of King instead of Lord of Ireland. Katharine Howard is executed on a charge of immorality. Panic and flight of the Scots at Solway Moss.
1543.	*July*. Henry marries his sixth and last wife, Katharine Parr. A treaty for the marriage of Prince Edward and Mary, Queen of Scots, is arranged with Scotland.
1544.	Invasion of Scotland under **Lord Hertford** (afterwards Somerset) and **Lord Lisle** (afterwards Warwick and Northumberland). Invasion of France by Henry in person. Capture of Boulogne. An Act is passed releasing the king from his debts (also a similar one in 1529).

[Notes.]

(a) GENEALOGY OF THE HOWARDS.

John, created Duke of Norfolk. Killed at Bosworth, 1485.
|
Thomas, Earl of Surrey (restored to the dukedom 1514), won the battle of Flodden 1513, d. 1524.

- Thomas, Duke of Norfolk, d. 1554.
  | Henry, Earl of Surrey, beheaded 1547.
    | Thomas, Duke of Norfolk, beheaded 1572. (Great-grandfather of Lord Stafford, executed in 1680.)
- Sir Edward, Admiral, killed at Brest, 1513.
- Edmund. Katharine m. Henry VIII.
- William, created Lord Howard of Effingham.
    | Charles, second Lord Howard of Effingham, created Earl of Nottingham 1596, (defeated Spanish Armada), d. 1624.
- Elizabeth
    | Anne Boleyn m. Henry VIII.
- Thomas Boleyn, created Earl of Wiltshire.

(b) GENEALOGY OF THE DUDLEYS AND THE SYDNEYS.

Edmund Dudley (minister of Henry VII.).
|
John Dudley (Viscount Lisle, 1542; Earl of Warwick, 1547), created Duke of Northumberland, 1551.

- Robert Dudley, younger son, created Earl of Leicester, 1563.
- Guildford Dudley (m. Lady Jane Grey), executed 1554.
- Mary m. Sir Henry Sydney, Lord Deputy of Ireland, d. 1586.
    | Sir Philip Sydney, d. 1586, m. Frances, daur. of Sir F. Walsingham.
    | Robert Sydney, created Earl of Leicester 1618. (Grandfather of Algernon Sydney, who was executed 1683.)

(c) GENEALOGY OF THE SUFFOLKS.

Mary m. Charles Brandon, Duke of Suffolk.

- Frances m. Henry Grey, Duke of Suffolk d. 1559.
    | Jane m. Guildford Dudley, executed 1554.
    | Katharine m. Edward Seymour (son of the Protector).
      | Lord Beauchamp.
        | William Seymour m. Arabella Stuart.
- Eleanor.
    | Margaret m. Henry Stanley, Earl of Derby.

FOREIGN.

1545-63. The Council of Trent.
1546. Death of Luther.
1547. Francis I. of France dies, and is succeeded by Henry II. Complete defeat of the Protestants by Charles V. at Mühlberg.

1548. Mary, Queen of Scots is sent to France.

1552. Peace of Passau.

1545.	*A benevolence of not less than twenty pence in the pound on land and tenpence on goods is exacted.*
1546.	The Duke of Norfolk and the Earl of Surrey, his son (*a*), are committed to the Tower for treason.
1547.	Surrey is executed. *Jan.* Henry dies.

EDWARD VI., 1547—1553 (6 Years).

Born 1537.

	Hertford (now created Duke of Somerset) is made Protector.
	An ecclesiastical visitation is directed, to order the use of English in services and to pull down images. Bonner and Gardiner protesting, are imprisoned.
	The Protector invades Scotland to enforce the treaty of marriage of 1543, and defeats the Scots at the **battle of Pinkie**.
	The newly-made treasons of Henry VIII. and the Act (about proclamations) of 1539 are repealed.
	Severe Acts against vagrancy are passed in Parliament.
1549.	The **"First Prayer-Book of Edward VI."** is approved, and the **"Act for Uniformity of Service"** passed in Parliament.
	Lord Seymour, brother of Somerset, is condemned for treason by attainder *without being heard in his own defence*, and beheaded.
	A rebellion in Norfolk, under Ket, and other places, against those, especially the newly-made nobles, who had enclosed common land is put down by Warwick.
	A rebellion in Devon and Cornwall demanding the restoration of the old Liturgy is put down by Russell.
	The French besiege Boulogne.
	Somerset having lost credit during the rebellions, is forced to submit to the Council and resign his Protectorship. **John Dudley** (*b*), Earl of Warwick, gains the chief influence in the Council.
1550.	The Council make peace with France and Scotland and restore Boulogne.
1551.	Great distress is caused by wholesale depreciation of the coinage. The Princess Mary is forbidden the use of the Mass.
	Warwick now becomes Duke of Northumberland. Somerset is sent to the Tower, charged with high treason.
1552.	**Somerset is executed.**
	Parliament enacts that no one shall be convicted of treason without the evidence of two witnesses, who must both appear.
	A second **Act of Uniformity** and second **Prayer-Book** are issued.
1553.	The king (sixteen years old) falls ill. Northumberland persuades him to bestow by will the succession on **Lady Jane Grey** (*c*). *July.* Edward dies.

[Notes.]   *FOREIGN.*

1554-56. Charles V. resigns his dominions in Italy, the Netherlands, and Spain to his son Philip II.

1555. The Religious Peace of Augsburg arranges the religious affairs of Germany.

1556. Act of Supremacy repealed by the Irish Parliament.

1557. The first Covenant signed at Edinburgh.

1558. Mary, Queen of Scots, marries Francis, the Dauphin of France.

Charles V. resigns the empire, which passes to his brother Ferdinand.

(a) GENEALOGY OF THE GUISES.

René II., Duke of Lorraine.

- Antony, Duke of Lorraine, d. 1544.
  - Francis, Duke of Guise, murdered 1563.
    - Henry, Duke of Guise, murdered 1588.
- John, Cardinal, d. 1550.
  - Charles, Cardinal, d. 1574.
- Claude, Duke of Guise, d. 1550.
  - Claude, Duke of Aumale, killed 1573.
  - Louis, Cardinal, d. 1578.
    - Louis, Cardinal, murdered 1588.
  - Mary, m. James V. of Scotland.
    - Mary, Queen of Scots.
  - Charles, Duke of Mayenne, d. 1611.

MARY, 1553—1558 (5 Years).

Born 1516; Married, 1554, Philip of Spain.

1553. Lady Jane Grey is proclaimed.
Mary flies to the Howards in Norfolk. Northumberland's army deserts him. Mary advances to London.
Northumberland, Lady Jane Grey, and her husband are committed to the Tower. **Northumberland is executed.**
Bonner is made Bishop of London, and Gardiner Lord Chancellor.
The laws concerning religion passed in Edward's reign are annulled in Parliament.
Negotiations are opened for the marriage of the queen to Philip of Spain.

1554. Rebellion of Sir Thomas Wyatt. It fails. Sir Thomas Wyatt, **Lady Jane Grey, and her husband, father, and uncle are executed.**
The Princess Elizabeth is sent to the Tower.
July. **Marriage of the queen with Philip.**
Cardinal Pole comes to England. **All statutes against the Pope since the twentieth year of Henry VIII. are repealed** (but the monastic lands remain in the hands of their present owners).

1555. **The persecuting statutes of Henry IV. and V. against heretics are revived.** Hooper and many others are burnt as heretics.
Thirty-seven members of the Commons secede from Parliament.
Aug. Philip leaves England. *Oct.* Latimer and Ridley are burnt.

1556. **Cranmer is burnt.**
Cardinal Pole, papal legate, is made Archbishop of Canterbury.
The Dudley conspiracy on behalf of Elizabeth fails.

1557. Stafford's attempt upon Scarborough with French help fails.
Philip comes to England and persuades Mary to declare war against France.
The Spaniards and English defeat the French at St. Quentin.

1558. **Calais is besieged and captured by the French under the Duke of Guise** (*a*).
The French are defeated at Gravelines by the Spanish, who are assisted by the English fleet.
Nov. Death of Mary and of Cardinal Pole.

ELIZABETH, 1558—1603 (45 Years).

Born 1533.

Elizabeth retains Mary's Council, adding **Sir William Cecil** to their number.
Elizabeth forbids unlicensed preaching, and allows part of the Liturgy to be used in English. A new Prayer-Book is prepared.
Elizabeth refuses Philip's offer of marriage.

[Notes.]

(a) All ecclesiastical jurisdiction was annexed to the Crown; it was ordained that no foreign potentate should exercise any power or authority in this kingdom; and the queen was empowered to exercise her power through Commissioners.

(b) GENEALOGY OF FRENCH KINGS FROM HENRY II. TO HENRY IV

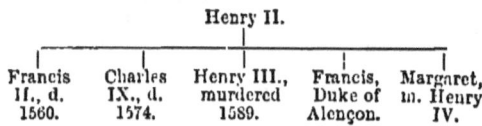

(c) This Act imposed the oath of supremacy on every member of the House of Commons (and thus excluded Catholics from that House), but not on the Peers (see 1678). It also bound many others to take the oath when tendered to them.

(d) GENEALOGY OF DARNLEY.

James IV. m. Margaret Tudor m. Earl of Angus.

James V. m. Mary of Guise.   Margaret m. Earl of Lennox.

Mary, Queen m. Lord Darnley.   Charles.
of Scots.
James I.   Arabella Stuart
of England.   m. William
                    Seymour.

In his lectures as Lady Margaret Professor he had attacked the government of the English Church. In 1572 he published "An Admonition to the Parliament," calling upon it to reform the abuses in the Church.

Henry of Navarre was a descendant in the younger branch of Robert of Clermont, the fourth son of St. Louis. The elder branch became extinct in the person of the Constable Bourbon, killed at Rome in 1527. Henry's immediate ancestry was as follows:—

Charles, Duke of Vendôme, d. 1557.

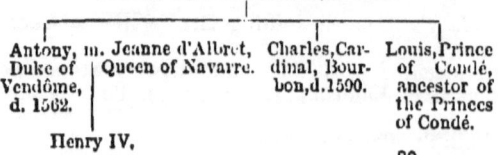

FOREIGN.

1559. John Knox returns to Scotland from Geneva. Treaty of Château Cambrésis between Spain and France.
Henry II. of France dies, succeeded by Francis II. (b), who dies 1560.
War breaks out in Scotland between the regent Mary of Guise and the Reformers.
1561. Mary, Queen of Scots, now a widow, returns to Scotland.
1565. Mary marries Darnley (d).
1566. Murder of Rizzio at Holyrood. Birth of James.
1567. Murder of Darnley. Mary marries Bothwell. Mary is forced to abdicate and imprisoned, is succeeded by her son, James VI.
1568. Insurrection of the Netherlands begins.
Civil war in France from 1566 to 1570 closed by peace at St. Germain.
1571. Don John of Austria defeats the Turks off Lepanto.
1572. Massacre of St. Bartholomew.
1574. Charles IX. of France dies, succeeded by Henry III.
1576. Henry of Navarre puts himself at the head of the Protestants in France (f).
The Catholics of France form a league.
1579-1580. Rebellion of Desmond in Munster is assisted by the Spaniards; but is finally suppressed in 1583, and is followed by extensive colonization.

80

1559.	Parliament meets. **The Act of Supremacy** (a) **is passed,** with penalties for refusing it. **The Act of Uniformity is passed** establishing the revised Prayer-Book. [See *Summary: The Reformation*, p. 241.] Peace is made with France. **Parker is made Archbishop of Canterbury.**
1560.	Elizabeth sends help to the Scottish Reformers. The regent of Scotland dies, and by the treaty of Edinburgh it is agreed that the French troops shall leave Scotland.
1562.	Elizabeth sends help to the French Huguenots. A severe Act is passed against Roman Catholics (c).
1563.	The Thirty-nine Articles are drawn up and signed by Convocation. Arthur and Edmund Pole (the last of the Yorkists) are convicted of treason and imprisoned till their deaths. [See *Summary: York and Lancaster*, p. 264.] The advanced Protestants denounce vestments.
1564.	Archbishop Parker and the queen enforce uniformity. Many of the London clergy refuse to obey, and, supported by **Dudley, Earl of Leicester,** leave the Church.
1566.	Peace is made with France. The Commons resolve to petition the queen to marry, but are commanded by her to discuss the matter no further. *Paul Wentworth moves to know whether her command is not against their liberties.*
1568.	**Mary, Queen of Scots,** having escaped from Lochleven Castle and been defeated at Langside, takes refuge in England. **Mary's case is investigated before a conference at York.** Mary is consigned to Tutbury.
1569.	Norfolk is committed to the Tower for proposing to marry Mary. **Insurrection in behalf of the old religion and of Mary** under the Earls of Northumberland and Westmoreland in Yorkshire and the northern counties. It is suppressed with great cruelty.
1570.	The Pope Pius V. issues a bull releasing Elizabeth's subjects from their allegiance. Cartwright, a leader of the Puritan party, is expelled from his professorship at Cambridge (e).
1571.	A marriage is proposed between Elizabeth and Henry of Anjou (afterwards King of France). Parliament passes severe Acts against Romanists and against the introduction of papal bulls. **The Puritans propose in Parliament alterations in religion,** and Strickland, the mover, is ordered by the Council not to appear again in his place in Parliament.
1572.	The Ridolfi plot having been discovered, Norfolk is executed. Parliament proposes an attainder against Mary, and is forbidden to proceed by the queen.
1575.	The Netherlanders offer the sovereignty of Holland and Zealand to Elizabeth, who declines.
1576.	**Grindal** succeeding Parker, becomes Archbishop of Canterbury.
1577.	Grindal is sequestered from his see for declining to suppress the "Prophesyings" of the Puritans.
1580.	A Jesuit mission under Campion and Parsons to reconvert England arrives.

[Notes.]

(a) *High Commission Court.*—"It consisted of forty-four commissioners, twelve of whom were bishops, many more privy councillors, and the rest either clergymen or civilians. This commission, after reciting the Acts of Supremacy, Uniformity, and two others, directs them to inquire from time to time, as well by the oaths of twelve good and lawful men as by witnesses, and all other means they can devise, of all offences . . . committed contrary to the tenor of the said several Acts and statutes" (*Hallam*).

(b) William of Nassau, Prince of Orange, took his title from the Principality of Orange near the Rhone, which had been acquired by his family by marriage. His descendants were—

His sons, Maurice, d. 1625, and Frederick Henry, d. 1647.

William II., m. Mary, daughter
d. 1650.   of Charles I.
           of England.

William III. of England.

(c) The Speaker of this Parliament, in answer to his request for liberty of speech, is told that it is granted, "but not to speak every one what he listeth, or what cometh into his brain to utter, their privilege was Ay or No. Wherefore, Mr. Speaker, her majesty's pleasure is that if you perceive any idle heads . . . which will meddle with reforming the Church and transforming the Commonwealth, and do exhibit bills to such purpose, that you receive them not until they be viewed and considered by those who it is fitter should consider of such things."

FOREIGN AND COLONIAL.

1584. William of Orange (b) accepts the sovereignty of Holland and Zealand, but is assassinated the same year, and his son Maurice succeeds with the title of Stadtholder.
1585. Raleigh's first colony is founded in America (no permanent settlement).
1588. Henry III. flies from Paris and joins Henry of Navarre.
1589. Henry III. of France is murdered by Jacques Clement, and is succeeded by Henry of Navarre (Henry IV.).
1590. Henry IV. defeats the League at the battle of Ivry.
1592. The Presbyterian Church established in Scotland by an Act of the Scottish Parliament.
1593. Henry IV. becomes a Catholic.
1598. Henry IV. grants toleration to the Protestants by the Edict of Nantes.
Treaty of Vervins between France and Spain.
Death of Philip of Spain. Succeeded by Philip III.
1600. **First charter granted to the East India Company.**

1581.	Francis, Duke of Anjou (formerly Alençon), younger brother of Henry III., comes to England to negotiate as to his marriage with Elizabeth.
	Campion is tried for high treason and executed.
1583.	**Whitgift** succeeds Grindal as Archbishop of Canterbury, and persecutes the Puritans.
	The "High Commission Court" is placed on a permanent footing (*a*). [See note (*a*), p. 80.]
1584.	An association is formed with the sanction of Parliament to protect Elizabeth from assassination, and a strict watch is set over Mary.
1585.	**Treaty between Elizabeth and the Netherlands.** Leicester is sent to their assistance.
1586.	Leicester is made Stadtholder. Babington's conspiracy is detected. Battle of Zutphen. Death of Sir Philip Sydney.
	Trial of Mary, Queen of Scots, by special commission.
	Leicester returns without success from the Netherlands.
1587.	**Mary, Queen of Scots, is executed.**
	Pope Sixtus V. issues a new bull, and proclaims a crusade against Elizabeth. He sends his benediction to the forces prepared by Philip of Spain against England.
	[The Marprelate tracts grossly abusing the hierarchy are circulated at this time.]
	Sir Francis Drake makes an expedition to Cadiz, and destroys part of Philip's armament.
	Peter Wentworth is committed to the Tower for submitting questions to the Speaker touching the liberties of the House.
1588.	*July.* **Defeat of the Spanish Armada.**
	Death of Leicester.
1589.	Expedition to Portugal to support Antonio against Philip of Spain.
1590.	**Death of Walsingham.**
1591.	English forces are sent under Essex to help Henry IV. of France.
	Eleven judges remonstrate against illegal commitments by the Privy Council.
1592.	A second expedition is sent to help Henry IV.
1593.	Acts with penalties are passed against both Puritans and Romanists (*c*).
1595.	Tyrone (O'Neal), assisted by Philip of Spain, rebels, and Sir John Norris is sent against him.
1596.	Expedition to Cadiz under **Essex** and Howard.
1597.	Failure of expedition under Essex and Raleigh against Spain.
	Philip makes propositions for peace.
1598.	Death of Sir John Norris in Ireland, and defeat of Bagnal by O'Neal.
	Death of Burleigh.
1599.	Essex is sent to Ireland against O'Neal. He fails, returns to England, and is put into custody for a time.
1600.	Essex intrigues with James of Scotland, and with Romanists and Puritans.
1601.	**Insurrection of Essex. His execution.**
	Spaniards land in Ireland and fortify Kinsale.
	Debate in Parliament on monopolies. The queen consents to their abolition.

[Notes.]

(*a*) This provided for the appointment, in every parish, of the churchwardens and from two to four householders, nominated by the justices of the peace, as overseers of the poor. These persons might levy a rate on land and use it (1) to set to work indigent children and able-bodied men out of work; (2) to relieve people who could not work, and had no near relatives to support them; (3) to erect houses of correction for vagabonds, and to put out pauper children as apprentices.

(*b*) *Millenary Petition.*—It was subscribed by 825 clergymen, and stated objections to the use of the surplice, of the cross in baptism, and the ring in marriage, the reading of the Apocrypha, non-residence of ministers, etc.

(*c*) The chief points urged were the right of the Commons to control their own elections (violated by James' Proclamation and the rejection of the member for Buckinghamshire), and the right of the members to freedom from arrest (violated by the imprisonment of Sir Thomas Shirley for a private debt).

(*d*) Under the heading "King" Cowell wrote: "He is above the law by his absolute power, and though for the better and equal course in making laws, he do admit the Three Estates unto Council, yet this in divers learned men's opinion is not of constraint, but of his own benignity, or by reason of the promise made upon oath at the time of his coronation."

FOREIGN AND COLONIAL.

1605. Barbados, our oldest colony, founded.

1608. **First permanent English settlement in America** made at Jamestown by the **Virginia Company.**

1609. A treaty is made between the Dutch and the Spaniards which practically secures the independence of the former.

The disputed succession to Juliers and Cleves begins the troubles which lead to the Thirty Years' War.

Henry IV. of France murdered by Ravaillac at the moment when he was setting out for Germany to aid the Protestant Union. Succeeded by Louis XIII.

1611. The colonization of Ulster by natives of England and Scotland begins to be carried out.

1612. Episcopacy is authorized in Scotland by the Scottish Estates.

[1601—1612] ENGLISH.

1601.	The first regular Poor Law (*a*) is passed.
1602.	O'Neal submits, and is pardoned.
1603.	*March.* Elizabeth dies.

JAMES I., 1603—1625 (22 YEARS).
Born 1566; Married, 1589, Anne of Denmark.

James reaches London from Scotland in May. [See *Summary: Scotland, Part II.*, p. 248.] The Millenary Petition (*b*) is presented to James. Ten of those who present it are committed to prison.

The Main Plot to change the government, and possibly to place Arabella Stuart [see note (*d*), p. 80] on the throne, and the Bye Plot to obtain toleration are discovered. Sir Walter Raleigh and others are imprisoned.

1604.	**The Hampton Court Conference** between the bishops and the representatives of the Puritans is held. The Authorized Version of the Bible is ordered to be made.

Whitgift dies, and is succeeded by **Bancroft** as Archbishop of Canterbury.

The First Parliament of James *vindicates its privileges* (*c*), *and presses for persecution of the Catholics.*

Peace is concluded with Spain.

The Gunpowder Plot is projected against both king and Parliament.

1605.	**The Gunpowder Plot is discovered.**
1606.	Parliament increases the severity of the laws against Catholics.
1607.	A bill for a Union between England and Scotland is rejected in the Commons, who, however, repeal the hostile border laws.

The enclosure of commons leads to disturbances, headed by "Captain Pouch."

1608.	*The judges having decided in Bates' case (the case of "Impositions") that the king might regulate the customs, a new book of rates largely increasing them is issued.*
1610.	*The Commons remonstrate against the "Impositions," the High Commission Court, and Royal Proclamations.*

The failure of the plan of the younger Cecil (now Salisbury) for the commutation of feudal dues (by the arrangement called "The Great Contract") is caused by the refusal of Parliament.

Cowell's law dictionary "The Interpreter" (*d*), which ascribes absolute power to the king, is censured by the Commons.

Bancroft dies, and is succeeded by **Abbott** as Archbishop of Canterbury, who, though of Puritan tendencies, increases the severity of the High Commission Court. Dissolution of Parliament.

1611.	The order of Baronets is instituted by James as a means of raising money.

Arabella Stuart is imprisoned in the Tower for marrying William Seymour [see note (*c*), p. 76], and dies, 1615.

1612.	Princess Elizabeth is betrothed to the Elector Palatine and married the next year.

Death of Salisbury, the younger Cecil. The Treasury is

[Notes.]

(a) This Parliament was called by the advice of certain courtiers, who having undertaken to provide obsequious members, received the nickname of "Undertakers."

(b) An impeachment is a trial where the House of Commons is the prosecutor and the Lords are the judges. An Act of Attainder is a bill by which a person is attainted of treason and condemned by Parliament.

(c) Their protest was to the effect that "their liberties and privileges were the undoubted birthright of the subjects of England: the State, the defence of the realm, the Church, the laws and grievances were proper matters for them to debate: members have liberty of speech, and freedom from all imprisonment for speaking on any matters touching Parliament business."

(d) "A subsidy was an income tax of 4s. in the pound upon the annual value of lands, and a property tax of 2s. 8d. in the pound upon the actual value of goods. Those whose lands were not worth 20s. a year, or whose personal property was not worth 60s. in value, were not taxed, and the lands were rated very low" (*King and Commonwealth*).

(e) Tonnage was a tax of 1s. 6d. to 3s. on every tun of wine or beer, and poundage of 6d. to 1s. on every pound of dry goods, except staple commodities, exported or imported.

(f) In his memoirs of the first Parliament of Charles I. Sir John Eliot, in mentioning the bills which received the king's assent, says, "The Bill of Tonnage and Poundage was respited, and yet those levies made." (See Forster's "Life of Eliot," vol i. p. 309.)

FOREIGN AND COLONIAL.

1614. The French Estates-General meet and declare Louis XIII. to be of age. This is the last meeting before 1789.

1618. The General Assembly of Scotland passes the Articles of Perth, imposing much more ceremonial. The Thirty Years' War begins.

1619. The Bohemians choose Frederick of the Palatinate as their king.

1620. Landing of the first Puritan settlers at Plymouth in America. The Protestants are defeated at the battle of Prague.

1621. Philip III. of Spain dies, and is succeeded by Philip IV.

1623. Several English traders are massacred by the Dutch at Amboyna, one of the Molucca Islands.

1624. Richelieu becomes first minister of France (to 1642).

1612.	placed in Commission. **Robert Carr, Viscount Rochester** (afterwards Earl of Somerset), becomes the king's chief adviser. Death of Prince Henry at the age of nineteen.
1614.	**The second Parliament of James** (*a*), called "*The Addled Parliament,*" *meets, and after refusing a supply till it had dealt with the king's imposition of customs, is dissolved. Several members are imprisoned.*
1616.	Sir Walter Raleigh is released from the Tower, and allowed to go to South America.
	Somerset and his wife are tried and convicted of the murder of Overbury.
	Suspension and deprivation of Coke, the chief justice.
	Villiers, afterwards Duke of Buckingham, becomes chief favourite of James.
1618.	Execution of Sir Walter Raleigh, nominally for treason, in reality for his quarrels with the Spaniards.
1619.	James refuses to assist his son-in-law the Elector Palatine, who has been elected King of Bohemia.
1620.	Negotiations with Spain concerning the marriage of Prince Charles.
1621.	**The third Parliament** of James meets. The Commons impeach(*b*) Sir Giles Mompesson for holding monopolies. **Bacon, Lord Chancellor**, is impeached, and deprived of the great seal.
	Nov. Parliament reassembles, and the Commons make a protest against the violations of their liberties (*c*)*. The king tears it out from their journal with his own hand.*
1622.	*On the dissolution of Parliament, Coke,* **Pym,** *Selden, and two others are imprisoned.*
1623.	Prince Charles and Buckingham go to Madrid, and treaties are drawn up.
	On their return to England, Buckingham procures the breaking off of the match, and thus obtains popularity.
1624.	**The fourth Parliament of James** votes supplies, and war is declared with Spain. *Monopolies are finally declared illegal in Parliament.* Lord Middlesex, the Lord Treasurer, is impeached and condemned for bribery.
	A treaty of marriage for Prince Charles is arranged with France.
1625.	*March.* James dies.

CHARLES I., 1625—1649 (24 Years).

Born 1600; Married, 1625, Henrietta Maria of France.

June. Charles marries Henrietta of France.
First Parliament of Charles. The Parliament grants two subsidies (*d*), but a bill granting tonnage and poundage (*e*) for one year instead of for life is dropped in the House of Lords (*f*).
Eight ships which had been sent to Richelieu in pursuance of the treaty with France are used against Rochelle.
Parliament, adjourned from London, meets at Oxford.
Dr. Montague, royal chaplain, is censured in Parliament for a work of Arminian tendencies.

[Notes.]

FOREIGN AND COLONIAL.

1626. Christian IV. of Denmark defeated at Lutter by Tilly.

1628. *Oct.* Fall of La Rochelle and the political power of the Huguenots.

(*a*) He had said that no subject could refuse a tax or loan without peril of damnation.

(*b*) *Petition of Right:—*
1. That no freeman be required to give any gift, loan, benevolence, or tax without common consent by Act of Parliament.
2. That no freeman be imprisoned or detained contrary to the law of the land.
3. That soldiers or mariners be not billeted in private houses.
4. That commissions to punish soldiers and sailors by martial law be revoked and no more issued.

1629. The Massachusetts Bay Company formed, which founds a (second) Puritan colony in America.

1625.	Parliament, refusing to grant supplies, is dissolved. The expedition to Cadiz, for which money had been provided by forced loans, fails to take that town or to intercept the Spanish treasure fleet.
1626.	*Feb.* **Second Parliament of Charles** meets, many members of the last Parliament being excluded by being appointed sheriffs, and a writ being withheld from the Earl of Bristol. Three committees are appointed—for privileges, for religion, and for the state of the kingdom. Sir Dudley Digges and **Sir John Eliot** impeach Buckingham on behalf of the Commons. *They are sent to the Tower, but are released on Parliament refusing to continue its business.* *June.* The Commons continuing the impeachment of Buckingham, and refusing to grant supplies, Parliament is dissolved. *Money is collected by forced loans, and tonnage and poundage illegally levied.*
1627.	Drs. Sibthorp and Mainwaring preach in favour of the king's prerogative. War is declared against France in the interest of the Huguenots, and money is collected by forced loans. The expedition to the isle of Rhé, off Rochelle, under Buckingham proves a failure. Five gentlemen (including Edward Hampden) are imprisoned (for refusing forced loans) under a Privy Council warrant issued by royal command. Their case is argued before the judges, and decided against them. Poor men are pressed for the army and navy under martial law, and billeted on the refractory gentlemen.
1628.	*March.* **The third Parliament of Charles meets.** The Commons, after having been irritated by the Court, throw the blame of all their grievances on Buckingham. By request of the Commons, Mainwaring's sermons are condemned by proclamation (*a*). *After various conferences with the Lords, the Commons, led by Wentworth and Pym, draw up the* **PETITION OF RIGHT** (*b*), *which passes the Lords and is presented to the king, who after some hesitation assents to it,* June. Parliament now grants five subsidies. *June* 26. Parliament is prorogued. **Laud** is translated from Bath and Wells to London, and becomes the king's chief adviser in ecclesiastical matters. About the same time favours are shown to Mainwaring. Preparations for a second expedition against France are made. **Wentworth (afterwards Strafford)** comes over to the side of the king, and is soon made President of the Council of the North. [See 1537.] *Aug.* **Buckingham is assassinated at Portsmouth** by Felton. Tonnage and poundage are illegally collected as before. Alderman Chambers is imprisoned for non-payment of customs duties, and for insolent words spoken before the Council.
1629.	*Jan.* The adjourned Parliament meets and discusses its grievances.

FOREIGN AND COLONIAL.

1632. Gustavus Adolphus, King of Sweden, who landed in Germany 1630, defeats Wallenstein at Lützen, but falls on the field.

1633. The choice of the Lords of the Articles in the Scottish Parliament is put into the hands of the bishops by Charles.

During his term of office Wentworth reformed the Irish Church and the Civil Service, made the army efficient, introduced the linen manufacture, got a grant of money from the Irish Parliament, and began to reclaim for the Crown large tracts of land in Connaught with a view to colonization.

1634. Murder of Wallenstein.

1637. The Scots resist the introduction of a new Liturgy drawn up by Laud.

1638. The Second Covenant is drawn up, and Episcopacy in Scotland is condemned by the Glasgow Assembly. The Covenanters prepare for war.

1639. *Aug.* The Scottish Parliament meets, formally abolishes Episcopacy, and makes fresh preparations for war.

Madras is acquired, first English territory in India.

(*a*) Rockingham Forest was extended from six miles to sixty. It appeared as if the greater part of England would soon be considered as having been forest-land in former days.

(*b*) The king, says Correro the Venetian, moves among the rocks by which he is surrounded, slowly but surely. The judges explain the laws in his favour, as there are no parliaments to contradict them: and his subjects do not then venture to withstand him. "With the key of the laws he seeks to open the entrance to absolute power" (*Ranke*).

1629.	Finally, March 2, the Speaker refuses, by the king's order, to read a remonstrance of Sir John Eliot on tonnage and poundage, and on religion. He said he had orders to adjourn, but was held in his chair till Holles had passed a resolution that they who make innovations in religion, or who exact or pay subsidies not granted by Parliament, are enemies of the kingdom. Parliament is now adjourned till March 10, and then dissolved. Meantime, on March 5, *Sir John Eliot and others are sent to the Tower.* **[Eleven years of arbitrary government follow.]**
1630.	*April.* Peace is made with France. [About this time Wentworth, Laud, Coventry, Weston, and Noy form the king's ministry.] *Nov.* Peace is made with Spain. Dr. Leighton is by sentence of Star Chamber pilloried and imprisoned for writing against prelates. Large sums are being collected from the gentry by distraint of knighthood.
1632.	**Sir John Eliot dies in the Tower.**
1633.	The nobility are irritated by an inquiry into the extent of royal forests and alleged encroachments, conducted by Lord Holland, chief justice in eyre (*a*). The city of London is irritated by the confiscation of its settlements in Ulster and a heavy fine in Star Chamber for alleged mismanagement. The merchants are irritated by the grant to companies of the sole right of selling soap, starch, beer, and other articles. *June.* The king goes to Scotland to be crowned. *July.* **Wentworth is appointed Lord Deputy of Ireland.** *Aug.* **Laud becomes Archbishop of Canterbury.**
1634.	*A writ for ship-money drawn up by Noy, carefully following the ancient precedents, is addressed to maritime towns and counties, and on the pretext of defending the coast against pirates, a collection is made without complaint.*
1635.	*A new writ of ship-money after Noy's death, extending the tax to inland towns and counties, is issued.* Archbishop Laud holds a visitation, in which he endeavours to give greater prominence than before to ritual.
1637.	*The judges, asked by the king, give their opinion that the king can legally order his subjects to pay ship-money if the kingdom is in danger* (*b*). **John Hampden** *having refused to pay ship-money, judgment is given against him by a majority of the judges (after long arguments before them).* Prynne, a barrister, Burton, a clergyman, and Bastwick, a physician, are condemned in the Star Chamber for their writings, and pilloried, and have their ears cut off. Williams, Bishop of Lincoln, who had favoured the Puritans, is imprisoned for libel, and suspended by the High Commission Court.
1639.	The king advances to Berwick. The Scots, assisted by money

[Notes.]

(a) The Scottish army was to be disbanded; the English fleet was to withdraw from the Firth; the king's castles were to be handed back to him; a free General Assembly was to meet in August, and a Parliament directly afterwards, and for the future Parliaments were to be regularly summoned.

(b) *Triennial Act:*—
1. Every Parliament was to be *ipso facto* dissolved at the end of three years from the first day of its session, unless then actually sitting, and in that case, then on its first subsequent prorogation or adjournment.
2. A Parliament must be summoned within three years from the dissolution of the last Parliament, and must not be prorogued within fifty days of its meeting without its own consent. Provision is made for the elections being made by the people in default of the king's issuing the writs.

(c) *Strafford's Impeachment.*—He was accused on twenty-eight counts which concerned his conduct towards England, Ireland, and Scotland. The chief was that he had incensed his majesty against the members of the late Parliament, telling him "they had denied to supply him, and that his majesty having tried the affections of his people, and been refused, he was absolved from all rules of government, and that he had an army in Ireland which he might employ to reduce this kingdom" (*State Trials*). The Lords refused to admit as evidence a paper found by Sir Harry Vane, which supported his father's evidence on this charge. For which cause the Commons brought in a bill of attainder.

FOREIGN AND COLONIAL.

1641. The Incident (or design of Charles to arrest Argyll and Hamilton) in Scotland.

Oct. 23. The Irish Rebellion breaks out, and is followed by dreadful massacres and disorders, in which Ireland was computed to have lost one-third of its population, and to have been thrown back many years in trade and civilization.

1639.	from France, advance to the Border, *June.* The pacification of Berwick is concluded (*a*).
1640.	**The fourth Parliament of Charles** meets. *Pym makes a speech reciting the illegal acts of the Crown since the last Parliament.* The king, on condition that he would give up ship-money, demands an immediate subsidy, and the Commons seeming likely to refuse, Parliament is dissolved, *May* 5.
	Convocation, having granted a subsidy, sits after the dissolution, and passes canons asserting the divine right of bishops.
	Aug. The Scots invade England, win the battle of Newburn, and advance into Yorkshire. *The king summons a Great Council of peers at York.* Negotiations with the Scots are opened at Ripon, and then transferred to London.
	Oct. 22. **The High Commission Court sits for the last time.**
	Nov. **The fifth Parliament of Charles** meets (Lenthal Speaker). The Commons impeach Lord Strafford, who had remained in England at the king's request.
	Prynne, Burton, Leighton, Chambers, and others are released by Parliament and compensated.
	Finch, the Lord Chancellor, is impeached, but flies to Holland.
	The recent canons of Convocation are declared to be illegal.
	Laud is impeached and committed to custody.
1641.	A commission is issued by the Commons to deface and demolish in churches images, altars, and monuments.
	Feb. The **Triennial Act** is passed (*b*).
	March 10. The Commons bring in a bill to exclude the bishops from the House of Lords, which is passed May 1.
	March 22. Strafford's trial begins in the House of Lords (*c*). A bill of attainder against him is passed by the Commons, April 21.
	May 3. The plot to bring up the army to rescue Strafford is announced by Pym to the Commons.
	May 7. The Lords pass the bill of attainder against Strafford.
	May 10. The king consents to the attainder.
	The king agrees that Parliament shall not be adjourned or dissolved without its own consent.
	May 12. **Strafford is executed.**
	May 27. A bill for the complete abolition of Episcopacy ("**The Root and Branch Bill**") is read in the Commons.
	June 21. A grant of tonnage and poundage for two months is made, which is afterwards renewed.
	July. Statutes are passed *abolishing the Court of Star Chamber (and therewith the Council of the North and the Court of Wales) and the High Commission Court, and the King's Council is deprived of the power of arbitrary imprisonment and jurisdiction.* [See Summary: The Council, p. 266.]
	Statutes are also passed against ship-money, distraint of knighthood, and illegal custom duties, and the extent of the royal forests is fixed.
	Aug. The English and Scottish armies are disbanded.
	Aug. The king goes to Scotland attended by a committee of the Commons.
	Sept. 9 to Oct. 20. Recess of Parliament.

[Notes.]

(a) The Grand Remonstrance consisted of 206 clauses, in which were related the unconstitutional and foolish acts of the government since the beginning of the reign, and remedies were demanded. It was, in fact, a vindication of the Parliament and an appeal to the people.

(b) *The Propositions.*—These propositions demanded that obnoxious counsellors be dismissed; that all the chief officers of State should be approved by the Parliament, should take an oath to abide by the laws, and hold their offices *quamdiu se bene gesserint;* that the king's children be not married without the consent of Parliament, and that their guardians be such as Parliament approves; that all transactions of State be agreed upon by the Council; that the laws against Catholics be enforced and the liturgy be reformed; that the regulations for the militia be accepted; that the fortresses should be put into the hands of men approved by Parliament; that the king's forces should be discharged; that the five members should be secured from further molestation; and that an alliance should be made with the Dutch.

(c) Essex, fifty years of age, was the son of the Earl of Essex executed in 1601. He was divorced from his wife in order that she might marry the Earl of Somerset in 1614. He had served abroad, and had lost much property by the extension of the forests.

1641.	*Nov.* 22. **THE GRAND REMONSTRANCE** (*a*) *passes the Commons by a majority of eleven, and is ordered to be printed.* *Dec.* 30. The Commons impeach the bishops, who had signed a protest against the Acts passed by the House of Lords in their absence. [At this time **Falkland** and **Colepepper** take office under the king. **Hyde** (afterwards Clarendon) only refuses in order better to serve the king's interests in the Commons.]
1642.	*Jan.* 3. The attorney-general charges Lord Kimbolton (afterwards Manchester) and five members of the Commons (John Hampden, Pym, Holles, Haselrig, Strode) with high treason in the House of Lords. *Jan.* 4. **The king comes in person to the House of Commons and demands the five members, who have escaped to the city.** *Jan.* 10. **Charles leaves London (not to return till 1649).** *Feb.* The queen goes over to Holland with the crown jewels to collect forces. The king agrees to the exclusion of the bishops from the House of Lords. *March* 9. The Commons having requested the king to place the charge of fortified places and the command of the militia in their hands, the king, after many conferences, finally refuses at Newmarket. *March* 22. The Lords order Sir John Hotham to receive no forces into Hull without an order from both Houses. *April* 23. Hotham refuses to admit the king into Hull. Both sides begin to raise forces, the Parliament through the lord-lieutenants, the king by commissions of array. *May.* Falkland, Hyde, and others withdraw from Parliament to the king, and many such absentees are deprived of their seats. *June* 2. The Parliament sends nineteen propositions to the king at York, which he rejects (*b*). *July.* **Essex** (*c*) is appointed captain-general of the Parliamentary forces. *Aug.* 1. *The Commons make an order for levying tonnage and poundage.* *Aug.* 22. The king sets up his standard at Nottingham. *Aug.* 31. Stage plays are ordered to cease by Parliament. *Sept.* 1. The Commons finally resolve to abolish bishops and other ecclesiastical officers. *Sept.* 20. The king establishes his headquarters at Shrewsbury. Essex places garrisons in the line of towns from Northampton to Worcester to bar the approach of the king to London. Charles, having outmarched Essex, turns to meet him at **Edgehill**, October 23. Indecisive battle. Charles marches towards London, by Oxford. Essex retreats to Warwick, and then comes to London. *Nov.* 13. The king obtains Brentford after a sharp fight. The armies face one another at Turnham Green. *Nov.* 15. The king retreats, and takes up winter quarters at Oxford. Essex takes up his quarters round Thame. *Dec.* *A tax on property and incomes is levied through the whole kingdom by the Parliament.*

[Notes.]

(a) These counties were Suffolk, Norfolk, Cambridge, Essex, Hertford, Huntingdon, and, afterwards, Lincolnshire.

(b) Now spelt Adwalton.

(c) It was agreed that the Parliament should pay the Scots a certain sum for their equipments, and a monthly subsidy so long as they remained in England.

FOREIGN AND COLONIAL.

1643. Louis XIII. dies, succeeded by Louis XIV.
A "New England Confederation" is formed in America of Massachusetts, Plymouth, Connecticut, and Newhaven.

Sept. The Marquis of Ormond makes a peace (the Cessation) with the Irish, and sends over troops to England.

1644. Montrose with a body of Highlanders and Irish Royalists defeats Lord Elcho at Tippermuir and captures Perth.

1643.	The Association of the Eastern Counties (*a*) is regulated by ordinance. *June* 6. Edmund Waller's plot against Parliament is discovered. War is carried on for the most part in four different districts—(1) by the main forces on the road from Oxford to London, (2) in Yorkshire, (3) in the west, and (4) in the eastern counties. (1) *June* 18. Hampden is defeated and mortally wounded at **Chalgrove Field**, and the main Parliamentary army becomes much disorganized. (2) *June* 30. At **Atherton Moor** (*b*), near Bradford, **the Fairfaxes** are defeated by the "Papist" army under Newcastle. The elder Fairfax takes refuge in Hull. The younger (Sir Thomas) passes over to Lincolnshire. (3) *July* 13. At **Roundway Down**, near Devizes, Waller, with the Parliamentary forces of the west, is utterly defeated, and Bristol is sacked by **Prince Rupert**, July. (4) *July* 25. **Cromwell**, with the army of the eastern counties, wins the battle of **Gainsborough**. The king now proposes to march on London, which is fortified by the citizens, with all his forces, but Newcastle refusing to leave Yorkshire till Hull is taken, Charles forms the siege of Gloucester. *Sept.* 5. Essex raises the siege of Gloucester. The king tries to intercept him on his march to London. First battle of **Newbury** indecisive, September 20. **Falkland is killed.** Essex continues his march to London. The king retreats to Oxford for the winter. *Sept.* 25. Parliament makes an agreement with the Scots for assistance, and signs **THE SOLEMN LEAGUE AND COVENANT.** *Oct.* 10. Manchester, Cromwell, and Sir T. Fairfax defeat Newcastle's forces at **Winceby** in Lincolnshire. *Oct.* 11. The siege of Hull is raised. *Dec.* 8. **Death of Pym.**
1644.	*Jan.* 19. The Scottish army, 21,000 strong, crosses the Border (*c*). *Jan.* 22. The king summons a Parliament at Oxford. *Jan.* 25. Sir T. Fairfax defeats the Irish contingent at Nantwich. In the north, Newcastle moves north to resist the Scots, but on the advance of Fairfax retreats to York, where he is besieged by the allied armies. In the south, Essex and Waller attempt to besiege the king in Oxford. He escapes to Worcester, and Essex marches into the west. The king detaches Rupert to the north, and having defeated Waller at **Cropredy Bridge**, *June* 29, pursues Essex. In the north, Rupert, evading the allied army, raises the siege of York, and with Newcastle is utterly defeated by the allies under Alexander Leslie (Earl of Leven), Fairfax, Manchester, and Cromwell, at **Marston Moor**, *July* 2. In the west, the king out-generals Essex, who is forced to abandon his army, which surrenders at Lostwithiel, *Aug.* Essex having collected a new army, and being reinforced by

[Notes.]

(a) The Commons demanded (1) the establishment of Presbyterianism ; (2) the appointment of the officers of the militia by themselves ; (3) the renewal of the war with Ireland.
The king would grant (1) a limitation of the power of the bishops by councils of the lower clergy ; (2) that for three years the officers of the militia should be nominated by a commission, half of whom were to be named by himself, and afterwards the appointment of officers was to be in his hands ; (3) that permanent peace should be made in Ireland.

(b) This battle brought to a close the fighting in the open field, and the Parliamentary leaders spent the next two years in capturing the strong places which still held out for the king. Charles wanders from place to place.

(c) This Assembly consisted of ten peers, twenty members of the House of Commons, one hundred and twenty-one divines, and six deputies of Scotland. Presbyterians and Independents were present, but the Baptists were excluded.

(d) 1. To reduce the army.
2. To deprive of their commands all members of the Parliament.
3. That all officers should take the Covenant.
4. That a sixth only of the arrears of pay should be paid to the soldiers.

FOREIGN AND COLONIAL.

1645. *Feb.* Montrose gains a victory over Argyll at Inverlochy.

May. Montrose gains another victory at Aldern.

July. Montrose defeats Baillie at Alford.

Aug. Montrose again defeats Baillie at Kilsyth.

Sept. 13. Montrose is utterly routed by David Leslie at Philiphaugh.

1644.	Manchester and Cromwell, an attempt was made to cut off the king on his return to Oxford. *Oct.* 27. **Second battle of Newbury** indecisive. **The Independents bring the Self-denying Ordinance into Parliament.**
1645.	*Jan.* 1. Sir John Hotham and his son are executed for a plot formed in 1643 to deliver Hull to the king. *Jan.* 10. **Archbishop Laud is beheaded.** Negotiations (*a*) are opened at Uxbridge with the king, *Jan.* 30: are broken off. *Feb.* 21. *April* 3. The Self-denying Ordinance (depriving members of Parliament of civil or military office) passes the Lords. Essex, Manchester, and Waller give up their commissions. **The Parliamentary army is remodelled at Windsor, and put under the command of Sir Thomas Fairfax.** *May* 10. The services of Cromwell, though a member of Parliament, are retained by Act of Parliament for forty days, and this Act is renewed from time to time. The king withdraws to Chester. Fairfax and "the new model" advance to the siege of Oxford. Charles marches south and storms Leicester, and hesitates whether to relieve Oxford or march against the associated counties. Fairfax marches north, is joined by Cromwell with the Association horse, and totally defeats the king at the **battle of Naseby**, near Market Harborough in Leicestershire, *June* 14. (The king's baggage is taken, in which are found his letters to the queen and to the Irish rebels, which are published by the Parliament). Fairfax defeats Goring at Langport, *July.* *Sept.* 10. Bristol is surrendered by Prince Rupert. *Sept.* 23. Charles' forces are defeated at Rowton Heath, near Chester (*b*).
1646.	After fruitless negotiations at various times with the Parliament, the Scottish army in England, and the Independents, Charles, finding himself disappointed of help from Montrose in Scotland, **betakes himself to the Scottish army at Newark** (*May* 5), which retreats with him to Newcastle. *June* 24. Oxford surrenders to Fairfax. At Newcastle, Charles, urged by the queen, now in France, refuses to concede anything to the Parliament on the question of the militia or the Church.
1647.	The Parliament having agreed to pay £400,000 to the Scots for their expenses, the first payment is made *Jan.* 21 (see 1644). *Jan.* 30. **The king is given up at Newcastle to the Parliamentary Commissioners.** [**The Westminster Assembly of Divines** (*c*), which had been sitting constantly since 1643, had by this time established Presbyterianism, which was, however, only generally accepted in Middlesex and Lancashire.] The four ordinances are passed by Parliament (*d*). *March* 21. A great meeting of the officers is held at Saffron Walden to protest against the ordinances.

[Notes.]

FOREIGN AND COLONIAL.

(*a*) 1. Parliament was to be moved to Oxford and dissolved within three months.
2. Episcopacy was to be restored, but there was to be also complete toleration.
3. Bristol, Digby, Worcester, and Newcastle alone were to be excepted from the amnesty.
4. A reform was to be effected in the administration of justice, and imprisonment for debt was to be abolished.
5. The command of the forces by sea and land was to reside in Parliament for ten years.
6. The appointment to all the great offices was to be in the hands of Parliament.

(*b*) 1. Charles agreed to an amnesty for all members of the Parliament.
2. The appointment of officers and the command of the military forces of the kingdom was to be in the hands of Parliament for twenty years.
3. The appointment of the chief officers of State was to be in the hands of Parliament for twenty years.
4. Certain members of the Royalist party were reserved for punishment.
5. The bishops were to be suspended and the Presbyterian clergy established and endowed provisionally for three years.

(*c*) The Commons then resolved that whatever is enacted by them has the force of law without the consent of the king or the House of Lords. The members expelled by Colonel Pride were formally excluded from Parliament, Feb. 1, 1649.

1648. The Scottish moderate Presbyterian party in the Estates pass a vote that 40,000 men under Hamilton shall invade England in the king's interest.
Condé wins the battle of Lens.
The Peace of Westphalia concludes the Thirty Years' War.

1649. Prince Charles accepts the proposals of the extreme Covenanters under Argyll.

1647.	The Parliament passes a resolution that the army have no business to meddle with State affairs. *May*. The Presbyterian Commissioners from the Parliament attempt to disband the army. The army refuse, and arrange a general assembly of all the soldiers to meet on *June* 4 near Newmarket. *June* 2. The king is seized at Holmby House by Cornet Joyce, and conducted to Newmarket. *June* 10. The army have a great meeting at Triplow Heath, and an interview with the Parliamentary Commissioners, at which they demand the expulsion of eleven of the Presbyterian leaders. The army march towards London and place the king at Hampton Court. They make liberal proposals (*a*) to the king, who rejects them, and flies from Hampton Court to the Isle of Wight (*Nov.* 11), and there corresponds with the Scots, the Presbyterians, and the Royalists.
1648.	Royalist insurrections break out in Kent and in Wales. The fleet goes over to the side of Charles. Fairfax puts down the Royalists at Maidstone (*June*) and at Colchester (*Aug.*). Cromwell takes Pembroke Castle. *July* 5. **The Scottish army** enters England, and **is defeated by** Cromwell at **Preston** (*Aug.* 17), **Wigan,** and **Warrington.** *Sept.* The Parliament enter into negotiations with the king at Newport (Isle of Wight). The king agrees to their propositions (*b*). The army return to London and demand the punishment of the king. **Colonel Pride expels the Presbyterian majority from the House of Commons,** *Dec.* 6. The Independent minority (53 members) vote to bring the king to trial before a special or High Court of Justice. This is rejected by the House of Lords (12 members) (*c*).
1649.	*Jan.* 20. **The High Court of Justice meets.** *Jan.* 30. **The king is beheaded.**

THE COMMONWEALTH, 1649—1660
(11 Years).

[The publication of *Eikōn Basilikē*, giving an account of Charles' life in prison, produces a reaction of feeling in his favour.]
Feb. 6. A resolution is passed in the Commons that the House of Lords is "useless, dangerous, and ought to be abolished."
Feb. 7. It is resolved that government by a king or single person is "unnecessary, burdensome, and dangerous, and ought to be abolished." *Feb.* 15. A Council of State is appointed.
Hamilton, Holland, and Capel are executed.
Troops are ordered to Ireland. Insurrection of the Levellers, who are dispersed by Cromwell and Fairfax at Burford.
May 19. **An Act declaring and constituting the people of England to be a Commonwealth and free State passes, and is proclaimed.**
Aug. 2. Ormond is defeated by General Jones at Rathmines.

[Notes.]

(*a*) All land of the Irish in Ulster, Munster, and Leinster is confiscated and distributed among the adventurers, who had lent money for the war, and the soldiers of the Republic. Innocent Papists who had had no part in the rebellion were compensated by grants of land in Connaught.

(*b*) *Barebone's Parliament.*—So called from Praise-God Barbon, junior member for the city of London.
It proposed (1) to simplify the law, to abolish the Court of Chancery, to establish county courts for the recovery of small debts, to do away with imprisonment for debt, and to pay the judges by salaries instead of fees.
2. To transfer patronage in the Church to congregations, and do away with tithes.
3. To register births, deaths, and marriages, and to make all marriages take place before a magistrate; to set up a register for deeds affecting land, and to provide a better system of workhouses.
" In justice to Barebone's Parliament its reforms should be compared with the course of subsequent legislation. Of the reforms proposed by them, the larger number have been adopted, while others have been held advisable, if not practicable, in the present century" (*King and Commonwealth*).

FOREIGN AND COLONIAL.

1650. Montrose defeated and captured at Corbiesdale, executed May 21.
Charles goes to Scotland. An army is formed in Scotland of the extreme Covenanters, exclusive of the followers of Hamilton and the Royalists, and put under the command nominally of Alexander Leslie, Lord Leven, really of David Leslie.
1651. *Jan.* 1. Charles is crowned at Scone. He gets together a new army from the followers of Hamilton and the Royalists, and takes up a position at Stirling.
1652. Cromwellian settlement of Ireland (*a*).

[1649—1653] ENGLISH.

1649.   *Aug.* 15. **Cromwell lands in Ireland.**
Sept. 11. He storms and sacks **Drogheda** and (*Oct.* 12) Wexford.
1650.   Cromwell returns to England, leaving Ireton and Ludlow in command.
Fairfax having refused the command of the army against the Scots, it is accepted by Cromwell (*June* 25), who crosses the Tweed (*July* 16), advances to Edinburgh, and is forced to retreat to Dunbar for want of provisions. **Battle of Dunbar,** *Sept.* 3. The Scots are utterly routed.
Dec. Capture of Edinburgh.
1651.   *Aug.* Cromwell crosses the Forth, and Charles marches into England. He is pursued by Cromwell (who leaves Monk in command in Scotland) and defeated at the **battle of Worcester,** *Sept.* 3.
Charles, after many adventures, takes ship at Brighton and lands at Fécamp, *Oct.* 17.
Oct. 9. The Navigation Act, aimed against the Dutch (forbidding the importation of goods in any but English vessels or those of the country where they are made), is passed.
Nov. Parliament fixes November 3, 1654, as the day of its dissolution.
1652.   *Feb.* An Act of oblivion of all offences committed before the battle of Worcester is passed in Parliament.
May 19. The Dutch are defeated in a battle off Dover.
July. War is declared against the Dutch.
Aug. A bill is introduced to make the new House of Commons consist of four hundred members. All present members are to keep their seats, with a right of veto on newly elected members (Perpetuation Bill). The army remonstrate.
Nov. **Blake** is defeated by Tromp in the Dover roads.
1653.   The Parliament resolves that it will not proceed with the Perpetuation Bill till another conference has been held with the army.
April 20. Word is brought to the officers that the Parliament is passing the bill. Cromwell goes down to the House and expels the members.
Cromwell and the officers appoint a Council of State (nine army men and four civilians), which sends letters to the Independent ministers to consult with their congregations and send up the names of persons fitted to sit in Parliament.
From these names the Council select one hundred and thirty-nine to meet as a Parliament.
July 4. This Assembly of Nominees (**the " Little " or " Barebone's "**(*b*) **Parliament**) meets.
June and July. Important victories over Tromp and the Dutch fleet.
The Parliament propose to abolish the Court of Chancery, tithes, and Church patronage, and appoint a commission to reform the law.
But finding they cannot carry out these measures, they resign their power into the hands of Cromwell, *Dec.*
Dec. 16. **The " Instrument of Government,"** by which **Cromwell** is made **Lord Protector with a Council of**

[Notes.]   *FOREIGN AND COLONIAL.*

(a) The executive government was to consist of a Protector and a Council of State. The members of the Council were, in the first instance, named in the instrument, for life; but on the occurrence of a vacancy it was to be filled up by the Protector from a list of six persons nominated by the Parliament. The right of legislation was vested in Parliament; but the Protector might suspend the coming into operation of any Act for twenty days. Parliaments were to be held once in every third year; but they might not be dissolved till they had sat five months. The Protector was to be general by sea and land, but he was to decide questions of war and peace by the aid of his Council, and in case of war Parliament was to be immediately summoned.

(b) "The capture of Jamaica marks the period when the lawless rule of the buccaneers (in the plantations) began to be exchanged for the rule of European governments" (*Payne*).

1655. Capture of Jamaica (b).

(c) The House inquiring why the names of certain members were not returned, is answered that the Council have not refused to approve any who have appeared to them to be persons of integrity, fearing God, and of good conversation; and those who are not approved, his Highness hath given order to some persons to take care they do not come into the House.

(d) The executive government was to consist of a Protector and a Council of State. The members of the Council and the chief officers were to be nominated or removed with consent of Parliament. Parliament was to consist of two Houses, and meet at least once every three years. The Protector was to be general by sea and land. All Christian religions but Popery and Socinianism were to be tolerated. The Protector was allowed to name his successor. Had the army allowed Cromwell to receive the title of king, this would have in fact restored the old constitution in an amended form and with a new dynasty.

1653.	twenty-one (a), is published, and Cromwell is inaugurated in Westminster Hall.
1654.	*March* 20. A board of triers to examine the character of ministers nominated to livings by patrons is instituted by ordinance. *April* 5. **Peace is concluded with Holland.** *April* 12. England and Scotland are united by ordinance. *May.* Vowell and Gerard's plot to assassinate the Protector is discovered. *Aug.* 28. Commissioners are sent round to examine the character of clergy already in possession of livings. The Court of Chancery is reformed by ordinance. *Sept.* 3. **The first Protectorate Parliament** meets. [Four hundred members for England (many rotten boroughs being disfranchised and their members given to large but unrepresented towns, and the county representation being equalized according to population), thirty for Scotland, thirty for Ireland.] The republicans, headed by Vane, debate the question of government by "a single person." *Sept.* 12. Cromwell, after addressing the Parliament, allows those only to sit who would pledge themselves not to attempt to alter the form of government. About a hundred members are excluded.
1655.	*Jan.* 22. On the expiration of five lunar months Cromwell dissolves Parliament. *March* 10. Penruddock's rising at Salisbury. Penn and Venables fail to capture San Domingo, but take Jamaica from the Spaniards, *May.* *Aug.* Cromwell divides England into eleven military districts, each under a major-general. *Oct.* **Treaty with France** against Spain, providing that Prince Charles shall no longer live in France. The readmission of the Jews into England is discussed by the Council, but nothing is settled.
1656.	*Feb.* War is declared against England by Spain. *Sept.* 17. **The second Protectorate Parliament** meets. Above ninety republicans and Presbyterians are not allowed to take their seats (c). Cromwell interferes on behalf of the Vaudois subjects of the Duke of Savoy.
1657.	*March.* An offensive and defensive alliance is made with France. *March* 29. After some debate, Parliament offers the title of king to Cromwell, with a new constitution explained in the instrument called "**The Humble Petition and Advice**" (d). *April.* Spanish treasure fleet beaten off Cadiz. *May* 8. After several conferences, Cromwell refuses to accept the title of king by the request of the army, but accepts the Petition and Advice, *May* 25. *June* 26. The new constitution is inaugurated in Westminster Hall. Lambert refuses the oath to Cromwell, and is deprived of his post of general. Writs are sent out to the newly-created House of Lords.

[Notes.]

FOREIGN AND COLONIAL.

(a) *Richard Cromwell* died in 1712. His brother *Oliver*, a captain in the army, had been killed in 1644. His brother *Henry*, Deputy of Ireland 1656, died in 1674. Of his sisters, *Elizabeth* married Claypole, and died 1658; *Bridget* married (1) Ireton, (2) Fleetwood, and died 1681; *Mary*, Lady Fauconberg, died 1712; *Frances*, Lady Russell, died 1721.

(b) 1. An Act of amnesty for life, liberty, and property for all those not excepted by Parliament.
2. Liberty of conscience for all those whose views did not disturb the peace of the realm.
3. The settlement in Parliament of all claims to landed property.
4. The payment of arrears to Monk's army.

(c) All tenures of estates of inheritance in the hands of private persons (except copyhold tenures) were turned into free and common socage, and the same were for ever discharged from homage, wardship, values, and forfeiture of marriage, and other charges, incidents, and tenure, by knight's service, and from aids for marrying the lord's daughter, or for making his son a knight.

1659. By the Treaty of the Pyrenees Louis XIV. agreed to marry the Infanta Maria Theresa, who renounces her right to succeed to the Spanish crown.

1661. Death of Mazarin.

[1658—1661]   ENGLISH.

1658.   *Jan.* 20. Parliament meets in its reorganized form. The Commons debate their relation to the other newly-made House, and are dissolved by Cromwell, *Feb.* 4.
June. The English and French beat the Spaniards in the battle of the Dunes, and gain Dunkirk, which is surrendered to the English.
Sept. 3. **Cromwell dies, aged fifty-nine.**
Richard Cromwell is declared Protector by the Council.
To conciliate the army, Lambert is restored to his post.

1659.   *Jan.* Parliament meets, but does little business, and provokes the army.
April 22. Richard Cromwell, trusting to the promises of the army, dissolves the Parliament.
May 7. **The remains of the Long Parliament** ("the Rump") **are restored** by the army.
July. Richard (*a*) leaves Whitehall.
Aug. Booth's rising in Cheshire is put down by Lambert.
Oct. 12. **Lambert** and **Desborough** (Cromwell's brother-in-law) are dismissed by the Rump from their posts, and Fleetwood, Cromwell's son-in-law, becomes (a merely nominal) commander-in-chief.
Oct. 13. Lambert marches to Westminster and turns out the Rump.
Monk marches from Scotland, and Lambert is sent against him.
Dec. 26. The Rump resumes its sittings.

1660.   *Jan.* 3. Fairfax meets Lambert's army on Marston Moor and persuades his men not to fight against Monk, with whom he marches to London ; and Monk declares for a free Parliament.
March. 16. The Long Parliament dissolves itself, after appointing the new Parliament (or Convention) to meet on April 25.
April 25. **The Convention meets and invites Charles to return.**
May 25. Charles having issued at Breda certain promises (*b*), lands at Dover, and (*May* 29) enters London.

CHARLES II., 1660—1685 (25 YEARS).

Born 1630 ; Married, 1662, Katharine of Portugal.

[Clarendon, leading minister.]
An Act of Indemnity and Oblivion, excepting the regicides and five others, is passed.
Military tenures and feudal dues are abolished, as well as the right of purveyance (*c*).
Sept. The king's revenue is settled at £1,200,000 (to be made up by tonnage and poundage for life, and an hereditary excise levied in place of the feudal dues).
Oct. The trial of the regicides begins. Ten suffer death.
The army, except two regiments, is disbanded.
Dec. 29. The Convention Parliament is dissolved.

1661.   *Jan.* 6. Venner's plot is put down.

[Notes.]

(a) *Act of Settlement.*—(1) Adventurers who had received land in 1652, in consideration of money they had lent for the war, are confirmed in their lands. (2) Soldiers who had served the king before 1649 are to receive the value of five-eighths of their pay in land. (3) Soldiers of the Republic are confirmed in lands granted in 1652. (4) Innocent Papists who had not been even indirectly involved in the rebellion are to receive back their lands.
Act of Explanation, 1665.—Adventurers and soldiers gave up one-third of their lands.

(b) "They declared that there was no legislative power in either or both Houses without the king, and that the sole supreme command of the militia, and of all forces by sea and land, had ever been by the laws of England the undoubted right of the Crown; that neither House of Parliament could pretend to it, nor could lawfully levy any war, offensive or defensive, against his majesty" (*Hallam*, ii. p. 328).

(c) *Act of Uniformity.*—The Act included five points, which were made compulsory on all holders of livings—
1. Ordination by a bishop.
2. Assent and consent to the Book of Common Prayer.
3. The oath of canonical obedience.
4. Renunciation of the Solemn League and Covenant.
5. A declaration that it was unlawful to bear arms against the sovereign under any pretext whatever.

(d) The chief Nonconformist bodies besides the Roman Catholics were—
1. *The Presbyterians*, who had had a majority in the Long Parliament, and who in 1647 had succeeded in getting Presbyterianism established in England.
2. *The Independents* (at first often known as "Brownists"), who had been powerful during the Commonwealth through their strength in the army, and in 1658 had held a great meeting in which they had drawn up a declaration of faith and order.
3. *The Baptists*, who though they had seven congregations in London and forty in the provinces, had been excluded from the Westminster Assembly.
4. *The Society of Friends*, followers of George Fox.

(e) The clergy now lose their right of self-taxation (see 1295, note), and the franchise for members of the House of Commons becomes the right of clergymen by an Act passed 1664.

(f) *Repeal of the Triennial Act of* 1641.—Every clause of the bill is completely repealed, yet, "with an inconsistency not unusual in our statutes," a provision is added that in future Parliaments shall not be intermitted more than three years at most.

(g) "That supplies granted by Parliament are only to be expended for particular objects specified by itself became from this time an undisputed principle recognised by frequent and at length constant practice" (*Hallam*).

FOREIGN AND COLONIAL.

1661 and 1665. The Acts of Settlement and Explanation are passed in the Irish Parliament(a).

1661. In Scotland the old form of government is restored, Episcopacy established, and the persecution of the Covenanters begun. Execution of Argyll.

1662. Mile Act (similar to the Five-Mile Act) is passed by the Scottish Parliament.

1663. Irish ships are excluded from the privileges of English under the Navigation Act.

1664. Conquest of New Netherlands (granted to the Duke of York, and called New York), in America, from the Dutch.

1665 and 1680. Cattle, sheep, swine, or beef, mutton, pork, or bacon, and butter, forbidden to be exported from Ireland to England.

1668. *May* 2. Louis being checked by the Triple Alliance, makes peace with Spain at Aix-la-Chapelle.

1661.	*April.* **The conference at the Savoy** between the bishops and the Presbyterian ministers fails. [See *Summary: Ecclesiastical*, Part IV., p. 243.] *May* 8. A new Parliament, strongly Royalist, meets, confirms the acts of the Convention, and restores some prerogatives (*b*) to the Crown. *Dec.* **Corporation Act passed**, ordering all holders of municipal offices to renounce the Covenant, and take the sacrament according to the English form.
1662.	*May.* Charles marries Katharine of Portugal, receiving Bombay and Tangiers. *May* 19. **The Act of Uniformity** (*c*) **is passed**, enforcing the use of the Prayer-Book as at present composed. A great many ministers resign their benefices rather than take the oath (*d*). Lambert and Sir Henry Vane having been tried for treason, Lambert is imprisoned and Vane executed. Charles makes a declaration in favour of indulgence, promising to use his influence to get such an Act passed. *Nov.* **Dunkirk is sold to the French.**
1663.	**Convocation grants a subsidy (for the last time)** (*e*).
1664.	*The Triennial Act of* 1641 *is repealed* (*f*). **The Conventicle Act** is passed (forbidding religious assemblies other than those allowed by the Church of England).
1665.	*Feb.* War is declared against Holland. *June* 3. Victory by the Duke of York over the Dutch off Lowestoft. *Sept.* **The great plague of London** is at its height. *Oct.* Parliament grants £1,250,000 *to be spent on the war only* (*g*). *Oct.* 30. **The Five-Mile Act** is passed (forbidding ministers who had not subscribed the Act of Uniformity, or taken the oath of non-resistance, to teach in schools, or to settle within five miles of any corporate town).
1666.	*Jan.* 16. **Louis XIV. declares war against England,** and makes an alliance with the Dutch. *June* 1-4. A long and indecisive sea-fight against the Dutch under Prince Rupert and Albemarle (Monk). *July.* Victory over the Dutch. *Sept.* 2-6. **The great fire of London.** [*A committee is appointed by Parliament in this year to inspect the accounts of naval and other officials.*]
1667.	*May* 10. The French and Dutch fleets are defeated in the West Indies. *June.* The Dutch advance into the Thames and burn the ships at the mouth of the Medway. *July* 21. Peace with the Dutch. *Aug.* **Clarendon is dismissed,** impeached (*Nov.*), and flies to the Continent, and is sentenced to banishment. **The Cabal Ministry take office** (Clifford, Arlington, Buckingham, Ashley, Lauderdale).
1668.	*Jan.* 23. **The Triple Alliance** is formed between Holland, Sweden, and England against France. A bill for comprehension of Presbyterians in the Church and for toleration to other Nonconformists is defeated.
1669.	Sir George Carteret is dismissed from his office of Treasurer of the

[Notes.]

(a) The chief terms appear to have been—
1. Charles was to aid Louis in a war against the Dutch, for which he was to receive £300,000, and have the aid of thirty French ships
2. The province of Zealand and the adjacent islands were to be reserved for England.
3. Charles was to have £200,000 per year on condition that he declared himself a Catholic.
The last article was only known to Clifford and Arlington.

FOREIGN AND COLONIAL.

1670 and 1696. No goods to be imported from the colonies to Ireland.

1672. France invades Holland, great riots occur, and De Witt, the Grand Pensionary, is murdered by the mob, *Aug.* 4. William of Orange (aged twenty-two) becomes Stadtholder.

1669.	Navy *on the report of commissioners who had been appointed with very extensive powers to investigate the public accounts.*
1670.	The Conventicle Act of 1664 is renewed and made more stringent.
	May 20. **The secret Treaty of Dover** (*a*) is concluded between Charles and Louis.
	Dec. Sir John Coventry having spoken in Parliament against the profligacy of the court, is attacked by hired bullies.
1671.	In consequence an Act is passed to make malicious wounding a capital offence.
	Parliament votes £800,000 for the fleet. A difference between the Lords and the Commons about money bills arises. Parliament is prorogued first for a year, finally for twenty-one months.
1672.	*Jan.* 2. Notice is given that the principal of loans due this year is not to be paid, but only the interest (which amounts to a declaration of national bankruptcy).
	The Duke of York is publicly received into the Roman Catholic Church.
	March 15. **Declaration of Indulgence** (repealing all Acts against Nonconformists and Catholics) is proclaimed.
	March. Failure of the attempt on the Dutch treasure fleet.
	March. War declared against Holland by England and France.
	Battle of Southwold Bay against the Dutch indecisive.
1673.	Parliament meets, and forces Charles to withdraw the Declaration of Indulgence.
	Parliament passes **the Test Act** (which orders that all persons holding office under the Crown are to take the sacrament according to the rites of the Church of England, and make a declaration against transubstantiation).
	Clifford and the Duke of York, as Catholics, retire from their offices. **End of the Cabal ministry.** [Clifford retires from politics. Shaftesbury and Buckingham lead the Opposition. Lauderdale alone keeps his place in Scotland.]
	Sir Thomas Osborne (afterwards Earl of **Danby** and Duke of Leeds) becomes Lord Treasurer and leading minister.
1674.	*Jan.* Parliament meets and attacks Buckingham, Arlington, and Lauderdale.
	Feb. 7. Parliament passes resolutions against a standing army.
	Feb. 28. Peace is concluded with Holland.
1675.	Danby's bill, for making all placemen declare on oath that they consider resistance to the king unlawful, and that they will make no alteration in Church and State, passes through the Lords but is rejected by the Commons.
	Nov. For 500,000 crowns (to be paid as an annual subsidy) from Louis, Charles prorogues the Parliament for fifteen months.
	The coffee-houses are closed to prevent political discussion.
1677.	Parliament meets after fifteen months' prorogation.
	Shaftesbury, Salisbury, Wharton, and Buckingham, having questioned whether the prorogation of fifteen months did not necessarily dissolve the Parliament, are sent to the Tower by the House of Lords, and Shaftesbury remains there for a year.

[Notes.]

FOREIGN AND COLONIAL.

1678. *Aug.* 10. After long negotiations the Treaty of Nimwegen is made by France with Holland and Spain. [With the Empire, 1679.]

(*a*) This Act prevented Roman Catholic peers from sitting in Parliament for the first time (see 1562, note). It required members to make a declaration against certain Romanist doctrines, as well as to take the oath of supremacy.

(*b*) Temple's scheme was to interpose a powerful Privy Council between the king and the Parliament. Its members were to be men of weight and influence, and their united income was not to be less than £300,000. In practice it was found to be too large.

1679. Murder of Archbishop Sharp in Scotland. Defeat of the Covenanters at Bothwell Brigg.

(*c*) This statute contained no new principle. It simplified and made effectual the exercise of an ancient right. Its chief provisions were—
1. That any unconvicted prisoner, committed for any crime except treason or felony, may, during either term time or vacation, call upon the Lord Chancellor or any judge, under penalty of a fine of £500, to issue a writ of *habeas corpus* to the gaoler, ordering him, under penalty of a fine of £100, to bring up the body of the prisoner within not more than twenty days, and that the judge, on his appearance, shall release him on bail.
2. That no Englishman be imprisoned in Ireland, Scotland, the Channel Islands, or any other of the foreign dominions of the king.
3. That every person committed for treason or felony may, unless he be indicted in the next term or the next sessions of gaol delivery after his commitment, be, on prayer to the court, released on bail, unless it appear that the Crown's witnesses could not be produced at that time, and that if he be not tried in the second term or gaol delivery, he be discharged. See *Hallam*, vol. iii. ch. xiii.

1680. Death of Sivajee the Mahratta.

1677.	The Commons having voted a subsidy for the use of the navy, order it to be paid into the hands of their own receivers. Parliament demands the dismissal of the army. Nov. 4. **Mary, eldest daughter of the Duke of York, marries William of Orange.**
1678.	Parliament meets, votes for an increase in the army and navy for war with France, and grants £1,000,000. Charles collects an army. Louis, fearing that Charles is going to side with the Dutch, gives money to the members of the Opposition who are opposing the Government. During the negotiations between the Dutch and the French, Charles makes a **secret treaty with France** (the text written by Danby) for 6,000,000 livres to dissolve Parliament, to disband the army, and not to assist the Dutch if they continue the war. **Popish Plot.** Depositions of Titus Oates against the Papists. Parliament is immediately called. Both Houses address the king to dismiss the Duke of York from his counsels. Many trials of leading Roman Catholics. Nov. 30. An Act is passed for "disabling Papists from sitting in either House of Parliament" (a). An exception is carried in the Duke of York's favour by two votes. Louis, having no further need of Charles, now that peace has been made with the Dutch, discloses the treaty between Charles and himself. The Commons impeach Danby and five Catholic peers.
1679.	Jan. Parliament is dissolved, after sitting since 1661. March 6. Charles' third Parliament meets. The king rejects the Speaker (Edward Seymour) chosen by the House. The Parliament (having elected Serjeant Gregory Speaker) resumes proceedings against Lord Danby, who pleads the royal pardon. The Commons address the king on the illegality of this pardon, and demand justice from the Lords. April. **Danby is committed to the Tower.** Leading ministers, **Sunderland, Temple, Essex, Halifax.** Temple advises the formation of a Privy Council of thirty (b). May. The Commons resolve on a bill to exclude the Duke of York from the succession. The Exclusion Bill is then committed in the Commons. The king gives his consent to the **Habeas Corpus Act** (c). Parliament is prorogued and then dissolved. Oct. Charles' fourth Parliament is elected, and is prorogued seven times, finally till October 1680.
1680.	Many petitions are sent to the king urging him to assemble Parliament. Counter-petitions are sent up by those who "abhor" the Exclusion Bill; [from which came the names of "Petitioners" and "Abhorrers," afterwards changed into "Whigs and Tories."] Oct. The Commons resolve that it has always been the right of the subjects of England to petition for a Parliament. Nov. **The Exclusion Bill passes the Commons.** The proceedings against the four peers of 1677 are annulled by Parliament.

[Notes.]

(a) This decree was publicly burned by order of the House of Lords in 1700.

(b) GENEALOGY OF THE RUSSELLS.

Francis, 4th Earl of Bedford, d. 1641.
|
┌─────────────────────────┬─────────────────────────┐
William, 5th Earl,   Edward.
created Duke of |
Bedford 1694,   Edward, created Earl
d. 1700.   of Orford, d. 1727.
| Won the battle of
William, Lord Rus-   La Hogue.
sell, executed 1683.
|
Wriothesley,   2nd
Duke of Bedford,
d. 1711.
|
┌──────────────┬──────────────┐
Wriothesley,   John, 4th Duke,
3rd Duke.   Secretary of State
                temp. George III.,
                d. 1771. (Great-
                grandfather of
                Lord John, created
                Earl Russell.)

FOREIGN AND COLONIAL.

1681. Surprise of Strasburg by the French in time of peace.

1683. The charter of Massachusetts is annulled by the king.
The Turks besiege Vienna, but are repulsed by the Pole, John Sobiesky, and Charles, Duke of Lorraine.
Death of Colbert, the French minister.

1685. Argyll's insurrection in Scotland completely fails, and Argyll is executed.
Oct. 26. The Edict of Nantes is revoked, and the French Protestants and the Vaudois are very cruelly treated.

114

1680.	In consequence of a speech by George Savile, Marquis of Halifax, the **Exclusion Bill is rejected by the Lords.** *Dec.* Stafford [see note (a), p. 76], chief of the Popish victims, is beheaded.
1681.	*Jan.* The king by message declares that he never will assent to the Exclusion Bill. The Commons refuse to vote supplies. Parliament is dissolved. *March* 21. Charles' fifth Parliament meets at Oxford. Many of the members bring armed followers. The Commons again bring in the Exclusion Bill. Charles proposes that the government shall be carried on after his death in James' name by the Prince of Orange as regent for James. *March* 28. The Commons order the bill to be read a second time next day. Parliament is dissolved the same day, and does not meet again during the rest of the reign. Louis agrees to pay five million livres to Charles in the next three years. *Nov.* 24. The Government prosecutes Shaftesbury for treason, but the bill is ignored by the grand jury in London.
1682.	**The Duke of Monmouth** makes a progress through England, assumes royal state, and touches for the king's evil. The charters of London and other towns are examined by a decree of "quo warranto," and during the next two years are remodelled in the interests of the court. Shaftesbury goes to Holland, and dies, January 22, 1683.
1683.	*June.* The Ryehouse Plot (a plan entered into by Rumbold and some extreme Whigs to murder the king and the Duke of York) is discovered. Rumbold escapes to Holland. *July* 21. The University of Oxford passes a decree condemning the doctrine that resistance to a king is lawful (a). *July* 21. William, Lord Russell (b), is tried and executed for a supposed share in the Ryehouse Plot. Essex dies in prison. *Dec.* Algernon Sydney is also convicted and executed, unpublished writings of his being used for want of a second witness.
1684.	Monmouth is pardoned for his late proceedings, but is banished to Holland. Rochester is made President of the Council.
1685.	*Feb.* 6. The king dies.

JAMES II., 1685—1689 (4 Years).

Born 1633; Married { 1661, Anne Hyde.
{ 1673, Mary of Modena.

James declares in a speech to the Council that he will maintain the government, both in Church and State, as by law established.
[Ministry—**Rochester**, Lord Treasurer; **Halifax**, President of the Council; **Godolphin**, Chamberlain; and **Sunderland**, Secretary of State.]
James continues to levy the taxes which had been voted only for Charles' life. He receives £67,000 from France.
Titus Oates and Dangerfield, having been convicted of perjury, are cruelly punished. Baxter, the Presbyterian divine, is severely punished.

[Notes.]

FOREIGN AND COLONIAL.

1686. William of Orange forms the league of Augsburg to resist Louis XIV.

1688. Louis XIV. quarrels with the Pope, and invades Germany.

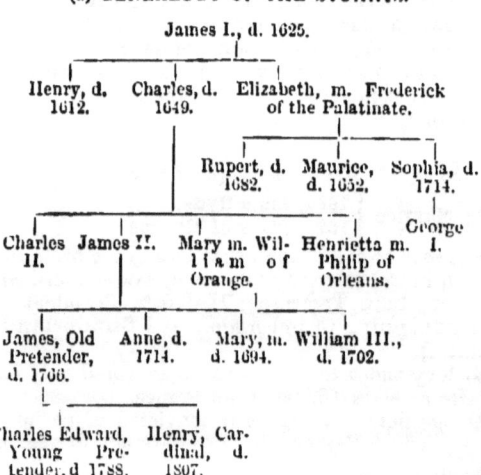

(a) GENEALOGY OF THE STUARTS.

[1685—1688] ENGLISH.

1685.
May 22. Parliament meets and gains the release of Danby and the Popish peers. Parliament votes the revenue of Charles II., with the addition of a tax on sugar and tobacco.
Insurrection of **Monmouth**, *June* 11. He lands in Dorsetshire, takes the title of king at Taunton, is **defeated at Sedgemoor, July 6,** and, having been captured in the New Forest, is executed, *July* 15.
His adherents are terribly punished by Colonel Kirke, and by Judge Jeffreys in the Bloody Assize.
Oct. 21. Halifax is deprived of his office.
Dec. **Sunderland** is made president of the Council as well as secretary.

1686.
June. Sir Edward Hales having received a commission in the army contrary to the Test Act, the judges give an opinion favourable to the dispensing power of the king. In consequence many Romanists receive commissions in the army and Church preferment.
July. A new court of Ecclesiastical Commission is set up. Compton, Bishop of London, is suspended by this court.
A camp of 13,000 troops is formed at Hounslow to overawe London.
Massey, a Romanist, is made Dean of Christ Church, Oxford.
The chapel at Whitehall is opened for the public celebration of Romanist rites.

1687.
Clarendon is recalled from Ireland, and succeeded by Tyrconnel. Rochester, having refused to change his religion, is removed from the Treasury, which is put in commission.
April. **The Declaration of Indulgence** is published, which suspends the penal statutes against the Roman Catholics and Protestant Dissenters.
Both **Oxford and Cambridge are attacked by the Ecclesiastical Commission.**
July 2. Parliament is dissolved, having been prorogued since *Dec.* 1685. *July* 3. James receives a Papal nuncio.
James having asked the lord-lieutenants to furnish a list of Papists and Nonconformists suitable for members of Parliament, many of them resign.

1688.
May 4. James issues the Declaration of Indulgence again, and orders the clergy to read it on *May* 20 and 27.
Archbishop Sancroft and six other bishops present their petition to be excused (*May* 18), and very few clergy read the Declaration.
June 10. A son, afterwards the Old Pretender, is born to James (a).
June 29, 30. **The seven bishops are tried and acquitted.**
June 30. A letter is sent to **William of Orange** asking him to bring an army and secure the liberties of the people, signed by Devonshire, Shrewsbury, Danby, Lumley, Compton, Bishop of London, Admiral Edward Russell, and Henry Sydney.
Sept. 30. **William of Orange issues his Declaration**, giving a list of James' bad acts, and declaring that, as husband of Mary, he was coming with an army to secure a free and legal Parliament, by whose decision he would abide.

[Notes.]

(a) *The Ministry.*—Danby, President of the Council; Halifax, Privy Seal; Nottingham and Shrewsbury, Secretaries; Godolphin, on the Treasury Board.

(b) *Repeal of the Acts of Settlement and Explanation.*—In their stead Parliament ordered—
1. That the heirs of all persons who had held land in Ireland should enter at once into their estates.
2. That those persons who had bought lands from the adventurers or soldiers since 1661 should receive compensation for the land they now lost.

(c) The Nonjurors did not become extinct till 1805.

(d) *Mutiny Bill.*—Its chief clauses set forth—
1. That standing armies and courts-martial were unknown to the law of England.
2. That on account of the special dangers of the time, no man mustered on pay in the service of the Crown should, on pain of death, or such lighter punishment as a court-martial should think sufficient, desert his colours or mutiny against his officers.

"These are the two effectual securities against military power: that no pay can be issued to the troops without a previous authorization by the Commons in a Committee of Supply, and by both Houses in an Act of Appropriation: and that no officer or soldier can be punished for disobedience, nor any court-martial held, without the annual re-enactment of the *Mutiny Bill*" (*Hallam*).

FOREIGN AND COLONIAL.

1689. Peter the Great becomes Czar of Russia.
Louis declares war against Holland.
March 14. A stormy session of the Convention begins at Edinburgh.
Edinburgh Castle holds out for James.
Dundee (Graham of Claverhouse) retires to Stirling with troops, summons a parliament, and then retires to Blair Athol.
The Convention expels the bishops, abolishes Episcopacy, passes the "Claim of Right," and William and Mary are proclaimed, *April.*
Dundee defeats Mackay at Killiecrankie, but is killed and is succeeded by Cannon, *July* 27.
Mackay gains some successes, and the Highlanders disperse.
In *Ireland* Tyrconnel unites the Irish against the English, increases the army, disarms the Protestants, who take refuge in Londonderry and Enniskillen.
March. James lands in Ireland.
May. He holds a parliament at Dublin.
(1) Repeals the Acts of Settlement and Explanation of 1661 and 1665 (b).
(2) Issues bad money.
(3) Passes a sweeping Act of Attainder.
July 30. Kirke raises the siege of Londonderry.
Colonel Wolseley defeats the Irish army at Newtown Butler, near Enniskillen, *Aug.*

[1688, 1689] ENGLISH.

1688.
The king in alarm restores many displaced officers, gives back the town charters, dissolves the Ecclesiastical Commission, restores the fellows of Magdalen College, Oxford, and removes Sunderland and Petre out of the Council.
Oct. 19. William sails from Holland, but is driven back by bad weather.
Nov. 2. **William** sails again, **lands at Torbay** (*Nov.* 5), and marches to Exeter.
Danby and Devonshire get up an insurrection in the north.
William advances slowly towards London. Churchill and many officers desert and bring over some of their troops.
Princess Anne flies to the northern insurgents.
Dec. 8. Commissioners for James and William meet at Hungerford.
Dec. 10. James sends away his wife and the Prince of Wales, and endeavours to escape to France, *Dec.* 11, but is recaptured and brought back to London, *Dec.* 12.
Dec. 17. **James** is escorted to Rochester, and **leaves the kingdom**, *Dec.* 23.
Dec. 19. **William arrives in London** and calls a meeting of the Peers, and of those persons who have been members of any of Charles II.'s Parliaments. They recommend a convention, which is called for *Jan.* 22.

1689.
Jan. 22. The Convention meets. After a long discussion both Houses agree to settle the throne on William and Mary, all the executive power resting with William. At the same time they sum up a statement of James' illegal acts, and claim the rights and liberties which he has infringed, in the **DECLARATION OF RIGHT.**
[See *Summary: Parliament, Part III.*, 1430-1689, p. 235.]
William and Mary having accepted the **Declaration of Right**, are declared king and queen, *Feb.* 13.

WILLIAM AND MARY, 1689—1702 (13 YEARS).

William, born 1650; married 1677.   **Mary** { Born 1662. Died 1694.

A ministry is formed (*a*). Twelve new judges are created.
Feb. 13. The Convention is made into a Parliament. The king's revenue is fixed at £1,200,000 per annum. A new oath of allegiance and supremacy is imposed on all place-holders in Church or State. Seven bishops and about 300 clergy refuse it, and form the body of "Nonjurors" (*c*).
A regiment mutinies and marches for Scotland, but is forced to capitulate, their lives being spared.
The annual **Mutiny Bill** (*d*) *is passed for the first time in consequence.*
War is declared against France. The **Toleration Act** is passed, but a bill for comprehending certain Nonconformists

[Notes.]

FOREIGN AND COLONIAL.

(*a*) *Bill of Rights.*
1. The pretended power of suspending or dispensing with the laws is illegal.
2. The late Court of Ecclesiastical Commission and all other such courts are illegal.
3. Levying money by pretence of prerogative without grant of Parliament is illegal.
4. Keeping a standing army in time of peace, unless with consent of Parliament, is illegal.
5. Subjects have a right to petition the king.
6. The election of members of Parliament ought to be free.
7. Freedom of speech and debate in Parliament ought not to be questioned in any court or place out of Parliament.
8. Excessive fines must not be imposed, and jurors in cases for high treason must be freeholders.
9. For redress of all grievances and for the strengthening of the laws Parliament ought to be held frequently.
10. William and Mary are declared King and Queen of England, and all who are Papists or who shall marry a Papist are declared incapable of possessing the Crown.

1690. Calcutta is founded, and Fort William soon afterwards built.

1691. A new East India Company established called "The English Company."
Ginkel having taken Athlone, which commands the passage of the Shannon, St. Ruth falls back to Aughrim. He is there defeated and killed.
Oct. 3. Limerick capitulates.
An Act passed by the English Parliament excludes Roman Catholics from the Irish Parliament.
Military execution is proclaimed in Scotland against all clans who have not laid down their arms and taken the oath of allegiance by *Dec.* 31.
1692. *Feb.* Massacre of Glencoe.
In the Parliament of this year, and in other Parliaments under William III. and Anne, very severe laws were passed against the Irish Catholics. (See note 1700.)

(*b*) GENEALOGY OF THE CHURCHILLS AND GODOLPHINS.

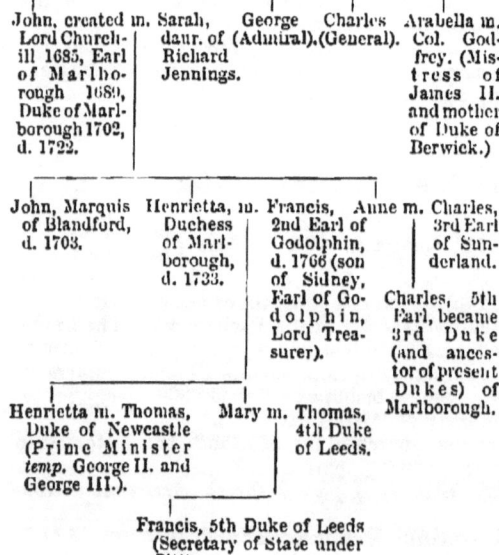

1689.	in the Church of England is postponed, and a bill for the repeal of the Test Act is rejected. *Oct.* Parliament meets and passes the **BILL OF RIGHTS** (*a*) as a statute.
1690.	The Whigs attempt to add to the Bill for restoring the charters of towns forfeited under Charles II. and James II. a clause to exclude from office all those who had been concerned in the surrender. It is thrown out by the Tories. The Indemnity Bill is coupled with numerous exceptions by the Whigs, and causes so violent a struggle between the parties that William is on the point of returning to Holland. *Jan.* Parliament is dissolved. *March.* The new Parliament meets, with a Tory majority. **Halifax** leaves the Government, and **Danby** (now Marquis of Carmarthen) takes the lead. The Abjuration Bill, to make all place-holders take an oath abjuring King James, is rejected in both Houses. *May.* An Act of Grace from the Crown grants an amnesty excluding only the regicides and about thirty others. *June.* William goes to Ireland. *June 30.* Herbert, Lord Torrington, is defeated at **Beachy Head** by the French, who burn Teignmouth. This national disgrace causes great excitement, and large offers of money and assistance are made to William. *July 1.* **Battle of the Boyne.** William is victorious. James flies to Waterford, and leaves Ireland for France. William and Lord Marlborough (*b*) subdue the south of Ireland: the Irish retreat beyond the Shannon. William having unsuccessfully besieged Limerick, returns. Godolphin becomes First Lord of the Treasury. Shrewsbury resigns. *Dec.* Torrington having been tried for his conduct at Beachy Head, is acquitted, but dismissed from the service by William, and is replaced by Russell.
1691.	Viscount Preston is tried, and convicted of plotting against the Government. William goes to the Continent in the summer.
1692.	Marlborough, suspected of treason, is dismissed from all his offices. William goes abroad. Louis and James collect a great fleet at Brest, and an army on the coast of Normandy, to invade England. James issues a declaration which excepts great numbers of Englishmen from pardon in case he is successful. Mary causes this declaration to be published with notes. *May.* **The French fleet is utterly defeated by Russell** [see note (*b*), p. 114] off **La Hogue.** *Aug. 4.* William is defeated at **Steinkirk.** The failure of an expedition against St. Malo causes a quarrel between Nottingham and Russell, who withdraws from command of the navy.
1693.	**The National Debt** is originated in a loan raised by Montagu.

[Notes.]

FOREIGN AND COLONIAL.

(a) *The Sunderlands.*—Robert Spencer, Earl of Sunderland, was minister to James II., and died in 1702. His son Charles, who married Anne, daughter of the first Duke of Marlborough (see p. 120), was minister under Anne and George I., and died 1722.

1693. A new charter is granted to the old East India Company.

(b) *Land Tax.*—This tax was used by the Long Parliament instead of the ancient subsidy (see note 1625), and was again resorted to after the Restoration. In 1692 the land of the country was regularly valued. After that time varying amounts in the £ were charged in various years till 1798, when the tax was made permanent at 4s. in the £, and landowners were permitted to redeem the tax by a single payment.

(c) *Bank of England.*—£1,200,000 was borrowed from certain capitalists, who in return were incorporated by Royal Charter as "The Governor and Company of the Bank of England," to trade solely in bills of exchange, bullion, and forfeited pledges.

1695. The Irish Parliament repeals all the Acts of James II.'s Parliament of 1689.

(d) *Expedition against Brest.*—It is now known from the Stuart papers that Marlborough himself disclosed the English plans to the enemy.

(e) *Licensing Act.*—This Act was first passed in 1662, and was renewed from time to time. By it the entire control of printing was vested in the government. Printing might only be carried on at London, York, and the universities, and the number of master printers was confined to twenty. The Secretary of State was also empowered to issue warrants for discovering and seizing libels against the government.

(f) *Trials for Treason.*—The prisoner is to have a copy of the indictment five days and a list of the jury two days before the trial, and his witnesses are to be examined on oath. Two witnesses are required to one overt act, or one to one, another to another overt act of the same kind of treason.

1697. Peter the Great visits England and learns shipbuilding at Deptford.
Accession of Charles XII., King of Sweden.
1698. A charter is granted to the new East India Company.
Act to forbid the export of Irish manufactured wool to any country whatsoever passed by the Irish Parliament.

(g) *Three Resolutions.*—(1) That the Commons would assist the king to prosecute the war with all possible energy. (2) That in no case should the value of the new coinage be changed. (3) That Parliament pledges itself to make good the deficiencies in the parliamentary funds voted in 1695.

(h) *Peace of Ryswick.*—France gives up all conquests made since the Treaty of Nimwegen, 1678, acknowledges William as King of England, and Anne as his successor.

1693.	The elder Sunderland (a) (now for the first time received at court) advises William to form a united Whig ministry, which is completed by 1697. Somers (a Whig) is appointed Lord Keeper. *June.* Great disaster to the Smyrna merchant fleet, which is almost entirely destroyed or captured by the French off Cape St. Vincent. *July.* William is defeated at **Landen**. New charter granted to the East India Company by the Crown. The land tax (b) of 4s. in the £, on the new valuation of 1692, produces about £2,000,000.
1694.	The Bank of England (c) is established. An expedition against Brest having been defeated by the French, and the general, Talmash, being killed (d), Marlborough is again employed; and after the death of Mary is faithful to William. The **Triennial Act** (*limiting the duration of Parliament to three years, and providing that three years shall not pass without a Parliament*) is passed. William gives his consent, which he had refused once before. *Dec.* **Death of Queen Mary.**
1695.	The Commons refuse to renew the Licensing Act (e). Lord Carmarthen (now Duke of Leeds) is proved to have been connected with dishonest practices in the granting of the East India charter, and is soon forced to retire. **Godolphin** is now the only other Tory in the ministry. *An Act to restrain and punish bribery in elections is passed.* *May.* The censorship of the press expires, and has never since been revived. *Oct.* **Surrender of Namur** to William, who returns home in triumph and calls a new parliament, in which the majority is strongly Whig.
1696.	*An Act is passed regulating trials for treason* (f). *Feb.* A plot, arranged by Sir George Barclay, to murder William, and a design to invade England managed by the Duke of Berwick [see note (b), p. 120], are discovered. An association is formed to avenge William's death in case of his murder, to support the succession of Anne, and to continue the war. The Habeas Corpus Act is suspended. A new coinage is issued under the management of Somers, Montagu, Locke, and Sir Isaac Newton. On the failure of the scheme of the Land Bank, the Bank of England advances to William £200,000. Parliament passes three resolutions (g) to secure the credit of England.
1697.	Execution of Sir John Fenwick by attainder for treason. On the retirement of **Godolphin** the ministry becomes wholly Whig. (**Montagu**, First Lord of the Treasury, **Russell**, **Somers**, and **Wharton** composing " the Junto.") The **Peace of Ryswick** (h) is signed amidst great rejoicings. The army is reduced to 10,000 men, by order of Parliament.

[Notes.]

FOREIGN AND COLONIAL.

(*a*) *First Partition Treaty.*—Spain, Indies, Netherlands to the Electoral Prince; Guipuscoa and Sicilies to France; Milan to the Archduke Charles.
(*b*) A reward of £100 is offered for information against any priest who exercises his religious functions, for which the penalty is imprisonment for life. Every Papist at the age of eighteen is to take the oaths of allegiance and supremacy, and subscribe the declaration against transubstantiation and the worship of saints, in default of which he is incapable of holding land by purchase or inheritance, and the property is to go to the next Protestant kin. No Catholic is to send his children abroad to be educated.
N.B.—This Act was rarely carried into practice.
(*c*) *Second Partition Treaty.*—Spain, Indies, Netherlands to Archduke Charles; Milan to France, to be exchanged for Lorraine.
(*d*) *Succession Act.*—The Crown to pass after Anne to the Electress Sophia and her Protestant descendants. The sovereign not to leave England without consent of Parliament. No foreigner to hold office or receive grants from the Crown. Public business to be done by the Privy Council, and resolutions to be signed by those members who advise them. No war to be made for the foreign dominions of the sovereign. *Judges are to receive fixed salaries, and cannot be removed except for conviction of some offence, or on the address of both Houses of Parliament.*
(*e*) *Kentish Petition.*—This implores the Commons "to drop their disputes, have regard to the voice of the people, and change their loyal addresses into bills of supply."
(*f*) The lesser ministers were Sir Charles Hedges, Secretary of State; Marquis of Normanby, Lord Privy Seal; the Earl of Pembroke, Lord President; the Earl of Jersey, Lord Chamberlain; Sir Edward Seymour, Comptroller of the Household; Sir John Leveson Gower, Chancellor of the Duchy of Lancaster; Howe, joint Paymaster of the Forces; Prince George of Denmark, Lord High Admiral; Duke of Devonshire, Lord Steward.
(*g*) *Methuen Treaty.*—English woollen goods to be admitted into Portugal. Duty on Portuguese wines to be less by one-third than that on French.

1699. The failure of the Darien scheme causes great irritation in Scotland against the English.
The shores of Australia are explored by Dampier, an Englishman.
1700. *Nov.* Charles II. of Spain dies, and Louis accepts the crown of Spain for his grandson Philip.
1701. Frederick I. becomes King of Prussia.
1703. The French and Bavarians defeat the Emperor's troops at Hochstädt and take Augsburg.
The Scottish Parliament passes a resolution that "the Presbyterian Church is the only true Church of Christ in the kingdom," and also passes certain resolutions limiting the authority of the Crown. (1) No king of England was to declare peace or war without the consent of the Scottish Parlia-

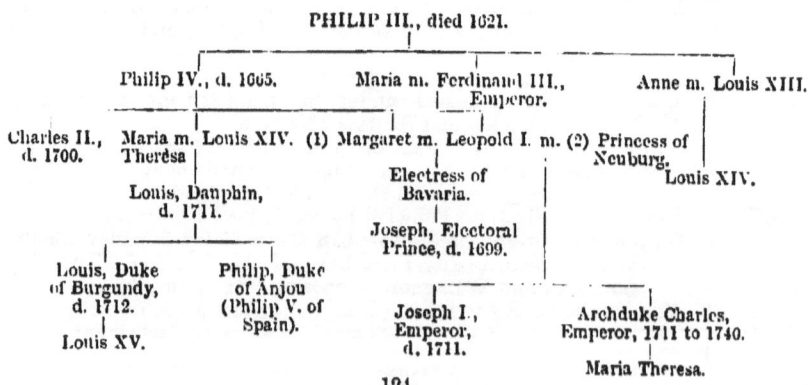

(*h*) PEDIGREE TO ILLUSTRATE THE WAR OF THE SPANISH SUCCESSION.

1698.	First Partition Treaty agreed upon between England, Holland, and France for dividing the Spanish dominions (a) and (h).
1699.	The Dutch guards are sent home. Parliament attacks William's grants of royal property to his Dutch favourites.
1700.	A bill for the resumption of these grants is passed by Parliament. A severe Act is passed against the Roman Catholics (b). Second Partition Treaty (c) made in consequence of the death of the Electoral Prince. **Death of William, Duke of Gloucester.** **William recalls Rochester and Godolphin** to the Cabinet.
1701.	**The Act of Settlement (or Succession Act) receives the royal assent** (d). The Tories in the Commons impeach Bentinck (Lord Portland), Russell (now Lord Orford), Somers, and Montagu (now Lord Halifax), and ask the king to dismiss the four lords before the impeachment. The four lords send a counter-address. The Kentish Petition (e) is presented by William Colepepper and four others, for which they are sent to prison. At the trial of Somers the Commons do not appear, and the Lords declare him acquitted. **Death of James II.** Louis XIV. acknowledges the Pretender as king. A new Parliament meets, with a great majority of Whigs.
1702.	**William dismisses his Tory ministers.** A bill is passed for attainting the Pretender. A bill is passed to uphold the Protestant succession, and imposing an oath to that effect on all holding employment in Church or State. *Feb.* 20. William falls from his horse and breaks his collar-bone. *March* 8. William dies.

ANNE, 1702—1714 (12 YEARS).

Born 1665; Married, 1683, Prince George of Denmark.

Marlborough, Nottingham (Secretary of State), **and Godolphin** (Lord Treasurer) become the chiefs of a combined ministry of Whigs and Tories (f).
May. War is declared against France.
Admiral Benbow is defeated in the West Indies.
The Spanish treasure-ships are destroyed in Vigo Bay.
Marlborough takes the command of the allies in the Netherlands and captures Liège.
In accordance with the wish of William III., commissioners meet to treat for a union between England and Scotland, but cannot agree.
Rochester (a Tory) is dismissed from office.

1703.	The Methuen Treaty is concluded with Portugal (g). Bonn, on the Rhine, is captured by the allies.

[Notes.]

(a) *Aylesbury Election Trial.*—In this trial a man of the name of Ashby brought an action against the returning officer for rejecting his vote, and the case came by appeal before the House of Lords, which the Commons regarded as a breach of privilege.

(b) The firstfruits of benefices, which had been finally granted to the Crown in 1559, are now placed in the hands of the governors of Queen Anne's Bounty for the augmentation of small livings.

(c) *Union of England and Scotland.*—(1) The title of the United Kingdom is to be Great Britain. (2) £398,000 are to be paid by England to Scotland, to pay off the Scottish debt, to indemnify the shareholders in the Darien Company, etc. (3) The Scotch are not to pay any of the terminable taxes which had been granted by the English Parliament. (4) The Established Church of Scotland and the Scottish laws and judicial procedure are to be preserved. (5) Forty-five members for Scotland are to sit in the House of Commons, and sixteen peers, chosen at each general election, to represent the peers of Scotland, are to sit in the House of Lords. (6) No new Scottish peers are to be created.

(d) By this Act members of Parliament appointed to offices under the Crown which had existed before October 25, 1705, must vacate their seats, but may seek re-election.

FOREIGN AND COLONIAL.

ment. (2) The appointment of the great officers was transferred to the Scottish Parliament. A bill of security was passed authorizing Parliament to name a successor from the family of Sophia, but not the one named by England, unless security was given for independence of trade and religion in Scotland. The last did not receive the royal assent.

1704. The Test Act extended to Ireland.
The royal assent is given to the Act of Security.

1705. It is agreed that commissioners should again meet to treat of a union between England and Scotland.
Louis of Baden defeats the French at Hagueneau.

1706. Prince Eugène wins the battle of Turin.

1707. Death of Aurungzebe, the Moghul.

1708. The old and new East India Companies are united. (A partial union had been effected in 1702.)

1709. Charles XII. of Sweden is defeated by the Russians at the battle of Pultowa.
By the Barrier Treaty the Dutch obtain the right of garrisoning a line of fortresses in the Spanish Netherlands.

1703.	The Aylesbury election trial produces a dispute between the Lords and the Commons (a).
1704.	Queen Anne's Bounty is instituted (b). Nottingham (a Tory) leaves the ministry. **Harley** and **St. John** (moderate Tories) join the ministry. *Aug.* Marlborough and Prince Eugène defeat Tallard and Maximilian of Bavaria at **Blenheim**, on the Danube. **Gibraltar** is captured by Admiral Rooke and Sir Cloudesley Shovel. Somers passes resolutions declaring that after Christmas 1705 all Scotchmen are to be regarded as aliens. Importation of Scottish goods to England is prohibited. The border towns are ordered to be put in a state of defence.
1705.	Sunderland is sent as English envoy to Vienna. Marlborough forces the French lines between Antwerp and Namur, but is prevented by the Dutch from fighting a battle near Waterloo. Lord Cowper becomes Lord Chancellor. Peterborough and the allies capture Barcelona. The Whigs have a majority in the new Parliament.
1706.	Commissioners are again appointed to treat for a union between England and Scotland. Galway and the allies occupy Madrid. Peterborough saves Barcelona. Marlborough and the allies defeat the French under Villeroi at **Ramillies** (*May*), and secure all Flanders except **Lille**, **Tournay**, **Mons**, and **Namur**. Sunderland (a Whig) is made Secretary of State. The terms of the Union between England and Scotland are agreed upon. Louis XIV. makes overtures for peace.
1707.	**THE BILL FOR THE UNION OF ENGLAND AND SCOTLAND PASSES THE ENGLISH PARLIAMENT** (c). [See *Summary : Scotland, Part III.,* p. 250.]
1708.	The allies in Spain are defeated by Berwick at Almanza. *An Act is passed preventing the holders of pensions from the Crown, or of offices created after October 25, 1705, from sitting in Parliament* (d). Harley and St. John leave the ministry. **Robert Walpole** joins it as Secretary at War. The French fleet is delayed by the illness of the Pretender, who has the measles, and on sailing to the Firth of Forth to support the Jacobites, is put to flight by Byng. Marlborough and Prince Eugène defeat the French under Vendôme at **Oudenarde** (*July*), and capture **Lille**. Minorca is captured by General Stanhope. Somers is made Lord President of the Council.
1709.	Louis XIV. again treats for peace, but his terms are rejected. **Tournay** is captured by Marlborough. Marlborough and Prince Eugène defeat Villars at **Malplaquet** (*Sept.*), and capture **Mons**. Marlborough asks to be made Captain-General for life, but is refused.

[Notes.]

(a) Dr. Sacheverell had preached two sermons, one at Derby, another in London, on "perils among false brethren," advocating non-resistance, reflecting on the Whig clergy, and attacking the ministers. The Commons voted the sermons scandalous and seditious libels.

(b) *The Conference at Gertruydenberg.*—Louis agreed to give up—(1) to the Dutch ten fortresses in Flanders for a barrier; (2) to the Empire, Luxembourg, Strasburg, Brisach; (3) to the Duke of Savoy, Exilles and Fénestrelles; (4) to England, Newfoundland. But though he would allow the Archduke Charles to be King of Spain, he refused to assist the allies to expel Philip from Madrid.

(c) *Tory Administration.*—Harley, Chancellor of the Exchequer; St. John and Lord Dartmouth, Secretaries of State; Sir Simon Harcourt, Lord Keeper; Rochester, Lord President; Bishop of Bristol, Privy Seal; Shrewsbury, Lord Chamberlain; Ormond, Lord-Lieutenant of Ireland.
In 1711 Harley is created Earl of Oxford, and becomes Lord Treasurer. In 1713, when several changes were made, Wyndham became Chancellor of the Exchequer.

(d) *Occasional Conformity Act.*—Any officer, civil or military, or any magistrate of a corporation, who having received the sacrament according to the Test Act of Charles II., should during his time of office attend any conventicle or dissenting meeting, is to forfeit £40, and be incapable of holding any office or employment in England. (The bill had been introduced in the years 1702, 1703, 1704, but thrown out each time by the Lords.)

(e) *The Treaty of Utrecht.*—Philip of France to be King of Spain, but the crowns never to be united. France to acknowledge the Protestant succession. Gibraltar, Minorca, and Newfoundland to be held by England. English to have the right of trading in slaves to America, and of sending one ship a year to the South Seas. The Catalans are left to their fate.

(f) *Schism Act.*—No person is to keep a public or private school unless he is a member of the Church of England and licensed by the bishop.
(Thirty-three peers signed a protest against the Act, including Somers, Halifax, Argyll, Nottingham, Wharton, Townshend, and five bishops.)

FOREIGN AND COLONIAL.

1711. Charles VI. succeeds his brother as Emperor.

1713. Schism Act extended to Ireland.
Frederick William I. becomes King of Prussia.

1714. Death of the Electress Sophia, *June* 8.

1710.	Dr. Sacheverell is impeached (*a*) by the Whigs, but escapes with a light sentence, and the trial creates a great Tory reaction. A conference is held between France and the allies at Gertruydenberg, but comes to nothing (*b*). Douay is captured by the allies. Stanhope wins the battles of Almenara and Saragossa over the French and Spaniards. *Aug.* **The Whig ministry is dismissed, and is replaced by a Tory administration led by Harley and St. John** (*c*).
1711.	*The Property Qualification Bill for members of the House of Commons is passed* (see 1858). Guiscard attempts to assassinate Harley in the Privy Council. Marlborough takes Bouchain in France. The Duchess of Marlborough, through the intrigues of Harley and Mrs. Masham, is dismissed from all her offices. Marlborough is accused of peculation and is dismissed. Robert Walpole is accused of peculation and sent to the Tower. The South Sea Company is formed to trade in the South Seas. An Act is passed against occasional conformity, dispossessing many dissenters of the offices which they held (*d*). *To get a majority in the Lords, twelve new peers are created.*
1712.	Ormond (a Jacobite) is made commander-in-chief. An Act of this year restores, in opposition to the feeling of the Scottish Church, the ancient rights of patronage, and thus leads ultimately to the great secession of 1843. The first stamp duty is imposed for the purpose of repressing libels. It lessens the circulation of cheap papers.
1713.	Negotiations are pending since January 1712 between England and France, which result in **the Treaty of Utrecht**, 13*th March* (*e*). Oxford (formerly Harley) and St. John intrigue to secure the succession of the Pretender, and make Ormond warden of the Cinque Ports.
1714.	The Electoral Prince of Hanover (afterwards George II.) is invited to England, and application is made for his writ as Duke of Cambridge. The Schism Act (*f*) is passed. Thirty-three peers protest. A quarrel arises between **Bolingbroke** (formerly **St. John**) and **Oxford** (formerly **Harley**), who is dismissed from his office. In a cabinet council, by arrangement of the Dukes of Shrewsbury, Argyll, and Somerset, **Shrewsbury** is raised to the office of Lord Treasurer, vacant by the dismissal of Oxford, and the Hanoverian succession is secured. *Aug.* 1. Death of Anne.

GEORGE I., 1714—1727 (13 YEARS).
Born 1660; Married, 1682, Sophia of Brunswick.

Till the arrival of the new king the government is carried on by the seven great officers of State and eighteen " Lords Justices " nominated by the king, and including, with the exception of Marlborough, the leaders of the Whig party.

Sept. George arrives in England.

[Notes.]

(a) *Whig Administration.*—Lord Townshend and General Stanhope, Secretaries of State; Walpole, Paymaster of the Forces; Lord Cowper, Chancellor; Earl of Nottingham, Lord President; Lord Orford, Admiralty; Duke of Marlborough, Ordnance and Commander-in-Chief; Pulteney, Secretary at War; Duke of Devonshire, Lord Steward; Duke of Shrewsbury, Lord Chamberlain; Earl of Sunderland, Lord-Lieutenant of Ireland.

(b) *The Riot Act.*—If twelve or more persons unlawfully and riotously assembled against the peace, do not disperse within one hour of being ordered to do so by proclamation in the king's name by a justice of the peace, sheriff, under-sheriff, mayor, or other lawful authority, they shall be guilty of felony; and if any are killed in resisting those who are charged to disperse them, no one shall be held guilty of their murder.

(c) Stanhope is First Lord of Treasury and Chancellor of the Exchequer, Sunderland and Addison Secretaries of State.
In 1718 Sunderland becomes First Lord of the Treasury, and Stanhope Secretary of State. Aislabie, Chancellor of the Exchequer.

(d) *Peerage Bill.*—Only six more peerages beyond the then number (178) to be created. Extinct peerages to be filled up. New peerages to be confined to heirs-male. The sixteen representative peers of Scotland to be replaced by twenty-five hereditary peers named by the Crown. (It was supported by Sunderland, Stanhope, and Argyll, but opposed by Walpole and his followers, as well as by the Tories.)

FOREIGN AND COLONIAL.

1715. *Sept.* 1. Death of Louis XIV.
Louis XV. succeeds under the regency of the Duke of Orleans.
Cardinal Dubois, minister.

1717. Charles XII. and Alberoni intrigue with the Jacobites against England.

1718. Death of Charles XII. of Sweden.

1719. Alberoni is dismissed by the King of Spain.
Toleration Act carried by the Irish Parliament.

1714.	**Townshend, Stanhope, and Walpole** become the heads of a new Whig administration (*a*).
1715.	*Jan.* Parliament, which has continued six months after the late queen's death, is dissolved. The new Parliament, with a large Whig majority, meets, *March.* Bolingbroke and Ormond retire to France to avoid prosecution, but are attainted. Oxford is impeached and committed to the Tower. The Riot Act (*b*) is passed in consequence of serious riots in the Midland counties and elsewhere. **The Earl of Mar in Scotland, Forster and Derwentwater in England, raise rebellions.** The leading English Jacobites are arrested. *Nov.* Forster is defeated and taken at Preston, and Mar fights the indecisive battle of Sheriff Muir against Argyll.
1716.	The Pretender comes over, but soon withdraws with Mar. Derwentwater and others are executed. Forster escapes from prison. **The Septennial Act,** *prolonging the duration of Parliament to seven years, but not longer, is passed. Thirty-one peers protest.* Ministerial crisis. Townshend having lost favour by opposing the king's Hanoverian schemes, is removed to the lord-lieutenancy of Ireland, and **Stanhope becomes chief minister.**
1717.	The Triple Alliance is made between England, France, and Holland to guarantee the Hanoverian succession. **Townshend, Walpole, and Pulteney** are obliged to resign their offices for opposing Stanhope (*c*). Oxford is tried and acquitted. A comprehensive Act of Grace is passed, and many political prisoners are released. Convocation, after the prorogation of this year, continues to be prorogued without doing business till 1850.
1718.	Admiral Byng defeats the Spanish fleet off Cape Passaro in Sicily. The Occasional Conformity and Schism Acts are repealed. England, France, Austria, and Holland form the Quadruple Alliance.
1719.	The Spaniards invade Scotland and are joined by some Highlanders, but are defeated at Glenshiel. *The Peerage Bill passes the Lords, but is rejected by the Commons* (*d*) *by 269 to 177.* [A statute is passed this year to enable the English Parliament to legislate for Ireland. This was repealed in 1782.]
1720.	Peace made with Spain. **The South Sea Company** purchase from the Government part of the national debt. The shares of the company rise to £1000 each, and then fall rapidly to £135. Great ruin ensues.
1721.	Walpole, who with Townshend had just rejoined the Government, restores public credit. The directors are prosecuted, and Stanhope dies (*Feb.* 1722). Sunderland has to resign, and dies in April 1722. Aislabie, Chancellor of Exchequer, is expelled the House.

[Notes.]

(a) *Walpole's Ministry.*—Walpole, First Lord of the Treasury and Chancellor of the Exchequer; Lords Townshend and Carteret, Secretaries of State; Earl of Macclesfield, Lord Chancellor; Lord Carleton, Lord President; Duke of Kingston, Privy Seal; Earl of Berkeley, First Lord of the Admiralty; Duke of Marlborough, Ordnance; Byng (afterwards Lord Torrington), Treasurer of the Navy; Duke of Argyll, Lord Steward; Duke of Newcastle, Lord Chamberlain; Pulteney, Cofferer of the Household.

(b) Malt tax was changed into a tax of threepence on each barrel of ale, then the national drink of Scotland; the brewers resisted, but in the end gave way.

(c) *Walpole's Excise Scheme.*—This was a scheme to transfer the taxes on tobacco and wine from the customs to the excise, *i.e.* instead of a customs duty levied at the port, a tax would be levied at the manufactory on the quantity made, and a licence would be required for the sale of the articles, and the manufactories and shops would be liable to inspection. In his dictionary, edition 1755, Johnson defined excise as "a hateful tax upon commodities, and adjudged, not by common judges of property, but by wretches hired by those to whom excise is paid."

(d) For their opposition to Walpole, Chesterfield is dismissed from his post of Lord Steward of the Household, and the Duke of Bolton and Lord Cobham are removed from the command of their regiments.

(e) The leaders of the Prince of Wales' political friends, called "the Leicester House Party," were Pulteney, Carteret, Chesterfield, Sandys, Sir T. Sanderson, Lyttelton, William Pitt, the Grenvilles, and Bubb Dodington, representing the opposition Whigs.
The Tory leaders were Wyndham, Shippen, Lord Polwarth, Sir John Hynde Cotton, Fazackerley, Sir Watkin Wynn, Lord Cornbury; and in the Lords, Gower, Bathurst, and Lichfield.

FOREIGN AND COLONIAL.

1723. Wood is allowed to issue a copper coinage in Ireland. Great agitation follows, and it is withdrawn next year.
Louis XV. begins to reign in person.
1725. Death of Peter the Great.
1726. Cardinal Fleury becomes chief minister of France.
1727. The elective franchise completely taken away from the Irish Roman Catholics.
There being no Triennial Act in Ireland, the Parliament elected this year sits till 1760.

1732. The colony of Georgia is founded.
1733-35. War of the Polish succession between Spain, France, and Savoy against Austria and Russia.

[1721—1737] ENGLISH.

PRIME MINISTERS. **WALPOLE** (*March* 1721).	⨯ **Walpole becomes First Lord of the Treasury and Prime Minister** (*a*).
1722.	A Jacobite conspiracy is discovered, and Atterbury, Bishop of Rochester, is sent to the Tower.
1723.	Atterbury is banished. Bolingbroke is allowed to return; he makes overtures to Walpole, which are rejected.
1724.	⨯ **Carteret**, not agreeing with Walpole, is sent to Ireland as Lord-Lieutenant. **Henry Pelham** becomes Secretary at War. **Newcastle** becomes Secretary of State. At Glasgow riots occur because the malt tax had been changed into a tax on beer (*b*).
1725.	Austria and Spain having concluded a treaty at Vienna against England, a counter-treaty is made at Hanover between England, France, and Prussia, and hostilities go on during the next two years. **Pulteney** joins the Opposition.
1727.	*June* 10. Death of George I.

GEORGE II., 1727—1760 (33 YEARS).

Born 1683; Married, 1705, Caroline of Anspach.

	⨯ Sir Spencer Compton is proposed as Prime Minister, but Walpole keeps his place, and increases the civil list. The Spaniards besiege Gibraltar without success. The first Annual Bill of Indemnity for not observing the Test and Corporation Acts is passed.
1728.	*The publication of Parliamentary debates is declared to be a breach of privilege* (*now and in* 1738).
1729.	**Peace with Spain is made at Seville.**
1730.	Lord Townshend has to withdraw, and leaves Walpole's ascendancy complete. [About this time **John** and **Charles Wesley** form their society at Oxford, which is joined later by Whitfield.]
1731.	By the second treaty of Vienna England guarantees the Pragmatic Sanction by which Maria Theresa is to succeed to the hereditary dominions of her father, Charles VI. Use of Latin in the courts of law is abolished. Carteret joins the Opposition.
1733.	Walpole brings in his excise scheme (*c*) and meets with violent opposition, in deference to which he abandons the measure (*d*).
1734.	Meeting of a new Parliament. Walpole's majority is somewhat reduced. Bolingbroke soon withdraws to France.
1736.	Porteous riots in Edinburgh. Captain Porteous is hanged by the mob.
1737.	The Prince of Wales becomes the centre of the opposition to Walpole (*e*).

[Notes.]

FOREIGN AND COLONIAL.

(a) By treaty the English and Spanish governments were allowed to search each other's ships for contraband goods, and as the English were constantly trying to establish an illegal trade with the Spanish colonies of South America, this right led to constant ill will between the two nations.

(b) At that time election petitions were tried by a committee of the whole House, and were regarded purely as party questions.

(c) Wilmington is the same as the Sir Spencer Compton who was asked by George II. to be Prime Minister in 1727.
Wilmington's Ministry.—Wilmington, First Lord of the Treasury; Pulteney in the Cabinet without office; Lord Hardwicke, Lord Chancellor; Sandys, Chancellor of the Exchequer; Lord Carteret, Duke of Newcastle, Secretaries of State; Earl of Winchilsea and Nottingham, Admiralty; Henry Pelham, Paymaster; Duke of Grafton, Lord Chamberlain.

(d) GENEALOGY OF THE CARTERETS AND GRANVILLES.

Sir Bevil Granville, killed at Lansdowne 1643.

Sir John, created Earl of Bath. Charles II.'s messenger from Breda to the Convention Parliament.

Jane m. Sir William Leveson Gower. | Grace, created Countess Granville, d. 1744. | m. George, Lord Carteret, d. 1695.
Sir John, created Lord Gower (ancestor of Dukes of Sutherland, and of the present Earl Granville). | John, Lord Carteret, succeeded as Earl Granville 1744, d. 1763. |

Robert, 2nd Earl Granville. | Louisa m. Thomas, 2nd Viscount Weymouth. | Sophia m. William, Earl of Shelburne, Prime Minister 1782-83.

Thomas, 3rd Viscount Weymouth, created Marquis of Bath. (Secretary of State *temp.* George III.)

(e) *Pelham's Ministry of* 1744.—Henry Pelham, First Lord of the Treasury and Chancellor of the Exchequer; Lord Hardwicke, Lord Chancellor; Duke of Newcastle and Lord Harrington, Secretaries of State. Duke of Bedford, Duke of Grafton, Duke of Devonshire, Duke of Dorset, and others. Earl of Chesterfield, Lord-Lieutenant of Ireland; Dodington, Treasurer of the Navy; Sir John Hynde Cotton, Treasurer of the Chamber till 1746.

1740. In this year and 1741 terrible famine in Ireland.
Death of the Emperor Charles VI., accession of Maria Theresa. Accession of Frederick the Great to the throne of Prussia, who at once claims and seizes Silesia. War between Frederick and Maria Theresa.
1741. Battle of Molwitz.
1742. By the advice of Carteret, Austria cedes Silesia to Prussia by the Treaty of Breslau.

1743. By the Treaty of Worms, England, Holland, Austria, Saxony, Sardinia agree to carry out the Pragmatic Sanction.
1744. Chesterfield becomes Lord Lieutenant of Ireland.
League of Frankfort formed between France and Prussia in opposition to the Treaty of Worms.

[1737—1744] ENGLISH.

PRIME MINISTERS. **WALPOLE.** 1737.	Quarrel between the king and the Prince of Wales, on the birth of the Prince's eldest daughter. **Death of Queen Caroline.**
1739.	Wesley develops his society, which becomes known as that of the Methodists, in London. Secession of the Opposition from the House of Commons. Walpole yields against his judgment to the wish of the king and nation, and makes war with the Spaniards in consequence of their use of the right of search (*a*). Capture of Porto Bello.
1740.	**Steady increase in the opposition to Walpole led by Pulteney, Carteret, and Sandys.**
1741.	Sandys and Carteret's motions for the dismissal of Walpole are thrown out by both Houses of Parliament. The neutrality of Hanover is declared. Failure of the English attack on Carthagena. Meeting of a new parliament.
1742.	**Walpole is defeated** on the question of the Chippenham election, and **resigns all his offices** (*b*).
LORD WILMINGTON (*c*).	**Wilmington** becomes nominal Prime Minister, and some members of the Opposition come into office, but there is no great change of policy. **Pulteney** loses much of his power by **retiring to the House of Lords as Earl of Bath**, and **Carteret** is virtually head of the Government. Walpole becomes Earl of Orford. A committee is appointed to inquire into the acts of the late Government. *The Place Bill, limiting the number of offices tenable by members of Parliament, is passed.*
1743.	England takes part in the war, and her troops, with the Hessians and Hanoverians, defeat the French at **Dettingen** (*June* 16) on the Main. The French withdraw from Germany.
HENRY PELHAM.	On the death of Wilmington (*July*) **Henry Pelham** becomes Prime Minister, and Carteret loses power.
1744.	Indecisive action off Toulon between the English and the French and Spanish fleets. The French fleet, which was prepared to support an expedition of Charles Edward to England, is so much damaged by a storm that the attempt is abandoned. Open war is declared between England and France. Return of Anson from his voyage round the world with over a million dollars' worth of treasure taken from the Spaniards. Carteret (who has now succeeded as **Earl Granville**) (*d*) leaves the ministry. **The "Broad Bottom"** (*e*) **administration** is formed by a coalition under the Pelhams.

[Notes.]

FOREIGN AND COLONIAL.

1745. Election of Maria Theresa's husband as Emperor with title of Francis I.
Treaty of Dresden, close of second Silesian war.

1746. Madras surrendered to the French.

(a) GENEALOGY OF THE FOX FAMILY.

Sir Stephen Fox, d. 1716.

- Charles, d. 1713.
- Stephen, created Earl of Ilchester.
- Henry, created Lord Holland (Paymaster-General *temp.* George II., III.), d. 1774.
  - Stephen, 2nd Lord Holland, d. 1774.
    - Henry Richard, 3rd Lord Holland, d. 1840.
  - Charles James Fox, b. 1749, d. 1806.

1748. Madras restored by the Treaty of Aix-la-Chapelle.

(b) *New Style.*—This had been introduced into Roman Catholic countries by Pope Gregory XIII. in 1582, but was not adopted in England till this year. By it the year 1752 was to begin on the 1st of January instead of the 25th of March, and eleven days were to be suppressed between the 2nd and 14th of September. The quarter days for Government purposes were, however, to be the 5th of April, 5th of July, 10th of October, and 5th of January.

(c) *Lord Hardwicke's Marriage Act.*—As it provided that, with the exception of Jewish and Quaker marriages, no marriage should be valid unless performed according to certain formalities by a clergyman of the Church of England, it was a great grievance to Nonconformists.

1751. Capture and defence of Arcot by Robert Clive, and surrender of Trichinopoly by the French (1752).

PRIME MINISTERS. HENRY PELHAM. 1745.	The English and their allies are defeated by the French at **Fontenoy**. Louisburg and the Isle of Cape Breton at the mouth of the St. Lawrence are taken from the French. *October. Sir F. Dashwood brings in an amendment (to the address), claiming for the people the "right to be freely and fairly represented in Parliament."* **Landing of Charles Edward Stuart** in the Highlands. He outwits Cope. Is proclaimed at Edinburgh. Defeats Cope at **Prestonpans**, *September* 21. Takes Carlisle, *November* 15; reaches **Derby**, *December* 4; and retreats, reaches Glasgow, *December* 25.
1746.	Defeats General Hawley at **Falkirk**, *Jan.* 17. Ministerial crisis. *Feb.* The ministry resign because the king will not admit **Pitt**. Granville fails to form a ministry. **The ministers return with Pitt as Vice-Treasurer of Ireland, a few months later Paymaster of the Forces. Henry Fox** (*a*) **becomes Secretary at War.** Charles Edward Stuart is finally defeated at **Culloden**, *April* 16. Highlanders are disarmed, forbidden to wear their national dress, and the hereditary jurisdiction of the Highland chiefs is abolished and compensation given (1747). Execution of Lords Kilmarnock and Balmerino.
1747.	Execution of Lords Lovat and Derwentwater (Charles Radcliffe). (Dr. Cameron executed, 1753.) [See *Summary : Jacobites*, p. 267.] Naval victories off Cape Finisterre and off Ushant. The Duke of Cumberland is defeated at Lauffeld, and **Bergen-op-Zoom is surrendered by the allies**.
1748.	Resignation of Chesterfield. **Peace of Aix-la-Chapelle.** All conquests made during the war are restored by both sides. France is to recognise Maria Theresa. The right of search is left unnoticed (see 1739).
1750.	Interest on the national debt is reduced to three per cent., and soon after the fourteen different kinds of stocks are consolidated into five.
1751.	Death of Frederick, Prince of Wales. The New Style is introduced on a motion of Lord Chesterfield (*b*). **Death of Henry St. John, Lord Bolingbroke.**
1752.	The year begins on *Jan.* 1, and eleven nominal days are omitted between *Sept.* 2 and *Sept.* 14.
1753.	Lord Hardwicke's Marriage Act to prevent clandestine marriages is passed (*c*).

[Notes.]

(*a*) *Duke of Newcastle's Ministry.*—Newcastle, First Lord of the Treasury; Lord Hardwicke, Chancellor; Legge, Chancellor of the Exchequer; Lord Holdernesse and Sir Thomas Robinson, Secretaries of State; Lord Anson, First Lord of the Admiralty; Earl Granville (Carteret), Lord President; Earl Gower, Lord Privy Seal; Duke of Grafton, Earl of Halifax, George Grenville; Hartington (succeeded as Duke of Devonshire), Lord-Lieutenant of Ireland.

(*b*) *Duke of Devonshire's Ministry.*—Devonshire, First Lord of the Treasury; Legge, Chancellor of the Exchequer; Earl Granville, Lord President; Earl Gower, Privy Seal; the Earl of Holdernesse and William Pitt, Secretaries of State. George Grenville, the Dukes of Rutland and Grafton also in the ministry. Charles Townshend, Treasurer of the Chamber; Duke of Bedford, Lord-Lieutenant of Ireland.

(*c*) *Newcastle's Ministry.*—Newcastle, First Lord of the Treasury; Legge, Chancellor of the Exchequer; Pitt and Holdernesse, Secretaries of State; Lord Temple, Lord Privy Seal; Granville, Lord President; Fox, Paymaster; George Grenville, Treasurer of the Navy; Lord Halifax, First Lord of Trade; Lord Anson, Admiralty; Duke of Devonshire, Lord Chamberlain; Charles Townshend, Treasurer of the Chamber.

(*d*) By this conquest the Ohio valley was secured, and the territories of Western America secured for England and not for France.

FOREIGN AND COLONIAL.

1754. French form the settlement of Fort Duquesne on the Ohio. War follows between the English and French colonists.

1756. Opening of the Seven Years' War. Defeat of Braddock at Fort Duquesne. Calcutta is captured by Surajah Dowlah. Tragedy of the Black Hole of Calcutta.

1757. Calcutta retaken. The battle of Plassy (*June* 23) secures Bengal for England. Victories of Rosbach and Leuthen for Frederick.

1758. Capture of Fort Duquesne (afterwards called Pittsburg) (*d*). Frederick defeats the Russians at Zorndorf, but is defeated by the Austrians at Hochkirchen.

1759. Ticonderoga and Crown Point captured. Accession of Charles of Naples to the throne of Spain. Frederick is defeated at Kunersdorf.

1760. The victory of Wandewash secures Madras, and completes the downfall of French power in India. Frederick wins at Torgau.

1761. Capture of Pondicherry by Coote (restored 1763). Family compact formed between France and Spain, *Aug*.

[1753—1761]   ENGLISH.

PRIME MINISTERS. **HENRY PELHAM.** 1753.	A bill for the naturalization of Jews is passed, but in consequence of the popular opposition is repealed next session.
1754. **DUKE OF NEWCASTLE.**	Death of Henry Pelham, who is succeeded as Prime Minister by the Duke of Newcastle (*a*).
1755.	Pitt refuses to support the payment of subsidies to Hesse and Russia, and is discharged from his post of Paymaster of the Forces. Henry Fox is made Secretary of State.
1756.	England makes an alliance with Prussia. War is declared between England and France. Byng (son of the Byng mentioned in 1718) fails to relieve Minorca.
DUKE OF DEVONSHIRE. 1757.	Resignation of Newcastle. The Duke of Devonshire becomes nominal Prime Minister (*b*), Pitt Secretary of State with real power. The bill for the establishment of a national militia is passed. Execution of Byng. Pitt is dismissed by the king, *April* 9. Newcastle tries to form a ministry without Pitt,
NEWCASTLE.	but fails, and has to receive Pitt, *June* 28 (*c*) The country is for eleven weeks without a government. *July.* Cumberland is defeated at Hastenbeck, and capitulates at Klosterseven.
1758.	Prince Ferdinand of Brunswick is made commander-in-chief of the English and Hanoverians. A series of small expeditions are made against Cherbourg and other places on the French coast. A subsidy of £670,000 begins to be paid yearly to Prussia. Naval victories off Carthagena and Basque Roads. Louisburg and Cape Breton taken.
1759.	Capture of Guadaloupe and bombardment of Le Havre. Victory of **Minden**; Ferdinand of Brunswick, in command of the allies, defeats the French under Marshal de Broglie. The capture of **Quebec** under General Wolfe ensures the conquest of Canada. Naval victories at Lagos and off Quiberon Bay.
1760.	*Oct.* 26. Death of George II.

GEORGE III., 1760—1820 (60 YEARS).
Born 1738 ; Married, 1761, Charlotte-Sophia of Mecklenburg-Strelitz.

1761.	Lord Bute is made Secretary of State. Pitt resigns because the rest of the ministry refuse to go to war with Spain.

[Notes.]

FOREIGN AND COLONIAL.

(a) "Nothing in his public life became him like the leaving of it" (Massey). He had reduced his own income from £25,000 to £6000 a year, yet refused a pension.

(b) *Lord Bute's Ministry.*—Bute, First Lord of the Treasury; Sir Francis Dashwood, Chancellor of the Exchequer; Earl Granville, President of the Council; Duke of Bedford, Privy Seal; Earl of Halifax, Admiralty; Earl of Egremont and George Grenville, Secretaries of State. Henry Fox, Lord Sandys, and others.

(c) The Dukes of Newcastle, Grafton, and Rockingham were deprived of their lord-lieutenancies; the Duke of Devonshire resigned his, and his name was struck off the list of the Privy Council by the king's own hand. The proscription reached even to inferior officials who had been promoted by the late Administration.

1763. Treaty of Hubertsburg closes Seven Years' War, and Frederick keeps Silesia.

(d) "The public still looked at Lord Bute through the curtain, which indeed was very transparent."

(e) *George Grenville's Ministry.*—Grenville, First Lord of the Treasury and Chancellor of the Exchequer; Duke of Marlborough, Privy Seal; Earls of Halifax and Egremont, Secretaries of State; Earl Gower, Lord Chamberlain; Earl of Sandwich, Admiralty; Lord Holland (Fox), Paymaster of the Forces; Lord Henley (afterwards Earl of Northington), Lord Chancellor; also Marquis of Granby and others.

(f) General Warrant, *i.e.* a warrant in which no name is inserted, but the officers may arrest whom they suspect.

1764. The defeat of the Nabob of Oudh at Buxar by Munro makes England the leading power in India.

(g) Bedford became President of the Council, an office vacant by the death of Lord Granville.

(h) *Stamp Act.*—A charge of so much on contracts, wills, and legal documents, levied by means of a stamp, as, for instance, a receipt stamp.

[1762—1765]   ENGLISH.

PRIME MINISTERS.	
NEWCASTLE. 1762.	A *Bribery Act is passed, in which pecuniary penalties are attached to the offence.* War is declared by England against Spain. **Newcastle resigns,** nominally because Bute refuses to continue the subsidy to Prussia, in reality because he is never consulted either in matters of policy or of patronage (*a*).
LORD BUTE.	Lord **Bute** becomes Prime Minister (*b*). Capture of Havannah, capital of Cuba. Capture of Manilla, capital of the Philippine Islands. Preliminaries of peace are signed at Fontainebleau. Several peers disapproving of the peace are deprived of their lord-lieutenancies (*c*). Fox, Paymaster of the Forces, receives a seat in the Cabinet, and secures a majority for the peace in the Commons (319 to 65), though strenuously opposed by Pitt. [During this year the secret service money amounted to £82,000.]
1763.	**The Peace of Paris** between England, France, Spain, and Portugal is **signed.** England keeps her conquests in America, including Canada, and gains considerable advantages in the West Indies. In India, Pondicherry is restored unfortified. *Unconstitutional dismissal of placemen for their votes in Parliament.*
GEORGE GRENVILLE.	Lord Bute, frightened by his unpopularity, resigns (*April*), and is succeeded by **George Grenville,** with Lords Egremont and Halifax (the Triumvirate) (*d*) (*e*). Proceedings are begun, under a general warrant (*f*), against **Wilkes** for number 45 of the *North Briton.* He is arrested, but released under Habeas Corpus Act, on the ground of his privilege, by Chief-Justice Pratt. *Wilkes is denied his privilege by Parliament, notwithstanding remonstrances of Pitt and a protest by seventeen peers.* Wilkes and the printers obtain damages against the king's messengers for illegal imprisonment. Attempt of the king to get Pitt to join Grenville. Coalition between Bedford and Grenville, known as **the Bedford ministry** (*g*).
1764.	Wilkes is expelled from the House of Commons. Great riots in favour of Wilkes. Grenville passes an Act imposing customs duties on the American colonies, and gives notice of the Stamp Act.
1765.	**The Stamp Act** (*h*) for America is passed, notwithstanding the protests of six colonies. The king shows the first symptoms of madness. In the proposed Regency Bill his mother's name is ex-

[Notes.]

FOREIGN AND COLONIAL.

(*a*) The princess's name was inserted by the House of Commons in spite of the ministers.

(*b*) *Marquis of Rockingham's Ministry.* — Rockingham, First Lord of the Treasury; Dowdeswell, Chancellor of the Exchequer; Earl of Winchilsea, Lord President; Duke of Newcastle, Privy Seal; Earl of Northington, Lord Chancellor; Duke of Portland, Lord Chamberlain; Duke of Rutland, Master of the Horse; General Conway and the Duke of Grafton, Secretaries of State; Earl Egmont, Admiralty; Marquis of Granby, Viscount Howe, Charles Townshend, and others.

(*c*) *Duke of Grafton's Ministry.*—Grafton, First Lord of the Treasury; Charles Townshend, Chancellor of the Exchequer; Earl of Northington, Lord President; Earl of Chatham, Lord Privy Seal; Lords Shelburne and General Conway, Secretaries of State; Lord Camden, Lord Chancellor; Marquis of Granby, Lord Hertford, and others.

(*d*) At this time the corporation of Oxford offer their representation for about £6000, for which the mayor and ten aldermen are imprisoned in Newgate, where they arrange the sale of their representation to the Duke of Marlborough and Lord Abingdon.

(*e*) The chief members of the Whig parties:—
Bedford's Party.—Bedford, Gower, Sandwich, Weymouth, Rigby.
Rockingham's Party.—Rockingham, Burke, Portland, Conway, Devonshire, Richmond, Lord John Cavendish, Sir George Savile, Dowdeswell, Keppel.
Chatham's Party.—Chatham, Shelburne, Camden, Dunning, Barré, Beckford, Alderman Townsend.
The Grenvilles.—Temple, George Grenville, James Grenville, Lord Lyttelton, Sir R. Lyttelton, Lord Suffolk, Augustus Hervey (afterwards Earl of Bristol), "Single-Speech" Hamilton.

(*f*) *North's Ministry.*—Lord North, First Lord of the Treasury and Chancellor of the Exchequer; Earl Gower, Lord President; Earl of Halifax, Privy Seal; Sandwich (Dec. 1770), Rochford, and Hillsborough (Colonies), Secretaries of State; Charles James Fox, a Junior Lord of the Admiralty till 1772, and of the Treasury, 1773 to 1774; Hawke, Admiralty; Barrington, Secretary at War; Rigby, Paymaster.
[In 1771 Sandwich became First Lord of the Admiralty and Grafton became Privy Seal. In 1778 Jenkinson became Secretary at War.]

1768. Captain Cook makes his first voyage to Australia and explores Botany Bay and the neighbourhood, which he visits 1770, and names New South Wales.
Octennial Act passed for Ireland.
1769. Corsica annexed to France.

1770. Disturbances at Boston.

PRIME MINISTERS. **GEORGE GRENVILLE.** 1765.	cluded (*a*); this irritates the king against Grenville. Through the Duke of Cumberland he applies to Pitt, who will not join without Lord Temple, who is pledged to Grenville.
LORD ROCKINGHAM. 1766.	*July.* The duke then goes to **Rockingham**, who forms a ministry (*b*). A Declaratory Act, stating that England has authority over the colonies both in legislation and taxation, is passed. Repeal of the American Stamp Act. Pitt strongly supports this measure, but repeatedly refuses to join the ministry. The House of Commons by resolution condemns all general warrants as illegal.
DUKE OF GRAFTON.	*July.* Fall of the Rockingham ministry. Pitt forms a strong government under the Duke of Grafton as nominal chief, and himself becomes Earl of Chatham (*c*). Chatham soon falls ill, and Grafton becomes real Premier.
1767.	Charles Townshend, Chancellor of the Exchequer, passes an Act for taxing American imports by various small customs duties (the total produce of which is estimated at not more than £40,000). Death of Charles Townshend. Lord North becomes Chancellor of the Exchequer.
1768.	At the general election (*d*) Wilkes having been at the bottom of the poll for the city is elected for Middlesex. Riots and disturbances in favour of Wilkes. He is imprisoned for his former libels. Chatham gets better, but leaves the government on grounds of general ill-health.
1769.	*Jan.* The first letter signed "Junius" appears in the *Public Advertiser.* *Feb.* 16. Wilkes is re-elected for Middlesex. *Feb.* 17. Wilkes is declared incapable of sitting in the present Parliament by 235 to 89. *March* 16. Wilkes again elected for Middlesex. The election declared void the next day. *April* 13. Wilkes elected for Middlesex (fourth time) by 1143 to 296 for Colonel Luttrell. *April* 16. Luttrell is seated in the House of Commons by 197 votes to 143.
1770. **LORD NORTH.**	Resignation of the Duke of Grafton. *Jan.* Lord Chatham is unable to get the Bedford section of the Whigs (*e*) to agree with him, and the king gives the seals to **Lord North** (*f*). Charles Yorke accepts the Chancellorship, and dies three days afterwards (probably by suicide). *March.* All the American import duties are removed except the tax on tea.

[Notes.]

FOREIGN AND COLONIAL.

(a) GENEALOGY OF THE GRENVILLES AND PITTS.

Hester, Countess Temple m. Richard Grenville.

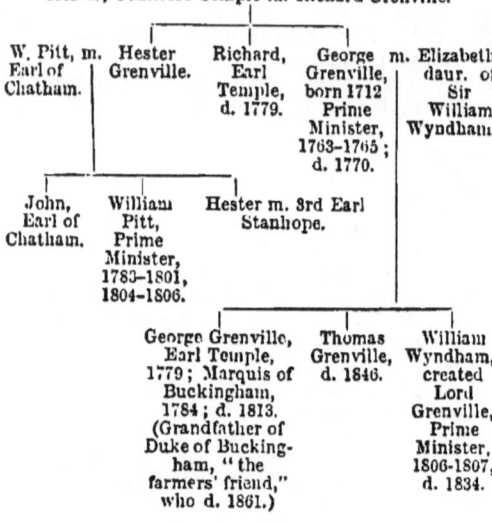

(b) This allows no descendants of George II. to make a legal marriage without the consent of the reigning sovereign, unless they are twenty-five years of age, and have given twelve months' notice to the Privy Council, and the marriage has not been petitioned against by Parliament.
To oppose this Act Charles James Fox gave up his place in the ministry.

(c) *Lord North's Regulating Act.* — (1) Establishes a supreme court, with Elijah Impey as chief judge. (2) Makes the governor of Bengal, Warren Hastings, Governor-General of India.* (3) Makes a new council of five, consisting of Barwell, Clavering, Monson, Francis, and the Governor-General.
The twenty-four directors elected by the proprietors of India stock appoint the Governor-General.

---

* Speaking more accurately, Warren Hastings, who had been President of the Bengal Council, was made Governor-General of Bengal, with certain powers of control over the President and Council of each of the other provinces. (By the Act of 1833 the supreme Government of India is vested in a "Governor-General of India in Council," but the governorship of Bengal becomes *ex officio* one of the functions of the Governor-General of India. In 1853 power was given to appoint a lieutenant-governor of Bengal.)

1772. First partition of Poland between Austria, Russia, and Prussia.
1773. The people of Boston board the ships and throw the tea overboard.
1774. The governor of Bengal, Warren Hastings, is made Governor-General of India.
The Assembly of Massachusetts meets for the last time (under the English Crown). It recommends a Congress of the different colonies, and is dissolved by Gage, the governor.
Congress meets at Philadelphia, and denies the right of Parliament to tax the colonies.
By a conciliatory policy, and the legal establishment of the Roman Catholic religion, the loyalty of Canada is secured.
Louis XVI. succeeds Louis XV. Turgot, minister.
1775. George Washington (of Virginia) is appointed commander-in-chief by the Americans.

144

PRIME MINISTERS. LORD NORTH. 1770.		An Act introduced by George Grenville (a) gives the hearing of election petitions to a committee of thirteen members (selected from forty-nine chosen by ballot, with one nominee from each party) instead of a committee of the whole House. Grenville dies, Nov. *May.* Lord Chatham in the course of a debate suggests the addition of a third member to every county. The printers and publishers of Junius' letters are tried and acquitted. *Lord Mansfield lays it down that the jury have not the right to decide whether the publication is libellous, but only whether it has been published.*
	1771.	*The attempt of the Commons to prevent the publishing of their debates is foiled by Alderman Wilkes and the Lord Mayor. Since this time the publication of debates, though still asserted to be a breach of privilege, has gone on with only occasional interruptions.*
	1772.	A bill to relieve Dissenting ministers from subscription to some of the Articles is rejected in the Lords now and in 1773. **The Royal Marriage Act is passed** (b). Lord Mansfield decides (in Sommerset's case) that slavery cannot exist in England.
	1773. 1774.	Lord North's Act for the regulation of India is passed (c). The petition of Massachusetts for the removal of its governor is rejected, and Franklin is insulted by Wedderburn at a meeting of the Privy Council. Charles James Fox is removed from office through the king's influence. The Boston Port Bill is passed closing the port of Boston. The constitution of Massachusetts is annulled. Charges brought against Clive during the passing of the Regulating Act prey on his mind and cause his suicide. Wilkes is elected for Middlesex and allowed to take his seat. He is also elected Lord Mayor. [In the general election of this year Gatton is sold for £75,000.]
	1775.	Lord Chatham speaks and the city of London petitions against the severe measures taken against the colonists, but the House of Lords rejects Lord Chatham's conciliatory proposals by 61 to 32. Burke's conciliatory motions are also rejected. *April.* Battle of **Lexington**, indecisive. Ticonderoga and Crown Point, which command the valley of the Hudson, are taken by the colonists. The British win the battle of **Bunker's Hill**.

[Notes.]

FOREIGN AND COLONIAL.

(a) He had always desired to effect a reconciliation, but was not willing to abandon the sovereignty of England.

(b) The penalties now repealed are—the perpetual imprisonment of priests for saying mass, the forfeiture of the estates of Roman Catholic heirs educated abroad to the next Protestant heir, and the prohibition to acquire land by purchase.

(c) The grant consisted of three propositions—(1) to allow free export of wool; (2) to allow a free export of glass and all kinds of glass manufactures; (3) to allow free-trade with all the British plantations on condition of equality of customs.

1776. *July* 4. Declaration of Independence by the United States. Congress meets and declares the thirteen colonies free and independent states.
Necker becomes chief minister of France.
1777. The French send help to the Americans.

1778. France recognises the independence of the United States and makes a treaty with them (arranged by Franklin).

1779. Dissenters admitted to office by an Act of the Irish Parliament.
Irish volunteers are formed.
Irish volunteers help the Parliament, and great excitement is caused in Dublin.
Free-trade is granted to Ireland (c).
1780. A French army lands in Rhode Island.
Hyder Ali invades the Carnatic.
Katharine of Russia forms the armed neutrality of Norway, Russia, and Sweden against England.

[1775—1780] ENGLISH.

PRIME MINISTERS.	
LORD NORTH. 1775.	Grafton resigns the Privy Seal ; Lord George Germaine (formerly Sackville) became Colonial Secretary. Numerous petitions are sent by the towns supporting or condemning the king's policy. The English defeat an American invasion of Canada.
1776.	**The English under Sir William Howe are forced to evacuate Boston.** *Wilkes' motion for parliamentary reform lost in the Commons.* Under General Howe the English drive the Americans from Long Island and **take New York.** The English take Rhode Island. The Whigs, disapproving of the government's American policy, cease to attend Parliament for a time.
1777.	Lord Chatham again speaks against the use of arms to subdue the colonists. (Motion rejected by 99 to 28.) The English win the battle of **Brandywine** and take **Philadelphia.** General Burgoyne marches down the Hudson from Canada to join Clinton from New York, but is forced to surrender at **Saratoga.**
1778.	The Duke of Richmond's motion to recognise the independence of the United States is opposed by Chatham in his last speech (*a*). Burke brings in his measure for the relief of Irish trade. *May* 11. **Death of Chatham.** Thurlow becomes Lord Chancellor. **Sir George Savile passes his measure for the relief of Roman Catholics** (*b*). The English evacuate Philadelphia. Naval fight off Ushant under Keppel, indecisive.
1779.	Anti-Popish riots in Scotland. Dissenting ministers and schoolmasters are at length relieved from subscription to any of the Thirty-nine Articles. Spain declares war against England. The French and Spanish besiege Gibraltar.
1780.	By an Act of the English Parliament many of the restrictions on Irish trade are annulled. *Great Yorkshire petition for economical reform presented (the beginning of the modern system of petitioning).* Middlesex and Westminster hold meetings in favour of retrenchment. Two peers (Lords Carmarthen and Pembroke), supporting Lord Shelburne's motion for an inquiry into public expenditure, are dismissed from their lord-lieutenancies. Rodney defeats the Spanish fleet off Cape St. Vincent and supplies Gibraltar, which, however, is again besieged. Burke brings in his bill for economical reform.

[Notes.]

FOREIGN AND COLONIAL.

(a) The Duke of Richmond's bill provided for annual Parliaments, manhood suffrage, and electoral districts.

1781. Hyder Ali defeated by Sir Eyre Coote at Porto Novo.

(b) "Twelve millions were borrowed upon terms so advantageous to the lenders that the price of the new stock rose at market from nine to eleven per cent. above par" (*Annual Register*, 1781).

(c) The Declaration of Right demanded—(1) the repeal of statute 6 of George I.; (2) the repeal of that part of Poynings' law which reserved the initiation of Irish legislation to the English Council; (3) the repeal of the Perpetual Mutiny Act for Ireland; (4) the recognition of the Irish House of Peers as a Court of Appeal in the last resort.

(d) *Marquis of Rockingham's Ministry.*—Rockingham, First Lord of the Treasury; Lord John Cavendish, Chancellor of the Exchequer; Lord Camden, President of the Council; Duke of Grafton, Privy Seal; Lord Thurlow, Lord Chancellor; Lord Shelburne and Fox, Secretaries of State; also Keppel, Burke, Dunning, and others.

1782. Grattan's Declaration of Right (c) accepted by the Irish Parliament, and statute 6 of George I. and the Permanent Mutiny Act repealed by the English.

Hyder Ali dies, and is succeeded by Tippoo Sahib.

(e) It was said that seventy elections depended on these officers, and that 11,500 officers were electors.

[1780—1782]   ENGLISH.

Prime Ministers.	
LORD NORTH. 1780.	Dunning carries his motion, "that the power of the Crown has increased, is increasing, and ought to be diminished" by 233 to 215. *June.* Lord George Gordon (President of the Protestant Association, formed in consequence of the concessions of 1778) leads riots against concessions to the Catholics. *The Duke of Richmond brings in a motion for reform, which is rejected* (a). The English under Lord Cornwallis defeat the colonists at Camden, and win various successes in the Southern States. Major André, who had been captured while negotiating the defection of Benedict Arnold, is hanged as a spy. War is declared against Holland.
1781.	Rodney captures St. Eustatia in the West Indies. Burke's bill for economical reform is lost on the second reading by 233 to 190. The Permanent Mutiny Bill (Ireland) is passed amidst protests by Fox and others. Fox's motion for terminating the war is lost by 172 to 99. **The English** under Lord Cornwallis win the battle of Guildford, but **are forced to surrender at Yorktown.** The French retake St. Eustatia. [Lord North issues this year a loan of £12,000,000 to defray the cost of the American war, by which supporters of the ministry make large sums of money (b).]
1782.	Minorca is taken by the Spaniards. *Feb.* Conway's motion for peace is lost by one. *March.* After other motions of want of confidence, which are nearly carried, **Lord North resigns.**
LORD ROCKINGHAM.	**Lord Rockingham's ministry comes into** power (d). **Rodney wins his great victory over Count de Grasse in the West Indies.** The civil list is divided into eight classes and regulated. Pensions from the civil list are restricted and secret pensions abolished. £72,000 is saved by abolishing useless offices. *Government contractors are excluded from the House of Commons, and revenue officers* (e) *are debarred from voting at elections.* All the former proceedings in connection with Wilkes' election for Middlesex, which had been often protested against by Chatham and others, are expunged from the journals of the House of Commons. Pitt's motion for reform is rejected by 161 to 141.

[Notes.]

(a) *Lord Shelburne's Ministry.*—Lord Shelburne (afterwards Marquis of Lansdowne), First Lord of the Treasury; William Pitt, Chancellor of the Exchequer; Lord Camden, President of the Council; Duke of Grafton, Privy Seal; Lord Grantham and Thomas Townshend, Secretaries of State; Keppel, Admiralty; Duke of Richmond, Ordnance; Lord Thurlow, Lord Chancellor; Henry Dundas and others.

(b) *Gilbert's Act.*—This Act allowed parishes or unions where the Act was adopted, by a vote of two-thirds of the owners and occupiers over £5 ratable value, to nominate three persons, of whom one was to be chosen by the justices to act as a paid guardian of the poor instead of the old overseers. The guardian is obliged to find work for any poor person willing and able to work who may apply to him, and to supplement his wages if needful out of the rates.

(c) A treaty acknowledging the independence of the United States was signed between them and Great Britain at Paris. The same day a treaty was signed at Versailles between Great Britain, France, and Spain, by which Pondicherry and Carical, with other possessions in Bengal, were given back to France and Trincomalee to the Dutch.

(d) *Duke of Portland's Ministry.*—Portland, First Lord of the Treasury; Lord North and Fox, Home and Foreign Secretaries; Lord John Cavendish, Chancellor of the Exchequer; Keppel, Admiralty; Viscount Townshend, Ordnance; Charles Townshend, Burke, Sheridan, also in the ministry. Great Seal in commission.

(e) *Fox's India Bill.*—Authority of the Company to be transferred to seven commissioners, nominated by Parliament for four years, after which time they were to be named by the Crown. The management of commerce to be in the hands of a committee of directors named by the proprietors.

(f) *Pitt's first Ministry.*—William Pitt, First Lord of the Treasury and Chancellor of the Exchequer; Earl Gower, Lord President; Marquis of Carmarthen and Earl Temple (the latter after four days succeeded by Lord Sydney), Secretaries of State; Duke of Richmond, Ordnance; Lord Thurlow, Chancellor; Henry Dundas, Treasurer of the Navy.

(g) *The course of the struggle between Pitt and the Opposition, in its detail, is as follows:—*

1783. Dec. 18. Dismissal of the Coalition Ministry. Pitt appointed Prime Minister.
Dec. 22. Resignation of Earl Temple.
Erskine's motion to address the king against a dissolution carried without a division.

1784. Jan. 12. Fox's motion to go into committee on the state of the nation carried by 232 to 193.
Lord Surrey's motion condemnatory of the use of the king's name and of the change of ministers carried by 196 to 54.
Jan. 16. Lord Charles Spencer's motion that the continuance of the ministry in office is contrary to constitutional principles, carried by 205 to 184.
Jan. 23. Pitt's East India Bill thrown out on the second reading by 222 to 214.
Jan. 26. Meeting at the St. Alban's Tavern under the presidency of Mr. Grosvenor, to promote a union of the parties.
Feb. 2. Mr. Grosvenor's motion for "an efficient, united, and extended administration," is carried without a division.
Coke's rider that the continuance of the ministers in office is an obstacle to such an Administration being formed, is carried by 223 to 204.
(*Continued on page 152.*)

FOREIGN AND COLONIAL.

1783. Russia takes the Crimea.
Flood's bill for parliamentary reform in Ireland is rejected.

[1782—1784]   ENGLISH.

PRIME MINISTERS. **LORD ROCKINGHAM.** 1782.	Irish difficulties are remedied by the repeal of 6 George I. and the Permanent Mutiny Bill of 1781, and other concessions, whereby Ireland obtains legislative independence.
LORD SHELBURNE.	**Death of the Marquis of Rockingham,** *July* 1. Lord Shelburne, Prime Minister (*a*). **Resignation of Fox and Burke. Pitt** becomes Chancellor of the Exchequer. The siege of Gibraltar, which had been defended by General Eliott against the French and the Spaniards, is finally raised. **England acknowledges the independence of the United States.** [See *Summary: American War of Independence*, p. 266]. Gilbert's Workhouses (*b*) Act is passed this year.
1783.	**Peace between France and England and between the United States and England is signed at Versailles** (*c*), *Jan.* A coalition is formed between Lord North and Fox, who carry amendments on the address to the Crown, and **Shelburne resigns,** *Feb.* 24.
DUKE OF PORTLAND.	*April* 2. After thirty-seven days' interval **the Coalition Ministry comes into power with the Duke of Portland as nominal Prime Minister** (*d*). *Pitt's resolution in favour of parliamentary reform is thrown out by a majority of* 144 (293 to 149). Fox's India Bill (*e*) is introduced into the House of Commons and passed. George III. authorizes Earl Temple to say that "whoever voted (in the Lords) for the India Bill was not only not his friend, but would be considered by him as an enemy." The Lords reject the bill. **The Coalition Ministry is dismissed,** *Dec.* 18.
WILLIAM PITT. 1784.	**William Pitt becomes Prime Minister,** forming a government from members of both parties, *Dec.* 23(*f*). Struggle of Pitt and the king against the Opposition led by Fox and North (*g*). Pitt's India Bill is rejected by a majority of eight. The Lords and the city of London support the ministry. The House of Commons address the king for the removal of ministers. A representation to the Crown to the same effect is carried by a majority of one only. The Mutiny Bill is passed. *March.* Parliament is dissolved. *May.* **Large majority for the ministers in the new Parliament.** One hundred and sixty friends of the Coalition lose their seats. Pitt by the Commutation Act reduces the duty on tea and spirits to prevent smuggling.

[Notes.]

(*Continued from page* 150.)

Feb. 4. Lord Effingham carries resolutions in the Lords condemnatory of the conduct of the Commons by 100 to 53.
Feb. 18. A motion for postponing the supplies carried by 208 to 196.
March 1. Fox's motion for an address for the removal of ministers carried by 201 to 189.
March 5. Fox's motion to postpone the Mutiny Bill to the 8th carried by 171 to 162.
March 8. Fox's motion for a representation to the king on the state of affairs carried by 191 to 190.
March 10. The Mutiny Bill passed without a division.
March 25. Parliament dissolved.

(*a*) *Pitt's India Bill.*—A new department of government is made, called the Board of Control, consisting of six members of the Privy Council, including one Secretary of State and the Chancellor of the Exchequer, with supreme authority over the administration of the Company civil and military. All business and patronage to be in the hands of the Company, but the Crown to have a veto in the case of appointment to the chief offices. The Board lasts till 1858. Lord Sydney is the first President of the Board, succeeded by William Grenville in 1790.

(*b*) *Sinking Fund.*—By this plan a sum of one million pounds, raised by extra taxes, was to be set apart and invested at compound interest towards paying off the national debt. Its fallacy was exposed in 1813. It was practically taking money out of one pocket to put it into the other, the nation having to pay the cost of the transfer.

(*c*) "He showed how the patriotism of a Nonconformist soldier might be rewarded with penalties and proscription; and how a public-spirited merchant would be excluded from municipal offices in his city which his enterprise had enriched, unless he became an apostate from his faith. The annual Indemnity Acts proved the inutility of penal laws while they failed effectually to protect Dissenters. . . . Lord North regarded the Test Act as 'the great bulwark of the constitution'" (*May*, iii. 100, 101).

(*d*) "Between 1788 and 1840 about 80,000 convicts were sent from this country to New South Wales under a system regulated by various Acts of Parliament and Orders in Council framed under their provisions" (*Arthur Mills*, "*Colonial Constitutions*").

(*e*) The principal managers of the impeachment were Burke, Fox, Sheridan, Windham, Sir Gilbert Elliot, General Burgoyne, Adam, Colonel North, and Fitzpatrick.

(*f*) These were—1. That no new peers should be created. 2. That no pension or place should be granted for life other than was necessary by law. 3. That the king's person should be left in the hands of the queen.

FOREIGN AND COLONIAL.

1785. Warren Hastings leaves India.

1786. Lord Cornwallis Governor-General of India (to 1793).

1787. Meeting of the Notables of France.
English settlement made at Sierra Leone.
France and Prussia interfere in the affairs of Holland in the interests of the Prince of Orange.
1788. First convict settlements made at Sydney and at Norfolk Island (*d*).
1789. Irish Parliament asks the Prince of Wales to assume the regency as his right.
May 5. The Estates General meet at Versailles, and the Revolution begins.
The Estates become the National Assembly.
The Bastille is stormed, *July* 14.

PRIME MINISTERS. WILLIAM PITT. 1784.		The India Bill is passed (*a*). Reforms in the Post Office. Letters are sent by fast mail-coaches and the privilege of franking curtailed. [*In this year, in consequence of the unfair exclusion of Fox from Parliament after the Westminster election, a bill is passed limiting the poll to fifteen days instead of forty, with other provisions.*]
	1785.	*Parliament meets for session in January instead of in the autumn, and has done so, as a rule, ever since.* Pitt proposes wise and liberal measures with a view of giving Ireland commercial freedom, but the jealousy and opposition of traders and others in the House of Commons force him to abandon them. *Pitt's motion for reform, in which he proposes to disfranchise thirty-six rotten boroughs returning seventy-two members, to compensate their owners, and to give the members to the counties and to London, is thrown out by 248 to 174.* Commissioners are appointed to inquire into the salaries of officials.
	1786.	Pitt passes his sinking fund (*b*), by which one million a year is to be set aside to accumulate at compound interest for the payment of the national debt. **Burke moves the impeachment of Warren Hastings**, and it is decided to prosecute him on the charge of injustice to the Rajah of Benares. A commercial treaty is made with France which abolishes most of the protective duties between the two countries.
	1787.	Beaufoy's motion (*c*) for the repeal of the Test and Corporation Acts is lost by 176 to 98. During the discussion of a motion for the payment of the Prince of Wales' debts, Fox denies the Prince's marriage to Mrs. Fitzherbert. The debts are paid. The Association for the Abolition of the Slave Trade is formed.
	1788.	*Feb.* 13. The trial of Warren Hastings in Westminster Hall begins (*e*). A bill is passed for the better regulation of slave-ships. *Nov.* The king's illness is made public. **Pitt supports the right of Parliament to settle the Regency.** Fox declares that the "heir-apparent has an inherent right to assume the reins of government."
	1789.	Pitt moves that the Prince of Wales should be invested with the royal authority subject to three conditions (*f*). *Feb.* 19. The king recovers, and great rejoicings are held all over the kingdom.

[Notes.]

FOREIGN AND COLONIAL.

(*a*) For Grenville's pedigree, see note 1770.

(*b*) Each province is to have a Governor and Council appointed by the Crown, and a representative Assembly. But the Government is independent of the Assembly, and only responsible to the Colonial Office.

1790. Storming of Ismail by Suwarrow.
1791. *April.* Death of Mirabeau.
June. Flight of the king to Varennes.
Aug. Conference at Pilnitz between the Emperor and the King of Prussia.
Oct. The Legislative Assembly is constituted.
Formation of the United Irishmen.

1792. Submission of Tippoo Sahib.
April. The Girondin Ministry declares war.
July. Austria and Prussia invade France.
Aug. Storming of the Tuileries.
September massacres.
Sept. 20. Cannonade of Valmy.
Sept. 21. Meeting of the National Convention. Declaration of the Republic.
Nov. Battle of Jemappes.
The disabilities of the Scottish Episcopalians are removed.
Many of the harshest disabilities of the Irish Catholics removed in this and the next year.

[1789—1792]   *ENGLISH.*

PRIME MINISTERS.
WILLIAM PITT.
1789.

Beaufoy's motion (see 1787) is again brought in and lost by only twenty (122 to 102). [A similar motion by Fox is lost next year by 294 to 105, and the subject of Tests is not resumed again for nearly forty years.]
Wilberforce, Burke, and Fox support resolutions condemnatory of the slave trade.
At Stockdale's trial for a libel on the House of Commons by publishing a defence of Warren Hastings, Erskine eloquently defends him, and he is acquitted.
William Wyndham **Grenville** (*a*) becomes Secretary of State instead of Lord Sydney (formerly Thomas Townshend).

1790.

Fox's declaration of his sympathy with the French Revolution produces a coolness between him and Burke.
Flood's motion for parliamentary reform is withdrawn without a division.
Quarrel with Spain about Nootka (now called St. George's) Sound.
Burke publishes his Reflections on the French Revolution.

1791.

The Canada Bill divides Canada into two provinces (*b*). It is the occasion of the open declaration of the quarrel between Burke and Fox.
Pitt fails in his attempt to prevent the Russians from encroaching on Turkish territory.
Fox brings in his Libel Bill (see 1792).
Mitford's bill, removing some of the disabilities of the Roman Catholics, is passed.
Resignation of the Duke of Leeds (formerly Carmarthen). Grenville becomes Foreign Secretary and **Dundas** Home Secretary.
Wilberforce's motion for the abolition of the slave trade, supported by Pitt and Fox, is rejected by 163 to 88.
The rioters of Birmingham, unchecked by the magistrates, destroy Dr. Priestley's house.

1792.

Pitt, in announcing the Budget, declares that he hopes for a durable peace.
April 23. **Warren Hastings is acquitted.**
A bill for the abolition of the slave trade passes the Commons, but is postponed by the Lords.
Fox's motion to repeal some of the disabilities of the Dissenters is thrown out.
Fox passes his Libel Bill, which places the liberty of the press under the protection of juries by allowing them to decide what constitutes a libel as well as the fact.
The Society of the Friends of the People is formed to promote parliamentary reform.
Thurlow has to resign (after having been Chancellor to

[Notes.]

FOREIGN AND COLONIAL.

1793. Jan. 21. Execution of Louis XVI.
War declared by France against England, Feb. 1.
Fall of the Gironde, June.
Insurrection of La Vendée.
Pondicherry taken from the French.
Sir John Shore Governor-General of India (to 1798).
An important Catholic Relief Bill passes the Irish Parliament (a).
Second partition of Poland.

(a) By the Act of 1793, Catholics in Ireland (not in Great Britain) may hold any commission in the army up to the rank of colonel. [To remedy this the Army and Navy Service Bill of 1807 is introduced, see 1807.]

(b) *Pitt's Ministry as reconstituted*, 1794.
Pitt, First Lord of the Treasury and Chancellor of the Exchequer; Loughborough, Chancellor; Earl of Chatham, Privy Seal; Lord Grenville, Foreign Secretary; Duke of Portland, Home Secretary; Windham, Secretary at War; Dundas, Secretary for War; Hawkesbury (afterwards Liverpool), Board of Trade.
[George Canning became Under Foreign Secretary in 1796, and Joint Paymaster, 1800; Huskisson, Under Secretary for War, 1795; Castlereagh, Secretary for Ireland, 1798.]

1794. Execution of Danton.
Lord Fitzwilliam becomes Viceroy of Ireland.
The United Irishmen apply to France, and prepare for rebellion.
Execution of Robespierre.
1795. Third partition of Poland.
First Orange Lodges formed in Ireland, but Orangemen had existed before.
Lord Camden succeeds Lord Fitzwilliam as Viceroy of Ireland.
The Directorate established.

[1792—1795] ENGLISH.

PRIME MINISTERS.
WILLIAM PITT.
1792.

every ministry since Lord North's except the Coalition of 1783), and is succeeded after a few months as Lord Chancellor by Wedderburn, Lord Loughborough.
Preparations for war.
Trial of Thomas Paine. He is defended by Erskine.

1793.

Lord Grenville passes his Alien Act for the supervision and, if necessary, the removal of aliens. Burke's dagger scene.
War is declared by England against France, *Feb.* 11.
England, Spain, and Holland join Austria and Prussia in the First Coalition.
Fox's resolution condemning the war lost by 270 to 44.
The Traitorous Correspondence Act is passed.
Troops are sent to Holland and to the south of France.
A Catholic Relief Act for Scotland is passed removing various disabilities.
Treaty of commerce with Russia.
[*The Society of Friends of the People offer to prove that about 200 members of Parliament are returned by towns with less than 100 electors, and that 357 members are returned by 154 patrons.*]
Mr. Grey's motion for parliamentary reform is opposed by Burke and Pitt, and thrown out by a large majority (232 to 41) this year, and again in 1797.
Trials for treason of Muir, Palmer, and others, who are condemned to transportation.
Toulon is abandoned.

1794.

The suspension of the Habeas Corpus Act is carried by 201 to 39 (the first time for England since 1745).
June 1. **Lord Howe gains a great victory over the French fleet.**
The Duke of Portland and some of the old Whigs join the ministry (*b*). A third Secretaryship of State (for War) established. Henry Dundas becomes Secretary *for* War. Windham is Secretary at War.
The Duke of York is defeated at **Bois-le-Duc.**
Horne Tooke, Hardy, Thelwall, and others are tried for treason, but acquitted.
A strong feeling in favour of peace is shown in the country.

1795.

Marriage of the Prince of Wales to Caroline of Brunswick. [An additional annuity of £65,000 a year is given him, which gradually pays off his debts of more than half a million.]
The suspension of the Habeas Corpus Act is continued. [It is in operation for eight years altogether.]

[Notes.]

FOREIGN AND COLONIAL.

GENEALOGY OF THE HOUSE OF HANOVER.

Sophia, granddaughter of James I., d. 1714.
|
George I. m. Sophia Dorothea of Zell.
d. 1727.
|
- George II. m. Caroline of Anspach. d. 1760.
- Sophia Dorothea m. Frederick William I. of Prussia.

- Frederick, m. Augusta of Saxe-Coburg. Prince of Wales, d. 1751.
- William, Duke of Cumberland, d. 1765.
- Frederick II., the Great.

- George III. m. Charlotte Sophia of Mecklenburg Strelitz, d. 1820.
- Edward, Duke of York, d. 1767.
- William Henry, Duke of Gloucester, d. 1805.

- George IV. m. Caroline of Brunswick, d. 1830.
  - Princess Charlotte, d. 1817.
- Frederick, Duke of York, d. 1827.
  - William IV. d. 1837.
- Edward, Duke of Kent, d. 1820.
  - Victoria.
- Ernest Augustus, Duke of Cumberland and King of Hanover, d. 1851.
  - George, King of Hanover, 1851-1866.
- Adolphus Frederick, Duke of Cambridge, d. 1850.
  - George, Duke of Cambridge.

(a) *Corresponding Societies Bill.*—"The series of repressive measures was now complete. The popular constitution of England was suspended" (*May*, ii. 330).

(b) The total sum spent in compensation to owners of disfranchised boroughs was £1,260,000. "A great end was compassed by means the most base and shameless" (*May*, iv. 332).

(c) *Union of Great Britain and Ireland.*—Four bishops sitting in annual rotation, and 28 representative temporal peers elected for life, and 100 commoners sat in the Imperial Parliament, and free-trade was established between the two countries. Irish peers are specially allowed to sit for any English seat in the House of Commons. One Irish peer only can be created when three Irish peerages have become extinct. This is to last till there are only 100 Irish peers.

(d) By proclamation dated November 5, 1800, the members of Parliament then sitting for England were declared to be members of the first Parliament of the United Kingdom of Great Britain and Ireland, to meet on January 22, 1801.

1796. Ceylon is taken from the Dutch. Buonaparte's campaign in Italy. Battles of Montenotte, Lodi, and Arcola.
1797. Peace of Campo Formio.
1798. Irish Rebellion. Arrest of O'Connor, Lord Edward Fitzgerald, and others. Lord Cornwallis succeeds Lord Camden. Insurrection breaks out. General Lake defeats the rebels at Vinegar Hill, *June* 21. French expedition to Egypt. French expedition under General Humbert lands in Ireland and surrenders. Lord Mornington (Marquis Wellesley), Governor-General of India (to 1805).
1799. Capture of Seringapatam. Death of Tippoo. Second Coalition. Buonaparte becomes Consul.
1800. The Bill for the Union of England and Ireland passes the Irish Parliament with the help of bribery (b). Napoleon completely defeats the Austrians at the battle of Marengo, *June*. Moreau defeats the Austrians at Hohenlinden, *Dec.*
1801. Peace of Lunéville signed between France and Austria.

[1795—1801] *ENGLISH.*

PRIME MINISTERS.
WILLIAM PITT.

1795. War having been declared against the Dutch, **the Cape of Good Hope is captured.**
Return of the British from Holland. Acquittal of Warren Hastings.
Fruitless expedition to Quiberon Bay.
Spain declares war against England.
The Treasonable Practices Bill and Seditious Meetings Bill are carried. Burke retires from Parliament this year, and dies 1797.

1796. The French expedition to Ireland is dispersed by a storm, and proves a complete failure.
Unsuccessful negotiations with the Directorate.

1797. Sir John Jervis and Nelson defeat the French and Spaniards off **Cape St. Vincent,** *Feb.* 14.
The Bank of England stops cash payments.
April. **The Mutiny at Spithead** is suppressed without difficulty.
May. **Mutiny at the Nore.** It is suppressed in *June.*
Admiral Duncan defeats the Dutch fleet off **Camperdown,** *Oct.*
Fox moves for the repeal of the Treason and Sedition Acts, but is supported by only forty-one persons.

1798. *May.* Fox's name is struck out of the list of Privy Councillors.
An income tax of 10 per cent. on incomes over £200 is imposed.
Aug. 1. Nelson utterly defeats the fleet which had conveyed Napoleon and his army to Egypt, in the **battle of the Nile.**
[There is a secession from Parliament of Fox and his friends this year, who consider Pitt's repressive measures dangerous to liberty (see 1776).]

1799. Sir Sidney Smith helps the Turks to hold **Acre** against Napoleon.
Pitt forms the Second Coalition. (England, Austria, and Russia chief members.)
The Duke of York takes command of the English expedition to **Holland,** and is defeated at **Bergen.**

1800. Lord Grenville rejects Buonaparte's proposals of peace.
The Corresponding Societies Bill is passed (*a*).
Lord Keith with the Austrians besieges Genoa.
July. **THE ACT FOR THE UNION OF GREAT BRITAIN AND IRELAND IS PASSED** (*c*).
[See *Summary : Ireland, Part II.,* p. 253.]
Malta is captured from the French.
The Armed Neutrality between Russia, Sweden, Denmark, and Prussia is revived. (See 1780.)

1801. *Jan.* The first Imperial Parliament of the United Kingdom meets (*d*).
Pitt proposes to pass a measure for the **relief of the Catholics.** The king opposes it, and **Pitt with**

[Notes.]

(a) Pitt created or promoted more than 140 peers during his ministry.

(b) *Addington's Ministry.*—Addington, First Lord of the Treasury and Chancellor of the Exchequer; Eldon, Lord Chancellor; Duke of Portland, Lord President of the Council; Earl of Westmoreland, Lord Privy Seal; Lord Pelham, Home Secretary; Lord Hawkesbury (afterwards Lord Liverpool), Foreign Secretary; Lord St. Vincent, First Lord of the Admiralty; Earl of Chatham, Ordnance; Lord Hobart, Charles Yorke, and others.

(c) In 1782 the office of Secretary of State for the Colonies, first made in 1768, had been abolished. From 1782 to 1801 the Colonial business had been transacted at the Home Office.

(d) *Treaty of Amiens.*—(1) England restores to France, Spain, and the Dutch all her conquests except Trinidad and Ceylon. (2) Malta is to be restored to the Knights of St. John. (3) The King of England gives up the title of King of France, held since the time of Edward III. There were other minor articles.

(e) *Pitt's second Ministry.*—Pitt, First Lord of the Treasury and Chancellor of the Exchequer; Lord Eldon, Lord Chancellor; Duke of Portland (succeeded by Addington), Lord President; Earl of Westmoreland, Lord Privy Seal; Lord Hawkesbury, Lord Harrowby (succeeded by Lord Mulgrave), Lord Camden (succeeded by Viscount Castlereagh), Home, Foreign, and War and Colonial Secretaries; Henry Dundas (Lord Melville), Admiralty; Duke of Montrose and others.

(f) *Lord Grenville's Ministry.*—Grenville, First Lord of the Treasury; Fox, Foreign Secretary; Lord Henry Petty, Chancellor of the Exchequer; Lord Erskine, Lord Chancellor; Lord Sidmouth, Privy Seal; Mr. Grey (afterwards Lord Howick), Admiralty; Lord Moira, Ordnance; Lord Spencer, Home Secretary; Windham, War and Colonial Secretary; Lord Minto, Board of Control; Sheridan, Lord Auckland, Lord Temple, Lord Chief-Justice Ellenborough, and others.
[A resolution is introduced into the Commons condemning the holding of a seat in the Cabinet by Chief-Justice Ellenborough.]

FOREIGN AND COLONIAL.

1801. Alexander I. becomes Emperor of Russia.
The departments of War and Colonies are united under one Secretary till 1854 (c).
1802. Trinidad annexed.
Treaty of Bassein in India. The Peishwah transfers his suzerainty to the East India Company.
1803. Penal settlement made at Hobart Town in Tasmania.
Sir Arthur Wellesley gains the battle of Assaye over the Mahrattas.
General Lake wins the battle of Laswaree.
1804. Buonaparte proclaimed Emperor.
1805. Napoleon prepares a large armament at Boulogne, and orders Villeneuve to entice Nelson to the West Indies, and then return to the Channel. The scheme fails.
Napoleon breaks up his camp at Boulogne, and gives up his expedition against England.
Third Coalition.
Capitulation of Ulm.
Battle of Austerlitz, *Dec.* 2.
Lord Cornwallis, Governor-General of India (*July* to *Oct.*), succeeded by Sir G. Barlow (to 1807).
Cape Colony finally taken from the Dutch.
1806. Mutiny of the Sepoys at Vellore suppressed.
Dissolution of the Holy Roman Empire.

[1801—1806] ENGLISH.

PRIME MINISTERS.		
ADDINGTON. 1801.		his friends resigns (*a*). *March.* **Addington forms a ministry** (*b*), but the illness of the king delays the proceedings.
	March.	Abercrombie defeats the French at **Alexandria**.
	April.	Nelson destroys the Danish fleet off **Copenhagen**, and the Armed Neutrality is broken up.
		Nelson fails in an attack on the French gunboats and batteries at Boulogne.
		Preliminaries of peace are signed, but are severely criticised by Pitt's friends in Parliament, headed by Lord Grenville.
1802.	*March.*	**Treaty of Amiens signed** (*d*).
		Perceval becomes Attorney-General.
		Buonaparte demands restraints upon the English press, and the dismissal from England of French persons obnoxious to him. His demands are refused.
1803.		Peltier is convicted of writing a libel on Buonaparte in London.
	May.	**Declaration of war.**
		Large bodies of volunteers are formed.
		Emmett and others are arrested, tried, and executed for insurrection at Dublin.
1804.		Short return of the king's illness.
		Pitt, Fox, and Grenville unite to oppose Addington's ministry.
WILLIAM PITT.		**Pitt forms a new administration,** *May* (*e*). The king refuses to have Fox, without whom Grenville declines office. Pitt agrees not to bring up the Catholic question.
		Wilberforce's bill for the abolition of the slave trade, passed by the Commons, is thrown out by the Lords.
		A bill is passed for providing additional forces.
		Spain declares war against England.
		Napoleon prepares to invade England.
1805.		Addington joins the ministry (as **Lord Sidmouth**).
		Nelson sails to the West Indies in pursuit of the French fleet
		Henry Dundas, Lord Melville, is accused of peculation in the navy, and is impeached.
		The Third Coalition is formed against France. (England, Russia, Austria, chief members.)
	July 22.	Sir Robert Calder fights the French and Spanish fleets off **Ferrol**.
	Aug.	Nelson returns to Portsmouth.
	Oct. 21.	The French and Spanish fleets are defeated off **Cape Trafalgar,** but **Nelson is killed.**
1806.		**Death of William Pitt,** *Jan.* 23.
LORD GRENVILLE.		Grenville and Fox unite to form **the ministry of "All the Talents"** (*f*).
		Fox opens negotiations with Napoleon.
		Trial of Lord Melville, who is acquitted.

161 L

[Notes.]

(a) *Berlin Decrees* (1) declared the British Isles in a state of blockade.
(2) Forbade France or any of her allies to trade with them.
(3) Declared all English property forfeited and all Englishmen in a state occupied by French troops prisoners of war.

(b) *Orders in Council.*—A series of orders were issued which prohibited all trade with French ports or ports occupied by French troops.

(c) *Slave Trade.*—It was abolished mainly by the efforts of Wilberforce, Clarkson, and Zachary Macaulay

(d) See note on 1793. The Act proposed that all who should enter his Majesty's service should enjoy the free and unrestrained exercise of their religion, so far as it did not interfere with their military duties. The king refused to admit Catholics to the staff, and to include dissenters in the provisions of the bill (*May*, iii. 128).

(e) *Duke of Portland's Ministry.*—Portland, First Lord of the Treasury; Perceval, Chancellor of the Exchequer; Canning, Foreign Secretary; Lord Castlereagh, War and Colonial Secretary; Lord Eldon, Lord Chancellor; Earl of Westmoreland, Lord Privy Seal; Hawkesbury, afterwards Earl of Liverpool, Home Secretary; Huskisson, Secretary to the Treasury; Sir Arthur Wellesley, Chief Secretary for Ireland; Earl Bathurst, Mr. Dundas, Lord Mulgrave, the Earl of Chatham, and others.

FOREIGN AND COLONIAL.

1806. Battle of Jena, *Oct.* 14.

1807. Battle of Eylau.
June 14. Battle of Friedland.
Napoleon begins to interfere in the Peninsula.
Treaty of Tilsit.
Lord Minto Governor-General of India (to 1813).
Invasion of Portugal by the French.

1808. Joseph Buonaparte becomes King of Spain.
Spaniards completely defeated at Burgos, Espinosa, and Tudela; and Madrid captured, *Dec.* 4.

1809. Battle of Aspern.
July 6. Battle of Wagram.

PRIME MINISTERS. **LORD GRENVILLE.** 1806.	Resolutions in favour of **abolition of the slave trade** proposed by Fox and Grenville and carried. General Stuart lands in Calabria and defeats the French at **Maida**. **Death of Fox**, *Sept.* 13. **Lord Howick**, formerly Mr. Grey, becomes Foreign Secretary, Thomas Grenville First Lord of the Admiralty, Tierney President of Board of Control. Napoleon issues his **Berlin Decrees** (*a*).
1807.	The Orders in Council (*b*) are issued in reply to the Berlin Decrees. Expedition of Sir John Duckworth against Constantinople. **The Act for the Abolition of the Slave Trade is passed** (*c*). The attempt to pass a bill relieving Catholic (and dissenting) officers in the army and navy (*d*) from their disabilities affronts the king and causes **the fall of the ministry** (*March*), who refuse to pledge themselves not to revive the Catholic question.
DUKE OF PORTLAND.	**The Duke of Portland becomes Prime Minister** (*e*). Motions are introduced that "ministers ought not to bind themselves by any pledge as to what advice they shall give the king," and "that it is impossible for the king to act without advice;" and the motions are lost. Parliament is dissolved. A Tory and Anti-Catholic majority returned. The "Orders in Council" produce much irritation in the United States, and the two countries gradually drift into war. (See 1812.) General Whitelocke is defeated in an expedition against **Buenos Ayres**, and is dismissed the service. An expedition against **Copenhagen** bombards the city and forces the surrender of the fleet. Heligoland is taken.
1808.	**The Spaniards rise against the French** and demand help from England. **Sir Arthur Wellesley** is sent to Portugal, and **the war in the Peninsula begins**. *Aug.* Sir Arthur Wellesley defeats the French at Roriça and **Vimiero**. Portugal is evacuated by the French in accordance with the **Convention of Cintra**. Great dissatisfaction in England at the terms granted to them, which Napoleon, however, blames Junot for accepting. Sir John Moore having taken the command of the English in Portugal, advances into Spain towards **Burgos** to relieve the Spaniards, *Dec.*
1809.	He retreats to **Corunna**, defeats the French, but is killed in the action, *Jan.* 16. Charges are brought against the Duke of York of maladministration in the army, and against **Castlereagh** and **Perceval** of parliamentary corruption.

[Notes.]

FOREIGN AND COLONIAL.

(*a*) *Perceval's Ministry.*—Perceval, First Lord of the Treasury and Chancellor of the Exchequer; Marquis of Wellesley, Foreign Secretary (succeeded by Castlereagh, 1812); Lord Liverpool, Colonial and War Secretary; Lord Eldon, Lord Chancellor; Lord Camden, Lord President; Ryder, Home Secretary; Robert Dundas (afterwards Lord Melville), President of the Board of Control; Lord Palmerston, Secretary at War; Peel, Under Colonial Secretary.

(*b*) The negotiations with Grey and Grenville failed because changes in the royal household were refused by the Prince.

1810. Mauritius taken from the French.

(*c*) *Lord Liverpool's Ministry.*—Liverpool, First Lord of the Treasury; Lord Castlereagh, Foreign Secretary; Lord Sidmouth, Home Secretary; Vansittart, Chancellor of the Exchequer; Lord Harrowby, Lord President of Council; Lord Westmoreland, Lord Privy Seal; Viscount Melville, First Lord of the Admiralty; Lord Eldon, Lord Chancellor; Earl of Buckinghamshire, Board of Control; Palmerston, Secretary at War; Huskisson, Woods and Forests (from 1814); Peel, Secretary for Ireland; Lord Bathurst, Earl of Mulgrave, Robinson, and others.

(*d*) GENEALOGY OF THE BENTINCKS AND CANNINGS.

William Bentinck, created Earl of Portland
(favourite of William III.), d. 1709,
great-grandfather of
William, 3rd Duke of Portland, Prime Minister,
1783 and 1807-9.
General John Scott.

Henrietta m. William Henry,   Lord William
           4th Duke, d.   Bentinck
           1854.   (Governor-
                               General of
                               India, 1828-
                               1835).

William Henry,   Lord George Bentinck
5th Duke, d.   (leader of the Pro-
1879.   tectionists), d. 1848.

Joan   m. George Canning,
(created Viscountess   Prime Minister
Canning).   1827.

Charles John, created Earl Canning
(Governor-General of India, 1856-1862).

1812. The United States declare war, and invade Canada, but without permanent success. Napoleon invades Russia. *Sept.* 7. Battle of the Borodino. Burning of Moscow. Crossing of the Beresina, *Nov.*

[1809—1812] ENGLISH.

PRIME MINISTERS. **DUKE OF PORTLAND.** 1809.	Sir Arthur Wellesley defeats Soult at **Oporto** and Victor at **Talavera**, but being unsupported by the Spaniards is obliged to retreat. A great expedition is sent to **Walcheren** under Lord Chatham, and proves a complete failure. **Canning and Castlereagh's** mutual recriminations lead to their resignation, and bring about a duel.
PERCEVAL.	**Resignation of the Duke of Portland, who dies a few weeks after. Perceval becomes Prime Minister** (a).
1810.	Sir Francis Burdett is sent to the Tower by the House of Commons for contempt, and great riots ensue. *Brand's motion for parliamentary reform is rejected by* 234 *to* 115 (also in 1812). *May.* Grattan's motion in favour of the Catholics is defeated by 104 (213 to 109). Lord Wellington defeats Masséna at **Busaco** (*Sept.*), and retires behind the lines of **Torres Vedras**, which Masséna cannot penetrate, and is forced to retreat (*Nov.*). The king's malady returns, and becomes permanent.
1811.	The **Regency Bill**, modelled on that of 1788, is passed, and **the Prince of Wales becomes Regent.** Sir Thomas Graham defeats Victor at **Barrosa**, and Masséna retires towards **Ciudad Rodrigo**. *May.* Wellington defeats Massena at **Fuentes d'Onoro** and takes Almeida. *May.* Beresford defeats Soult at **Albuera**, but fails to take **Badajos**. Luddite rioters destroy much machinery in Nottinghamshire and the Midland counties.
1812.	*Jan.* Wellington storms **Ciudad Rodrigo**. **Ministerial crisis. Lords Grenville and Grey** (formerly Howick) refuse to join Perceval. **Lord Wellesley resigns and Castlereagh becomes Foreign Secretary.** *April.* Wellington storms **Badajos**.
LORD LIVERPOOL.	**Bellingham assassinates Perceval** in the House of Commons. After negotiations with Lord Wellesley and with Canning, and also with Grey and Grenville (*b*), had failed, **Lord Liverpool becomes Prime Minister** (*c*), *June*, and Sidmouth Home Secretary. Canning (*d*), who in this year declares himself in favour of Catholic claims (a matter which becomes an "open question" in the ministry), carries his motion for the consideration of the laws affecting Catholics by 129. The United States declare war against England. The "Orders in Council" are revoked too late to prevent war.

[Notes.]

(a) In the next thirteen years upwards of 50,000 such debtors were set free from prison.

(b) *First Peace of Paris.*—The parties were France, Great Britain, Russia, Austria, and Prussia. France was allowed to retain the boundaries of 1792, with some additions. Great Britain was to keep Malta, but to restore all the colonies held by France on Jan. 1, 1792, except Tobago, St. Lucia, and Mauritius, and to restore all the Dutch colonies she held except Ceylon, the Cape, and part of (now British) Guiana. A general congress was to meet at Vienna within two months to complete these arrangements.

(c) *The Holy Alliance.*—The contracting parties declared their intention to conduct their domestic administration and foreign relations according to the precepts of Christianity, and bound themselves to observe three points—(1) To give mutual assistance for the protection of religion, peace, and justice; (2) to regard themselves as delegated by Providence to govern three branches of one Christian nation; (3) to admit any other Powers which should declare their adherence to the same principles. The Duke of Wellington said that "he thought the British Parliament would like something more precise." Its real object was to guarantee despotism against the insurrection of the subject.

(d) *Second Peace of Paris.*—France lost some of the territory granted by the first treaty. £28,000,000 was to be paid to the allies for the expenses of the war. The fortresses of the northern frontier were to be occupied by the allies for five years, and the garrison paid by France. All works of art requisitioned by Napoleon were to be restored to their owners.

FOREIGN AND COLONIAL.

1813. Battles of Lützen (*May*), Bautzen (*May*), and Dresden (*Aug.*).
The East India Company's charter is renewed, but trade with India is made free to all.
Nepaul war this and next year.
Oct. 16-19. Battle of Leipzig.
Lord Moira (Hastings) begins to act as Governor-General of India (to 1823).
1814. *March.* The Allies enter Paris.
April. Napoleon abdicates the Empire and retires to Elba.
A European Congress meets at Vienna.
1815. *Feb.* Napoleon escapes from Elba.
March. Louis XVIII. flies to Brussels.

1816. Lord Amherst's embassy to China.

Prime Ministers. **LORD LIVERPOOL.** 1812.	*July.* Wellington defeats Marmont in the battle of **Salamanca,** and advances to **Madrid.** He fails to take Burgos, and is forced to retreat. A bill is passed for the relief of insolvent debtors (*a*). Dissenting ministers are relieved from some penalties of the Conventicle Act, and Unitarians from other penalties in 1813.
1813.	The chief clause in Grattan's Catholic Relief Bill is rejected by 251 to 247. The bill is dropped. *June.* Wellington defeats Joseph at the **battle of Vittoria,** beats Soult at the **battle of the Pyrenees** (*July*), and storms **St. Sebastian** (*Sept.*). **Pampeluna** surrenders (*Oct.*).
1814.	English forces join the Prussians in Holland, and fail before Bergen-op-Zoom. Wellington invades France, and wins the battle of **Orthez** (*Feb.*), and defeats Soult at **Toulouse** (*April*), after an armistice had been signed between the French and the allies at Paris. **First Peace of Paris** (*b*). The allied sovereigns pay a state visit to the Prince Regent. An expedition is sent against Washington, which it burns, but the English are defeated on Lake Champlain. Lord Castlereagh represents England at the **Congress of Vienna.** Treaty of Ghent, by which peace is made between England and the United States.
1815.	An expedition is sent against New Orleans, but is repulsed (the signing of the treaty not being yet known). By a Corn Bill the importation of wheat for home consumption is positively forbidden when the price is under 80s. **On the receipt of the news that Napoleon had escaped from Elba (landing in France, March 1), Wellington and Blucher take the command of the allied forces in Belgium.** *June* 16. **Napoleon defeats the Prussians at Ligny, and Wellington defeats Ney at Quatre Bras.** *June* 18. **Wellington and Blucher completely defeat Napoleon at Waterloo.** *July.* Napoleon surrenders to the English at Rochefort, and is conveyed to St. Helena. *Sept.* The Holy Alliance (*c*) is made between Russia, Austria, and Prussia; but Lord Castlereagh refuses to accede to it. *Nov.* **Second Peace of Paris** (*d*). [See *Summary: French War,* p. 268.]
1816.	*May* 2. Marriage of Princess Charlotte (heiress presumptive) to Leopold of Saxe-Coburg.

FOREIGN AND COLONIAL.

(a) "The suspension of the Habeas Corpus Act formed part of Lord Sidmouth's repressive measures in 1817, when it was far less defensible than in 1794" (*May*, iii. 17).

(b) "A measure denounced in 1807 as a violation of the constitution and the king's coronation oath was now agreed to with the acquiescence of all parties" (*May*, iii. 143).

(c) This congress was really more important than the Holy Alliance, for it gave a practical turn to what had hitherto been a mere speculative union.

1818. Suppression of the Pindaries. Extinction of the Peishwahs.
Sept. Congress of Aix-la-Chapelle (c).

1819. Singapore occupied by the English.
After several victories Bolivar forms the Republic of Columbia.

PRIME MINISTERS.
LORD LIVERPOOL.
1816. Canning joins the Government as President of the Board of Control.
Riots in the east of England in agricultural districts.
A motion in the Lords for relief of Catholics is rejected by four.
Aug. Humiliation of the Dey of Algiers by Lord Exmouth's bombardment, and release of many Christian slaves.
Dec. The Spa Fields riots are suppressed.

1817. [50,000 of Cobbett's *Political Register* are now sold weekly.]
Parliament is opened. Outrage on the Prince Regent.
Secret committees of both Houses are appointed to deal with the alleged disaffection of part of the nation.
A bill to suspend the Habeas Corpus Act is passed (*a*) in the Lords by 150 to 35, in the Commons by 265 to 103.
The march of the Blanketeers from Manchester.
An Act to prevent seditious meetings is passed.
The Military and Naval Officers' Oath Bill is passed. It opens all ranks in the army and navy to Catholics and Dissenters (*b*).
March. **The "Sidmouth Circular"** to the lord-lieutenants authorizing magistrates to apprehend persons accused of libellous publications is issued.
May. Grattan's motion for relief of Catholics is lost in the Commons by 245 to 221, in the Lords by 142 to 90.
Sir. F. Burdett's motion for reform is lost by 265 to 77.
June. The "Derbyshire Insurrection" breaks out.
Nov. 6. Death of Princess Charlotte.
Dec. William Hone is tried for libel. He defends himself, and notwithstanding Lord Ellenborough's efforts, is acquitted.

1818. The suspension of the Habeas Corpus Act is repealed.
Secret committees are again appointed.
The Bill of Indemnity for those who had been engaged in arrests on suspicion or in the dispersal of meetings since *Jan.* 1817 passes both Houses. A protest in the Lords is made by ten peers.
A motion for the repeal of the Septennial Act, supported by **Romilly and Brougham,** *is lost by* 117 *to* 42.
Burdett's motion for annual parliaments and universal suffrage is rejected by 106 *to* 0 (Burdett and Cochrane tellers for the motion).
The renewal of the Alien Bill is carried after much discussion and opposition.
£1,000,000 is voted by Parliament to build new churches.
Parliament is dissolved by the Regent without notice.

1819. Birth of Princess Alexandrina Victoria (afterwards Queen Victoria).

[Notes.]

FOREIGN AND COLONIAL.

(a) *The Six Acts.*
Nov. 29. Introduced by the Lord Chancellor:—
1. An Act to prevent delay in the administration of justice in cases of misdemeanour.
Nov. 29. By Lord Sidmouth:—
2. An Act to prevent the training of persons to the use of arms and to the practice of military evolutions and exercise.
3. An Act for the more effectual prevention and punishment of blasphemous and seditious libels.
4. An Act to authorize justices of the peace in certain disturbed counties to seize and detain arms collected and kept for purposes dangerous to the public peace, to continue in force until the 25th of March 1822.
Dec. 3. By Lord Castlereagh:—
5. An Act to subject certain publications to the duties of stamps upon newspapers, and to make other regulations for restraining the abuses arising from publication of blasphemous and seditious libels.
Dec. 17. By Lord Sidmouth. Nov. 29. In Commons by Lord Castlereagh:—
6. An Act for more effectually preventing seditious meetings and assemblies [out-of-doors], to continue in force until the end of the session of Parliament next after five years from the passing of the Act.

1820. Congress at Troppau, afterwards at Laybach.
Revolution in Spain.

(b) Plunket (Grattan having died in 1820) had carried his motion for a committee by 227 to 221. The bill is supported by Canning, and read a second time by 254 to 243.

(c) It was originally proposed to give the seat to Leeds, but the county of York was substituted by the Lords.

1821. *May.* Death of Napoleon Buonaparte.
Outbreak of insurrections in Greece, and the Danubian Principalities.
Congress of Verona.

(d) *The Grenville Party.*—Marquis of Buckingham, Lord Grenville, Thomas Grenville, Charles Wynn, Dr. Phillimore Sir George Nugent, Sir Watkin Wynn, William Fremantle.

PRIME MINISTERS **LORD LIVERPOOL** 1819.	Motions in favour of Catholic relief are defeated in the Commons by 243 to 241, in the Lords by 147 to 106. Riots and large meetings of working classes to petition for reform. Wager of Battle is abolished. Peel's Act passed for the resumption of cash payments. Proclamations against seditious meetings. *Aug.* **Manchester reform meeting** in St. Peter's Fields. Attack of yeomanry. Arrest of Hunt and others. *Nov. 23.* Parliament is assembled. Debates on the "Manchester Massacre." Majorities for ministers (381 to 150 in the Commons). **The Six Acts** (*a*) are brought in and carried after strenuous opposition in both Houses. *Lord John Russell proposes resolutions in favour of reform, which are rejected.* [In this year Hunt and his followers assume for the first time the name of Radical Reformers.]
1820.	*Jan. 29.* Death of George III.

GEORGE IV. 1820—1830 (10 YEARS).

Born, 1762; Married, 1795, Caroline of Brunswick.

Feb. The name of the queen is omitted in the liturgy. The Cato Street conspiracy to assassinate ministers is discovered.
Execution of Thistlewood and other conspirators.
June. The queen arrives from the Continent.
July. **A bill of pains and penalties against the queen is brought in by Lord Liverpool.**
Canning resigns his office at the Board of Control.
Brougham defends the queen.
Decreasing majorities for the bill. It is abandoned amidst popular rejoicings.
Sir J. Mackintosh passed a bill by which shoplifting to the amount of 5s. ceased to be a capital crime. [See note *a*, p. 186.]

1821. The Catholic Relief Bill is passed by the Commons (*b*), but thrown out by the Lords by 159 to 120.
A bill to disfranchise Grampound is carried. The two seats are given to the county of York (*c*).
July. Coronation of George IV. The queen is refused admission to Westminster Abbey, and dies, *Aug.*

1822. The Grenville party (*d*) join the Government. Wellesley becomes Lord-Lieutenant of Ireland.
Jan. **Retirement of Lord Sidmouth from office. Peel succeeds him as Home Secretary.**
Feb. Parliament is opened.

[Notes.]

FOREIGN AND COLONIAL.

(a) The Navigation Acts had been passed in 1651, 1661, and 1662. By them no goods of any kind might be imported into English dominions from Asia, Africa, America, Russia, and Turkey, and very few from other European countries, except in English vessels, or in vessels belonging to the country where the goods were made. Their object was to encourage British shipping at the expense of the Dutch.

(b) Combinations to intimidate employers were made illegal in 1825. By section 3 of the Act of that year any person who by violence shall wilfully or maliciously force any master to make any alteration in his mode of regulating business shall be liable to imprisonment with hard labour for two months. The avowed policy of the Act was to define the combinations that were legal, and to make all others illegal.

1823. Spain is invaded by France and the constitution abolished.
The Greeks obtain several victories.
Lord Byron arrives in Greece.
Lord Amherst Governor-General of India (to 1828).

1824. Jan. The English are worsted in the Ashantee war.
Death of Byron in Greece.
War with Burmah. Rangoon is taken.
Sept. Death of Louis XVIII. of France; succeeded by his brother, Charles X.
1825. The independence of Colombia, South America, recognised by England.
Death of Alexander, Emperor of Russia, succeeded by Nicholas.

PRIME MINISTERS. LORD LIVERPOOL 1822.	*March* 27. **Canning** is appointed Governor-General of India. Lord J. **Russell's** motion "that the present state of representation requires serious consideration" is rejected by 105 (269 to 164). Canning's bill to admit Catholic peers to sit in the House of Lords is passed by the Commons and rejected by the Lords by 171 to 129. *June.* Brougham makes a motion declaring that the influence of the Crown is destructive of the independence of Parliament, and asserts that it has largely increased since Dunning's resolution in 1780 (see 1780). (Motion rejected by 216 to 101.) *Aug.* 12. **Suicide of Lord Londonderry** (formerly **Castlereagh**). *Sept.* **Canning**, about to start for India is made **Foreign Secretary.**
1823.	17,000 *freeholders of Yorkshire petition for reform.* Robinson becomes Chancellor of Exchequer in the place of Vansittart (Lord Bexley). **Huskisson** becomes President of Board of Trade. Huskisson carries his Reciprocity of Duties Bill, thus largely modifying the effects of the Navigation Acts (*a*). Peel's Currency Act comes into operation. *May.* Two moderate measures of Catholic relief pass the Commons, but one is rejected and the other dropped by the Lords. The freedom of the South American republics is now fully recognised by England. [**The Catholic Association** (Ireland) is formed this year.]
1824.	The Acts arranging for the fixing of wages of Spitalfields weavers are repealed. The total repeal of all Acts limiting the free travelling about of workmen is carried. All laws controlling the combinations of either masters or workmen are repealed. (This Act is altered in the next year (*b*).) The duties on silk and on wool are largely reduced.
1825.	[This year a motion was passed in the Commons that it is expedient that provision be made by law for the maintenance of the Roman Catholic clergy in Ireland.] The Catholic Association is suppressed by a bill in Parliament limited to three years. Sir F. Burdett's Catholic Relief Bill carried in the Commons by 248 to 227 (third reading), is rejected in the Lords by 178 to 130. The Duke of York speaks against it.

[Notes.]

(a) *Court of Chancery.*—Hume stated in a debate connected with this matter that he thought it the greatest curse that ever fell on a nation to have such a Chancellor [*i.e.* Lord Eldon] and such a Court of Chancery as this country was visited with. Grenfell said if his honourable friend had stated that the Lord Chancellor was a curse to the country, he had done that which was not altogether becoming in him or any other member to do. If his honourable friend had said that the Court of Chancery was a curse to the country, he had stated that which no man conversant with the subject could deny.

(b) *Canning's Ministry.*—Canning, First Lord of the Treasury and Chancellor of the Exchequer; Lord Lyndhurst, Chancellor; Sturges-Bourne, Home Secretary; Lord Dudley, Foreign Secretary; Duke of Portland, Lord Privy Seal; William, Duke of Clarence, Lord High Admiral; Huskisson, Treasurer of the Navy and President of the Board of Trade; Lord Anglesey, Ordnance; Lord Palmerston, Secretary at War; Lord Goderich, Colonial and War Secretary; Lord Harrowby, President of the Council.

(c) Lord Eldon, who now retires, had been Lord Chancellor (with the exception of one year, 1806-1807) for twenty-six years.

(d) *Lord Goderich's Ministry.*—Goderich, First Lord of the Treasury; Lord Lyndhurst, Chancellor; Herries, Exchequer; Lord Lansdowne, Home Secretary; Lord Dudley, Foreign Secretary; Huskisson, War and Colonial Office; Duke of Portland, Lord President of the Council; Earl of Carlisle, Lord Privy Seal; Tierney, Master of the Mint; Grant, President of the Board of Trade; Bourne, Woods and Forests; Palmerston, Secretary at War; Stanley, Under Colonial Secretary.

(e) By the efforts of Huskisson, Lord Althorp, instead of Herries, Chancellor of the Exchequer, was named President of a Finance Committee. Both Huskisson and Herries threatened to resign, and Lord Goderich, overcome by the difficulty, resigned himself.

(f) *Duke of Wellington's Ministry.*—Wellington, First Lord of the Treasury; Lord Lyndhurst, Lord Chancellor; H. Goulburn, Chancellor of Exchequer; Mr. (Sir Robert in May 1830) Peel, Home Secretary; Lord Dudley, Foreign Secretary; Huskisson, Colonial and War Secretary; Palmerston, Secretary at War; Grant, Board of Trade.

(g) " The annual Indemnity Acts, though offering no more than a partial relief to dissenters, left scarcely an argument against the repeal of laws which had been so long virtually suspended " (*May*, iii. 157). Protests in the Lords against the repeal are signed by Cumberland, Eldon, Newcastle, Redesdale, and seven other peers.

(h) "*Canningites.*"—Huskisson, Lord Dudley, Palmerston, Charles Grant, Lamb, Lord Eliot, Duke of Portland, Lord George Bentinck, J. Evelyn Denison, Frankland Lewis.

FOREIGN AND COLONIAL.

1826. Storming of Bhurtpore by Lord Combermere.
Annexation of Assam.
Treaty of Akierman between Russia and Turkey.
Dec. The Regent and Cortes of Portugal apply to England for help.

1828. War between Russia and Turkey. Russians take Varna; have to retire.
Lord William Bentinck Governor-General of India (to 1835).

[1825—1828] ENGLISH.

PRIME MINISTERS. LORD LIVERPOOL. 1825.	A commission is appointed to inquire into the administration of the Court of Chancery (a). Great money panic in England. Crash of joint-stock companies and banks.
1826.	The house-tax on houses under £10 rent, and the duty on houses with less than seven windows, are abolished. Riots in Lancashire to destroy power-looms. *June.* Dissolution of Parliament. *Dec.* Troops are embarked to assist Portugal against Spain if necessary. They anchor in the Tagus, but are not required.
1827.	*Jan.* Death of the Duke of York. Illness and **resignation of Lord Liverpool.**
CANNING.	*April.* **Canning becomes Prime Minister** (b), and is joined by some of the Whigs. The Duke of Wellington and Peel refuse to join him. They, with Lord Eldon, retire (c). Treaty of London between England, France, and Russia for the pacification of Greece.
LORD GODERICH.	Death of **Canning**, *Aug.* 8. **Lord Goderich** (formerly Robinson) becomes Prime Minister (d). *Oct.* Battle of **Navarino.** Destruction of Turco-Egyptian fleet.
1828.	**Lord Goderich resigns,** unable to arrange difficulties within the Cabinet (e).
DUKE OF WELLINGTON.	The **Duke of Wellington becomes Prime Minister** (f). Lord John Russell's motion for the repeal of the **Test and Corporation Acts** (g) is carried in the Commons by 237 to 193, and a bill founded on it passes both Houses. The duties on foreign corn are regulated in accordance with a sliding scale. A bill for disfranchising Penryn and giving its members to Manchester passes the Commons, but is lost in the Lords. The Government opposing the transference of the franchise from East Retford to Birmingham, and Huskisson voting against Government, his offered resignation is accepted. He is followed by **Lord Palmerston, Dudley, Grant, Lamb** (afterwards **Lord Melbourne**), and other "Canningites" (h). Sir F. Burdett's resolution for committee on Catholic claims is carried in Commons by 272 to 266. The Lords refuse to concur by 181 to 137. **O'Connell** is elected for the county of Clare, but cannot sit, being a Catholic. The Catholic Association is revived in this year.

[Notes.]

FOREIGN AND COLONIAL.

1829. Settlement made in Western Australia.
The Russians advance to Adrianople. France and England intervene.
Treaty of Adrianople between Russia and the Porte.
The Sultan acknowledges the independence of Greece.
The French begin the conquest of Algeria.

(a) Roman Catholics are admitted by a new oath to Parliament, and almost all civil and political offices except those of Regent, Lord Chancellor, and Lord-Lieutenant of Ireland are opened to them.
Peel said, "The credit belongs to others and not to me; it belongs to Mr. Fox, to Mr. Grattan, to Mr. Plunket, to the gentlemen opposite, and to an illustrious and right honourable friend of mine who is now no more."
Protests in the Lords are signed by Cumberland, Eldon, Sidmouth, Newcastle, Bexley, and thirty-four other peers.

(b) The reason urged for this Act was that by the creation of small freeholds a large number of dependent voters had been created who were subject to the influence either of the landlords or the priests.

1830. Revolution in Paris.
July 27. The "Three Days" begin.
Arrival of Charles X. in England.
Revolt and independence of Belgium.
The crown of Greece offered to Leopold of Saxe-Coburg and refused.

(c) He said that the Legislature and system of representation deservedly possessed the full and entire confidence of the country.

(d) *Lord Grey's Ministry.*—Grey, First Lord of Treasury; Lord Brougham, Lord Chancellor; Lord Althorp, Chancellor of Exchequer; Lord Melbourne, Home Secretary; Lord Palmerston, Foreign Secretary; Lord Lansdowne, President of Council; Lord Durham, Lord Privy Seal; Sir J. Graham, Admiralty; Lord Goderich, War and Colonial; Stanley, Chief Secretary for Ireland; Charles Wynn, Secretary at War; Spring Rice and E'lice, Secretaries to the Treasury. Grant, Lord Holland, Lord Auckland, Lord John Russell, Duke of Richmond.
[Macaulay became Secretary to the Board of Control in 1832.]

DUKE OF WELLINGTON. 1829.	*Feb.* In the king's speech, after a reference to the disorders in Ireland caused by the revival of the Catholic Association, Parliament is recommended to consider whether the disabilities of Catholics cannot be removed. Peel now resigns his seat for Oxford (*Feb.* 4), but stands again. He is defeated by Sir R. Inglis by 146 votes. *Feb.* An Act suppressing the Catholic Association is passed. *March* 3. The king finding that the supremacy oath is to be altered, refuses his consent to the bill for Catholic Emancipation, but on the resignation of the Duke of Wellington, Peel, and the Chancellor, he gives his consent in writing. *March* 5. **The Catholic Relief Bill is carried in the Commons** (*a*). (Third reading 320 to 142.) Duel between the Duke of Wellington and Lord Winchilsea. *April.* **The bill passes the Lords.** (Third reading 213 to 109.) [See *Summary: Catholic Relief*, p. 270.] *The Act disfranchising 40s. freeholders in Ireland and raising the qualification to £10 is passed* (*b*). O'Connell is re-elected for Clare. He agitates for repeal of the Union between England and Ireland in this and following years. [The annual Act for suspending the militia ballot is passed this year for the first time.]
1830.	*Feb.* Meeting of Parliament. Lord John Russell's *proposal to enfranchise Leeds, Birmingham, and Manchester is rejected by* 188 to 140. *June* 26. **Death of George IV.**

WILLIAM IV., 1830—1837 (7 Years).

Born 1765 ; Married, 1818, Adelaide of Saxe-Meiningen.

	July 24. Parliament is dissolved, and meets in *Nov.* *Sept.* Death of **Huskisson** at the opening of Liverpool and Manchester Railway. Recognition of Louis Philippe by England. The Duke of Wellington asserts that the House of Commons needs no reform (*c*). Parnell's motion on the Civil List is carried against the ministry by 29 (233 to 204). **The Duke of Wellington resigns**, *Nov.*
LORD GREY.	Lord Grey becomes **Prime Minister** (*d*), and forms a ministry out of the old Whigs and the followers of Canning and Grenville. *He at once stipulates that reform shall be a Cabinet measure.*

[Notes.]

FOREIGN AND COLONIAL.

1831. Leopold of Saxe-Coburg becomes King of Belgium. He is supported by a British fleet.
Dec. Repeal of the Hereditary Peerage Decree in France.

(a) "This prosecution nearly brought to a close the long series of contests between the Government and the press" (*May,* ii. 379).

1832. Otho, son of the King of Bavaria, is made King of Greece.

PRIME MINISTERS.
LORD GREY.
1831.

March 1. **The Reform Bill is introduced by Lord John Russell.**
After a debate of seven nights, seventy-one speakers having spoken, leave is given to bring in the bill.
March 21. The bill is carried on the second reading by a majority of 302 to 301.
April. General Gascoyne's amendment, that the number of members of Parliament for England and Wales ought not to be diminished, is carried in committee by 8 (299 to 291) against the Government.
The king is persuaded by the ministers to dissolve.
April 22. **Parliament is suddenly dissolved** by him in person, with a view of preventing Lord Wharncliffe's address in the Lords against a dissolution being carried.
June. **The new Parliament meets. (Reformers in a great majority.)**
The Reform Bill is carried (second reading) by 136 (367 to 231).
£30,000 is voted towards the support of undenominational national schools in Ireland.
Sept. 22. **After many weeks of discussion and obstruction the Reform Bill passes the Commons by 345 to 236, but is rejected (Oct. 8) in the Lords by 41 (199 to 158).**
Several members of the House of Lords are insulted by the mob. Lord Ebrington's vote of confidence in ministers is carried by 329 to 198.
Nottingham Castle is burned down, and there are disturbances elsewhere.
Riots in Bristol and destruction of property.
A proclamation is issued for the repression of political unions.
Cobbett is prosecuted by the Attorney-General (for inciting to violence by his writings), but unsuccessfully, the jury not being able to agree (*a*).
Dec. Parliament meets. **A third Reform Bill is brought in** and is carried (second reading) by 162 in the Commons.
Adjournment for Christmas.
Many outrages in Ireland this year, especially owing to the collection of tithes, which now becomes in many places impossible.
An Ecclesiastical Commission of this year reports on the revenues of the English Church.

1832.

Jan. Parliament resumes work.
March. **The Reform Bill passes the Commons.**
April 14. **In the Lords the second reading is carried by 9** (184 to 175). Protests signed by 77 peers.

[Notes.]

(a) The National Union (on May 3) stated that if the Lords threw out the bill there was reason to expect that the payment of taxes would cease, that other obligations of society would be disregarded, and that the ultimate consequence might be the utter extinction of the privileged orders.
(b) This was a motion of Lord Lyndhurst that the consideration of the disfranchising clauses should be postponed till the enfranchising clauses had been first considered. Lord Grey stated that he should consider its success fatal to the measure.
(c) *The Reform Bill of* 1832.—This measure disfranchised fifty-six nomination boroughs which returned 111 members, took away one member from thirty others, and two from Weymouth and Melcombe Regis, thus leaving vacant 143 seats. It gave 65 additional members to the counties, two members each to Manchester, Leeds, Birmingham, and nineteen large towns, including the metropolitan districts, and one member each to twenty-one other towns, all of which had been previously unrepresented. In the counties copyholders and leaseholders for years were added, as voters, to the 40s. freeholders, and tenants-at-will paying £50 a year (the Chandos clause) were enfranchised. In the towns a £10 household franchise was established, and the rights of freemen to vote were restricted. [See *Appendix III*.]
(d) The number of members for Scotland is increased from 45 to 53, of whom 30 sit for counties, and 23 for cities and burghs. The county franchise is given to all holders of property worth £10 a year, and to some classes of leaseholders. The burgh franchise is given to all £10 householders.
(e) The number of members for Ireland is increased from 100 to 105; franchise, same changes as in England (but see 1829), except that the county occupation franchise is £20 (reduced to £12 in 1850, when the borough franchise was reduced to £8).
(f) In 1813 private persons had been allowed to trade with India. The monopoly of the China trade is now taken from the Company. The Company's commercial property is sold, but its dominion over India is confirmed for twenty years.
(g) Lord Grey stated that during 1832 over 9000 crimes had been committed, all connected with and growing out of the disturbed state of the country.
(h) Two archbishoprics and eight bishoprics were suppressed. Many ecclesiastical incomes were reduced and many sinecures swept away, and a commission was appointed to administer surplus revenues. At first it was proposed in the bill that any surplus beyond that applied to church building, etc., should be applied to such purposes as Parliament might direct. This, however, involving the vexed question of "appropriation," was abandoned by ministers.
(i) This loan was ultimately surrendered as a free gift.
(j) Children under nine years of age not to be employed. Women and young persons under eighteen not to work more than twelve hours.
(k) This grant was voted annually up to 1839, when it was increased. It was dispensed to the National Society and the British and Foreign School Society by the Treasury.
(l) It received a special impetus from the assize sermon preached by Keble at Oxford on the action of the Irish Church Commission in dealing with the Irish Church.

FOREIGN AND COLONIAL.

1833. The East India Company's charter is renewed. It becomes now a political body, not commercial (*f*).

1834. Discontent in the Legislative Assembly in Canada.
The *Zollverein* or Commercial Union of Germany is formed, including all German States except Austria.

PRIME MINISTERS.
LORD GREY.
1832.

The Easter recess follows.
April 21. Great meeting of political unions at Birmingham. Numbers estimated at 150,000 (*a*).
May 7. **A motion in committee adverse to the bill carried in the Lords by 35** (*b*) (151 to 116). The king refusing to create new peers, **ministers resign. The Duke of Wellington fails to make a ministry.**
Ministers again propose to the king to create new peers if necessary. The king consents, and intimates to the Opposition peers his intention to do this if necessary.
June. **THE REFORM BILL PASSES THE LORDS BY 106 TO 22** (*c*). [See *Summary: Parliament, Part IV.*, p. 237, and *Summary: Reform,* p. 275.]
Reform Bills are passed for Scotland (*d*) and Ireland (*e*).
Dec. Dissolution of Parliament.

1833.

Jan. **The first reformed Parliament meets.** [Estimated strength of parties—Conservatives, 172; Liberals, etc., 486.]
An Act is passed enabling Quakers, Moravians, and Separatists, on entering the House of Commons, to substitute an affirmation for an oath.
March. A Coercion Act for Ireland (*g*) is passed giving special powers to prevent disturbances.
Morning sittings are adopted by the Commons for despatch of business.
A motion for reducing the malt-tax is carried in the Commons. Lord Althorp tenders his resignation, which is not received, and the motion is rescinded.
The Church Temporalities (Ireland) Act, reducing and reforming the Irish Church and appointing a commission, is carried (*h*).
The Act for the Emancipation of Slaves passes the Lords, *Aug.* [Abolition of slavery in the colonies from *Aug.* 1, 1834, with a compensation to owners of £20,000,000.]
A bill is passed on the subject of Irish tithes for collecting arrears of tithe and giving the clergy £1,000,000 on loan (*i*) in compensation for arrears.
An Act is passed renewing the Bank charter.
An Act is passed regulating the work of children in factories (by Lord Ashley) (*j*).
An Act is passed making an education grant of £20,000 (*k*).
The Jewish Relief Bill passes the Commons, but is rejected by the Lords in this and several following years till 1858.
The Tractarian movement in the English Church dates from this year (*l*).

1834.

Hume's motion on the Corn Laws is defeated by 157.

[Notes.]

(a) The poor-rates had reached the sum of £8,600,000, and in many places were equal to or even greater than the annual rent of the land itself.
The new law confined relief to destitution, instituted the workhouse test to detect imposture, forbidding outdoor relief to the able-bodied. It united parishes into unions, and union workhouses were substituted for parish workhouses.

(b) They are succeeded by Spring Rice, Colonial and War Secretary; Carlisle, Privy Seal; Auckland, Admiralty; and Conyngham, Postmaster-General.

(c) *Lord Melbourne's Ministry.*—Lord Melbourne, First Lord of the Treasury; Lord Brougham, Lord Chancellor; Littleton, Irish Secretary; Wellesley, Lord Lieutenant; Lord Althorp, Chancellor of Exchequer; Lord Duncannon, Home Secretary; Lord Palmerston, Foreign Secretary; Spring Rice, Colonial and War Secretary; Poulett Thomson, Board of Trade; Ellice, Secretary at War; Lord J. Russell, Paymaster; Sir George Grey, Under Colonial Secretary.

(d) "All the accustomed grounds for dismissing a ministry were wanting. There was no immediate difference between them and the king, there was no disunion among themselves, nor were there any indications that they had lost the confidence of Parliament" (*May*, i. 146).

(e) *Sir Robert Peel's Ministry.*—Sir R. Peel, First Lord of the Treasury and Chancellor of the Exchequer; Lord Lyndhurst, Lord Chancellor; Goulburn, Home Secretary; Duke of Wellington, Foreign Secretary; Earl of Aberdeen, War and Colonial; Sir H. Hardinge, Secretary for Ireland; Herries, Secretary at War; Lord Wharncliffe, Privy Seal; Earl de Grey, Admiralty; Alexander Baring (Lord Ashburton, 1835), Board of Trade; Lord Haddington, Lord-Lieutenant of Ireland; Praed and Sidney Herbert, Secretaries of the Board of Control; W. E. Gladstone, Under Secretary for the Colonies.

FOREIGN AND COLONIAL.

1835. Lord Heytesbury appointed Governor-General of India by Peel, but the appointment cancelled by the Whigs, and Lord Auckland sent out in his place.

Kaffir war. The eastern province of South Africa becomes independent.

Colonel de Lacy Evans, with English volunteers, helps Queen Isabella of Spain against her uncle, Don Carlos.

PRIME MINISTERS. LORD GREY 1834.	Ripon's bill for relieving the bishops of their legislative and judicial functions in the House of Peers is refused by 125 to 58. **The Poor Law Amendment Act is carried** (on second reading) by 319 to 20 (a). *April.* The monster demonstration in London by trades-unionists passes by without disturbance. O'Connell's motion for the repeal of the Union is thrown out by 523 to 38. *May* 27. Ward moves that the Church Establishment in Ireland exceeds the wants of the population, and ought to be reduced. Stanley, Sir J. Graham, the Duke of Richmond, and Lord Ripon leave the Government on the Irish Church question (b). *May* 28. The king assures the Irish bishops, when presenting him with a birthday address, that he will defend their Church. *June* 2. Lord Althorp meets Ward's motion by announcing a special commission of inquiry (composed of laymen) into the revenues of the Irish Church, and the motion is lost by 396 to 120. The Irish Land-Tax Bill, proposing a substitute for tithes, is thrown out in the Lords by 189 to 122. **Resignation of Lord Althorp** (who did not wish the Coercion Bill to pass entire).
LORD MELBOURNE.	**Resignation of Lord Grey. Lord Melbourne becomes Prime Minister** (c), with the previous Cabinet, including Lord Althorp, *July* 17. The Irish Coercion Act is renewed in a modified form. The **Central Criminal Court** is established. **Lord Althorp becomes Lord Spencer. Lord Melbourne is suddenly dismissed by the king** (d), *Nov.* 15. The Duke of Wellington acts for Sir R. Peel during his return from abroad.
SIR R. PEEL.	*Dec.* **Sir R. Peel forms an administration** (e). Parliament is dissolved. [New charter granted to the Bank of England this year.] An Ecclesiastical Commission is issued to inquire into matters of income, patronage, and territorial divisions in the English Church. In the Tamworth Manifesto Sir R. Peel indicates his principles and the reforms which he desires.
1835.	*Feb.* New Parliament meets. The Conservatives gain largely. [Estimated strength of parties—Conservatives, 273; Liberals, 380. Various reforming bills are introduced, and the ministry is beaten on several occasions.

[Notes.] | FOREIGN AND COLONIAL.

(a) *Lord Melbourne's Ministry.*— Melbourne, First Lord of the Treasury, Great Seal in Commission (till 1836, then Pepys, Lord Cottenham); Lord Duncannon, Lord Privy Seal; Spring Rice, Chancellor of the Exchequer; Lord J. Russell, Home Secretary; Lord Palmerston, Foreign Secretary; Lord Glenelg (formerly Charles Grant), War and Colonial; Lord Howick, Secretary at War; Mulgrave (afterwards Marquis of Normanby), Lord-Lieutenant of Ireland; Lord Morpeth, Chief Secretary for Ireland.

(b) The corporation of London alone is exempted from the operation of this Act.

1836. Lord Auckland Governor-General of India (to 1842).
South Australia is first colonized, capital Adelaide.

(c) It provided for the commutation of tithes in kind into a rent-charge upon the land payable in money, and reckoned according to the average price of corn for the seven preceding years. The great tithes were levied on corn and grass, the small tithes on other produce. By the bill of 1836 commissioners were appointed to carry out a commutation.

(d) Under the Ecclesiastical Commissioners the establishments of some cathedrals have been reduced, and the surplus applied to the augmentation of small livings and to other purposes. Ancient dioceses have been rearranged and new ones created.

1837. Natal is founded by Dutch settlers, placed under English rule in 1841.
Rebellion in Canada.

PRIME MINISTERS. SIR R. PEEL. 1835.	Sir R. Peel, assisted by Lord J. Russell, resists successfully the efforts of many county members and others to repeal the malt-tax. (Motion defeated by 350 to 192.) *April.* **Lord J. Russell carries his motion** involving the appropriation of the surplus revenues of the Irish Church to general moral and religious purposes by 285 to 258. *April* 8. **Sir R. Peel resigns.**
LORD MELBOURNE.	**Lord Melbourne becomes Prime Minister** (*a*). *June.* Another Ecclesiastical Commission is issued. *Sept.* **The Municipal Reform Act is finally passed** (*b*). (First elections under it in *Nov.*) The Irish Tithe Bill, embodying the appropriation clauses, is passed by the Commons by 319 to 282. In the Lords the appropriation clauses are rejected by 138 to 41, and the bill accordingly abandoned.
1836.	*Feb.* A committee on agricultural distress is appointed, sits four months, and makes no report. Nonconformists are allowed to celebrate their marriages in their own chapels (see 1753). *June.* The Irish Municipal Bill having been carried in the Commons by 61, is altered by the Lords and ultimately rejected by the Commons. The Bill for Tithe Commutation in England is passed (*c*). *Aug.* The Irish Tithe Bill having been carried in the Commons, its "appropriation clause" is rejected by the Lords by 138 to 47, and the bill is abandoned. *The Division Lists of the House of Commons now begin to be published for the first time by the House itself.* The newspaper stamp duty is reduced to one penny in this year. The Ecclesiastical Commissioners are incorporated in this year (*d*).
1837.	*March.* Grote's motion for the ballot is thrown out by 265 to 153. *April.* Resolutions are passed about the disturbed state of Canada. The Government Church-Rates Abolition Bill being carried by 5 only in the Commons (287 to 282), is abandoned by the ministers. *May.* The Irish Tithe Bill (introduced for the fifth time) is afterwards dropped owing to the dissolution. The Irish Municipal Bill is again defeated in the Lords. *June* 20. **Death of William IV.** [The Duke of Cumberland becomes King of Hanover.]

[Notes.]

FOREIGN AND COLONIAL.

(a) "From the Restoration to the death of George IV. no less than 187 capital offences were added to the criminal code. Year after year until his untimely death Sir Samuel Romilly struggled to overcome the obduracy of men in power. The Commons were on his side, but the Lords, under the guidance of their judicial leaders, were not to be convinced. It was computed that from 1810 to 1845 upwards of 1400 persons had suffered death for crimes which had since ceased to be capital" (*May*, iii.).

(b) The position of ministers had really been strengthened by the results of the commission. It was shown that the State Church included little more than one-tenth of the people, that in 150 parishes there was not one Protestant, and in 860 parishes less than 50. The Lords had taken their stand upon a principle, and were not to be shaken. The settlement of tithes could no longer be deferred, and any concession from the Lords was hopeless. But the retirement of the Whigs from a position which they had chosen as their own battlefield was a grievous shock to their influence and reputation.

(c) *The People's Charter.*—1. Universal suffrage. 2. Vote by ballot. 3. Annual Parliaments. 4. Payment of members. 5. Abolition of the property qualification. 6. Equal electoral districts.

(d) The object of the bill was to suspend the constitution of Jamaica for five years in consequence of difficulties made by the Assembly in connection with the emancipation of slaves. The bill was opposed by Hume and the Radicals as well as by Sir R. Peel.

(e) *Melbourne Ministry reconstituted in* 1839.—Francis Baring, Chancellor of the Exchequer; Marquis of Normanby, Home Secretary; Lord J. Russell, Colonial and War Secretary; Labouchere, President of the Board of Trade; Macaulay, Secretary at War; Lord Ebrington, Lord-Lieutenant of Ireland; Sir George Grey, Judge Advocate-General.

(f) The bill excited much opposition, especially because it was supposed that inspection was an unwarranted interference.

1838. Dost Mahommed receives a Russian mission at Cabul. Declaration of war against the Afghans.

1839. Capture of Candahar.
Annexation of Aden.
New Zealand is first permanently colonized (and included in the colony of New South Wales).
Beginning of the China War.

1840. Blockade of Canton by English fleet.
Transportation of convicts to New South Wales is discontinued.
A popular constitution is granted to Canada, and the two Canadas united.

[1837—1840]   ENGLISH.

PRIME MINISTERS.
LORD MELBOURNE.
1837.

1838.

1839.

1840.

VICTORIA, 1837—

Born, 1819; Married, 1840, Albert of Saxe-Coburg.

Numerous remissions of capital punishment are carried on the recommendation of the Criminal Law Commission. The use of the pillory is wholly abolished (a).
July. Parliament is dissolved.
Nov. New Parliament meets. [Estimated strength of parties—Conservatives, 310; Liberals, 348.]
Jan. Lord Durham is appointed Governor-General of Canada, amidst general approval.
The ministers announce the placing of the Irish tithe question on a new footing, which implies the abandonment of the appropriation clauses. The bill passes both Houses (b).
The Irish Poor Law Act is passed.
The Irish Tithes Commutation Act, commuting tithes into a permanent rent-charge, is passed.
Villiers' motion to consider the Corn Laws is thrown out by a large majority (300 to 95).
An Act against non-residence of clergy is passed.
The ministry having disallowed an ordinance issued by Lord Durham in Canada, after violent attacks from Lord Brougham (*Oct.*), Lord Durham resigns and leaves Canada.
[In this year **the People's Charter** is finally agreed upon and adopted by the Chartists (c).]
The Irish policy of ministers condemned in the Lords is approved in Commons by 22 votes.
May. The Jamaica Bill (d) is carried by 5 votes only in favour of the Government.
The ministers resign.
Sir Robert Peel, invited to form a ministry, **declines to accept office,** on the Queen's refusing to admit proposed changes in the ladies of the bedchamber.
Lord Melbourne takes office again (e).
July. **Rowland Hill's new postage scheme** (for a time a fourpenny, then a penny postage rate) is adopted as part of the Budget and passed.
The Government bring in a bill to increase the education grant (first made in 1833), to place it under the control of a committee of Privy Council, and to subject the aided schools to inspection. It is carried by a majority of 2 only (*f*) (275 to 273).
Nov. Chartist insurrection at Newport led by Frost and others.
Feb. The Queen marries Prince Albert of Saxe-Coburg.
April. Sir J. Y. Buller's motion of want of confidence in the Government rejected by 308 to 287.

187

[Notes.]

(a) Fifty-eight corporations were abolished, ten were reconstituted. Any borough with 3000 population might obtain a charter of incorporation.

(b) Messrs. Hansard had been sued for a libel for matter published in a parliamentary report. The Court of Queen's Bench decided against the House of Commons. The bill now passed is to the effect that such actions shall be stayed on an affidavit that any paper the subject of such action has been printed by order of Parliament.
Sir Robert Peel said, "Do you believe that slavery would have been abolished unless we had published to the world the abuses and horrors of slavery?"

(c) *Sir Robert Peel's Ministry.*—Sir R. Peel, First Lord of the Treasury; Lord Lyndhurst, Lord Chancellor; Goulburn, Exchequer; Sir J. Graham, Home Secretary; Lord Aberdeen, Foreign Secretary; Lord Stanley, War and Colonial; Lord Ripon, President of the Board of Trade (succeeded by Gladstone); Sir H. Hardinge, Secretary at War; Sir E. Knatchbull, Paymaster; Duke of Wellington, Leader of the Lords; Gladstone, Vice-President of Board of Trade; Lord Wharncliffe, President of Council; Duke of Buckingham, Lord Privy Seal; Earl de Grey, Lord-Lieutenant of Ireland; Lord Eliot (afterwards Earl of St. Germans), Chief Secretary for Ireland; Sidney Herbert, Secretary to the Admiralty.

FOREIGN AND COLONIAL.

1841. Hong-Kong ceded to England by treaty. The treaty is disavowed and war recommences.
Nov. Insurrection at Cabul.
Murder of Burnes and others.
Hong-Kong is ceded to England.
New Zealand becomes a separate colony.

1842. *Jan.* Evacuation of Cabul. Massacre of the army in the Khyber.
Aug. The Treaty of Washington (better known as the Ashburton Treaty) is signed.
Aug. After various defeats of the Chinese, the Treaty of Nankin, between China and England, is concluded.
Sept. Cabul reoccupied.
Lord Ellenborough Governor-General of India (to 1844).
1843. Annexation of Scinde. Battles of Meeanee and Hyderabad.

[1840—1843] ENGLISH.

PRIME MINISTERS.	
LORD MELBOURNE. 1840.	*Aug.* **The Irish Municipal Act** (*a*) passes after six years' controversy and difficulties between the House of Commons and the House of Lords. *In the matter of Stockdale* v. *Hansard, which began in* 1837 *and involved a question of privilege, a bill is passed preventing the recurrence of the difficulty* (*b*). The agitation for the repeal of the Union is renewed in Ireland. *Sept.* The allied squadron takes St. Jean d'Acre.
1841.	[The barrenness of the Queen's Speech excites much discontent.] **Free-trade agitation** during the spring under the leadership of **Cobden.** Meetings at Manchester, London, and elsewhere. *May.* After a discussion of eight days on the sugar duty and the Government's proposal of a fixed duty on corn, the Sugar Duty Bill of the ministers is rejected by a majority of 36 in a house of 598. **A motion by Sir R. Peel of want of confidence in the ministry is carried by 1 vote** (312 to 311). The ministry advise a dissolution. *June.* Parliament is dissolved. *Aug.* The new Parliament meets. [Estimated strength of parties—Conservatives, 367 ; Liberals, 286.] **Ministers are defeated both in Lords and Commons by large majorities** (168 to 96 in the Lords, 360 to 269 in the Commons). **Lord Melbourne resigns.**
SIR R. PEEL.	*Sept.* **Sir R. Peel forms a ministry** (*c*). [He is joined by seceders from Lord Grey's ministry— Lord Ripon, Lord Stanley, and Sir J. Graham.] Parliament meets, *Sept.* 16 ; is prorogued, *Oct.* 7. The Duke of Buckingham, well known to be opposed to any change in the Corn Laws, leaves the Cabinet.
1842.	*Feb.* Anti-Corn Law League bazaar at Manchester. Peel carries his sliding scale. [See *Summary: Corn Laws,* p. 272.] Russell and Melbourne's amendment for a fixed duty lost by 349 to 226 in Commons, and 207 to 71 in Lords. Villiers and Brougham's amendment for total repeal lost by 393 to 90, and 109 to 5. Sir R. Peel proposes and carries a revision of the customs tariff, the repeal of many duties, and the substitution of **an income-tax** for a limited period.
1843.	Lord Howick's motion for a committee to inquire into the cause of the prevailing distress is thrown out. A Government bill for compulsory education of pauper and factory children is introduced, but, being opposed by dissenters jealous of Church influence, has to be abandoned (*June*).

[Notes.]

(a) The Secession included more than one-third of the Scotch clergy. On census Sunday, eight years later, in 1851, 228,758 persons attended morning service of the Established Church, 253,482 that of the Free Church.

(b) The *Anti-Corn Law League* had been formed in 1838. Lord Melbourne, then Premier, in the course of a debate in 1839 had said, "To leave the whole agricultural interest without protection, I declare before God that I think it the wildest and maddest scheme that has ever entered into the imagination of man to conceive."

(c) The amount of security upon which the bank may issue notes is to be £14,000,000. Above that sum the notes must correspond to the amount of bullion, and a full statement of the accounts of the bank is to be given week by week to the Government for publication.

(d) *History of the Corn Laws up to* 1815:—
Exportation of corn was entirely forbidden previous to 1436; the first prohibition by Act of Parliament was in 1360. In 1436 exportation was permitted when the price was below 6s. 8d. per quarter, increased to 10s. in 1562. Export duties of varying amounts were imposed by Acts of 1570, 1593, 1604, 1623, 1656, 1660, 1663, and 1670, the last being 5s. 4d. per quarter when the price was at 53s. 4d. In 1689 the export duties were abolished, and a bounty of 5s. paid on exportation when the price was under 48s. The Act of 1773 prohibited exportation above 44s., giving bounty of 5s. below that price. In 1791 the prohibitory price was raised to 46s., and in 1804 to 54s., the bounty ceasing at 48s. In 1814 the bounties were abolished, and exportation permitted without duty.
Importation was forbidden, by an Act of 1463, when the price was under 6s. 8d. per quarter. In 1670 the following scale of duties was imposed—
    8s. per qr. when price is between 53s. 4d. and 80s.
    16s.   "   "   "   44s. and 53s. 4d.
    21s. 9d. "   "   at 44s. and under.
By an Act of 1773 foreign corn was admitted at a nominal duty of 6d. when the price reached 48s., 2s. 3d. when it was between 44s. and 48s., 24s. 3d. when at 44s. and under. The Act of 1791 increased the respective limits to 54s. and 50s., and that of 1804 to 66s. and 63s.
(For further history, see *Corn Law Summary*, p. 272.)

FOREIGN AND COLONIAL.

1844. The Boers being forced to submit, Natal is declared a British colony.
Recall of Lord Ellenborough. He is succeeded by Sir H. (afterwards Lord) Hardinge, Governor-General of India (to 1848).
1845. *Nov.* War declared against the Sikhs.
Dec. Battles of Moodkee and Ferozeshah.

PRIME MINISTERS. SIR R. PEEL. 1843.	*March.* The House of Commons decline to entertain the petition of the General Assembly of Scotland (on the vexed question of patronage and the right of the civil courts in spiritual jurisdiction) by a majority of 135. *May.* **Great Secession from the Scottish Church.** Establishment of the Free Church in Scotland (*a*). The Irish Arms Act is passed. **Disraeli** and Smythe, leaders of the "Young England" party, speak against the Government. Anti-Corn Law League (*b*), led by Cobden and Bright, begins monthly meetings in Covent Garden Theatre. Feargus O'Connor (who opposes at this time the efforts of the Anti-Corn Law League) issues his land scheme. A monster repeal meeting at Clontarf, near Dublin, is forbidden by a Government proclamation. **O'Connell and other repeal leaders are arrested.**
1844.	Trial of O'Connell. He is sentenced to a year's imprisonment and a fine of £2000. This sentence is reversed by the House of Lords on a technical error in the indictment (*Sept.*). Mainly owing to a revival of commercial prosperity there is a surplus this year, and further duties are remitted. Inquiry into the opening of Mazzini's letters at the Post Office. *July.* Sir R. Peel's Bank Charter Act is passed (*c*).
1845.	**Gladstone** leaves the ministry because the views of Government on the Maynooth grant, with which he now agrees, are at variance with his formerly published work on Church and State. Sir R. Peel proposes to renew the income-tax for three years. Takes 430 articles out of the tariff of duties, and reduces the sugar and other duties. A motion in favour of the agricultural interest, and demanding protection for all native industries, is supported by ultra-protectionists, and **Disraeli** states that under existing circumstances a Conservative government is an organized hypocrisy. Sir R. Peel's Maynooth Act is passed augmenting and putting on a permanent basis the grant to Maynooth College (passed in Commons by 317 to 184). Sir R. Peel founds the Queen's Colleges in Ireland for the improvement of education without religious distinction. *Oct.* Newman, hitherto with Dr. Pusey, a leader of the Tractarian movement, joins the Church of Rome. [The harvest for the first time since Sir R. Peel came into office is very bad.] The Irish potato crop fails. *Dec.* **Sir R. Peel,** proposing to his colleagues to **repeal the Corn Laws** (*d*), on the dissent especially of Lord Stanley, **resigns.**

[Notes.]

(a) *Sir R. Peel's Ministry reconstituted.*—In Jan. and Feb. 1846 Gladstone became Colonial and War Secretary; Lord Haddington, Privy Seal ; Lord Ellenborough, Admiralty; Earl of Lincoln, Secretary for Ireland ; Lord Canning, Woods and Forests; Earl St. Germans, Postmaster-General.
In Feb. 1845 Dalhousie had become President of Board of Trade, and Sidney Herbert Secretary at War.

(b) *Leading Protectionists.*—Lord Stanley (afterwards Derby), Lord G. Bentinck, Disraeli, Buckingham, Richmond, Stanhope, Malmesbury, Newcastle, Rutland, Granby, Sibthorp, Christopher, Henley, Miles, Newdegate, Spooner, Sir R. Inglis, Sir J. Buller, George F. Young, Bankes, Lord J. Manners.

(c) "He passed this last measure of his political life amid the reproaches and execrations of his party. He had assigned the credit of the Catholic Relief Act to Mr. Canning, whom he had constantly opposed, and he acknowledged that the credit of this measure was due to 'the unadorned eloquence of Richard Cobden,' the apostle of free-trade, whom he had hitherto resisted " (*May*, ii. 213).

(d) *Lord John Russell's Ministry.*—Lord John Russell, First Lord of Treasury; Lord Cottenham, Lord Chancellor ; Sir C. Wood, Chancellor of Exchequer ; Sir George Grey, Home Secretary ; Lord Palmerston, Foreign Secretary ; Lord Lansdowne, President of the Council; Earl of Minto, Lord Privy Seal; Earl Grey, Colonial and War Secretary; Fox Maule, Secretary at War; Sir J. Hobhouse, Board of Control; Lord Auckland, Admiralty; Earl of Clarendon, President of Board of Trade ; Milner Gibson, Vice-President; Morpeth (afterwards Carlisle), Woods and Forests; Macaulay, Paymaster.

(e) *Population of Ireland.*—1841 . . . 8,175,124
1851 . . . 6,552,385
1861 . . . 5,798,564
1871 . . . 5,411,416
1881 . . . 5,174,836

(f) Sir R. Peel said, "The best reparation that can be made to the last Government will be to assist the present Government in passing this law."

(g) Cobden says during the debate on this matter, "While the House frets over its sevenpence in the pound, the poor are paying twice that number of *shillings* in the pound in the great staples of their consumption. For every 20s. the working classes expend on tea they pay 10s. of duty, for every 20s. they expend on sugar they pay 6s. of duty, on coffee 8s., on soap 5s., on beer 4s., on tobacco 16s., on spirits 14s. . . . Both for the sake of trade and for the sake of the people you must diminish your expenditure or increase the amount of your direct taxation."

(h) *Treason Felony Act.*—By this, writing or speaking with a view to excite sedition was constituted a new crime called treason felony, which could be punished by penal servitude.

(i) Mitchel, Smith O'Brien, Meagher, and Gavan Duffy belonged to the Young Ireland party, usually associated with the *Nation* newspaper, founded in 1842; but Mitchel had this year set on foot the *United Irishman* which openly advocated rebellion.

FOREIGN AND COLONIAL.

1846. Jan. Feb. Battles of Aliwal and Sobraon. Treaty of Lahore, and end of first Sikh war.

1847. The carrying out of the Spanish marriages under the influence of France causes coldness between France and England.
1848. Feb. Revolution in France. Abdication of Louis Philippe.
March. He arrives in England.
March. Insurrections in Austria, Italy, and elsewhere.
Revolutions in Spain, Poland, Hungary, and Italy.
Dec. Louis Napoleon is declared President-elect of the French Republic.
Lord Dalhousie Governor-General of India (to 1856).
The Boers of the Orange Republic (or Free State) are forced to acknowledge the sovereignty of England.
[The Orange Republic is separated from England again in 1853.]
An attempt this year, by Order in Council, to transport convicts to the Cape of Good Hope is foiled by the colonists.

PRIME MINISTERS. SIR R. PEEL. 1845.	Lord J. Russell fails to form a cabinet, as Lords Grey and Palmerston will not act together. Sir R. Peel resumes office (a). Lord Stanley leaves him and is replaced by Gladstone. Great meeting of Anti-Corn Law League at Manchester, £60,000 subscribed in an hour and a half.
1846.	**SIR R. PEEL PROPOSES THE GRADUAL REPEAL OF THE CORN LAWS, AND CARRIES THE INTRODUCTION OF COMPLETE FREE-TRADE IN CORN** (to take final effect after three years). He is opposed both by protectionists (b) and by some free-traders. The bill is finally carried by 327 to 229, third reading, Sir R. Peel having frequently ascribed the honour of the measure to Cobden and his associates(c). The bill is carried in the Lords by 47 (second reading, 211 to 164). [See *Summary: Corn Laws*, p. 272.] Protest signed by 89 peers. On their Irish bill demanding additional repressive powers the Government are defeated through the influence of the protectionists by 73 (292 to 219). *June.* Sir R. Peel resigns.
LORD JOHN RUSSELL.	Lord John Russell becomes Prime Minister (d). Potato famine in Ireland, followed by wholesale emigration (e).
1847.	The Government grant £10,000,000 for the relief of Ireland. Fielden's Factory Bill, limiting the work of those under eighteen to ten hours a day and eight hours on Saturday, is passed. Parliament is dissolved. *Nov.* **The new Parliament meets.** Rothschild returned for London (the first Jew elected). [Estimated strength of parties — Conservative Free-traders, 105; Protectionists, 226; Liberals, 325.] [Disraeli soon becomes established as leader of the Opposition in the Commons (Lord G. Bentinck leading till his death in 1848).] Government has to ask for a Coercion Bill for Ireland similar to that for which Sir R. Peel was turned out. It is passed by a large majority (f). [The Poor Law Board is constituted this year.]
1848.	Lord J. Russell proposes a large increase of the income-tax, but has to abandon his proposal. The income-tax remains at 7d. in the pound (g). *April.* The Chartist meeting in London for the presentation of their monster petition, after exciting much alarm, turns out a failure. Treason Felony Act passed (h). Mitchel convicted of treason felony, Smith O'Brien and Meagher discharged without a verdict (i).

[Notes.]

FOREIGN AND COLONIAL.

1849. Capture of Mooltan.
Battle of Chillianwallah.
Battle of Goojerat.
Annexation of the Punjab. End of second Sikh war.
Rebellion in Hungary under Kossuth crushed by the aid of Russia.
French troops occupy Rome.
1850. Sir C. Napier resigns command of Indian forces owing to the action of Lord Dalhousie.
Victoria is made a separate colony, with Melbourne as capital.
The Australian Colonies Bill is passed. [In the course of the next few years representative governments are formed for New South Wales, Victoria, South Australia, and Van Diemen's Land.]
Great gold discoveries in Australia and California.

(a) The Queen's memorandum to Lord Palmerston :—
"The Queen requires, first, that Lord Palmerston will distinctly state what he proposes in a given case, in order that the Queen may know as distinctly to what she is giving her royal sanction. Secondly, having once given her sanction to a measure, that it be not arbitrarily altered or modified by the minister. Such an act she must consider as failing in sincerity towards the Crown, and justly to be visited by the exercise of her constitutional right of dismissing that minister. She expects to be kept informed of what passes between him and the foreign ministers, before important decisions are taken, based upon that intercourse; to receive the foreign despatches in good time; and to have the drafts for her approval sent to her in sufficient time to make herself acquainted with their contents before they must be sent off."

(b) Under the influence of the League in 1852, fifty tenant-right advocates were elected, and Crawford's Tenant-Right Bill of 1852 was introduced; but when Sadleir and Keogh joined the Aberdeen ministry the old sectarian rivalry broke out, and the League fell to the ground.

[1848—1851]   *ENGLISH.*

PRIME MINISTERS.	
LORD JOHN RUSSELL. 1848.	*May.* Jewish Disabilities Bill passed by Commons, thrown out by Lords by 163 to 128. *July.* The Habeas Corpus Act is suspended in Ireland. An abortive attempt at insurrection under Smith O'Brien is put down, and the leader transported. Gavan Duffy discharged without a verdict.
1849.	The Irish Encumbered Estates Court is established, in accordance with an Act of last year, to facilitate the sale of encumbered properties. Rothschild is re-elected, but not allowed to sit. Navigation laws repealed by 275 to 214 in the Commons, and 173 to 163 in the Lords. [See note 1823.] Piræus blockaded by the Mediterranean fleet in support of Finlay and Don Pacifico.
1850.	Disraeli, ascribing the agricultural distress to the establishment of free-trade, asks for a committee of inquiry. He is supported by Gladstone and opposed by Peel. His motion is lost by only 21 (273 to 252). A motion to repeal the window-tax wholly is lost by 3 only. A motion to repeal the malt-tax is lost by 124. *The Queen sends a memorandum to Lord Palmerston as to business between the Crown and a Secretary of State (a).* Roebuck's motion of confidence in the policy of the Government towards Greece is opposed by Sir Robert Peel, but carried by 310 to 264. *July* 2. **Death of Sir R. Peel.** Irish Tenant League, including men of all parties, is formed (*b*). *Sept.* 30. A Papal Bull creating Roman Catholic bishops in England is issued. It causes much excitement. Convocation meets for business (for the first time since 1717) this year.
1851.	Disraeli's motion that Government ought to introduce measures to alleviate agricultural distress is lost by only 14 (281 to 267). *Feb.* 17. The Budget causes much dissatisfaction. *Feb. Locke King's motion for assimilating county to borough franchise is supported by some Liberals, and carried against the Government by 100 to 52.* *Feb.* **Lord J. Russell resigns.** *Feb.* **Lord Stanley** (became Lord Stanley by courtesy 1834, summoned to the Peers in his father's lifetime 1844, succeeded as Earl of Derby *June* 1851) **is unable to form a Ministry.** *March.* **Lord J. Russell returns to office.** *Locke King's bill is thrown out by 299 to 83.* *May.* Opening of the Great Exhibition. *July.* The Ecclesiastical Titles Act (Great Britain and Ireland) is passed, declaring the Papal Bull of 1850

[Notes.]

(a) "It was a protest against an Act of the Pope which had outraged the feelings of the people of England, but as a legislative measure it was a dead letter" (*May*, iii. 235). It is repealed in 1871.

(b) *Lord Derby's Ministry.*—Lord Derby, First Lord of the Treasury; Lord St. Leonards (formerly Sir E. Sugden), Chancellor; Disraeli, Chancellor of the Exchequer; Walpole, Home Secretary; Lord Malmesbury, Foreign Secretary; Earl of Lonsdale, President of Council; Lord Salisbury, Privy Seal; Sir J. Pakington, Colonial and War Secretary; Herries, Board of Control; William Beresford, Secretary at War; Henley, Board of Trade; Earl of Hardwicke, Postmaster-General; Duke of Northumberland, Admiralty; Lord Naas, Secretary for Ireland; Lord Stanley, Under Foreign Secretary; Lord J. Manners, Chief Commissioner of Works.

(c) *Lord Aberdeen's Ministry.*—Lord Aberdeen, First Lord of the Treasury; Lord Cranworth, Lord Chancellor; Gladstone, Chancellor of the Exchequer; Lord Palmerston, Home Secretary; Lord John Russell, Foreign Secretary till Feb. 1853 (succeeded by Clarendon), then in Cabinet without office till June 1854; Duke of Newcastle, Colonial Secretary; Sidney Herbert, Secretary at War; Sir C. Wood, Board of Control; Cardwell, Board of Trade; Lord Canning, Postmaster-General; Sir J. Graham, Admiralty; Sir A. Cockburn, Attorney-General; Sir R. Bethell, Solicitor-General; Lord St. Germans, Lord Lieutenant of Ireland; Lord Granville, President of Council (succeeded by Lord J. Russell, June 1854, on becoming Chancellor of the Duchy of Lancaster); Duke of Argyll, Privy Seal; Robert Lowe, Secretary to the Board of Control.

FOREIGN AND COLONIAL.

1851. Dec. 2. The *coup d'état* in Paris.

1852. Jan. Louis Napoleon installed as Prince-President of the French Republic.
Second war in Burmah.
Annexation of Pegu.
Dec. The President of the French is declared Emperor as Napoleon III.
A constitution is given to each of six different colonies in New Zealand.

1853. The Kaffir war is brought to a close, having lasted for two years.
British Kaffraria is annexed.
July. Conference at Vienna.
July. Russian troops pass the Pruth.
Oct. Turkey declares war against Russia.
Defeat of the Russians at Oltenitza.
Nov. Destruction of a Turkish fleet at Sinope by Russia.

PRIME MINISTERS. **LORD** **JOHN RUSSELL.** 1851. 1852. **LORD DERBY.** **LORD ABERDEEN.** 1853.	null and void, and imposing a fine of £100 on all who try to carry it into effect (*a*). **Lord Palmerston's resignation is required by Lord J. Russell**, *on the ground of his having exceeded his authority as Secretary of State in his communications on his own authority to France with reference to the recognition of the* coup d'état *of Dec. 2.* Lord Granville becomes Foreign Secretary. *Feb.* Lord Palmerston carries an amendment to the bill for organization of the militia (arising out of fears of Napoleon III.) by 11 (136 to 125). **Lord J. Russell resigns.** *Feb.* **Lord Derby becomes Prime Minister** (*b*). *A Bribery Act is passed providing for inquiry into corrupt practices on the appointment of a commission.* Crawford's bill to secure and regulate the tenant-right of Ulster, to secure compensation for improvements, and to limit the power of eviction in certain cases, is thrown out on the second reading by 167 to 57. *July.* Dissolution of Parliament. *Sept.* Death of the Duke of Wellington. *Nov.* **New Parliament meets.** [Estimated strength of parties — Conservatives, 299; Liberals, 315; Peelites, 40.] **Disraeli's** Budget is much criticised, and is defeated by 305 to 286. *Dec.* Lord Derby resigns. *Dec.* **Lord Aberdeen becomes Prime Minister,** forming a **Coalition ministry** of Whigs and Peelites (*c*). [In this and other years great improvements were effected in the method of procedure both in Common Law and Equity.] *April.* **Gladstone introduces his first budget.** He points out the use of the income-tax in case of war. He proposes to retain it for one year at 7*d.* in the £, and gradually to diminish it so that it will expire in 1860. He abolishes the duties on soap, reduces 133 other taxes (the total amount of proposed remissions being estimated at over five millions), and imposes a succession duty. Union of England and France to protect Turkey against Russia. *April.* The Jewish Disabilities Bill is again rejected by the Lords. *July.* A conference of the four Powers, Great Britain, France, Austria, and Prussia, at Vienna, concerning the affairs of Russia and Turkey begins. *July.* The advertisement duty repeal is carried by Milner Gibson against the Government by 200 to 169.

[Notes.]

(a) The powers of the Company are only continued till Parliament shall otherwise provide. The Court of Directors is to contain six nominees of the Crown. The Civil Service is thrown open to competition.

(b) Franchise to be reduced to £10 in counties and £6 (rating) in boroughs. Educational, savings-bank, and other "fancy" franchises.

(c) GENEALOGY OF THE NAPIERS.

Francis, 5th Lord Napier.

William, 6th Lord Napier (great-grandfather of Francis, 9th Lord Napier, governor of Madras).	Charles. Sir Charles, Admiral (Acre, 1840; Baltic Fleet, 1854), d. 1860.	George m. Lady Sarah Lennox.
Sir Charles, General (conqueror of Scinde, 1843), d.1853.	Sir George, General	Sir William (author of "History of Peninsular War"), d. 1860.

(d) "In 1801 Lord Hobart succeeded to the office, and the departments of War and Colonies were united under one secretary. This arrangement continued till 1854, when, in consequence of the war with Russia, and the accumulated duties devolving on the Colonial Office, it was thought expedient to appoint a distinct Chief Secretary of State to preside over each department" (A. Mills, "Colonial Constitutions," p. 13).

(e) *Lord Palmerston's Ministry.*—Lord Palmerston, First Lord of the Treasury; Lord Cranworth, Chancellor; Duke of Argyll (succeeded by Lord Harrowby), Privy Seal; Lord Granville, President of Council; Gladstone, Exchequer; Sir George Grey, Home Secretary; Lord Lansdowne, Cabinet without office; Earl of Clarendon, Foreign Secretary; Sidney Herbert, Colonial Secretary; Lord Panmure (formerly Fox Maule), War Secretary; Sir C. Wood, Board of Control; Cardwell, Board of Trade; Lord Harrowby, Duchy of Lancaster; Lord Canning (succeeded by Duke of Argyll), Postmaster-General; Sir J. Graham, Admiralty; Earl of St. Germans, Lord-Lieutenant of Ireland; Sir J. Young, Secretary for Ireland; Sir A. Cockburn, Attorney-General; Sir R. Bethell, Solicitor-General; Sir W. Molesworth, Commissioner of Works.
On the resignation of the Peelites (Gladstone, Graham, St. Germans, Cardwell, Herbert, and Young) Sir G. C. Lewis became Chancellor of the Exchequer; Lord J. Russell, Colonial Secretary; Lord Stanley of Alderley, President of the Board of Trade; Sir C. Wood, First Lord of the Admiralty; Vernon Smith, President of Board of Control; Earl of Carlisle, Lord-Lieutenant of Ireland; Horsman, Secretary for Ireland (succeeded by Henry Herbert, 1857); Bouverie, Vice-President Board of Trade (succeeded by R. Lowe).

FOREIGN AND COLONIAL.

1854. Unsuccessful siege of Silistria by the Russians (*May*).
The first Cape Parliament meets. (A responsible government is not instituted till 1874.)
Colonial and War Secretaryships divided and a fourth Secretary of State appointed (d).
Newcastle retains the War Secretaryship. Sir G. Grey takes the Colonial Office.

1855. Sardinia joins England and France against Russia.
March. Death of the Emperor Nicholas of Russia. Succeeded by Alexander II.
The conference of the European Powers at Vienna proves a failure, because Russia refuses to agree to any limit being placed on the size of the Black Sea fleet.

PRIME MINISTERS. **LORD ABERDEEN.** 1853.	*Aug.* A new India Bill is passed, the last charter of the East India Company is granted (*a*). [See note 1773.]
	Dec. Lord Palmerston resigns, really because he does not consider the Government's policy towards Russia sufficiently decided.
	The English fleet is ordered to enter the Black Sea.
	Lord Palmerston resumes office.
1854.	*Feb.* **The ultimatum of England and France is sent to St. Petersburg.**
	March. A *Reform Bill* (*b*) *is introduced by Lord J. Russell, but ultimately withdrawn.*
	Gladstone in his Budget proposes to double the income-tax for six months (this to be renewed if necessary) to meet the war expenditure.
	The Corrupt Practices Act, providing for publication of accounts after parliamentary elections, and restraining candidates from paying any expenses except through authorized agents, is carried.
	March. The Baltic fleet under Sir C. Napier (*c*) is despatched.
	June. War and Colonial Secretaryships divided.
	June. The allied armies land at Varna under Lord Raglan and Marshal St. Arnaud.
	Sept. **The allied armies land in the Crimea.**
	Sept. 20. Battle of the **Alma**.
	Oct. 17. The siege of **Sebastopol** begins.
	Oct. 25. Battle of **Balaclava**.
	Nov. 5. Battle of **Inkerman**.
	Dec. Parliament is assembled. Lord Derby charges the ministry with great mismanagement of the war.
	[The bad administration of the war is denounced strongly in the *Times* and by the public.]
1855.	*Jan.* **Resignation of Lord J. Russell**, whose views as to the presence of a War Minister in the House of Commons had not been carried out.
	Roebuck's motion to inquire into the conduct of the war is carried by 157 (305 to 148).
	Jan. **Lord Aberdeen resigns.**
	Lord J. Russell and Lord Derby are unable to form administrations.
LORD PALMERSTON.	**Lord Palmerston becomes Prime Minister** (*e*).
	Gladstone, Sir J. Graham, S. Herbert, and other "Peelites" leave the ministry.
	The last penny of the newspaper duty is repealed.
	June. Further bombardments of Sebastopol.
	Death of Lord Raglan, succeeded by General Simpson.
	July. **Resignation of Lord J. Russell**, who had succeeded Sidney Herbert, on notice being given of a motion expressing want of confidence in him for his action at the conference at Vienna.

[Notes.]

FOREIGN AND COLONIAL.

1856. Annexation of Oudh.
Lord Canning Governor-General of India [Viceroy 1858] (to 1862).
Seizure of the lorcha *Arrow* by the Chinese.
Sir M. Seymour bombards Canton.

1857. *March.* Treaty of peace between England and Persia signed at Paris.

PRIME MINISTERS. LORD PALMERSTON. 1855. 1856.	*Sept.* 8. **Fall and evacuation of Sebastopol.** *Nov.* Surrender of General Williams after his long defence of Kars. *A committee of the Lords report against the power of the Crown to admit life peers to Parliament, which it attempted to do in the case of Sir James Parke created Baron Wensleydale.* The Government yield the point. *March* 30. **Treaty of peace finally signed at Paris** between Russia and Turkey, England, France, and Sardinia. *April.* Lord John Russell's motions involving a scheme of national education are rejected (260 to 158). *May.* Miall's motion in favour of Irish Church disestablishment rejected by 70 votes (163 to 93). The education vote of this year is £451,000. A paid Minister of Education is appointed to act as Vice-President of the Council.
1857.	In the Budget the income-tax is reduced from 1s. 4d. to 7d. in the £ (proposed for three years). *March.* Cobden's motion condemning the violent measures resorted to in the affair of the *Arrow* in China, and approved by Government, is carried by 16 votes (263 to 247). **Lord Palmerston** gives notice of a dissolution and **appeals to the country.** Bright and Gibson are rejected at Manchester, and Cobden at Huddersfield. *April.* **New Parliament** meets. [Estimated strength of parties—Liberals, 366 ; Conservatives, 287.] **Indian mutiny.** Outbreaks at **Meerut and Delhi, Lucknow and Cawnpore.** *June.* Destruction of the Chinese fleet. *July.* Death of Sir H. Lawrence at Lucknow. The massacre at **Cawnpore.** *Sept.* **Capture of Delhi. Relief of Lucknow** under Generals Havelock and Outram, who, joining the garrison, await further relief. *Nov.* **Final relief of Lucknow** under Sir Colin Campbell, commander-in-chief. Death of Havelock. Commercial panic in England. Suspension of Bank Charter Act. *Dec.* Parliament meets. The Bank Charter Indemnity Act is carried. *Dec.* Capture of Canton by English and French. In punishment for the mutiny Sepoy rebels are blown from the guns.
1858.	Orsini attempts to assassinate the Emperor of the French. [There is much irritation in France against England for harbouring assassin refugees, and much irritation

[Notes.]

(a) *Lord Derby's Ministry.*—Lord Derby,* First Lord of the Treasury; Lord Chelmsford,* Lord Chancellor; Lord Salisbury,* President of Council; Lord Hardwicke,* Privy Seal; Disraeli,* Chancellor of the Exchequer; Walpole,* Home Secretary; Lord Malmesbury,* Foreign Secretary; Lord Stanley* (succeeded by Sir E. Bulwer Lytton), Colonial Secretary; General Peel,* War Secretary; Lord Ellenborough,* Board of Control (succeeded by Lord Stanley); Henley,* Board of Trade; Sir J. Pakington,* Admiralty; Lord J. Manners,* Chief Commissioner of Works; Lord Colchester, Postmaster-General; Sir F. Kelly, Attorney-General; Cairns, Solicitor-General; Lord Naas, Irish Secretary; Hardy, Under Home Secretary; Lord Carnarvon, Under Colonial Secretary; Eglinton, Lord-Lieutenant of Ireland.

* In the Cabinet.

(b) *India Bill.*—The territories and powers of the Company are transferred to the Crown. India is to be administered by a Secretary of State for India and a Council of fifteen members. The Board of Control is abolished.

(c) By the year 1859 church-rates had been refused in no less than 1525 parishes or districts.

(d) *Proposed Reform Bill.*—County and borough franchise to be assimilated, the latter remaining as before. Lodgers at £20 per annum to have votes. Educational and other "fancy" franchises. Voting-papers to be allowed.

(e) Sotheron Estcourt succeeded Walpole as Home Secretary; Lord Donoughmore became President of the Board of Trade; Lord March (afterwards Duke of Richmond), President of Poor Law Board; Sir Stafford Northcote, Secretary to the Treasury.

(f) *Lord Palmerston's Ministry.*—Lord Palmerston,* First Lord of the Treasury; Lord Campbell,* Lord Chancellor (succeeded by Bethell (Lord Westbury) in 1861); Earl Granville,* President of Council; Duke of Argyll,* Privy Seal; Gladstone,* Chancellor of the Exchequer; Sir G. Lewis,* Home Secretary (succeeded by Sir G. Grey); Lord John Russell* (created Earl Russell 1861), Foreign Secretary; Duke of Newcastle * (succeeded by Cardwell), Colonial Secretary; Herbert,* War Secretary; Sir C. Wood,* Indian Secretary; Milner Gibson,* Board of Trade; Sir G. Grey,* Duchy of Lancaster; Duke of Somerset,* Admiralty; C. P. Villiers,* Poor Law Board; Earl of Elgin * (succeeded by Stanley of Alderley*), Postmaster-General; Cardwell (succeeded by Sir Robert Peel), Irish Secretary; Lowe, Vice-President of Council (succeeded by H. A. Bruce); Laing (succeeded by Frederick Peel, and in 1865 by Childers), Secretary to the Treasury; Lord Carlisle, Lord-Lieutenant of Ireland (succeeded by Lord Wodehouse 1864).
Sir G. Lewis became War Secretary in 1861, and died in 1863 (succeeded by Earl de Grey and Ripon*); Cardwell * became Chancellor of the Duchy of Lancaster in 1861, and was succeeded by Lord Clarendon 1864.

* In the Cabinet.

FOREIGN AND COLONIAL.

1858. Gladstone is sent as commissioner to the Ionian Islands.
Nov. The Queen of England is proclaimed Sovereign of India, Lord Canning receiving the title of Viceroy as well as Governor-General.
War with China resumed.

1859. War declared by France and Sardinia against Austria. The Austrians are defeated at Magenta and Solferino.
July. The Treaty of Villafranca brings to a close the war between France and Austria.
Lombardy ceded to Sardinia. Tuscany, Parma, and Modena unite themselves to Sardinia, but Savoy and Nice are ceded to France.
Queensland is made a separate colony (Brisbane capital), with a representative government.

[1858, 1859] ENGLISH.

PRIME MINISTERS. **LORD PALMERSTON.** 1858.	in England about the threats of certain French colonels and others.] Lord Palmerston introduces a bill transferring the government of India from the East India Company to the Crown. *Feb.* Lord Palmerston's Conspiracy to Murder Bill (relating to Orsini's late attempt on the Emperor), making conspiracy to murder a felony, is defeated on Milner Gibson's amendment by 19 votes. **Lord Palmerston resigns.**
LORD DERBY	**Lord Derby becomes Prime Minister** (*a*). *March.* **Capture of Lucknow** under Sir C. Campbell and Outram. Final suppression of rebels in India. Campaign of Sir H. Rose in Central India. *May. A bill abolishing the property qualification for English and Irish members of Parliament is introduced and afterwards passed.* *June.* A new India Bill (*b*) is introduced, and afterwards carried. Secretaryship of State for India constituted; Lord Stanley first Secretary. *June.* A treaty is arranged between England and China at Tien-Tsin. A bill for the abolition of church-rates is passed in the Commons and thrown out in the Lords (*c*). *July.* The admission of Jews to Parliament is at last, after many years' effort made by the House of Commons and resisted by the Lords, effected by a bill enabling either House by resolution to modify its oath, which is carried by 143 to 97.
1859.	*Feb.* Lord Cowley is sent to Vienna to mediate between France and Austria concerning Italy. *Disraeli announces the proposals of the Government on the reform of the franchise (d).* [*Walpole and Henley had retired on account of these proposals (e).*] *March.* **Defeat of the ministry** on the second reading of their Reform Bill by 39 votes (330 to 291). *April.* **Dissolution of Parliament.** *May.* The formation of volunteer rifle corps is sanctioned by the War Office. A declaration of neutrality in the war about to begin between Italy and Austria is issued by the Government. *May.* The **new Parliament** meets. [Estimated strength of parties—Conservatives, 305; Liberals, 348.] *June.* **The ministry is defeated** in the amendment to the address by 13 votes (323 to 310). *June.* **The Queen wishes Lord Granville to undertake the formation of a ministry.**
LORD PALMERSTON.	*June.* **Ultimately Lord Palmerston becomes Prime Minister** (*f*).

[Notes.]

FOREIGN AND COLONIAL.

(a) County franchise to be reduced to £10, boroughs to £6.

(b) "The object and intended effect of this Act was to substitute, in the relation of landlord and tenant, for the just and equitable principles of common law or custom, the hard commercial principle of contract, and to render any right of the tenant, either as to duration of tenancy or compensation, dependent on expressed or implied contract" (*Quoted by Barry O'Brien from Finlason's "Land Tenure,"* p. 106).

1860. Capture of Pekin. Treaty with China. Garibaldi frees Sicily and Naples, who decide to join Sardinia, and in March 1861 Victor Emmanuel is declared King of Italy by the Italian Parliament.

1861. *Jan.* 1. Accession of William I., King of Prussia. Bismarck becomes his chief adviser. The Boers of the Transvaal form themselves into a separate state.
Jan. to *May.* Secession of ten of the states of the American Union, who form the Confederate States.
April. Beginning of the American Civil War.
June. Death of Cavour.
July. Defeat of the Federals by the Confederates at the battle of Bull's Run.
1862. After a long series of engagements Lee and Jackson force M'Clellan to retire behind the James River.
Lord Elgin Viceroy of India (to 1863).
Parliament resolves (on the motion of A. Mills) that those colonies which enjoy self-government shall be responsible for their own military defence.

PRIME MINISTERS. **LORD PALMERSTON.** 1859.	[Cobden refuses the office of President of Board of Trade, which is offered him.] Budget. Gladstone adds 4d. in the £ of income-tax to incomes over £150. The Phœnix Club, under O'Donovan Rossa and Stephens, having become the nucleus of Fenianism, Rossa and others are tried and condemned, but released.
1860.	*Jan.* A treaty of commerce between France and England, negotiated by **Cobden**, is signed. *Feb.* The Government scheme for remission of wine duties is introduced. *March.* **A Government Reform Bill** is introduced by Lord J. Russell, but withdrawn later (*a*). *April.* A Church-Rates Abolition Bill carried in the Commons but thrown out in the Lords. *A Government bill abolishing the paper duty is carried on the second reading by* 245 *to* 192, *third reading by only* 219 *to* 210. *It is afterwards rejected by the Lords by* 193 *to* 104. *This causes much excitement in the Commons, as it is practically, though not in technical form, a Money Bill.* Ultimately Lord Palmerston moves and carries resolutions which indicate that in future the Commons can guard their powers by so framing their bills as to make a repetition of the late proceeding impossible. An Act is passed to base the relation of landlord and tenant in Ireland on contract and not on tenure (*b*).
1861.	*The Government make no mention of reform in the royal speech.* *Locke King's and Baines's motions for the reduction of the franchise are respectively negatived, the former by* 248 *to* 229, *the latter by* 279 *to* 154. *The whole financial scheme of Government being embraced in one bill, the Lords are obliged to pass the abolition of the paper duty. Ten peers protest.* The Church-Rates Abolition Bill is thrown out in the Commons by the Speaker's casting vote (274 on each side). Under the Bankruptcy Act of this year the imprisonment of common debtors is abandoned and many debtors in confinement are set free. *Nov.* Forcible seizure of the Confederate Commissioners Slidell and Mason when under British protection on the West India mail steamer *Trent.* On remonstrance from England the American Government consent to restore them. Congress pass a vote of thanks to Captain Wilkes for the seizure. *Dec.* **Death of the Prince Consort.**
1862.	Gladstone reduces the duty on tea to 1s. in the pound. Central Relief Committee for the Lancashire distress,

[Notes]

FOREIGN AND COLONIAL.

1863. Death of Lord Elgin. Succeeded by Sir John Lawrence as Viceroy of India (to 1869).
July. Lee defeated at Gettysburg.
General Grant captures Vicksburg on the Mississippi.
1864. Indecisive battle between Grant and Lee in the Wilderness.

(a) *Lord Russell's Ministry.*—Lord Russell,* First Lord of the Treasury; Lord Cranworth,* Lord Chancellor; Lord Granville,* President of Council; Duke of Argyll,* Privy Seal; Gladstone,* Chancellor of the Exchequer; Sir George Grey,* Home Secretary; Lord Clarendon,* Foreign Secretary; Earl de Grey* (succeeded by Lord Hartington*), War Secretary; Cardwell,* Colonial Secretary; Sir C. Wood* (succeeded by Earl de Grey), Indian Secretary; Milner Gibson,* Board of Trade; Goschen, Vice-President of Board of Trade; Lord Stanley of Alderley,* Postmaster-General; Villiers,* Poor Law Board; Duke of Somerset,* Admiralty; Chichester Fortescue, Irish Secretary; Wodehouse, Lord-Lieutenant of Ireland; Forster, Under Colonial Secretary; Hartington, Under War Secretary; Dufferin, Under Secretary for India.
In *Jan.* 1866 Goschen* was made Chancellor of the Duchy of Lancaster, Monsell becoming Vice-President of the Board of Trade. In the following month, on the resignation of Wood, De Grey and Ripon became Secretary for India; Hartington,* War Secretary; Dufferin, Under Secretary for War; and Stansfeld, Under Secretary for India.

* In the Cabinet.

(b) *Proposed Reform Bill.*—County franchise, £14 rental; borough franchise, £7 rental; lodgers paying £10 clear annual value.

(c) *Chief Adullamites.*—Lowe, Horsman, Earl of Lichfield, Lord Elcho, Earl Grosvenor, Lord Dunkellin, Lord R. Grosvenor, Laing, Doulton, Major Anson.

1865. War against Denmark. Schleswig ceded to Prussia, Holstein and Lauenburg to Austria.
Grant forces Lee to surrender at Richmond.
Murder of President Lincoln.
Insurrection of negroes in Jamaica.

1866. *June.* War declared by Prussia and Italy against Austria, Hanover, Bavaria, and Hesse.
Austrians defeat the Italians at Custozza.
July 3. Defeat of the Austrians at Königgratz (Sadowa).
Bavarians and Hessians defeated at Kissingen, Hanoverians at Laugensalza.
North Germany becomes united under the leadership of Prussia.

[1862—1866] ENGLISH.

PRIME MINISTERS.		
LORD PALMERSTON.		owing to the cotton famine, established. (The weekly loss of wages at one time was estimated at £168,000.)
1862.		
	July.	The **Alabama** is allowed to leave the Mersey under pretence that she is going for a trial trip.
1863.		**Marriage of the Prince of Wales** to Princess Alexandra of Denmark.
		The Ionian Islands resolve in favour of separation from England and union with Greece, to which England consents.
1864.		Gladstone takes 1d. off the income-tax, but refuses to repeal the malt-tax.
	April.	Locke King's County Franchise Bill (by 254 to 227) and Baines Borough Franchise Bill (by 272 to 216) are thrown out.
		A motion of want of confidence in ministers, on the ground of their lowering the influence of England by their behaviour in reference to the Danish war, is lost by 18 in Commons (313 to 295), carried by 9 in the Lords (177 to 168).
1865.		The Poor Law Union Chargeability Bill is carried.
		Reduction of the income-tax from 6d. to 4d., and of the duty on tea to 6d. in the pound.
		Resignation of the Lord Chancellor (Westbury) after a motion of censure passed in the House of Commons, succeeded by Cranworth.
	July.	**Dissolution of Parliament.**
		General election. **Gladstone is defeated at Oxford University.**
	Oct.	**Death of Lord Palmerston.**
LORD RUSSELL.	Nov.	**Lord Russell becomes Prime Minister** (a).
		[The severe action of Governor Eyre in Jamaica this year produces later on much discussion in England. He is superseded by the Government. He is prosecuted, but the grand jury find no bill, and he is reimbursed for his expenses from the public funds.]
1866.	Feb.	The **new Parliament is opened.**
		Gladstone becomes leader of the House of Commons. [Estimated strength of parties—Conservatives, 294; Liberals, 361.]
		A bill suspending the Habeas Corpus Act in Ireland passed in both Houses.
	March.	**The Government Reform Bill is introduced by Gladstone** (b).
		After many evenings' debate the Government Reform Bill is carried by 5 votes only (the division being 283 Conservatives and 32 Liberals against 318 Liberals and 2 Conservatives, including tellers), the small majority being chiefly owing to **the seceding** Liberal "**Adullamites**" (c), led by Lowe.
		The Government Distribution of Seats Bill is introduced.

[Notes.]

(a) *Lord Derby's Ministry.*—Lord Derby,* First Lord of the Treasury; Lord Chelmsford,* Lord Chancellor; Duke of Buckingham,* President of Council; Lord Malmesbury,* Privy Seal; Disraeli,* Chancellor of the Exchequer; Walpole,* Home Secretary; Lord Stanley,* Foreign Secretary; Lord Carnarvon,* Colonial Secretary; General Peel,* War Secretary; Lord Cranbourne* (succeeded as Marquis of Salisbury 1868), Indian Secretary; Sir Stafford Northcote,* Board of Trade; Lord Devon,* Duchy of Lancaster; Lord J. Manners,* Commissioner of Works; Sir J. Pakington,* Admiralty; Hardy,* Poor Law Board; Duke of Montrose, Postmaster-General; Lord Naas, Chief Secretary for Ireland; S. Cave, Vice-President of Board of Trade; Marquis of Abercorn, Lord-Lieutenant of Ireland; Cairns (created Lord Cairns 1867, Earl Cairns 1878), Attorney-General; Ward Hunt, Secretary to the Treasury.

In *March* 1867 Buckingham* became Colonial Secretary; Pakington,* War; Corry,* First Lord of the Admiralty; Duke of Marlborough,* President of the Council; Northcote,* Secretary for India; Duke of Richmond,* President of Board of Trade.

In *May* 1867 Walpole resigned office, remaining in the Cabinet; Devon* became President of Poor Law Board; Hardy,* Home Secretary; Wilson Patten, Chancellor of the Duchy of Lancaster.

* In the Cabinet.

(b) *Reform Bill of* 1867 (*England*).— In boroughs household suffrage was established, with a lodger franchise of £10; in the counties a £12 occupation franchise was established. In boroughs returning three members, each voter was only allowed to give two votes. [For redistribution of seats see *Appendix III.*]

Reform Bills of 1868 (*Scotland and Ireland*):—
Scotland.—To provide seven additional seats for Scotland a further disfranchisement was effected in England. The Scotch occupation franchise in counties was reduced to £14.
Ireland.—The borough franchise was reduced from £8 to £4.

Disraeli's Ministry.—Disraeli,* First Lord of the Treasury; Lord Cairns,* Lord Chancellor; Duke of Marlborough,* President of Council; Lord Malmesbury,* Privy Seal; Ward Hunt,* Chancellor of the Exchequer; Gathorne Hardy,* Home Secretary; Lord Stanley,* Foreign Secretary; Duke of Buckingham,* Colonial Secretary; Sir J. Pakington* (created Lord Hampton 1874), War Secretary; Sir Stafford Northcote,* Indian Secretary; Duke of Richmond,* Board of Trade; Corry,* Admiralty; Lord J. Manners,* Commissioner of Works; Colonel Patten (succeeded by Colonel Taylor), Duchy of Lancaster; Duke of Montrose, Postmaster-General; Lord Mayo (formerly Naas), Chief Secretary for Ireland (succeeded by Colonel Patten); S. Cave, Vice-President of Board of Trade; Abercorn, Lord-Lieutenant of Ireland.

In *Sept.* 1868 Wilson Patten succeeded Mayo as Secretary for Ireland, Colonel Taylor becoming Chancellor of the Duchy.

* In the Cabinet.

FOREIGN AND COLONIAL.

1867. By the British North America Act, Canada, Nova Scotia, and New Brunswick are united into the "Dominion of Canada."

1868. Abyssinian expedition.

[1866—1868]   ENGLISH.

PRIME MINISTERS. LORD RUSSELL. 1866.	*May.* Commercial panic in the City. The Bank Charter Act is suspended. **June. The Government is defeated by 11 (315 to 304) on Lord Dunkellin's amendment to the Reform Bill to substitute rating for rental. The ministry resign** (*June*).
LORD DERBY. 1867.	Lord Derby becomes Prime Minister (*a*). Reform demonstrations and riot in Hyde Park. *Feb.* **The new Government's Reform Bill is brought forward by Disraeli.** *March.* General Peel, Lord Carnarvon, and Lord Cranbourne resign on the Reform Bill question. Gladstone indicates various changes in the Government measure which will be necessary to make it a sound measure. Most of these are ultimately adopted. Mill's amendment in favour of female suffrage is rejected by 196 to 73. A clause granting minority representation to "three-cornered" constituencies is inserted by the Lords, on the motion of Lord Cairns, and accepted by the Commons. *July.* **The Reform Bill is read a third time without opposition.** *Aug.* **The Reform Bill passes the Lords** (protest signed by Lord Ellenborough) (*b*). *Sept.* Rescue of Fenian prisoners at Manchester. *Nov.* Parliament is called together to sanction the Abyssinian expedition to rescue English prisoners from King Theodore. *Dec.* Fenian outrage at Clerkenwell Prison, the explosion causing the loss of twelve lives. Trades-union outrages in Sheffield and elsewhere.
1868. DISRAELI.	Lord Derby resigns (*Feb.*). **Disraeli becomes Prime Minister** (*c*). Gladstone moves resolutions advocating the disestablishment of the Irish Church. *The Lords abandon the practice of voting by proxy.* *Election petitions are transferred from the House to be decided by the judges.* Gladstone carries a bill for the abolition of compulsory Church-Rates. *April.* Capture of Magdala, in Abyssinia, by British troops. **Gladstone carries his first resolution** (against the Government) by 65 (265 to 330). **Disraeli tenders his resignation, but agrees to appeal to the new constituencies in the autumn.** *June.* Gladstone's bill for suspending the exercise of

[Notes.]

(a) *Gladstone's Ministry.*—Gladstone,* First Lord of the Treasury; Lord Hatherley* (Page Wood), Lord Chancellor; Lord de Grey and Ripon* (created Marquis of Ripon 1871), President of Council; Earl of Kimberley* (formerly Lord Wodehouse), Privy Seal; Robert Lowe* (created Viscount Sherbrooke 1880), Chancellor of the Exchequer; Bruce* (created Lord Aberdare 1873), Home Secretary; Lord Clarendon,* Foreign Secretary; Lord Granville,* Colonial Secretary; Cardwell* (created Viscount Cardwell 1874), War Secretary; Duke of Argyll,* Indian Secretary; J. Bright,* Board of Trade; Lord Dufferin,* Duchy of Lancaster; Lord Hartington,* Postmaster-General; Childers,* Admiralty; Chichester Fortescue (created Lord Carlingford 1874), Secretary for Ireland; Earl Spencer, Lord-Lieutenant; Grant Duff, Under Secretary for India; Forster,* Vice-President of Privy Council (Cabinet 1870); Goschen,* Poor Law Board; Layard (succeeded by Ayrton 1869), Works.
On Lord Clarendon's death in 1870 Lord Granville* became Foreign Secretary; Lord Kimberley,* Colonial Secretary; Lord Halifax* (Sir C. Wood), Lord Privy Seal.
In *Jan.* 1871 Chichester Fortescue* succeeded Bright at the Board of Trade, Hartington* becoming Secretary for Ireland; Monsell, Postmaster-General; Knatchbull-Hugessen, Under Colonial Secretary; Lefevre, Under Home Secretary.
In *March* 1871 Goschen* succeeded Childers at the Admiralty; Stansfeld* became President of Poor Law Board; Baxter, Secretary to the Treasury; Lefevre, Secretary to the Admiralty; and Winterbotham, Under Home Secretary.
In *May* 1872 Childers* succeeded Dufferin as Chancellor of the Duchy, and in the same year Lansdowne succeeded Northbrook as Under War Secretary.
In *Oct.* 1872, on the resignation of Hatherley,* Roundell Palmer (created Lord Selborne), became Lord Chancellor.
In 1873 Ripon, Childers, Monsell, and Baxter retired; Bright* re-entered the ministry as Chancellor of the Duchy; Gladstone* took the Chancellorship of the Exchequer; Bruce* (created Lord Aberdare) was made President of the Council; Lowe,* Home Secretary; Ayrton, Judge Advocate-General; Adam, First Commissioner of Works; Dodson, Secretary to the Treasury; and Lyon Playfair, Postmaster-General.
* In the Cabinet.

(b) *Irish Church Act.*—By this Act—(1) The Irish Church was disestablished and became a free Episcopal Church, governed by a synod of clergy and laity. (2) The old Ecclesiastical Courts were abolished. (3) The Irish bishops lost their seats in the House of Lords. (4) The Maynooth grant to the Catholics and the *Regium Donum* to the Presbyterians were commuted. (5) The fabrics of the churches and cathedrals were handed over to the new Church. (6) All private endowments given since 1660 were handed over to the new Church. (7) The clergy and officials attached to the Church were compensated for their life-int. rest. (8) The remaining funds were to be applied, at the discretion of the Government of the day, to the relief of unavoidable suffering.
(c) See note (*a*), p. 212.
(d) See note (*b*), p. 212.

FOREIGN AND COLONIAL.

1869. Lord Mayo Viceroy of India (to 1872).
Nov. Opening of the Suez Canal.
Meeting of the Œcumenical Council at Rome, which declares (next year) the dogma of the infallibility of the Pope.
1870. *May.* Futile invasion of Canada by the Fenians.
July. War declared by France against Prussia.
Aug. Red River expedition.
Aug. Right wing of the French defeated at Wörth, the left at Forbach.
Aug. 14-18. Battles round Metz result in the siege of that town.
Sept. 1, 2. Battles round Sedan result in the surrender of the Emperor of the French and Macmahon's army.
Sept. Proclamation of the French Republic. Siege of Paris formed.
Sept. Italian troops enter Rome.
Oct. Surrender of Metz.
Oct. Prince Gortschakoff issues a circular stating that Russia will no longer be bound by the Treaty of 1856.

[1868—1870] ENGLISH.

PRIME MINISTERS. DISRAELI. 1868.	patronage in the Irish Church passes the Commons but is thrown out by the Lords. The Irish Reform Bill is passed, reducing the borough franchise, but leaving that of the counties unchanged. No redistribution of seats is effected. The Scottish Reform Bill is passed, giving seven additional members and reducing the franchise in counties and burghs. [*July* 31. End of the last Parliament elected under the Reform Bill of 1832.] *Nov.* **General election.** [Estimated strength of parties—Conservatives, 265; Liberals, 393.]
GLADSTONE.	*Dec.* **Resignation of Disraeli. Gladstone becomes Prime Minister** (*a*).
1869.	*March.* **A measure is introduced for the disestablishment and partial disendowment of the Irish Church** (*b*), the commutation of the Maynooth grant and the *Regium Donum*, and the subsequent organization of the Episcopal Church in Ireland. Second reading is passed by 368 to 250 (*March*), third reading by 361 to 247 (*May*); the second reading passes the Lords by 179 to 146 (*July*). The United States reject the settlement of the Alabama claims proposed by Lord Clarendon and Reverdy Johnson. The shilling duty still levied upon corn is abolished by Lowe's budget. The Endowed Schools Bill, founded on the report of the Schools Inquiry Commission, is passed, and the Endowed Schools Commission is appointed. The Scottish Education Bill, as amended by the Commons, is rejected by the Lords. Earl Russell's Life Peerage Bill is rejected by the Lords on the third reading by 106 to 77. The University Tests Abolition Bill is passed by the Commons, but rejected by the Lords by 91 to 54, and again in 1870. O'Donovan Rossa elected for Tipperary: his election is declared void, no felon being eligible.
1870.	*Feb.* **The Irish Land Act** (*c*) is introduced by Gladstone, and having passed both Houses of Parliament (second reading in the Commons by 442 to 11), receives the Royal Assent (*Aug.*). *Feb.* **The Elementary Education Act** (*d*) is introduced by Forster, and passes the second reading without a division. In committee the Cowper Temple clause is admitted by the Government, and the bill, after much opposition from the Nonconformists, headed by the "Birmingham League," passes the third reading, and is accepted by the Lords.

[Notes.]

(a) *Irish Land Act.*—By this Act—(1) The Ulster Tenant Right and similar customs in other parts of Ireland received a legal status. (2) New rights were conferred on tenants with reference to compensation for disturbance by the act of the landlord, except in the case of eviction for non-payment of rent. (3) Compensation was given for improvements. (4) Facilities were given for the loan by Government of two-thirds of the purchase-money to tenants desirous of buying their holdings from landlords who are willing to sell.

(b) *Elementary Education Act.*—By this Act, while the system of Government grants to schools supported by voluntary subscriptions is preserved, facilities are granted for the election, in districts where school accommodation is deficient, or where it is desired by the inhabitants, of a school board, which has the power to levy a rate and to erect and manage schools. All schools where religious instruction is given, and which receive a grant, are obliged to conform to a conscience clause. By the Cowper Temple clause " all catechisms and distinctive dogmatic formularies are excluded from rate-supported schools."

(c) *Objects of the Home Government Association* (from their resolutions):—
" It is hereby declared, as the essential principle of this Association, that the objects, and *the only objects*, contemplated by this Association are—
" To obtain for our country the right and privilege of managing our own affairs, by a Parliament assembled in Ireland, composed of her Majesty the Sovereign, and her successors, and the Lords and Commons of Ireland;
" To secure for that Parliament, under a federal arrangement, the right of legislating for and regulating all matters relating to the internal affairs of Ireland, and control over Irish resources and revenues, subject to the obligation of contributing our just proportion of the imperial expenditure;
" To leave to an Imperial Parliament the power of dealing with all questions affecting the Imperial Crown and Government, legislation regarding the colonies and other dependencies of the Crown, the relations of the United Empire with foreign states, and all matters appertaining to the stability of the Empire at large;
" To attain such an adjustment of the relations between the two countries, without any interference with the prerogatives of the Crown, or any disturbance of the principles of the Constitution."

FOREIGN AND COLONIAL.

1871. King William of Prussia takes the title of German Emperor.
Jan. 30. Capitulation of Paris.
Feb. Peace signed between France and Germany.
March 18. Outbreak of the revolt of the Commune in Paris. The second siege of Paris, by the Versailles troops, lasts from March 18 to May 21.

1872. Lord Mayo, Viceroy of India, is murdered. He is succeeded by Lord Northbrook (to 1876).
The Emperor of Germany by arbitration assigns the island of St. Juan, on the western coast of North America, to the United States.

[1870—1872] ENGLISH.

PRIME MINISTERS.
GLADSTONE.
1870.

Peace Preservation Act (Ireland) is passed.
Beaumont's bill for removing the bishops from the House of Lords is rejected by 158 to 102.
On the death of Lord Clarendon Lord Granville becomes Foreign Secretary (*July*); Lord Kimberley, Colonial Secretary; and Forster enters the Cabinet.
Aug. The majority of appointments in the Civil Service are thrown open to competition.
The Commander-in-chief is declared to be subject to the authority of the Secretary for War.
The Home Government Association (c), afterwards the Home Rule League, founded in Ireland.
A treaty is made with France and Germany to secure the neutrality of Belgium.

1871.

Jan. In the conference on the Treaty of Paris of 1856 England agrees to the abrogation of the clause which secured the neutrality of the Black Sea.
Feb. The Ballot Bill is introduced, and passes the second reading by 326 to 232 in the Commons, but is rejected by the Lords.
April. Lowe's proposed tax on lucifer matches is received with great disfavour and is withdrawn.
The bill to abolish religious tests at the Universities of Oxford and Cambridge is passed again by the Commons, and now passes the Lords.
May. The Treaty of Washington, by which it is agreed to submit the Alabama claims to arbitration, is concluded with the United States.
The bill for the better regulation of the army and the land forces of the Crown, which included among its provisions the abolition of the system of purchasing commissions in the army, passes the Commons. In the Lords, however, a motion of the Duke of Richmond postponing the purchase clause is carried. By the advice of ministers the Royal Warrant legalizing purchase is cancelled by the Queen. The Lords then pass the bill.
An Act is passed by which the Crown resumes the authority over the militia, yeomanry, and volunteers, which had formerly been vested in the lords-lieutenant of the counties.
Miall's motion to disestablish the remaining Established Churches of the United Kingdom is rejected by 374 to 89 (in 1873 by 356 to 61).
The dangerous illness of the Prince of Wales calls forth strong manifestations of loyalty.
[The Local Government Board, superseding and embodying the Poor Law Board of 1847, is constituted this year.]

1872.

The **Ballot Bill** having been again passed by the

[Notes.]

FOREIGN AND COLONIAL.

(a) *Irish University Bill.*—It was proposed (1) to combine Trinity College, Dublin, Maynooth, and the Colleges of Cork and Belfast into a new University capable of granting degrees; (2) to hand over the Theological Faculty of Trinity College, Dublin, to the Free Episcopal Church; (3) to exclude theology, moral philosophy, and history from the curriculum of the new University; (4) to create for the new University a governing body nominated in the first instance by the Act, but ultimately by the Crown, the Council, the Senate, and the Professors jointly; (5) to provide the funds of the new University partly from existing funds and partly from fees and Government aid.

(b) *Disraeli's Ministry.*—Disraeli,* First Lord of the Treasury; Lord Cairns,* Lord Chancellor; Duke of Richmond,* Lord President of the Council; Lord Malmesbury,* Lord Privy Seal; Lord Derby,* Foreign Secretary; Lord Salisbury,* Secretary for India; Lord Carnarvon,* Colonial Secretary; Gathorne Hardy * (Viscount Cranbrook 1878), Secretary for War; Cross,* Home Secretary; Ward Hunt,* Admiralty; Sir Stafford Northcote,* Chancellor of the Exchequer; Lord John Manners,* Postmaster-General; Lord Sandon, Vice-President of the Council; Duke of Abercorn, Lord-Lieutenant of Ireland; Sir M. Hicks Beach, Secretary for Ireland; Sir Charles Adderley (Lord Norton 1878), President of the Board of Trade; Sclater Booth, President of Local Government Board; Clare S. Read, Secretary of Local Government Board; Hon. R. Bourke, Under Secretary for Foreign Affairs; Lord George Hamilton, Under Secretary, India Office; W. H. Smith, Secretary to the Treasury.

In *July* 1876, on the resignation of Malmesbury, Lord Beaconsfield took the Privy Seal in addition to the First Lordship of the Treasury.

In *Nov.* 1876 Duke of Marlborough became Lord-Lieutenant of Ireland.

In *Aug.* 1877, on the death of Ward Hunt, W. H. Smith* became First Lord of the Admiralty, and F. Stanley Secretary to the Treasury.

In *Feb.* 1878, on the resignation of Lord Carnarvon, Hicks Beach* became Colonial Secretary, and Lowther* Secretary for Ireland; at the same time Northumberland * became Privy Seal.

In *April* 1878, on the resignation of Derby and Adderley, Salisbury* became Foreign Secretary; Hardy* (created Viscount Cranbrook), Secretary for India; F. Stanley,* War Secretary; Lord G. Hamilton, Vice-President of Privy Council; Sandon, President of the Board of Trade; Edward Stanhope, Under Secretary for India.

* In the Cabinet.

1873. The Ameer of Afghanistan is made dissatisfied by the result of some negotiations at Simla because the Viceroy refused to enter into a defensive alliance with him.

1874. War with Ashantee in defence of the Gold Coast Settlements is concluded.

PRIME MINISTERS. GLADSTONE. 1872.	Commons, is at length passed by the Lords, with a clause limiting its operation to eight years. The Geneva tribunal awards over £3,000,000 to the United States as damages due from England for the escape of the Alabama and other vessels employed by the Confederate States. A licensing Act is passed for the regulation of the sale of intoxicating liquors. *Nov.* A new commercial treaty made with France, somewhat modifying Cobden's treaty of 1860.
1873.	*Jan.* Death at Chislehurst of Napoleon III. *Feb.* Irish University Bill introduced. **The Supreme Court of Judicature Act** passes both Houses of Parliament. [See *Summary: Law Courts,* p. 256.] *March.* The Irish University Bill (*a*) is rejected on the second reading by 287 to 284. Ministerial crisis. **Gladstone resigns, but Disraeli refuses to take office.** Gladstone then agrees to remain in office, and the ministry is soon after reorganized. Lowe becomes Home Secretary; Gladstone Chancellor of the Exchequer as well as First Lord of the Treasury; Bruce, created Lord Aberdare, President of the Council; Bright, who had retired through ill-health (*Dec.* 1870), returns as Chancellor of the Duchy of Lancaster (*Sept.*) instead of Childers. Fawcett's Bill for the Abolition of Religious Tests at Dublin University is passed. *Nov.* The Irish Home Government Association hold a great meeting at Dublin, where the title of Home Rule League is taken. [See note 1870.]
1874. DISRAELI.	*Jan.* 24. Gladstone suddenly announces the dissolution of **Parliament.** *Feb.* General election. **Gladstone resigns and Disraeli becomes Prime Minister** (*b*). *Feb.* The new Parliament meets. [Estimated strength of parties — Conservatives, 350; Liberals, 244; Home Rulers, 58.] (During the last Parliament the Conservatives had lost 9 seats, the Liberals 32.) Lay patronage in the Scottish Church is transferred by Act of Parliament from the patrons to the male communicants of each kirk. A Licensing Act is passed, which slightly modifies the Act of 1872. *May.* Trevelyan's Bill for assimilating the County to the Borough Franchise is rejected by 287 to 173. The Public Worship Regulation Act is passed. *July.* Butt's motion on Home Rule is rejected by 458 to 61. Lord Sandon's Endowed Schools Act Amendment Bill

[Notes.]

FOREIGN AND COLONIAL.

(a) *Agricultural Holdings Act.*—It arranged for the compensation of agricultural tenants for unexhausted improvements in cases where landlords and tenants have not objected to coming under the Act.

1875. *Feb.* Colony of Fiji is constituted.
A central government is established for the whole of New Zealand.
July. Outbreak of the insurrection in Herzegovina.
Oct. The Prince of Wales starts on his Indian tour, and returns (*May*) 1876.
Andrassy Note submitted to the Powers by Austria.

1876. *Jan.* Lord Lytton becomes Viceroy (to 1880).
Carlist rebellion in Spain finally put down.
May. An insurrection in Bulgaria is put down by the Turks with great cruelty.
Abdul Aziz deposed in favour of Murad V., who in turn is deposed (*Aug.*) in favour of Abdul Hamid.
June. The Servians and Montenegrins declare war against Turkey, but are worsted.
Nov. In consequence of an ultimatum from Russia the Turks grant an armistice of six weeks to the Servians and Montenegrins. A Russian army is concentrated on the frontier.
Dec. Meeting of a European conference at Constantinople. New constitution proclaimed by Turkey.

Prime Ministers.	
DISRAELI. 1874.	is passed in a modified form, and transfers the powers of the Endowed Schools Commissioners to the Charity Commissioners.
1875.	*Jan.* Gladstone retires from the leadership of the Liberal party, and is replaced by the **Marquis of Hartington.**
	John Mitchel, who had been convicted of treason felony in 1848, and who had escaped from Tasmania, is re-elected member for Tipperary, *but the election was held void on the ground that a felon cannot sit in the House of Commons,* and the Dublin Court of Common Pleas assigns the seat to Captain Moore, the defeated candidate.
	The Artisans' Dwelling Act, introduced by Cross, is passed.
	The Regimental Exchanges Act is passed.
	The Peace Preservation Act (Ireland) is passed.
	Resolutions passed in the House of Commons that for the future strangers be excluded, not at the request of a single member, but on the vote of the majority of the House. The Speaker, however, still retains his power of closing the House.
	The Agricultural Holdings Act is passed (*a*).
	The Land Transfer Act, permitting holders of land, whether qualified or possessory, to register their titles, is passed.
	The Government having intimated their intention of allowing the Merchant Shipping Bill to drop, Plimsoll makes a personal attack upon some members of the House, and is forced to apologize. The Government then proceed with their bill, which is passed.
	A Slave Circular is issued, which orders officers to surrender slaves who have escaped on board a British man-of-war, when it is within the limits of the country from which they have escaped, on the demand being supported by the necessary proofs, and, in a revised version (*Oct.*), it is ordered that when the personal danger is over, the officer is no longer to permit the slave to remain on board.
	Nov. 1. The **High Court of Justice,** constituted by the Act of 1873, holds its first sitting.
	England purchases a number of shares in the Suez Canal.
1876.	*Jan.* Changes made in the relations between the Secretary of State for India and the Viceroy lead to the resignation of Lord Northbrook, who is succeeded by Lord Lytton.
	England agrees to the Andrassy Note, urging reform upon the Turks.
	The Additional Titles Bill, which enables the Queen to add to her other titles that of Empress of India, is passed.

[Notes.]

FOREIGN AND COLONIAL.

1876-78. Severe famine is prevalent in India.

(a) *County Franchise Bill.*—In 1872 it had been rejected by 148 to 70; in 1873 it was talked out; in 1874 it was rejected by 287 to 173; in 1875 by 268 to 166; in 1876 by 264 to 165. (In 1878 it was rejected by 271 to 219, in 1879 by 291 to 226.)

1877. *Jan.* 1. The Queen is proclaimed Empress of India at Delhi.
The proposals of the Conference of Constantinople rejected by Turkey.
April 12. Transvaal annexed.
April 24. Russian troops cross the Pruth and the Asiatic frontiers of Turkey. They are joined by the Roumanians and cross the Danube (*June*). For a time the Turks are successful, especially at Plevna; but after a severe defeat in Asia, Kars fell (*Nov.*), and Plevna (*Dec.*). The Russians then are joined by the Servians and Montenegrins. They advance through Bulgaria and threaten Constantinople (*Jan.* 1878).

PRIME MINISTERS. DISRAELI. 1876.		*April.* Dixon's bill for the establishment of compulsory school boards is rejected by 281 to 160. *May.* England refuses to accede to the Berlin Note, which urges upon Turkey the necessity of fulfilling her promises of reform. *May.* Lord Granville's resolution on the Burials question rejected by 148 to 92. *May.* The British fleet is sent to Besika Bay.
LORD BEACONSFIELD.		*Aug.* Disraeli is created **Earl of Beaconsfield**. Appellate Jurisdiction Act passed. An Elementary Education Act is passed, giving facilities for indirect compulsion. *Sept.* Gladstone, at Blackheath, advocates autonomous government for the Christian provinces of Turkey, and many meetings are held in the country to express indignation at the Bulgarian atrocities. *Sept.* 21. Lord Derby writes to Sir Henry Elliot at Constantinople, ordering him to lay before the Porte Baring's report on the Bulgarian atrocities, and to demand the punishment of the offenders. **Lord Salisbury** attends the European Conference at Constantinople. The Conference makes proposals for reform to Turkey, which are forestalled by the proclamation of a parliamentary constitution.
1877.		Failure of the Conference at Constantinople, and return of Lord Salisbury. England agrees to a European Protocol on Turkish affairs, which leads to no results. A South African Bill, to permit the colonies of Natal and the Cape of Good Hope, the Orange Free State and the Transvaal, to form a confederation, is introduced and ultimately passed. *April.* Shaw's motion for a select committee to inquire into the causes of the demand for Home Rule is rejected by 417 to 67. *May.* Gladstone's resolutions condemning the action of Turkey in regard to Lord Derby's note of September 1876 are rejected by 354 to 223. *June. Trevelyan's motion for extending county franchise is rejected by 274 to 218 (a).* *July.* During the debates on the South African Bill some of the Irish members, under Parnell, begin a series of manœuvres calculated to obstruct the business of the House of Commons, and on July 27 and 28 the House sits for twenty-six hours. Sir Stafford Northcote passes his *resolutions to the effect that when a member has been twice declared out of order by the Speaker, or by the Chairman of Committees, a motion may be made that the member be not heard during the remainder of the debate, and after the member complained of has been heard in*

[Notes.]

(a) *Treaty of San Stephano.*—The chief provisions of this treaty were these: A new self-governing state of Bulgaria was created, with a port on the Ægean Sea, and Russia received an accession of territory in Asia.

(b) *Treaty of Berlin.*—By this treaty (1) Bulgaria, north of the Balkans, was constituted an independent, autonomous, and tributary principality; (2) Bulgaria, south of the Balkans (Eastern Roumelia), was retained under the direct rule of the Porte, but was granted administrative autonomy; (3) the Porte retained the right of garrisoning the frontiers of Eastern Roumelia, but with regular troops only; (4) the Porte agreed to apply to Crete the organic law of 1868; (5) Montenegro was declared independent, and the seaport of Antivari was allotted to it; (6) Servia was declared independent, and received an accession of territory: (7) Roumania was declared independent, and received some islands on the Danube in exchange for Bessarabia; (8) Kars, Batoum, and Ardahan were ceded to Russia; (9) the Porte undertook to carry out without further delay the reforms required in Armenia; (10) in the event of the Greeks and the Porte not being able to agree upon a suggested rectification of frontier, the Powers reserved to themselves the right of offering their mediation.

(c) *Treaty of Gundamak.*—For £60,000 a year the Ameer agreed to receive an English envoy at Cabul, and to surrender the Kurum, Pishin, and Sibi valleys.

(d) *Irish University Act.*—By this Act (1) an examining body is created with power to confer degrees upon all approved persons, irrespective of their place of education; (2) these graduates, with the existing graduates of the Queen's University, are to form the Convocation of the new University; (3) the Senate of the new University are empowered to frame a scheme of exhibitions, prizes, and fellowships, and to ask Parliament to make a grant for their support.

FOREIGN AND COLONIAL.

1878. *March.* Treaty of San Stephano (a) signed by Russia and Turkey. Freedom of the native press abolished in India.
June. Meeting of the Berlin Congress, and Treaty of Berlin.
Shere Ali having received a Russian embassy at Cabul, a British envoy is sent, but is stopped at the Afghan frontier (*Sept.*). Invasion of Afghanistan. Capture of Ali Musjid and the Peiwar heights. Flight and death (1879) of the Ameer.

1879. Outbreak of the Zulu war. Defeat of the English at Isandhlwana (*Jan.*).
May. Treaty of Gundamak signed with Yakoob Khan, the new Ameer (c).
July. English victory over the Zulus at Ulundi.
Sept. The English envoy at Cabul, Sir Louis Cavagnari, having been murdered, the English again invade Afghanistan. English victory at Charasiab, and entry of Cabul.
Dec. Severe fighting in the neighbourhood of Cabul.

PRIME MINISTERS. LORD BEACONSFIELD. 1878.	*explanation, it be put to the vote without further debate.* *Jan.* 24. The British fleet is ordered to Constantinople. **Lord Carnarvon resigns.** Lord Derby threatens to resign. The order is countermanded. Vote of credit of £6,000,000 demanded from Parliament. *Feb.* The Fleet is sent to Constantinople. *March* 28. **Lord Derby leaves the ministry.** Lord Salisbury becomes Foreign Secretary. Lord Cranbrook (formerly Gathorne Hardy) becomes Indian Secretary, and Colonel Stanley Secretary for War. *April.* The reserves are called out. *April* 12. Adjournment of Parliament for Easter. *April* 13. Native troops from India ordered to Malta. Great agitation takes place against war with Russia. *May* 23. Hartington's motion condemning the employment of Indian troops out of India is rejected by 347 to 226. *May* 28. Death of Earl Russell. *May* 30. Secret treaty signed with Russia, agreeing to the annexation by Russia of Batoum, Kars, and Bessarabia, and the division of Bulgaria into two districts. *June.* **Lord Beaconsfield and Lord Salisbury attend the Congress of Berlin.** *June.* Secret treaty made with Turkey, agreeing to the occupation of Cyprus by the British on a guarantee for the integrity of the Asiatic dominions of Turkey. *July.* **Treaty of Berlin signed** (*b*). *Dec.* Parliament is summoned on account of the declaration of war against Afghanistan. A vote of censure on the Afghan policy of the Government is lost by 328 to 227.
1879.	Very severe distress in England owing to depression of trade. The Army Discipline and Regulation Bill is passed. The Irish University Act is passed (*d*). The office of Public Prosecutor is created. A commission is issued to inquire into the causes of agricultural depression. *Oct.* The Irish Land League is formed by Davitt. Anti-rent agitation begun in Ireland. Davitt and two other leaders are arrested, but released on bail. Gladstone visits Scotland and speaks against the Government.
1880.	Very severe distress both in England and Ireland. In consequence of the protraction of the debates on the Address and on the Distress Bill by the Irish members, a resolution is passed *enabling the House to suspend any member who has been named by the Speaker as guilty of wilful obstruction, and ordering*

[Notes.]

(a) *Gladstone's Ministry.*—Gladstone,* First Lord of the Treasury and Chancellor of the Exchequer; Lord Selborne,* Lord Chancellor; Lord Spencer,* President of the Council; Duke of Argyll,* Privy Seal; Lord Northbrook,* Admiralty; Sir W. Harcourt,* Home Secretary; Lord Granville,* Foreign Secretary; Childers,* War Secretary; Kimberley,* Colonial Secretary; Hartington,* Secretary for India; Bright,* Duchy of Lancaster; Chamberlain,* Board of Trade; Dodson,* Local Government Board; Forster,* Chief Secretary for Ireland; Fawcett, Postmaster-General; Adam, First Commissioner of Works; Wolverton, Paymaster; Mundella, Vice-President of Council; Osborne Morgan, Judge Advocate-General; Grant Duff, Under Colonial Secretary; Sir C. Dilke, Under Foreign Secretary; Lefevre, Secretary to the Admiralty; Earl Cowper, Lord-Lieutenant of Ireland.

In *Nov.* 1880 Lefevre became First Commissioner of Works, and Trevelyan Secretary to the Admiralty.

In *May* 1881, on the Duke of Argyll's resignation, Lord Carlingford* (Chichester Fortescue) became Privy Seal.

In *Aug.* 1881 Courtney succeeded Grant Duff as Under Colonial Secretary, and Lord Rosebery became Under Home Secretary.

In *May* 1882, on the resignation of Lord Cowper, Lord Spencer* became Lord-Lieutenaut of Ireland, and on the resignation of Forster, Lord F. Cavendish became Chief Secretary for Ireland. On the murder of Lord F. Cavendish, Trevelyan became Chief Secretary.

In *Dec.* 1882 Childers,* became Chancellor of Exchequer; Lord Hartington* War Secretary; Lord Derby* became Colonial Secretary; Lord Kimberley,* Secretary for India; Sir Charles Dilke * succeeded Dodson as President of the Local Government Board; Dodson* became Chancellor of the Duchy of Lancaster (Bright having retired in July).

In *March* 1883 Lord Carlingford became Lord President of Council.

In *Oct.* 1884 Trevelyan * became Chancellor of the Duchy of Lancaster, and Campbell-Bannerman, Chief Secretary for Ireland.

In *Nov.* 1884 Shaw Lefevre became Postmaster-General (on Fawcett's death).

In *Feb.* 1885 Lord Rosebery* became Privy Seal and Chief Commissioner of Works, and Shaw Lefevre * entered the Cabinet.

* In the Cabinet.

(b) In the late Parliament, at its dissolution, there were 351 Conservatives, 250 Liberals, and 51 Home Rulers.

(c) *Compensation for Disturbance Clause.*—It allotted to tenants evicted for non-payment of rent the compensation due to them had they left for other causes, and its operation was limited to the years 1880 and 1881. [See note 1870.]

FOREIGN AND COLONIAL.

1880. Marquis of Ripon, Viceroy of India.

April. In Afghanistan English victorious at Ahmed Kiel. *July* 22. Abdurrahman is recognised as Ameer.

July. English are defeated at Maiwand by Ayub Khan, son of Shere Ali. March of Roberts from Cabul to Candahar, and victory of Pir Paimal.

The Berlin Conference decided that Dulcigno should be handed over by Turkey to Montenegro, and that Greece should receive an accession of territory. To enforce this decision the allied fleet sails to Dulcigno, which is handed over to the Montenegrins (*Nov.*).

Turkey agrees to hand over part of Thessaly to Greece, and the Greek troops take possession (*Aug.*).

The Boers of the Transvaal revolt (*Dec.*).

[1880, 1881] *ENGLISH.*

PRIME MINISTERS. LORD BEACONSFIELD. 1880. GLADSTONE. 1881.	that if a member be suspended three times in one session, his suspension shall continue for a week, and as much longer as the House shall determine. The Relief of Distress Act for Ireland is passed. A bill introduced by Cross for consolidating the London Waterworks causes a great rise in the value of the shares of the companies. *March.* **Dissolution of Parliament** and general election. *April.* **Resignation of Lord Beaconsfield.** The Queen sends for Lord Hartington, and the next day for Lord Granville and Lord Hartington. Gladstone is then called upon to form a ministry (*a*). *April* 29. Meeting of the new Parliament. [Estimated strength of parties—243 Conservatives, 349 Liberals, 60 Home Rulers (*b*).] Goschen is despatched on a special mission to Constantinople. A circular is sent by Lord Granville to the European Powers proposing a conference to secure the fulfilment of the unfulfilled parts of the Treaty of Berlin. Bradlaugh having been elected for Northampton, and claiming to make an affirmation of allegiance instead of taking the oath, is allowed, after long discussion, to do so on his own responsibility, but it is decided by the courts of law that he is not eligible to make such an affirmation. Government announce their intention of not renewing the Irish Peace Preservation Act. A second Relief of Distress Act for Ireland is passed. A clause of this Act, known as the compensation for disturbance clause (*c*), is passed by the Commons by 303 to 237, but is rejected by the Lords by 282 to 51 (*Aug.*). The malt tax is abolished by Gladstone and a tax on beer substituted. Sir Wilfrid Lawson's resolution in favour of "Local Option" is carried by 229 to 203. The Burials Bill, granting relief to Nonconformists, is carried (second reading) by 196 to 77. The Ground Game Act is passed to secure farmers' crops from the depredations of hares and rabbits. The Employers' Liability Act is passed. Great agitation in Ireland, in consequence of evictions for non-payment of rent, organized by the Land League. Many agrarian outrages. Prosecution of Parnell and others for conspiring to incite breaches of the law. *Jan.* 6. Parliament meets. In the Irish State trial of Parnell and others the jury cannot agree upon a verdict and are discharged.

[Notes.]

(a) *Irish Land Bill.*—It provides that (1) any existing tenant may sell his interest in his holding to the best bidder, and that the purchaser acquires all the rights of the seller as a *present tenant*. (2) Every present tenant (or his assignee) has a right to apply to a court to fix a *judicial rent*, subject to statutory conditions. This judicial rent cannot be altered for fifteen years ; nor can the tenant be disturbed (except by his own act). At the end of fifteen years the tenant can apply for another term, subject to revision of rent. (3) The breach of any of the *statutory conditions* involves the determination of the *present tenancy* by compulsory sale, and the new tenant comes in without the rights of a *present tenant*.
(Future tenants are those who enter into tenancies not now existing.)
These are the main provisions, and there are details giving special safeguards — (1) English-managed estates are exempted from the Act. (2) The landlord may object to a new tenant, and he has rights of pre-emption and resumption under conditions to be judged by the court. There are also provisions for the establishment of peasant proprietors, of perpetual leaseholders on fee-farm rent, for assisting emigration, and for the benefit of the labourers.
[See notes on 1860, 1870, and 1880.]

(b) " Two regiments of the line and two regiments of militia constitute one territorial regiment of four battalions : these new regiments take their title from the country or district of their depôt, and in every respect they are assimilated as much as possible."—*Childers.*

FOREIGN AND COLONIAL.

1881. The English troops, advancing to the Transvaal, are defeated at Laing's Nek (*Jan.*) and Majuba Hill (*Feb.*).
March. An armistice made with the Boers, who agree to accept self-government under the suzerainty of Great Britain.
March. Assassination of Alexander, Czar of Russia.
Candahar is handed over to the Ameer of Afghanistan.
April. The French land troops in Tunis, and occupy all Tunisian territory.
Sept. Death of President Garfield from the wound of an assassin.
Sept. Ayoub Khan is defeated by Abdurrahman Khan.
Nov. Gambetta becomes Prime Minister of France.
1882. *Jan.* Fall of Gambetta.
Arabi Bey (afterwards Arabi Pasha), a colonel in the Egyptian army, having become Under-Secretary for War, begins to plot against the power of the Khedive and the influence of England and France in Egyptian affairs.
April. A plot is discovered in Egypt to assassinate Arabi Pasha, the head of the army and leader of the national party in Egypt.
May. Arabi Pasha convokes the Notables because the sentence up-

PRIME MINISTERS.
GLADSTONE.
1881.

Protection for Life and Property (Ireland) Bill introduced by Forster. *Feb.* 2. After a sitting of forty-one hours, largely occupied by obstruction, the Speaker declares that "a new and exceptional course is demanded," and at once puts the first reading of the bill, which is carried.
Feb. 3. Thirty-six Irish members, defying the Speaker's authority, are one by one suspended and removed from the House.
Feb. Resolutions are carried giving the Speaker special powers to restrict discussion when "urgency" has been voted in debate.
March. Protection of Life and Property Bill, and Peace Preservation (Ireland) Bill, passed.
April. Irish Land Bill introduced by Gladstone. Resignation of the Duke of Argyll.
April. Death of **Lord Beaconsfield.**
Aug. The **Irish Land Bill** (a) passes the Commons, and after some alteration in detail by the Lords, receives the Royal Assent.
The Regulation of the Forces Act and the Army Act are passed (b).
Oct. 13. Arrest of Parnell and other members of the Land League. Issue of the No-Rent Manifesto (*Oct.* 18). Proclamation of the Land League as "an illegal and criminal association" (*Oct.* 20).

1882.

Feb. Bradlaugh is forbidden, by 286 to 228, "to go through the form of repeating the words of the oath."
Feb. 17. The Lords appoint a committee, by 96 to 53, to "inquire into the Irish Land Act, and its effect on the condition of the country."
Feb. 20. Gladstone brings in his first rule on procedure in the House of Commons.
Feb. 21. Bradlaugh takes the oath on a copy of the New Testament which he had brought with him, and is expelled, by 297 to 80, for violating the orders of the House, and a new writ for Northampton is ordered.
Feb. 27. Gladstone's motion condemning the House of Lord's committee on the Irish Land Act is carried by 300 to 167.
March 2. Bradlaugh is re-elected for Northampton. The resolution of February in his case is reaffirmed.
May. Resignation of Lord Cowper and Forster, Lord-Lieutenant and Chief Secretary for Ireland.
Gladstone announces that Parnell, Dillon, and O'Kelly, three Irish members, have been released, and that a measure is to be brought in "to strengthen the law and remove the difficulties in the way of the administration of justice."

[Notes.]

(a) *Extract from Lord Granville's despatch to Lord Dufferin, July 11.*

"Her Majesty's Government look upon the action thus taken (the Admiral's notice on July 10th that he would open fire in twenty-four hours unless the forts, on which hostile preparations had been made, were disarmed) as no more than a matter of simple and legitimate self-defence. The military authorities at Alexandria had persisted in preparations of a threatening character in defiance of the orders of the Sultan, of the wish of the Khedive, and in contravention of their own explicit assurances. . . . Her Majesty's Government now see no alternative but a recourse to force to put an end to a state of affairs which has become intolerable. In their opinion it would be most convenient . . . that the force to be so employed should be that of the sovereign power. If this method of procedure should prove impracticable, in consequence of unwillingness on the part of the Sultan, it will become necessary to devise other measures. Her Majesty's Government continues to hold the view . . . that any intervention in Egypt should represent the united action and authority of Europe."

(b) The object of the Bill was to entitle tenants to receive compensation from landlords for certain kinds of improvements on the termination of their tenancies, without power to the parties to contract out of the Act.

FOREIGN AND COLONIAL.

on those who plotted against him had been commuted by the Khedive.
May 20. English and French fleets arrive at Alexandria.
May 26. Resignation of the ministry of Arabi Pasha, who keeps command of the army.
June 7. Dervish Pasha arrives in Egypt, sent by the Sultan, but fails to re-establish the Khedive's authority.
June 11. Outbreak in Alexandria and murder of some Europeans.
Arabi Pasha banished from Egypt for life.
Dec. Death of Gambetta.

1883. French War with Madagascar begins.
Nov. 1. The army of Hicks Pasha was almost destroyed in the Soudan by the forces of the Mahdi.

1884. The Ilbert Bill passed by the Legislative Council of India.

Prime Ministers.	
GLADSTONE. 1882.	*May* 4. Lord Spencer becomes Lord-Lieutenant and Lord F. Cavendish Chief Secretary for Ireland. *May* 6. Murder of Lord F. Cavendish and of Burke, the Permanent Secretary, in Phœnix Park, Dublin. Trevelyan becomes Chief Secretary. *May* 11. The Prevention of Crimes Bill (Ireland) is introduced; passes second reading by 383 to 45. *May* 15. The Arrears Bill (Ireland) is introduced; passes second reading by 269 to 157. *June* 30 and *July* 1. All-night sitting of the House of Commons. Suspension of twenty-five Irish members for obstructing the passage of the Prevention of Crimes Bill through committee. *July* 11. Fortifications of Alexandria bombarded and destroyed by the British fleet (*a*). *July* 15. Bright leaves the ministry. *Aug.* Landing of British army in Egypt, and occupation of Suez Canal. *Sept.* 13. Complete defeat of Arabi's army at Tel-el-Kebir by the British army under Sir Garnet Wolseley. Arabi taken prisoner at Cairo. Autumn session of Parliament. *Nov.* 10. Gladstone's resolution on Procedure in the House of Commons (arranging for the closing of debate, under certain conditions, provided that the motion for closing be not decided in the affirmative unless supported by more than 200, or opposed by less than 40 and supported by more than 100, members) is carried by 304 to 260. Several other Procedure Rules are passed.
1883.	*Feb.* Healy and Davitt imprisoned for six months, of which they served four. *March.* Explosion at Local Government Board Offices. Explosives Bill passed through Parliament. *March.* Two Grand Committees appointed in the House of Commons, one for Law and Justice, the other for Trade, Shipping, and Manufactures. *April.* Trial of Invincibles for murder of Lord F. Cavendish and Burke. Five men are convicted. *May* 3. Affirmation Bill rejected by 292 to 289. *May.* Government proposals as to a second Suez Canal ultimately abandoned in consequence of great opposition. The Corrupt Practices Bill is passed. The Agricultural Holdings Bill (*b*) is passed. The Bankruptcy Bill and the Patent Law Bill (after passing through the Grand Committee) are passed.
1884.	*Jan.* General Gordon is sent by the Government to Khartoum to arrange for the withdrawal of the Egyptian garrisons from the Soudan.

[Notes.]

(a) *Lord Cairns' amendment was as follows*:—"That this House, while prepared to concur in a well-considered and complete scheme for the extension of the franchise, does not think it right to assent to the second reading of a Bill having for its object a fundamental change in the electoral body, which is not accompanied by provisions which will ensure the full and free representation of the people, or by any adequate security that the Bill shall not come into operation except on an entire scheme."

FOREIGN AND COLONIAL.

1884. New Convention with the Transvaal signed.

Annexation of Merv by Russia.

French war with China.

Sir C. Warren is despatched to Bechuanaland.

Lord Dufferin appointed Viceroy of India.

Cleveland elected President of the United States.

1885. *Jan.* 26*th*. Fall of Khartoum.

[1884—1885.] ENGLISH.

PRIME MINISTERS.
GLADSTONE.
1884.

Feb. Bradlaugh, having administered the oath to himself, is excluded from the precincts of the House. He resigns his seat, and is re-elected by an increased majority.
Feb. Vote of Censure on Government for conduct of Egyptian affairs carried in Lords by 181 to 81, and lost in the Commons by 311 to 262.
Feb. Baker Pasha's native army routed near Trinkitat, south of Suakim. Fall of Sinkat and Tokar.
Feb. and Mar. Defeats of Osman Digna by Gen. Graham.
Feb. 29. Franchise Bill introduced (based on uniform household and lodger franchise in counties and boroughs).
March. A Royal Commission appointed on the Housing of the Poor.
April 27. Lord J. Manners' amendment to the Franchise Bill lost by 340 to 210.
May 2. Second Vote of Censure on Government for conduct of Egyptian affairs defeated in Commons by 303 to 275.
May 16. Lord C. Hamilton's amendment to leave out Ireland from the Franchise Bill beaten by 332 to 137.
June. A Conference, about the affairs of Egypt, of representatives of the Great Powers, assembles under the presidency of Lord Granville, but breaks up without result.
July 6. Cairns' amendment (a) to the second reading of the Franchise Bill in the Lords is carried by 205 to 146.
Gladstone announces his intention to bring forward the Franchise Bill again in an Autumn Session.
Many demonstrations for and against the action of the House of Lords are held throughout the country.
Lord Wolseley is sent to Egypt, and enters the Soudan (Aug.) with British troops.
Oct. 23. Opening of Autumn Session.
Oct. 24. Franchise Bill re-introduced in unaltered form. Second reading carried by 372 to 232. The Bill passes the third reading without a division. A compromise between the Houses is effected, and a Redistribution Bill is drafted by the leaders of both parties in consultation. The Franchise Bill becomes law on Dec. 6th.

1885.

Jan. 14. Gen. Herbert Stewart defeats a large force of Arabs at Abu Klea.
Jan. 19. After severe fighting, a position is secured at Gubat, where steamers from General Gordon arrive.
Jan. 24. Dynamite explosion at the Tower and the House of Commons.
Jan. 26. Khartoum is surrendered to the Mahdi, and Gordon is killed.

[Notes.]

FOREIGN AND COLONIAL.

(a) *The Redistribution Scheme was as follows :—*
  1. All boroughs with pop. under 15,000 disfranchised and merged in county districts.
  2. All towns with pop. under 50,000 to be represented by one member only.
  The effect of this change was to extinguish 160 seats. Towns between 50 and 165,000 inhabitants to be represented by 2 members; and with these exceptions and that of the City of London, the system of single member districts to be universal.
  (See Appendix III.)

(b) *Salisbury's Ministry.*—Lord Salisbury,* Foreign Secretary; Lord Halsbury,* Lord Chancellor; Lord Cranbrook,* President of the Council; Lord Harrowby,* Privy Seal; Sir M. Hicks Beach,* Chancellor of the Exchequer; Sir R. Cross,* Home Secretary; Sir F. Stanley,* Colonial Secretary; W. H. Smith,* War Secretary; Lord R. Churchill,* Secretary for India; Duke of Richmond,* Secretary for Scotland; Lord George Hamilton,* Admiralty; Lord Iddesleigh,* First Lord of the Treasury; Lord Carnarvon,* Lord-Lieutenant of Ireland; Lord Ashbourne,* Lord Chancellor of Ireland; Stanhope,* Board of Trade; Lord J. Manners,* Postmaster-General; Balfour, Local Government Board; Chaplin, Duchy of Lancaster; Sir H. Holland, Vice-President of the Council; Plunket, Works and Public Buildings; Ritchie, Secretary to the Admiralty; Bourke, Under Foreign Secretary; Sir R. Webster, Attorney-General; Sir J. Gorst, Solicitor-General; Sir W. Hart Dyke, Chief Secretary for Ireland.
In *Jan.* 1886 Lord Carnarvon resigns the Lord-Lieutenancy, and Sir W. Hart Dyke, the Chief Secretaryship of Ireland; W. H. Smith becomes Chief Secretary, and Lord Cranbrook War Secretary.

* In the Cabinet.

1885. *May.* Riel's rebellion in Manitoba put down by the Canadian forces.

June. Death of the Mahdi.

Sept. Union of Bulgaria and Eastern Roumelia under Prince Alexander effected.

Nov. Upper Burmah invaded by British troops, and King Theebau dethroned.

Nov. Servians invade Bulgaria, but are repulsed.

PRIME MINISTERS. **GLADSTONE.** 1885.	*Jan.* 28. Sir C. Wilson approaches Khartoum with a small force in two steamers, but, finding that he is too late, retires. *Feb.* British troops are sent to Suakim to cross the desert to Berber. A Colonial force arrives from New South Wales to give assistance in Egypt. The Berber expedition is abandoned later on. The Mahdi's influence breaks down, and the troops are gradually withdrawn from the Soudan. *Feb.* 24. Considerable difficulties arise in connection with the Afghanistan Boundary Commission. Russia refuses to withdraw from advanced posts. *Feb.* 26. Vote of Censure on Egyptian policy of Government lost by 302 to 288 in Commons, and carried in Lords by 189 to 68. *March* 16. An agreement between Russia and England is drawn up. *March* 30. Russian forces occupy Penjdeh, after an engagement with the Afghans. In view of possible war with Russia, war preparations are actively pushed forward. *April* 21. Gladstone asks for a vote of credit of 11 millions, 4½ for the Soudan, 6½ for special military and naval preparations. *May* 4. Gladstone announces that Russia and England are ready to refer their differences to the arbitration of a friendly state. The Redistribution Bill is considered in detail, and finally passes in June (*a*). Gladstone announces that some provisions of the Crimes Act (Ireland) will be re-enacted, and an Irish Land Purchase Bill introduced. *June* 8. Sir M. Hicks Beach's resolution (condemning the Budget proposals for an increase of the Beer and Spirit duties and the Death duties) is carried by 264 to 252 (39 Irish Home Rulers voting in the majority). Gladstone resigns. Salisbury becomes Prime Minister (*b*).
SALISBURY.	A Land Purchase (Ireland) Bill, commonly called Lord Ashbourne's Bill, is passed. The Crimes Act (Ireland) is not renewed. A Criminal Law Amendment Act for the protection of young girls is passed. *Nov.* 21. Irish Nationalists ask Irish voters to vote against Liberal candidates. *Nov. and Dec.* General Election. Estimated results: Liberals 335, Conservatives 249, Irish Home Rulers 86. *Dec.* Rumoured acceptance by Gladstone of the principle of Home Rule.

[Notes.]

(a) *Gladstone's Ministry.*—Gladstone,* First Lord of the Treasury and Privy Seal; Lord Herschell,* Lord Chancellor; Lord Spencer,* President of the Council; Sir W. Vernon Harcourt,* Chancellor of the Exchequer; Childers,* Home Secretary; Lord Rosebery,* Foreign Secretary; Lord Granville,* Colonial Secretary; Campbell Bannerman,* War Secretary; Lord Kimberley,* Secretary for India; Trevelyan,* Secretary for Scotland; Lord Ripon,* Admiralty; Morley,* Chief Secretary for Ireland; Mundella,* Board of Trade; Chamberlain,* Local Government Board; Heneage, Duchy of Lancaster; Lord Wolverton, Postmaster-General; Sir Lyon Playfair, Vice-President of Council; H. Fowler, Financial Secretary to the Treasury; Hibbert, Secretary to the Admiralty; Broadhurst, Under Home Secretary; Bryce, Under Foreign Secretary; Osborne Morgan, Under Colonial Secretary; Sir U. J. Kay-Shuttleworth, Under Secretary for India; J. Collings, Secretary to the Local Government Board; Sir Charles Russell, Attorney-General; Sir Horace Davey, Solicitor-General; Lord Aberdeen, Lord-Lieutenant of Ireland.
In *March* Stansfeld* becomes President of Local Government Board, and Lord Dalhousie, Secretary of Scotland, Chamberlain and Trevelyan having resigned.
* In the Cabinet.

(b) *Home Rule Bill for Ireland.*—The following are some among the chief provisions of the Bill:—
An Irish Legislature to sit in Dublin, with the Queen as its head, to consist of 309 members, 103 in the first order (with property qualification, and elected on £25 franchise) and 206 in the second order, the two orders to sit together and, unless a separate vote is demanded, to vote together. If the two orders disagree, the matter is vetoed for three years. If then carried by the second order it shall be decided by a majority of both orders.
The Lord-Lieutenant to be appointed by the Crown, not as the representative of a party. His office cannot be altered by the Irish Legislature; he can assent to or veto any Bill. The Executive to be constituted as in England. All constitutional difficulties to be settled by the Privy Council, whose decision is final.
The prerogatives of the Crown to be untouched. All matters concerning peace or war, Foreign and Colonial relations, trade, navigation, post, and telegraphs, coinage, army, navy, and reserve forces, to remain in the hands of the Imperial Parliament.
The Irish Legislature not to establish or endow any religion, or to prohibit religious freedom.
The customs and excise to be levied by the British Treasury.
The rights of existing civil servants, judges, and other permanent officials and police to be safe-guarded.
The Irish Legislature can raise and pay a police force.
The Irish members not to sit at Westminster except when summoned back for special purposes. This Act not to be altered unless they are so summoned back (28 to the Lords, 103 to the Commons).
Ireland to pay one-fifteenth as her portion of interest on National Debt, of Army, and Navy, and Civil Service charges, and £1,000,000 toward present Irish Constabulary till superseded.

(c) For notes (c) (d) (e) See p. 234.

FOREIGN AND COLONIAL.

1886. Annexation of Upper Burmah to the British Empire formally proclaimed.

Peace signed between Servia and Bulgaria.

April. Greece is restrained by the Great Powers from attacking Turkey.

May. Socialist riots in Chicago.

227 e

[1886.]   ENGLISH.

PRIME MINISTERS.
SALISBURY.
1886.

Jan. 12. Parliament meets.
Bradlaugh takes the oath, and the question is allowed to drop.
Royal Commission on Elementary Education Acts appointed.
Lord Carnarvon resigns the Lord-Lieutenancy of Ireland, and Sir W. Hart Dyke the Chief Secretaryship. W. H. Smith goes to Ireland as Chief Secretary.
Jan. 26. Lord R. Churchill announces that the Government will introduce a Bill to suppress the National League.
Jesse Collings's Amendment to the Address, regretting that no measure about allotments for labourers had been announced, is carried by 331 to 252.
Lord Hartington, Goschen, and 16 other Liberals voting in the minority.
Lord Salisbury resigns, and Gladstone forms a Government (*a*), Feb. 1st.

GLADSTONE.

Feb. 8. A meeting of unemployed is held in Trafalgar Square, which ends with a procession westwards and the pillaging and wrecking of many shops.
Feb. 18. Parliament meets.
Feb. 25. Scotch Crofters Bill introduced, and afterwards passed.
March 26. Chamberlain, Trevelyan, Heneage and Collings leave the Government owing to their disapproval of Gladstone's proposed Irish Policy.
April 8. Gladstone introduces the Home Rule Bill for Ireland (*b*).
April 14. Meeting of Unionist Liberals and Conservatives at Her Majesty's Theatre. Speeches by Lord Hartington, Lord Salisbury, and others.
April 16. Gladstone introduces the Land Purchase Bill (*c*).
May 1. Manifesto issued by Gladstone to his constituents (*d*).
May 5. At a meeting of the National Federation of Liberal Associations, otherwise known as the Birmingham Caucus, Chamberlain's party are defeated.
May 10. Second Reading of Home Rule Bill moved.
May 14. Meeting at Devonshire House of about seventy Liberal members who disapprove of the Bill.
May 15. Lord Salisbury states his alternative policy (*e*).
May 27. Meeting of Liberals at Foreign Office, at which Gladstone, after dealing with the question of the supremacy of Parliament and the retention of Irish members, says that those who do not altogether agree with the Bill may vote for its second reading, and are not bound to vote for the Land Purchase Bill—and that the Bill, if passed, shall be re-introduced in the autumn.

[Notes.]

(c) *Land Purchase Bill.*—Irish landlords are to have the option of selling, their tenants having no power to force or prevent the sale. The price to be fixed by a Land Commission; the normal price to be 20 years' purchase of the *net* rental (outgoings estimated at 20 per cent.); in exceptional cases it may rise to 22 years, and may fall below 20 years. If the land is nearly valueless the State Authority may refuse the offer. In certain cases, where the annual value is below £4, the State Authority may become the owner.

When the price is fixed the tenant shall become the freeholder, subject to the payment of a terminable annuity (of which he may pay off the whole or part at any time) for 49 years, equal to 4 per cent. on the capitalised value at 20 years' purchase of the former rent. The annuity is to be collected by the State Authority, and the surplus applied to the purposes of the Irish Government.

The British Treasury to advance a sum not exceeding £50,000,000 up to March 1890. The Irish State Authority to pay 4 per cent. on the loan (the stock to be redeemed by a terminable annuity for 49 years). To obtain security for the loan, the British Government is to appoint a Receiver-General, through whose hands the whole of the Irish Revenues shall pass.

(d) "On the side adverse to the Government are found, as I sorrowfully admit, in profuse abundance, station, title, wealth, social influence, the professions, or the large majority of them—in a word, the spirit and power of class. These are the main body of the opposing host. Nor is this all. As knights of old had squires, so in the great army of class each enrolled soldier has, as a rule, dependants. The adverse host, then, consists of class and the dependants of class. ... We have had great controversies before this great controversy—on free trade, free navigation, public education, religious equality in civil matters, extension of the suffrage to its present basis. On these and many other great issues the classes have fought uniformly on the wrong side, and have uniformly been beaten by a power more difficult to marshal, but resistless when marshalled—by the upright sense of the nation."

(e) "My alternative policy is that Parliament should enable the Government of England to govern Ireland; apply that recipe honestly, consistently, and resolutely for twenty years, and at the end of that time you will find that Ireland will be fit to accept any gifts in the way of local government or repeal of coercion laws that you may wish to give her. What she wants is government—government that does not flinch, that does not vary; government that she cannot hope to beat down by agitations at Westminster; government that is not altered in its resolutions or its temperature by the party changes which take place at Westminster."

(a) *Salisbury's Ministry.*—Lord Salisbury,* First Lord of the Treasury; Lord Iddesleigh,* Foreign Secretary; Lord Halsbury,* Lord Chancellor; Lord Cranbrook,* President of the Council; Lord Cadogan,* Privy Seal; Lord R. Churchill,* Chancellor of the Exchequer; Matthews,* Home Secretary; Stanhope,* Colonial Secretary; W. H. Smith,* War

FOREIGN AND COLONIAL.

1886. *June.* French flag hoisted at the New Hebrides.
Members of families who have reigned in France expelled from that country by a vote of the Chambers.

July. Russia closed Batoum as a free port.

Aug. Prince Alexander of Bulgaria seized by conspirators and conveyed across the frontier.

Sept. Prince Alexander returns to Sophia, but abdicates in deference to the wishes of Russia.

[1886—1887.]   ENGLISH.

PRIME MINISTERS.
GLADSTONE.
1886.

SALISBURY.

1887.

June 7. The Second Reading of the Home Rule Bill is lost by 341 to 311, 93 Liberals voting in the majority. Very serious riots take place in Belfast.
June 25. The Session ends, and an appeal to the country is made.
July. General Election. Estimated result: 316 Conservatives, 191 Home Rule Liberals, 78 Liberal Unionists, 85 Irish Home Rulers.
Gladstone resigns. Lord Salisbury becomes Prime Minister (*a*). He urges Lord Hartington to form a Ministry, but Lord Hartington declines.
Aug. 5. Parliament meets, Lord R. Churchill becomes leader of the House of Commons.
Aug. 19. Lord R. Churchill announces that Sir R. Buller will be sent to the West of Ireland; that a Royal Commission will be appointed to inquire into the working of the Land Acts of 1881 and 1885, and another Royal Commission to inquire into the resources of Ireland. He says that in February the Government hope to bring forward definite proposals on Local Government in Ireland
Sep. 21. Parnell's Tenant's Relief Bill (providing for abatement of rent of tenants whose rent was fixed before 1885, if proved unable to pay, and if half the rent and arrears were paid) rejected by 297 to 202.
Sir M. Hicks-Beach tries to bring pressure to bear upon landlords to stay evictions.
Oct. 17. The "Plan of Campaign" is announced at Woodford, on Lord Clanricarde's estate in Galway, where the tenants were being threatened with evictions for not paying rents which they said were impossible. It is formally published in *United Ireland*, Oct. 23. See (*b*), p. 227 *i*.
Dec. 23. Lord Randolph Churchill's resignation is announced, on the ground that he is not supported in a policy of retrenchment.
Jan. 3. Goschen accepts the post of Chancellor of Exchequer.
Jan. 13. Evictions on title at Glenbeigh carried out with great severity.
Jan. 14. Meeting of Round Table Conference (a conference on Irish affairs between Lord Herschell, Sir W. V. Harcourt, Morley, Chamberlain, and Sir G. Trevelyan, which ultimately came to nothing).
Jan. 27. Parliament meets. W. H. Smith becomes leader of the House of Commons.
Feb. 17. The Debate on the Address brought to a close by the Closure.
Feb. 21. New Rules of Procedure (closing debate by a bare majority, on the motion of any member, if the

227 *h*

[Notes.]

Secretary; Loru Cross,* Secretary for India; Lord G. Hamilton,* Admiralty; Lord Ashbourne,* Lord Chancellor of Ireland; Sir M. Hicks-Beach,* Chief Secretary for Ireland; Lord Stanley of Preston,* Board of Trade; Lord J. Manners,* Duchy of Lancaster; Ritchie,* Local Government Board; Raikes, Postmaster-General; Sir H. Holland, Vice-President of the Council; Plunket, Works and Public Buildings; Jackson, Financial Secretary to the Treasury; Sir J. Fergusson, Under Foreign Secretary; Sir J. Gorst, Under Secretary for India; Baron de Worms, Secretary to Board of Trade; Long, Secretary to Local Government Board; Sir R. Webster, Attorney-General; Sir E. Clarke, Solicitor-General; A. J. Balfour, Secretary for Scotland; Lord Londonderry, Lord-Lieutenant of Ireland.

In *Jan.* 1887, Goschen* became Chancellor of the Exchequer, Lord R. Churchill having resigned; Mr. W. H. Smith* became First Lord of the Treasury; Stanhope,* War Secretary; Lord Salisbury,* Foreign Secretary (Lord Iddesleigh declining to remain in the Cabinet); Sir H. Holland,* Colonial Secretary.

In *March* A. J. Balfour* became Secretary for Ireland (Sir M. Hicks-Beach having resigned); Lord Lothian became Secretary for Scotland.

* In the Cabinet.

(*b*) The following are extracts from the document which expounded the Plan of Campaign.

"The first question they have to consider is:—1. *How to meet the November demand.*—In a few weeks at most the agents will issue intimations from the rent office. . . . Should combinations be formed on the lines of branches of the National League, or merely by estates? By estates decidedly. Let branches of the National League, if they will, take the initiative in getting the tenantry on each estate to meet one another. . . . A Committee consisting, say, of six, and the chairman, should then be elected, to be called a Managing Committee, and to take charge of the half-year's rent of each tenant should the landlord refuse it. Every one present should pledge himself, (1) to abide by the decision of the majority; (2) to hold no communication with the landlord or any of his agents, except in presence of the body of the tenantry; (3) to accept no settlement for himself which is not given to every tenant on the estate. . . . Thus practically a half-year's rent of the estate is put together to fight the landlord with. This is a fund which, if properly utilised, will reduce to reason any landlord in Ireland.

"2. *How should the Fund be employed?*—The answer to this question must, to some extent, depend upon the course the landlord will pursue; but in general it must be devoted to the support of the tenants who are dispossessed either by sale or ejectment. It should be distributed by the Committee to each evicted tenant in the proportion of his contribution to the fund. But not one penny should go in law costs. . . . The fullest publicity should be given to evictions, and every effort made to enlist public sympathy. That the farms thus unjustly evicted will be left severely alone, and every one who aids the evictors shunned, is scarcely necessary to say. But a man who tries boycotting for a personal purpose is a worse enemy than the evicting land-

FOREIGN AND COLONIAL.

1887. *March.* Bill for increasing the German army passed by the Reichstag.

April. Imperial Conference composed of delegates from each of the Self-Governing Colonies was held at the Foreign Office under the Presidency of Sir Henry Holland to discuss matters of common interest.

July. Prince Ferdinand of Coburg elected Prince of Bulgaria by the Sobranje.

Oct. Italy joins in alliance with Austria and Germany.

[1887.]   ENGLISH.

PRIME MINISTERS.
SALISBURY.
1887.

consent of the Chair is obtained, provided at least 200 are in favour of it) introduced, and, urgency having been obtained for it, carried *March* 18 by 262 to 41.
Feb. 24. Jury fail to agree in trial of Dillon and others for conspiracy.
March 5. Sir M. Hicks-Beach resigns office of Chief Secretary of Ireland and is succeeded by Balfour.
March 22. Urgency demanded for Criminal Law Amendment Bill (Ireland), and carried by 349 to 260.
April 21. Budget introduced, the sum allotted for the annual National Debt payment is reduced by two millions, and a penny is taken off the income-tax.
May 2. Colonial Conference assembles at Colonial Office.
May 6. The House of Commons refuse to treat an article in the *Times* on Dillon as a breach of privilege, and Gladstone's motion for a Select Committee is rejected by 317 to 233.
June 17. After prolonged discussion on the Crimes Bill in Committee, clause 6 only having been reached, in accordance with previous notice, the remaining fourteen clauses are put without discussion, and the Bill reported. See (*a*), p. 227 *l*.
June 21. Celebration of the Queen's Jubilee.
July 14. Second Reading of Irish Land Bill. Important change, involving reduction of rents that had been fixed, introduced later, after strong representations by Liberal Unionists, and a meeting at the Carlton. The Bill passes in August. See (*b*), p. 227 *l*.
July 24. Eighteen counties proclaimed under the Crimes Act.
Aug. 19. Proclamation of the National League announced. Gladstone's motion for an address against the proclamation beaten by 272 to 194 (*Aug.* 26).
The Allotments Act (admitting the principle of compulsion), the Coal Mines Regulation Act, and Merchandise Marks Act are passed this Session.
Sep. 9. Nationalist meeting at Mitchelstown. The police, driven back by the people, fire from barracks, and kill one man and fatally wound two others.
Sep. 16. Parliament prorogued.
Sep. 20. Proclamation issued for suppression of National League in Clare, and parts of Galway, Kerry, Cork, and Wexford.
Oct. 31. W. O'Brien, Irish M.P., sentenced to three months imprisonment for inciting tenants to resist eviction.

[Notes.]

lord, and should be expelled from any branch of the League or combination of tenants. . . . No landlord should get one penny rent anywhere, or on any part of his estate, wherever situated, so long as he has one tenant unjustly evicted. Tenants should be the first to show their sympathy with one another, and prompt publicity should be given to every eviction, that the tenants of the evictor, wherever he holds property, may show their sympathy. Such a policy indicates a fight which has no half-heartedness about it, and it is the only fight which will win."

(a) Criminal Law and Procedure Act (Ireland):—

1. Resident Magistrates may, by order of the Attorney-General, hold inquiries and examine witnesses upon oath when felonies, misdemeanours, or other offences are shown, upon sworn information, to have been committed in a proclaimed district.
2. Two Resident Magistrates may try persons accused of certain crimes under the Act, and may sentence them to not more than six months' imprisonment, with hard labour.
3. The venue may be changed for trial of a crime committed in a proclaimed district.
4. The Lord-Lieutenant, in Council, may declare that any district in Ireland is proclaimed. Such proclamation shall expire if either House of Parliament present an address against it.
5. If the Lord-Lieutenant is satisfied that any dangerous Association exists in any part of Ireland, he may specially proclaim it, provided that such proclamation must be laid before Parliament (if sitting) within seven days, or (if in vacation) that it expire within seven days, unless Parliament has in the meantime been summoned to meet within twenty days. The Lord-Lieutenant may prohibit or suppress any such proclaimed Associations; and persons taking part in meetings of such Associations, or publishing accounts of them, shall be guilty of offences under the Act.

(b) Land Law (Ireland) Act:—

1. Leaseholders, with certain exceptions, are to have the benefits of the Land Act of 1881.
2. When proceedings for ejectment are brought, the defendant may apply to the court for a fair rent. The judicial rent may commence on the date of application to the court.
3. In certain cases a written notice shall be substituted for the execution of an ejectment.
4. Provisions are made to facilitate purchase
5. A re-adjustment of judicial rents fixed before 1886, with reference to the price of agricultural produce in 1887, 1888, 1889, is provided for.
6. The court is to have power to stay evictions, and to order payment by instalments when tenants are unable, through no fault of their own, to pay either rent or other debt.

Feb. 21. Earl of Onslow appointed Secretary to the Board of Trade in place of Baron de Worms, who was promoted to the Under-Secretaryship of the Colonies.

April. Sir Michael Hicks-Beach becomes President of the Board of Trade.

FOREIGN AND COLONIAL.

1887. *Dec.* M. Carnot elected President of the French Republic in succession to President Grévy.
1888. *Jan.* 24. Centenary of New South Wales celebrated.
Feb. German army increased by 700,000 men (thus raising it to above 2 millions).
Feb. 8. Lansdowne becomes Viceroy of India.
Feb. 15. The Fisheries Treaty signed at Washington, by Bayard (U.S.A.), Chamberlain (Great Britain), and Sir C. Tupper (Canada), determining the conditions on which fishing should be carried on off the North-West Coast of America. This was vetoed by United States Senate on August 21 by 3 votes (30 to 27).
March 9. The German Emperor, William I., died: succeeded by Frederick III.
June 15. The German Emperor, Frederick III., died: succeeded by his son, William II.

Aug. 30. Treaty for the Abolition of Sugar Bounties signed at the Foreign Office by all the Plenipotentiaries excepting those of France, Sweden, and Denmark, but not brought before Parliament.

PRIME MINISTERS.
SALISBURY.
1887.

1888.

Nov. 13. Serious conflict between the police and certain persons who attempt to hold a meeting in Trafalgar Square.
Dec. Several Irish M.P.'s, including T. D. Sullivan, Lord Mayor of Dublin, imprisoned under the Crimes Act.
Feb. 9. Parliament met.
New Rules of Procedure providing for the assembly of the House at three o'clock instead of four, and for adjournment of ordinary public business at midnight (no opposed business to be taken after that time, and the House, in all but exceptional cases, to stop business at 1 A.M.) introduced and afterwards carried.
March. Procedure Rule carried providing that the Closure may be applied if 100 members vote in the majority.
March 9. Goschen's scheme for reducing the interest on certain portions of the National Debt from 3 per cent. to $2\frac{3}{4}$ per cent. until April 5th, 1903, and thereafter to $2\frac{1}{2}$ per cent. until April 5th, 1923, introduced and afterwards passed.
March 19. Local Government Bill (England and Wales) introduced and afterwards passed. See (*a*), p. 228.
March 26. Goschen introduces his Budget Statement: the realised surplus for the year (£2,165,000) being the largest since 1873-74. Reduction of a penny in the income-tax.
April. Serious conflicts between Nationalists and police at Loughrea and other places. W. O'Brien imprisoned for taking part in the National League meeting at Loughrea.
June 19. Government defeated by 248 to 218 on an Amendment to the Local Government Bill, moved by J. Morley, transferring the appointment of chief constables to the County Council and the Quarter Sessions jointly.
Withdrawal of the Licensing Clauses of the Local Government Bill by the Government.
Second reading of the Channel Tunnel Bill rejected by 307 to 165.
July. W. H. Smith introduces Special Commission on "Parnellism and Crime" Bill: afterwards passed.
Aug. 11. Parnell lodged notice of an action against the *Times* to be tried in Scotland, and claiming £50,000 damages.
Aug. 13. Parliament adjourned to November 6th for an Autumn Session.
Aug. 16. The evictions in Co. Wexford vigorously resisted by the tenants and their friends.

[Notes.]

(a) This bill assimilated the government of counties to that established in municipal boroughs in 1834, on the basis of household suffrage. The governing body to consist of councillors, elected by a direct vote for three years, and aldermen, elected for six years by the councillors, the management of the police and appointment of chief constables being intrusted to a Joint-Committee of the Council and Quarter Sessions. Certain large boroughs were treated as counties.

FOREIGN AND COLONIAL.

Oct. 30. Certain territories in New Guinea annexed to the British Dominions.
Nov. 6. General Harrison elected President of United States.
Dec. 20. Defeat of the Arabs near Suakim by the Black Brigades supported by British and Egyptian troops.
1889. *Jan.* Gefcken indicted for high treason for publishing Frederick III.'s Diary.

June 28. The Portuguese Government took forcible possession of the Delagoa Bay Railway.

[1888—1889.] ENGLISH.

Prime Ministers.
SALISBURY.
1888.

1889.

Sep. 17. The Special Commission on "Parnellism and Crime" met for the first time.
Nov. 6. Parliament re-assembled.
Irish Land Purchase Bill, voting 10 millions sterling on lines of Ashbourne Act (1885), carried.
Dec. 24. Parliament prorogued.
Jan. The County Councils met for the first time, and elected their Chairmen and Aldermen.
Feb. 21. Parliament met.
Feb. 25. Richard Pigott, from whom the *Times* had obtained the alleged letters of Parnell and others, which formed one section of the articles on "Parnellism and Crime," disappeared from London, his evidence having altogether broken down. A warrant for his apprehension was issued. On Feb. 27th, before the Parnell Commission, Pigott's confession of forgery having been read, the Attorney-General, on behalf of the *Times*, withdrew the case founded upon the letters. Pigott committed suicide in Madrid on March 1st, whither he had been tracked by the police.
March 7. The Naval Defences Bill introduced, authorising an expenditure of £21,500,000 in building 70 additional ships representing a tonnage of 318,000; afterwards passed.
April 8. Local Government Bill for Scotland introduced, and afterwards passed.
April 9. Motion to establish a National Parliament in Scotland for the control of Scotch affairs negatived by 200 votes to 79.
April 15. Goschen's Budget Statement showed a deficit of £1,900,000, owing to the increased charges for the Navy and for the Local Government. This was met by diverting from the National Debt £1,000,000 of the saving effected by the conversion, by the imposition of a new death duty of 1 per cent. on estates of £10,000 and upwards, and by a slight change in the incidence of the beer duty.
June 3. Bills introduced for the Improved Drainage of Ireland, also Light Railways extension, and read for a first time, and subsequently passed.
July 22. The question of Royal Grants having been referred to a Select Committee, the compromise suggested by Gladstone, under which the Prince of Wales was to receive an increase of income of £36,000 a year, out of which he was to provide for his children, was ultimately accepted by the Government, Labouchere's amendment being defeated by 398 to 116, and J. Morley's amendment "that no adequate grounds have been shown for the proposal" by 355 to 134.

[Notes.]

FOREIGN AND COLONIAL.

Aug. 3. Attack and defeat by General Grenfell of the Dervishes' troops at Wad-el-Njumi.

Aug. 14. Boulanger and his associates convicted of misappropriating public money.

Nov. 15. A revolution in Brazil. The Emperor expelled, and a Republic declared.

1890. *Feb.* Bismarck resigned the Chancellorship of the German Empire.

West Australia Constitution Bill passed.

Treaties with Germany, France, Portugal, and Italy as to the African territories and spheres of influence are passed.

Aug. Heligoland handed over to Germany in accordance with treaty arrangements in Africa.

[1889—1890.] *ENGLISH.*

PRIME MINISTERS.
SALISBURY.
1889.

June—Aug. Acts for the Prevention of Cruelty to, and Better Protection of, Children passed.
•An Act for the more effectual prevention and punishment of bribery in public bodies passed.
Aug. 19. A strike of labourers employed at the docks in and near London commenced; 75,000 men joined the movement, and the whole shipping trade of London was paralysed, but a settlement was arrived at which much improved the position of the dock labourers.
Aug. 26. W. O'Brien imprisoned for inciting tenants on the Ponsonby estates not to pay their rents.
Aug. 30. Parliament prorogued.
Oct. 30. Charter granted to the British South African Company.

1890.

Feb. 12. Parliament meets. Breach of privilege resolution as to *Times* charges and Irish members rejected by 260 to 212.
March. Debate on the Special Commission. Gladstone's amendment rejected by 260 to 212, and the report is ordered to be printed in the journals of the House of Commons.
Balfour's Land Purchase Bill introduced.
Tithes Bill introduced.
April. Goschen's Budget takes 2d. a lb. off the tea duty, adds 6d. a gallon to the spirit duty, and 3d. to the beer duty.
April. New Education Code issued, abolishing the system of payment by results. The right of a school to the lowest fixed grant of 12s. 6d. per head to be determined not by the attainments of individual pupils, but by the general condition of the school.
May. Local Taxation (Customs and Excise) Bill introduced. The part of the Bill which provided for the extinction of licences after compensation had been given finally withdrawn at the end of June. The money arranged under the Budget arrangements for the purpose permissively granted to Technical and Intermediate Education (July and August).
Aug. Act passed to provide further facilities for the construction of certain railways in Ireland.
Police Act and Housing of Working Classes Amendment Act passed.
W. O'Brien and Dillon prosecuted for their action connected with New Tipperary, and sentenced in their absence to six months' imprisonment each. After the opening of the trial they escape to America to raise funds.
Nov. The Archbishop of Canterbury gives judgment in the case of the Bishop of Lincoln, who had been accused of Ritualistic practices.

[Notes.] FOREIGN AND COLONIAL.

PRIME MINISTERS.
SALISBURY.
1890.

Nov. 25. Parliament meets.
Nov. 25. The Irish Parliamentary Party re-elect Parnell their Sessional Chairman.
Irish Land Purchase and Congested Districts Bills introduced by Balfour.
Tithe Act introduced by Hicks-Beach.
In consequence of events arising out of the case O'Shea *v.* O'Shea and Parnell, a majority of the Irish Parliamentary Party renounce the leadership of Parnell, and elect Justin M'Carthy their Sessional Chairman.

[Notes.] *FOREIGN AND COLONIAL.*

[   ]   *ENGLISH.*

Prime Ministers.

[Notes.] | *FOREIGN AND COLONIAL.*

] *ENGLISH.*

Prime Ministers.

PART II.

SUMMARIES.

SECTION A.
SUMMARIES WHICH EXTEND MORE OR LESS OVER THE WHOLE COURSE OF THE HISTORY.

SECTION B.
SUMMARIES WHICH BELONG TO SPECIAL PERIODS.

SECTION A. SUMMARIES WHICH EXTEND MORE OR LESS OVER THE WHOLE COURSE OF THE HISTORY.

	PAGE
Parliament, Part I. (Preliminary) to 1295	233
,, ,, II. 1295-1430	233
,, ,, III. 1430-1689	235
,, ,, IV. 1689-1832	237
,, ,, V. 1832-1881	238
Ecclesiastical, Part I. To 1070	239
,, ,, II. 1070-1527	239
,, ,, III. 1527-1559. The Reformation	241
,, ,, IV. 1559-1661. Section A, Church; Section B, Nonconformists	243
,, ,, V. 1661-1881. Section A, Church; Section B, Nonconformists	244
Wales, 577-1543	246
Scotland, Part I. To 1290	247
,, ,, II. 1290-1603	248
,, ,, III. 1603-1707	250
,, ,, IV. 1707-1881	252
Ireland, ,, I. To 1494	252
,, ,, II. 1494-1801	253
,, ,, III. 1801-1881	254
Law Courts, 1107-1881	256
Army, 1073-1881	257

SECTION B. SUMMARIES WHICH BELONG TO SPECIAL PERIODS.

Gradual Union of England into one Kingdom, 449-827	259
The Northmen in England, (1) 787-897; (2) 907-937; (3) 980-1017	259
The Union of Normandy and England, 1002-1071	261
Struggle between the Kings and the Feudal Nobility, 1074-1174	262
Laws, Codes, and Charters up to the time of the Great Charter, c. 600-1215	262
The Hundred Years' War between England and France, 1338-1453	262
York and Lancaster, 1385-1563	264
The Council to 1641	266
American War of Independence, 1764-1783	266
Jacobites, 1691-1807	267
French War, 1793-1815	268
Catholic Relief, 1778-1829	270
Corn Laws, 1815-1846	272
India, 1600-1881	273
Reform, 1745-1881	275

SECTION A.

SUMMARIES WHICH EXTEND MORE OR LESS OVER THE WHOLE COURSE OF THE HISTORY.

PARLIAMENT.—PART I. (PRELIMINARY) TO 1295.

REPRESENTATION UP TO 1295.

1070. The laws of the English are declared by twelve men elected from each shire.
1085. Domesday survey is taken by inquest, each hundred and township appears by representative jurors.

1198. A carucage is assessed before knights elected in behalf of the shire.
1213. First united representation of townships on the royal demesne. Four men and the reeve are summoned from each township to the assembly at St. Albans.
Four discreet men of each shire are summoned to the Oxford Council.
1215. By an article of the Great Charter the assizes are to be held before four knights of the shire chosen by the shire. The articles of the Great Charter are to be carried out by twelve sworn knights from each shire, chosen in the county court.
1254. First summons to Parliament by royal writ of two knights of the shire.
1265. A parliament meets, to which are summoned two knights from each shire, and for the first time representatives from cities and boroughs.

1295. *First complete and model Parliament of the Three Estates.* Besides the barons and prelates, one proctor is summoned for the clergy of each cathedral, and two for the clergy of each diocese, two knights from each shire, two citizens from each city, and two burgesses from each borough.

TAXATION UP TO 1295.

991. Danegeld paid by the advice of the Witan for the first time.
1084. Danegeld is demanded by William I. at three times the old rate.
1159. Scutage first regularly instituted.
1163. A quarrel between Henry II. and Becket on a matter of taxation, probably the exaction of Danegeld.
1188. Saladin tithe. First tax upon personal property.
1193. Richard I.'s ransom is raised by five different kinds of taxes.
1198. St. Hugh, Bishop of Lincoln, refuses to pay money to support the war in France, considering himself bound to render military service in England only.

1215. The clauses about aids and scutages in the Great Charter give control over taxation to the Great Council.
1216. The clause about taxation is omitted in the re-issue of the Great Charter.
1237. A grant of a thirtieth of movables is made by the National Council.
1283. Two provincial councils, with representatives from both clergy and laity, meet at York and Northampton, and make various grants.
1294. The clergy are forced to grant one-half; the barons and knights of the shire grant one-tenth; by a separate negotiation one-sixth is collected from the towns.
1295. The Three Estates, in a complete Parliament, make their various grants.

PARLIAMENT.—PART. II. 1295—1430.

Structure.

[For numbers of Lords and Commons see Appendix II. and Appendix III.]

1322. The wages of members of the House of Commons are fixed at 4s. a day for a knight, and 2s. for a citizen or burgher.

233

SUMMARIES.

1332. The knights of the shire are first definitely recorded as deliberating apart from the lords and prelates, and in the next year as sitting with the citizens and burgesses.
1406. Regulations about elections in the county court are made in Parliament, with a view of preventing the sheriff from making a false return.
1430. The election of knights of the shire is regulated, the vote being restricted to persons possessing freeholds worth 40s. a year.

Financial Powers.

1297. By "Confirmatio Cartarum" the collection of any taxes without consent of Parliament is forbidden.
1332. An order for the collection of tallage is issued probably for the last time, the power of levying it being once more and finally abolished in 1340.
1362. Enactment that no subsidy should be set on wool by the merchants or any other body without consent of Parliament.
1373. Tonnage and poundage is formally granted by Parliament for two years, and from this time becomes a regular parliamentary grant.
1377. Walworth and Philipot are appointed treasurers of the parliamentary grant.
1385. Scutage appears nearly for the last time.
1398. The Shrewsbury Parliament grants customs to Richard II. for life.
1406. The Commons insist upon a proper audit of their grants. (From this time the right is never disputed by the Lancastrian kings.)
1407. The right of the Commons only to originate money grants is conceded.

Legislative Powers.

1322. The principle that what concerns the whole realm must be treated by a complete Parliament is stated. The Commons now finally gain a share in legislation.
1389. The Commons pray that the Chancellor and the Council may not, after the close of Parliament, make any ordinance contrary to the common law.
1414. It is agreed by Parliament and king that statutes shall be made without alteration of the petitions on which they are based.

Judicial Powers.

1341. In the case of John Stratford, Archbishop of Canterbury, the Lords insist that a peer must be judged in full Parliament, and before his peers.
1376. The Good Parliament impeaches the ministers.
1386. Impeachment of Suffolk (Michael de la Pole).

Privilege.

1376. John of Gaunt throws into prison Peter de la Mare, Speaker of the Commons. He is released by Richard II., and elected Speaker of Richard's first Parliament.
1397. Haxey's case. Interference by Richard II. with the Commons' freedom of debate.
1407. Henry IV. has to concede perfect freedom of deliberation by both Houses on money grants.

Relations of Parliament and King.

1310. Appointment of the Lords Ordainers.
1327. Renunciation of allegiance to Edward II.

SUMMARIES.

1377. Appointment of provisional government for Richard II. in Parliament.
1386. Council of Eleven appointed for Richard II. by Parliament.
1398. The Parliament of Shrewsbury delegates its authority to eighteen of its members.
1399. Parliament deposes Richard II.
1404. The Commons request Henry IV. to name twenty-two counsellors as his great and continual council. [A similar request is made in 1406 and 1410.]
1422. The Privy Council is nominated as a Council of Regency for Henry VI. by Parliament.

PARLIAMENT.—PART III. 1430—1689.

Structure.

[For numbers of Lords and Commons see Appendix II. and Appendix III.]

1539. On the dissolution of the monasteries the mitred abbots cease to sit in the House of Lords.
1604. The right of the House of Commons to control its own elections is established.
1641. The Triennial Act (see note) is passed.
1649. The House of Lords is abolished.
1653. The Assembly of Nominees (or Barebones Parliament) meets.
1654. In accordance with the Instrument of Government a House of Commons is chosen, to consist of four hundred members for England and Wales, thirty for Scotland, and thirty for Ireland.
1657. In accordance with the Petition and Advice writs are sent out by the Protector to summon a new House of Lords.
1661. The new Parliament is chosen, and meets in accordance with the ancient practice.
1664. The Triennial Act is repealed, though it is provided that Parliament should not be intermitted above three years at the most.
1689. The election of members of Parliament ought to be free. Parliament ought to be held frequently (Bill of Rights).

Financial Powers.

1449. The Commons attempt to tax the clergy, but the king refers their proposal through the Lords Spiritual to Convocation.
1484. The practice of exacting benevolences is abolished by Parliament.
1523. The House of Commons (of which Sir T. More is Speaker) refuses to grant the whole of a grant of money claimed by Wolsey in person.
1544. An Act is passed releasing the king from his debts.
1545. A benevolence of not less than 1s. 8d. in the £ on land and 10d. on goods is exacted.
1601. Debate in Parliament on monopolies. The queen consents to their abolition.
1610. The Commons complain of the Book of Rates, which had largely increased the customs.
1624. Monopolies are finally declared illegal in Parliament.
1626. Money is collected by forced loans, and tonnage and poundage illegally levied.
1628. Charles I. assents to the Petition of Right, and Parliament grants five subsidies.

SUMMARIES.

1629. The Speaker refuses, by the king's order, to read a remonstrance of Sir John Eliot on tonnage and poundage.
1634. A writ for ship-money drawn up by Noy, carefully following the ancient precedents, is addressed to maritime towns and counties, and a collection made without complaint.
1635. A new writ of ship-money after Noy's death, extending the tax to inland towns and counties, is issued.
1636. The judges give their opinion that the king can legally order his subjects to pay ship-money, if the kingdom is in danger.
1637. John Hampden refuses to pay ship-money. Judgment is given against him by a majority of judges after long argument.
1641. Statutes passed against ship-money, distraint of knighthood, and illegal customs.
1642. *Aug.* 1. The Commons make an order for levying tonnage and poundage.
Dec. A tax on property and incomes is levied through the whole kingdom by the Parliament.
1665. Parliament grants £1,250,000 to be spent on the Dutch war only (see note).
1666. A committee is appointed by Parliament to inspect the accounts of naval and other officials.
1677. The Commons having voted a subsidy for the use of the navy, order it to be paid into the hands of their own receivers.
1689. Levying money by pretence of prerogative is illegal. (Bill of Rights).

Legislative and Judicial Powers.

1450. Impeachment of Suffolk.
c. 1460. At the end of Henry VI.'s reign, bills, in the form of statutes, are introduced instead of petitions, to get over the evils of manipulation or saving clauses.
1461. A bill of attainder is passed against Henry VI. and Margaret.
1539. The king's proclamations are declared to be as valid as Acts of Parliament (repealed 1547).
1540. Thomas Cromwell is condemned by bill of attainder without being heard in his defence.
1610. The Commons complain of royal proclamations.
1621. Revival of impeachment in the cases of Mompesson and Bacon.
1689. The pretended power of suspending or dispensing with the laws is illegal (Bill of Rights).

Privilege.

1453. The Duke of York arrests Thorpe, the Speaker of the Commons. In the next Parliament they assert their privilege in his behalf, but he remains in prison.
1571. Strickland, proposing alterations in religion, is restrained by the Council from appearing in Parliament.
1588. Wentworth is committed to the Tower for questions to the Speaker touching the liberties of the House.
1604. First Parliament of James vindicates its privilege of freedom from arrest.
1622. On the dissolution of Parliament, Coke, Pym, Selden, and two others are imprisoned.
1626. Many members of the last Parliament are excluded by being appointed sheriffs, and a writ is withheld from the Earl of Bristol.
Sir Dudley Digges and Sir John Eliot are sent to the Tower, but are released on Parliament refus-

SUMMARIES.

ing to continue its business and the judges deciding in their favour.
1629. Sir John Eliot and others are sent to the Tower.
1641. The members of the House of Lords establish their right to record protests.
1642. The king comes in person to the House of Commons and demands the five members.
1677. Shaftesbury, Salisbury, Wharton, and Buckingham, having questioned whether the prorogation of Parliament for fifteen months did not necessarily dissolve the Parliament, are sent to the Tower by the House of Lords, and Shaftesbury remains there for a year.
1679. The king rejects the Speaker chosen by the House.
1689. Freedom of speech and debate in Parliament ought not to be questioned in any court or place out of Parliament (Bill of Rights).

Relations of Parliament and King.

1474. For eight years no Parliament sits except for forty-two days in 1478, the king having obtained an income for life from his earlier Parliaments.
1515. During the next thirteen years Parliament is only summoned once (*i.e.* in the year 1523).
1539. The king's proclamations are declared to be as valid as Acts of Parliament.
1604. The first Parliament of James I. vindicates its privileges.
1621. *Nov.* The third Parliament of James I. reassembles, and the Commons make a protest against the violations of their liberties. The king tears it out from their journal with his own hand.
1641. *Nov. 22.* The Grand Remonstrance passes the Commons by a majority of eleven, and on the next day is ordered to be printed.
1679. The Parliament resumes proceedings against Lord Danby, who pleads the royal pardon. The Commons address the king on the illegality of this pardon, and demand justice from the Lords.
1689. Declaration of Right, and Bill of Rights.

PARLIAMENT.—PART IV. 1689—1832.

Structure.

[For numbers of Lords and Commons see Appendix II. and Appendix III.]
(For history of reform see the Reform Summary, p. 275.)
1694. The Triennial Act limiting the duration of Parliament to three years, and providing that three years shall not pass without a Parliament, is passed. William III. gives his consent, which he had once before refused.
1695. An Act to restrain and punish bribery in elections is passed.
1707. An Act is passed preventing the holders of pensions from the crown or of offices created after October 25, 1705, from sitting in Parliament. Members of Parliament appointed to offices under the crown which existed before 1705 must vacate their seats, but are eligible for re-election.
1711. Property Qualification Bill for members of the House of Commons passed.

SUMMARIES.

1716. The Septennial Act, prolonging the duration of Parliament to seven years, but not longer, is passed.
1719. Peerage Bill, limiting the creation of peers, is passed by the Lords, but is rejected by the Commons.
1742. A Place Bill, limiting the number of offices tenable by members of Parliament, is passed.
1762. A Bribery Act passed in which pecuniary penalties are attached to the offence.
1770. George Grenville's Act gives the hearing of election petitions to a committee of thirteen members elected from forty-nine chosen by ballot, with one nominee from each party, instead of a committee of the whole House.
1782. Government contractors are excluded from the House of Commons. Revenue officers are debarred from voting at elections.
1784. A bill is passed limiting the duration of the poll to fifteen days instead of forty.
1818. A motion for the repeal of the Septennial Act is rejected.
1829. The Act disfranchising 40s. freeholders and raising the qualification to £10 is passed for Ireland.
1832. Reform Bills for England, Scotland, and Ireland (see Reform Summary, p. 275).

Privilege.

1703. The Aylesbury election trial produces a dispute between the Lords and the Commons.
1728 and 1738. The publication of parliamentary debates is declared to be a breach of privilege.
1763. Wilkes is denied his privilege by Parliament, notwithstanding remonstrances by Pitt and protest from seventeen peers.
1771. The attempt of the Commons to prevent the publishing of their debates is foiled by Alderman Wilkes and the Lord Mayor. Since this time the publication of debates, though still asserted to be a breach of privilege, has gone on with only occasional interruptions.

Relations of Parliament and King.

1711. To get a majority in the Lords twelve new peers are created by Harley.
1763. Unconstitutional dismissal of placemen by George III. for their votes in Parliament.
1780. Dunning carries his motion, "That the power of the Crown has increased, is increasing, and ought to be diminished."
1822. Brougham makes a motion declaring that the influence of the Crown is destructive of the independence of Parliament.

PARLIAMENT.—Part V. 1832—1881.

Structure.

[For numbers of Lords and Commons see Appendix II. and Appendix III.]

1852. A Bribery Act is passed providing for inquiry into corrupt practices on the appointment of a Commission.
1854. The Corrupt Practices Act providing for publication of accounts after parliamentary elections, and restraining candidates from paying any expenses except through authorized agents, is carried.

SUMMARIES.

1858. Property qualification for members of the House of Commons repealed.
1867. Reform Bill (see Reform Summary, p. 275).
1868. Election petitions are transferred from the House of Commons to be decided by the judges.
1877, 1880, 1881, and 1887. Resolutions are passed by the House of Commons to facilitate the progress of debate and prevent obstruction.

Privilege.

1840. In the matter of Stockdale *v.* Hansard, which began in 1837, and involved a question of privilege, a bill is passed preventing the recurrence of the difficulty (see note, 1840).
1860. The Lords throw out a bill abolishing the paper duty which had passed the Commons and was in technical form a money bill. In the next year the whole financial scheme of the Government is embodied in one bill, and the Lords are compelled to pass the abolition of the paper duty.
1875. Resolution passed in the House of Commons that for the future strangers be excluded not at the request of a single member, but on the vote of the majority of the House (the Speaker to retain his power of closing the House).

ECCLESIASTICAL.—PART I. To 1070.

597. Conversion of Ethelbert, King of Kent, by Augustine, Archbishop of Canterbury.
627. Conversion of Edwin by Paullinus.
633. Flight of Paullinus from York.
634. Aidan, from Iona, introduces Christianity at Lindisfarne, under King Oswald.
635. Birinus begins the conversion of Wessex.
664. Conference of Welsh and Roman priests at the Synod of Whitby. Roman ritual and time for keeping Easter are adopted.
668. Arrival of Theodore of Tarsus, Archbishop of Canterbury.
681. Wilfrid, driven from the archbishopric of York, converts the South Saxons.
687. Death of Cuthbert, Bishop of Lindisfarne.
787. Lichfield made an archbishopric with the leave of Pope Hadrian.
960. Dunstan becomes Archbishop of Canterbury.
975. Struggle between the secular clergy and monks begins.
1044. Robert of Jumièges (the first Norman bishop in England) is appointed Bishop of London.
1051. Robert of Jumièges made Archbishop of Canterbury.
1070. Stigand is deposed and Lanfranc made Archbishop of Canterbury. (For list of bishoprics see 1070.)

ECCLESIASTICAL.—PART II. 1070—1527.

1076. William I. refuses the demand of fealty made by Gregory VII.
1066-87. William I. forbids excommunications, calling of synods, or the receipt of Papal letters without his leave (see note 1076).

239

SUMMARIES.

1066-87. By an undated charter of William I.'s reign spiritual jurisdiction is separated from the secular courts of law and assigned to separate spiritual courts.
1093. Anselm is consecrated Archbishop of Canterbury.
1094. William II. refuses to give Anselm the temporalities of his see.
1097. Anselm, unable to bear the wickedness of William II., retires to Rome.
1100. Anselm is recalled.
1103. Anselm differs with Henry I. about investitures and leaves England.
1107. Anselm and Henry I. agree upon a compromise (see note).
1162. Becket elected Archbishop of Canterbury.
1163. Quarrel between Becket and Henry II. about the jurisdiction over criminous clerks.
1164. *Constitutions of Clarendon.*
1170. Murder of Archbishop Becket.
1206 to 1213. John's quarrel with Innocent III. about election of Langton as archbishop. England placed under an interdict.
1213. John receives Langton, and does homage for his kingdom to the Pope.
1215. John grants freedom of election to episcopal sees.
1226. The Pope's demand for a prebend from every cathedral and an equal contribution from every monastery is rejected.
1229. The Pope levies one-tenth of all the property of the clergy.
1256. The claim to "annates" is first made in England by Pope Alexander IV. for five years.
1279. *Statute of Mortmain* or *De Religiosis*, to check the bestowal of estates on religious foundations.
1295. Clergy first represented in a complete Parliament, but do not often attend as an Estate in Parliament (see note).
1296. The clergy, in accordance with the bull "Clericis Laicos," refuse to grant supplies, and are outlawed.
1301. The Pope claims Scotland as a fief of Rome.
1307. The Parliament of Carlisle asks for legislation against provisors, first-fruits, and other exactions of the Papacy.
1317. John XXII. "reserves" the appointment of eighteen episcopal sees in England in the next seventeen years.
1351. *The first statute of Provisors* to prevent encroachment by the Pope on patronage is passed.
1353. *First statute of Præmunire* to prevent usurpations of jurisdiction by the Pope.
1377. Wickliffe is cited to appear at St. Paul's.
1382. A statute passed against heretic preachers, but is repealed in the next Parliament.
1384. Death of Wickliffe.
1390. *Statute of Provisors* [re-enacting statutes of 1351 and 1362].
1391. *Statute of Mortmain* re-enacted.
1393. *The great statute of Præmunire.*
1395. The Lollards present a remonstrance to Parliament against the power of the clergy and the abuses in the Church.
1401. The Act *De Heretico comburendo* is passed by the Lords and clergy at the request of Archbishop Arundel. Execution of William Sawtre by royal writ [the first execution for Lollard heresy in England].
1410. The knights of the shire now (as well as in 1404) propose to confiscate the property of the Church.

SUMMARIES.

1414. Lollard meeting summoned at St. Giles' Fields; a new statute passed against the Lollards.
The property of priories belonging to foreigners is confiscated to the Crown by Parliament.
1417. Sir John Oldcastle, a leading Lollard, is captured and executed.
[Martin V. becomes Pope. During his papacy he "provides" as many as thirteen bishops in England in two years.]
1427. The Pope tries to suspend Archbishop Chichele from his legatine office because he will not procure the repeal of the statutes of Provisors. Chichele protests, and the bulls of suspension are seized by royal order.
1432. Beaufort is secured by statute against all risks of suffering "præmunire" for being cardinal.
1449. The Commons attempt to tax the clergy, but the king transmits their proposal through the Lords Spiritual to Convocation. [Practically, however, at this time and onwards, Convocation follows the example of the Commons in money grants.]
1515. Wolsey is created Cardinal and Lord Chancellor.
1517. Wolsey is made papal legate, with special licence from the king to accept the nomination.
1521. Henry VIII. receives from the Pope the title of Defender of the Faith for having written a work against Luther.
1523. Wolsey fails a second time to obtain the Papacy.

ECCLESIASTICAL.—PART III. 1527—1559.

THE REFORMATION.

1527. Henry VIII., having doubts about the legality of his marriage with Katharine of Aragon, submits the case to the Pope.
1528. A commission to Cardinals Wolsey and Campeggio to try the question of the king's marriage is granted by the Pope.
1529. Katharine appeals to the Pope, and the cause is finally avocated to Rome.
Fall of Wolsey.
Nov. The Seven Years' Parliament which carries out the severance from Rome now meets for the first time.
Parliament regulates the fees paid to clergymen, and forbids pluralities.
1530. Cranmer carries the opinions favourable to the divorce which had been received from the universities to the Pope.
1531. The clergy, incurring the penalty of "præmunire" and being fined for acknowledging Wolsey as papal legate, address Henry after much protest as "Head of the Church and Clergy so far as the law of Christ will allow."
Convocation make the first proposal to limit the Pope's power by petitioning the king and Parliament to abolish the payment of annates to the Pope.
1532. Parliament reforms the spiritual courts and strengthens the mortmain statutes.
An Act for restraining all appeals to Rome is passed.
1533. Cranmer is consecrated Archbishop of Canterbury, and declares Henry's marriage with Katharine void and that with Anne Boleyn legal.

SUMMARIES.

1534. An *Act forbidding the payment of annates to Rome* is passed and the election of bishops by a *congé d'élire* finally arranged. (See list of bishoprics, 1534.)
The clergy are forbidden to make laws binding on themselves without the king's consent. The legislative power of Convocation is thus practically suppressed.
An Act abolishing the authority of the Pope in England is passed. The Convocations of Canterbury and York declare that "the Bishop of Rome hath no greater jurisdiction conferred on him by God in the kingdom of England than any other foreign bishop."

1535. Henry formally takes the title of "*Supreme Head of the Church of England.*"
Fisher and Sir T. More are executed, practically for denying the king's supremacy.
Thomas Cromwell is appointed Vicar-General.

1536. Benefit of clergy is now restricted by Act of Parliament, and henceforth in the matter of jurisdiction clergy and laymen are on an equality.
The smaller monasteries and nunneries are dissolved and their property transferred to the Crown.
The English Bible is set up in the churches.

1539. All monasteries are now dissolved and granted to the king.
The Act of the Six Articles, with severe penalties for disobedience, is passed.

1540. Fall and execution of Thomas Cromwell.

1547. An ecclesiastical visitation is carried out to order the use of English in services and to pull down images; Bonner and Gardiner protesting, are imprisoned.

1549. The "First Prayer-Book of Edward VI.," together with the "Act for Uniformity of Service," is passed in Parliament.
A rebellion in Devon and Cornwall demanding the restoration of the old Liturgy is put down by Russell.

1552. A Second Act of Uniformity and Second Prayer-Book are issued.

1553. Bonner is made Bishop of London and Gardiner Lord Chancellor.
The laws concerning religion passed in Edward VI.'s reign are annulled in Parliament.

1554. Cardinal Pole comes to England. All statutes against the Pope since the twentieth year of Henry VIII. are repealed (but the monastic lands remain in the hands of their present owners).

1555. The persecuting statutes of Henry IV. and V. against heretics are revived. Hooper and many others are burnt as heretics.
Oct. Latimer and Ridley are burnt.

1556. Cranmer is burnt.
Cardinal Pole, now papal legate, is made Archbishop of Canterbury. (He dies in 1558.)

1558. Elizabeth forbids unlicensed preaching, and allows part of the Liturgy to be used in English. A new Prayer-Book is prepared.

1559. *The Act of Supremacy* is passed in Parliament, with penalties for refusing it.
The Act of Uniformity is passed establishing the revised Prayer-Book.
Parker is made Archbishop of Canterbury.

SUMMARIES.

ECCLESIASTICAL.—PART IV. 1559—1661.

A. CHURCH.

1563. The Thirty-nine Articles are drawn up and signed by Convocation.
1564. Archbishop Parker and the queen enforce uniformity.
1569. Insurrection in behalf of the old religion, and of Mary, Queen of Scots, under the Earls of Northumberland and Westmoreland. It is suppressed with great cruelty.
1570. The Pope Pius V. issues a bull releasing Elizabeth's subjects from their allegiance.
1571. Parliament passes severe Acts against Romanists and against the introduction of Papal bulls.
1576. Grindal succeeding Parker, becomes Archbishop of Canterbury.
1577. Grindal is sequestrated from his see for declining to suppress the "Prophesyings" of the Puritans.
1583. Whitgift succeeds Grindal as Archbishop of Canterbury, and persecutes the Puritans.
The "High Commission Court" is placed on a permanent footing.
1587. Pope Sixtus V. issues a new bull, and proclaims a crusade against Elizabeth. He sends his benediction to the forces prepared by Philip of Spain against England.
1604. The *Hampton Court Conference is held*. The Authorized Version of the Bible is ordered.
Whitgift dies, and is succeeded by Bancroft as Archbishop of Canterbury.
1610. Bancroft dies, and is succeeded by Abbot as Archbishop of Canterbury, who though of Puritan tendencies, increases the severity of the High Commission Court.
1625. Dr. Montague, royal chaplain, is censured in Parliament for a work of Arminian tendencies.
1627. Drs. Sibthorp and Mainwaring preach in favour of the king's prerogative.
1633. *Aug.* Laud becomes Archbishop of Canterbury.
1635. Archbishop Laud holds a visitation, in which he endeavours to give greater prominence than before to ritual.
1637. Williams, Bishop of Lincoln, who had favoured the Puritans, is imprisoned for libel and suspended by the High Commission Court.
1640. Convocation continues to sit after dissolution, grants a subsidy, and passes certain canons.
Oct. 22. The High Commission Court sits for the last time.
The recent canons of Convocation are declared to be illegal.

B. NONCONFORMISTS.

1563. The advanced Protestants denounce vestments.
1564. Many of the London clergy refuse to obey the Act of Uniformity, and leave the Church.

1570. Cartwright, a leader of the Puritan party, is expelled from his professorship at Cambridge.
1571. The Puritans propose in Parliamen alterations in religion, and Strickland, the mover, is imprisoned by Elizabeth.

1587. The Marprelate tracts grossly abusing the hierarchy are circulated at this time.
1593. Acts with penalties are passed against both Puritans and Romanists.

1606. Parliament increases the severity of the laws against the Catholics.

1630. Dr. Leighton is by sentence of Star Chamber pilloried and imprisoned for writing against prelates.

1637. Prynne, Burton, and Bastwick are condemned in the Star Chamber for their writings and pilloried.

1640. Prynne, Burton, Leighton, Chambers, and others released by Parliament and compensated.

SUMMARIES.

1641. A commission is issued by the Commons to deface and demolish in churches images, altars, and monuments.
March 10. The Commons bring in a bill to exclude the bishops from the House of Lords, which is passed *May* 1.
May 27. A bill for the complete abolition of Episcopacy ("The Root and Branch Bill") is read in the Commons.
July. The High Commission Court is abolished.
Dec. 30. The Commons impeach the bishops, who had signed a protest against the Acts passed by the House of Lords in their absence.
1642. *Sept.* 1. The Commons finally resolve to abolish bishops and other ecclesiastical officers.
1645. *Jan.* 10. Archbishop Laud is beheaded.

1654. Triers are appointed by ordinance, and commissioners are sent round to enquire into the characters of clergy already in the possession of livings.
1661. *April.* A conference at the Savoy between the bishops and the Presbyterian ministers fails.

1647. The Westminster Assembly of Divines, which had been sitting constantly since 1643, had by this time established Presbyterianism, which was, however, only generally accepted in Middlesex and Lancashire.
[1658. The Independents draw up a Confession of Faith at the Savoy.]
1661. *April.* The conference at the Savoy between the bishops and Presbyterian ministers fails.

ECCLESIASTICAL—PART V. 1661—1881.

A. CHURCH.

1662. *May.* The Act of Uniformity is passed enforcing the use of the Prayer-Book as at present composed.
1663. Convocation grants a subsidy (for the last time).
1664. An Act is passed ordering that the clergy should pay taxes like the laity, and that they should have the right of voting for members of Parliament.

B. NONCONFORMISTS.

1661. *Dec.* 21. Corporation Act passed ordering all holders of municipal offices to renounce the Covenant, and take the Sacrament according to the English form.
1662. *May.* A great many ministers resign their benefices rather than take the oath required by the Act of Uniformity.
1664. The Conventicle Act is passed forbidding unlawful assemblies for public worship.
1665. *Oct.* The Five-Mile Act is passed (forbidding ministers who have not subscribed the Act of Uniformity or taken the oath of non-resistance to settle within five miles of any corporation).
1668. An abortive attempt made to comprehend the Presbyterians in the Church.
1672. *March* 15. Declaration of Indulgence (repealing all Acts against Nonconformists and Catholics).
1673. Declaration of Indulgence withdrawn. Parliament passes the Test Act [which orders that all persons holding office under the Crown are to take the Sacrament according to the rites of the Church of England, and make a

SUMMARIES.

1686. *July.* A new court of Ecclesiastical Commission is set up. Compton, Bishop of London, is suspended by it. Massey, a Romanist, is made Dean of Christ Church, Oxford.
The chapel at Whitehall is opened for the public celebration of the Romanist rites.

1687. Both Oxford and Cambridge are attacked by the Ecclesiastical Commission.

1688. *May 4.* James orders the clergy to read the Declaration of Indulgence on May 20 and 27.
The seven bishops present their petition to be excused, May 18, and very few clergy read the Declaration.
June 29, 30. The seven bishops are tried and acquitted.
Sept. The Ecclesiastical Commission is dissolved.

1689. A new oath of allegiance and supremacy is imposed on all place-holders in Church or State. Seven bishops and about three hundred clergy refuse it, and form the body of "Nonjurors."

1704. Queen Anne's bounty is instituted.

1717. Convocation after this year continues to be prorogued without doing business till 1850.

declaration against Transubstantiation].

1678. Popish Plot. Depositions of Titus Oates against the Papists. Many trials of leading Roman Catholics.
An Act is passed disabling Papists from sitting in either House of Parliament.

1685. Baxter, the Presbyterian divine, is severely punished.

1686. The judges having given an opinion favourable to the dispensing power of the king, many Romanists receive commissions in the army and Church preferment.

1687. The Declaration of Indulgence is published, which suspends the penal statutes against the Roman Catholics and Protestant dissenters.
James having asked the lord-lieutenants to furnish a list of Papists and Nonconformists suitable for members of Parliament, many of them resign.

1689. The Toleration Act is passed.

1711. An Act is passed against occasional conformity dispossessing dissenters of any offices which they may hold.

1714. The Schism Act is passed.

1727. Yearly Act of Indemnity for dissenters who held office contrary to the Test and Corporation Acts begins to be passed.

1730. About this time the Wesleys form their society at Oxford.

1739. Wesley develops his society, which afterwards becomes known as that of the Methodists, in London.

1779. Dissenting ministers and schoolmasters relieved from subscription to any of the Thirty-nine Articles.
An Act is passed admitting dissenters to civil and military offices in Ireland.

1787. Beaufoy's motion for the repeal of the Test and Corporation Acts is lost by a large majority.

1789. Beaufoy's motion is again brought in, and lost by only twenty. [A similar motion by Fox is lost next year, and the subject of tests is not resumed again for nearly forty years.]

1812. Dissenting ministers are relieved from certain penalties of the Conventicle Act.

1813. Unitarians are relieved from some of their disabilities.

1828. Lord John Russell's motion for repeal of the Test and Corporation Acts passes both Houses.

SUMMARIES.

1831. An Ecclesiastical Commission for this year reports on the revenue of the English Church.
1833. The Tractarian movement dates from this year.
1834. A bill for relieving bishops from their legislative and judicial functions in the House of Lords is rejected.
An Ecclesiastical Commission is issued to inquire into matters of income, etc., in the English Church.
1835. Another Ecclesiastical Commission is issued.
1836. The bill for tithe-commutation in England is passed.
The Ecclesiastical Commissioners are incorporated.
1837. The Government Church-Rates Abolition Bill being carried by five only in the Commons, is abandoned by the ministers.
1838. An Act against non-residence of clergy is passed.
1845. J. H. Newman joins the Church of Rome.

1858. A bill for the abolition of Church-rates is passed in the Commons and thrown out in the Lords.
1868. Gladstone carries a bill for the abolition of compulsory Church-rates.

1874. Public Worship Regulation Act.

[For bishoprics of the English Church see notes 1070 and 1534.]

1829. [For Catholic relief see Summary, p. 270.]
1833. An Act is passed enabling Quakers, Moravians, and Separatists, on entering the House of Commons, to substitute an affirmation for an oath.
The Jewish Relief Bill passes the Commons, but is rejected by the Lords in this and several following years, until 1858.

1850. *Sept.* 30. A papal bull creating Roman Catholic bishops in England is issued. It causes much excitement.
1851. The Ecclesiastical Titles Act is passed, declaring the papal bull of 1850 null and void, and imposing a fine of £100 on all who try to carry it into effect.
1858. The admission of Jews to Parliament is at last (after many years' efforts made by the House of Commons, and resisted by the Lords) effected by a bill, enabling either House by resolution to modify its oath.
1870. In the Elementary Education Act a conscience clause is made compulsory on all schools receiving Government grants.
1871. Religious tests abolished at the Universities of Oxford and Cambridge.
1880. Burials Bill passed.

WALES. 577—1543.

577. Battle of Dyrham. The West Saxons divide the West Welsh from the North Welsh.
607. Battle of Chester. The Northumbrians divide the North Welsh from the Strathclyde Welsh.
779. Offa makes his dyke from the Dee to the Wye, to protect Shrewsbury and his other conquests from the Welsh.
836. The West Welsh with Northmen and West Saxons are defeated by Egbert at Hengist's Down.
916. The Welsh defeated by Ethelfleda.
922. The North Welsh seek Edward for lord.
924. The Strathclyde Welsh choose Edward for father and lord.
937. Strathclyde Welsh with Scots and Northmen from Ireland are defeated at Brunanburh.
1055. Expedition of Harold against the Welsh.
1063. Harold again invades Wales with Tostig. Griffith the king killed by his own men.

246

SUMMARIES.

1068. Wales ravaged by Harold's sons.
1090. William II. grants land in Wales to any one who will take it, and in consequence a war of conquest goes on for many years.
1105. Henry settles Flemings in Pembrokeshire.
1157 and 1165. Henry II.'s expeditions against Wales.
1174. During the rebellion against Henry II. the Welsh remain faithful.
1211. Wales, taking advantage of Innocent's threat to depose John, makes war.
1228. Series of petty wars against the Welsh, who throughout this reign support the opposition barons.
1277. Llewellyn having refused to swear allegiance to Edward, war breaks out. The Welsh are defeated. Llewellyn keeps only Anglesea and the district of Snowdon.
1282. The Welsh war breaks out again. David, brother of Llewellyn, deserts the English. Llewellyn is killed on the Wye.
1283. David is captured and executed.
1284. The Statutes of Wales settle the country.
1295. The rebellion of Madoc is suppressed.
1316. Welsh rebel, but are quickly suppressed.
1400. Rebellion of Glendower in Wales.
1402. Henry IV. invades Wales unsuccessfully.
1403. The Bretons land in Wales and burn towns on the coast in this and the next year, when the French king makes a treaty with Glendower.
1536. The union in matters of law, etc., between England and Wales is finally completed.
1543. Wales is divided into counties, and the Court of the Council of Wales and the Welsh Marches is erected (abolished 1641).

SCOTLAND.—Part I. To 1290.

c. 500. Scots invade Caledonia and expel the Picts from the west.
603. Defeat of the Scots by Ethelfrith at Dagsastan.
685. Egfrith defeated and killed by the Picts.
843. Union of Picts and Scots under Kenneth M'Alpin.
872. Northmen from Ireland ravage Scotland.
924. Constantine, King of Scots (900-943), chooses Edward to father and lord.
937. Constantine, King of Scots, is defeated at Brunanburh by Athelstan.
945. Edmund conquers Strathclyde, and gives it to Malcolm, King of Scots (943-954), on military tenure.
966. Edgar divides Northumbria, and grants Lothian to Kenneth, to be held by him as his man.
1031. Canute goes to Scotland, and Malcolm II. submits to him as his overlord. [Malcolm had obtained possession of Lothian, which had been apparently lost since Edgar's reign. He did homage for it as an English earldom.]
1054. Earl Siward, in the interest of Malcolm (afterwards III.), defeats Macbeth.
1056. Malcolm Canmore becomes King of Scotland.
1068. Malcolm III. (1057-93) makes peace and does homage for Cumberland.
1070. Malcolm III. marries Margaret, sister of Edgar Etheling.
1072. William I. invades Scotland, and Malcolm becomes his man.

SUMMARIES.

1091. William II. compels Malcolm III. to do homage.
1092. William II. takes possession of Cumberland.
1100. Henry I. marries Matilda, daughter of Malcolm III.
1138. David I. (1124-53) is defeated at the battle of the Standard, near Northallerton. David I. administers the northern counties till the end of the reign, his son Henry having received the earldom of Northumberland from Stephen.
1157. Henry II. causes Malcolm IV. to give up the northern counties, and to do homage for the earldom of Huntingdon, which David had held in right of his marriage with the daughter of Waltheof (see 1074).
1173. William the Lion joins the alliance against Henry II.
1174. The Scots invade England. William the Lion is captured at Alnwick. He is set free (by the Convention of Falaise), the castles of Lothian surrendered, and homage for Scotland exacted.
1189. Richard releases William the Lion from his engagement with Henry II.
1200. William the Lion does homage to John at Lincoln.
1209. John marches to the north, and receives such homage from the King of Scotland as was done before the Convention of Falaise.
1216. The King of Scots (Alexander II.) comes to Dover to do homage to Louis of France.
1221. Joan, sister of Henry III., marries Alexander.
1251. Alexander III. marries Margaret, daughter of Henry III.
1278. Alexander III. does homage to Edward for his English fiefs alone, and not for his kingdom.
1284. The Maid of Norway, granddaughter of Alexander III., is declared heir to the Scottish throne.
1286. Death of Alexander III.
1290. The Scotch consent to the marriage between Margaret, Maid of Norway, and Edward, Prince of Wales.
Death of Margaret.

SCOTLAND.—Part II. 1290—1603.

1291. Meeting at Norham with the Scots, who acknowledge Edward's claim to decide the question of the succession as overlord.
1292. Decision in favour of John Balliol, who accepts the throne as a vassal of England.
1293. Appeals against Balliol made to the English courts. Balliol is summoned to London to answer them.
1294. First alliance made between Scotland and France against England.
1295. First invasion of Scotland by Edward.
1296. Battle of Dunbar; surrender of Balliol, who is dispossessed, his kingdom treated as a forfeited fief, and John, Earl of Warrenne, is appointed guardian.
1297. Rising of Wallace. Battle of Cambuskenneth. Wallace is victorious, and assumes the post of guardian for Balliol.
1298. Second invasion by Edward. Defeat of Wallace at Falkirk. Edward attempts the constitutional union of England and Scotland.
1299. Comyn is placed by the Scots at the head of a regency for Balliol.

SUMMARIES.

1299. Pope Boniface claims Scotland as a fief of Rome.
1303. Scots under the Regent Comyn defeat the English.
1304. Comyn makes a treaty with Edward.
1306. Robert Bruce murders Comyn, and rebels. Bruce is crowned at Scone. Invasion of Scotland. Bruce defeated, and many of his adherents executed.
1310. Edward II. and Gaveston invade Scotland.
1311. Castle of Linlithgow taken by the Scots.
1312. Perth surprised by Robert Bruce.
1313. Roxburgh and Edinburgh taken by the Scots. Siege of Stirling by Robert Bruce.
1314. Edward II. invades Scotland. Battle of Bannockburn. English totally defeated.
1315. The Scots ravage Northumberland.
1316. Robert Bruce goes to Ireland to help his brother Edward.
1318. Robert Bruce retakes Berwick and ravages Yorkshire.
1323. Truce of thirteen years between England and Scotland.
1327. Scots invade England.
1328. Peace concluded between England and Scotland at Northampton, and the complete independence of Scotland is recognised.
1329. Death of Robert Bruce, succeeded by his son David, aged seven.
1332. Edward Balliol invades Scotland. His first expulsion from Scotland.
1333. Scots invade England. Siege of Berwick. Battle of Halidon Hill.
1334. Balliol's second expulsion from Scotland
1335. Edward III. and Balliol invade Scotland.
1336. The French help the Scots.
1346. Defeat of Scots at Nevill's Cross. Capture of David II.
1371. David II. is succeeded by his brother-in-law, Robert the Steward.
1385. Richard II. ravages Scotland, which had received help from France.
1388. Battle of Otterburn. The Scots are victorious, but Douglas is slain.
1402. The Scots invade England, are defeated at Homildon Hill by the Percies.
1405. James, heir to the Scottish crown, is captured by the English.
1406. Robert III. dies, and is succeeded by his son James, then a prisoner in England.
1417. Scots invade England.
1424. James I. is released by England and returns to Scotland.
1436. James I. is murdered, and succeeded by James II.
1449. War breaks out with Scotland, and a truce is made.
1460. James II. succeeded by James III.
1482. Richard, Duke of Gloucester, on behalf of his brother, Edward IV., helps the Duke of Albany in Scotland against James III. Edinburgh and Berwick are captured.
1488. James III. succeeded by James IV.
1502. James IV. marries Margaret, eldest daughter of Henry VII.
1513. Battle of Flodden Field. Defeat of the Scots and death of James IV.
1542. Panic and flight of the Scots at the battle of Solway Moss. Death of James V., succeeded by Mary, then a week old.
1543. A treaty for the marriage of Prince Edward and Mary, Queen of Scots, is arranged.
1544. Invasion of Scotland under Lord Hertford and Lord Lisle.

SUMMARIES.

1547. The Protector (Somerset) invades Scotland to enforce the treaty of marriage of 1543, and defeats the Scots at the battle of Pinkie.
1557. First Covenant signed at Edinburgh.
1559. John Knox returns to Scotland, and puts himself at the head of the Reformers.
1560. Elizabeth sends help to the Scottish Reformers against the French.
The Regent of Scotland dies, and by the treaty of Edinburgh the French troops leave Scotland.
1561. Mary, now a widow, returns from France.
1565. Mary marries Darnley.
1567. Murder of Darnley. Mary marries Bothwell.
Mary is forced to abdicate, succeeded by her son, James VI.
1568. Mary, having escaped from prison in Scotland, and been defeated at Langside, takes refuge in England. Mary's case is investigated before a conference at York. Mary is consigned to Tutbury.
1572. Parliament proposes an attainder against Mary, which is forbidden by the queen.
1586. Trial of Mary, Queen of Scots, by special commission.
1587. Mary is executed.
1592. Presbyterian Church established by an Act of the Scottish Parliament.
1603. James VI. of Scotland becomes James I. of England.

SCOTLAND.—PART III. 1603—1707.

1607. A bill for the Union between England and Scotland is rejected in the House of Commons.
1612. Episcopacy is authorized in Scotland by the Scottish Estates.
1618. The Articles of Perth, imposing much ceremonial in Scotland, are passed by the General Assembly.
1633. The choice of the Lords of the Articles is put into the hands of the bishops by Charles.
1637. The Scots resist the introduction by Laud of a new Liturgy resembling the English Prayer-Book.
1638. The Second Covenant is drawn up, and Episcopacy in Scotland is condemned by the Glasgow Assembly.
1639. The king advances to Berwick; the Scots, assisted by money from France, advance to the Border (*June*); the pacification of Berwick is concluded.
Aug. The Scottish Parliament meets, formally abolishes Episcopacy, and makes preparations for war.
1640. The Scots invade England, win the battle of Newburn, and advance into Yorkshire. Treaty of Ripon.
1641. The king goes to Scotland, attended by a committee of the Commons.
1643. *Sept.* 25. The English Parliament makes an agreement with the Scots for assistance, and signs the Solemn League and Covenant.
1644. The Scottish army enters England and takes an important part in the civil war.
1644-45. Montrose defends the king's cause in Scotland, but is defeated at Philiphaugh 1645.
1648. The Scottish moderate Presbyterian party in the Estates pass a vote that 40,000 men under Hamilton shall invade England in the king's interest, but are defeated at Preston.
1649. Prince Charles accepts the proposals of the extreme Covenanters under Argyll.

SUMMARIES.

1650. Montrose, defeated at Corbiesdale, is executed *May* 21.
Charles, having first signed the Covenant, goes to Scotland.
Cromwell crosses the Tweed (*July* 16), advances to Edinburgh, and is forced to retreat to Dunbar for want of provisions. Battle of Dunbar, *Sept.* 3. Scots utterly routed: Edinburgh surrendered.
Dec. Capture of Edinburgh.
1651. *Jan.* 1. Charles is crowned at Scone. He gets together a new army from the followers of Hamilton and the Royalists, and takes up a position near Stirling. He then marches into England, and is defeated at Worcester.
1654. Union of England and Scotland by ordinance, and free-trade between the two countries established.
1661. Old form of government re-established, and Episcopacy enforced with much persecution of the Presbyterians.
Lords of Articles revived (they had ceased in 1641).
Permanent militia established.
1679. Murder of Archbishop Sharp.
Rebellion of the Covenanters and battle of Bothwell Bridge.
1685. Rising and execution of Argyll.
1689. *March* 14. A stormy session of the Convention begins at Edinburgh. Edinburgh Castle holds out for James.
Dundee (Graham of Claverhouse) retires to Stirling with troops, summons a parliament, and then retires to Blair Athol.
The Convention expels the bishops, abolishes Episcopacy, passes the "Claim of Right," and William and Mary are proclaimed (*April*).
Dundee defeats Mackay at Killiecrankie, but is killed, and is succeeded by Cannon, *July* 27.
Mackay gains some successes, and the Highlanders disperse.
1691. Military execution is proclaimed in Scotland against all classes who have not laid down their arms and taken the oath of allegiance by *Dec.* 31.
1692. Massacre of Glencoe.
1699. The failure of the Darien scheme causes great irritation in Scotland against the English.
1702. In accordance with the wish of William III., commissioners meet to treat for a union between England and Scotland, but cannot agree.
1703. The Scottish Parliament passes a resolution that "the Presbyterian Church is the only true Church of Christ in the kingdom," and also passes certain resolutions limiting the authority of the Crown—(1) No King of England was to declare peace or war without the consent of the Scottish Parliament; (2) the appointment of the great officers is transferred to the Scottish Parliament. A Bill of Security is passed to name a successor to the throne from the family of Sophia, but not the one named by England, unless security was given for free trade and independence in religion. The last does not receive the royal assent.
1704. The royal assent is given to the Act of Security.
English Parliament passes the Alien Bill.
1706. It was agreed that commissioners should again meet to treat of a union between England and Scotland.
1707. The Act for the Union is passed, see 1707.

SUMMARIES.

SCOTLAND.—Part IV. 1707—1881.

1712. An Act of this year restores, in opposition to the feeling of the Scottish Church, the ancient rights of patronage, and this leads ultimately to the great secession of 1843.
1715. Rebellion in Scotland in favour of the Stuarts, and battle of Sheriff Muir.
1719. The Spaniards invade Scotland, and are joined by some Highlanders, but are defeated at Glenshiel.
1736. Porteous riots in Edinburgh. Captain Porteous hanged by the mob.
1745. Rebellion in Scotland in favour of the Stuarts, see 1745.
1746. Highlanders are forbidden to wear their national dress, and the territorial jurisdiction of the chiefs abolished, compensation being given.
Office of Secretary of State for Scotland is abolished.
1779. Anti-Popish riots in Scotland.
1843. *March.* The House of Commons decline to entertain the petition of the General Assembly of Scotland (on the vexed question of patronage, and the right of the civil courts in spiritual jurisdiction) by a majority of 135.
May. Great secession from the Scottish Church. Establishment of the Free Church in Scotland.
1874. The patronage of the Scottish Church is transferred by Act of Parliament to the male communicants of each kirk.

IRELAND.—Part I. To 1494.

c. 450. St. Patrick converts the Irish.
795. Invasion of Ireland by the Northmen.
1014. Brian Boru defeats Northmen at Clontarf, but his death plunges the country into anarchy.
1151. Irish Church organized by bull of Eugenius III.
1154. Ireland granted to Henry II. by the Pope.
1169. The Normans gain a footing in Ireland for the first time.
1171-72. Henry II. goes over to Ireland, and his supremacy is acknowledged.
1177. John, son of Henry, is nominated Lord of Ireland.
1295. Members for counties sent to the Dublin Parliament.
1315. Edward Bruce invades Ireland and defeats the colonists.
1316. Robert Bruce goes to the assistance of his brother.
1318. Edward Bruce is defeated and killed near Dundalk.
1331-38. English ordered to be used, and English officials only to be appointed.
1341. Burgesses appear as sitting in the Irish Parliament.
1366. Statute of Kilkenny (see note).
1394 and 1399. Richard II. goes to Ireland.
1459. Act passed by the Irish Parliament that it will be independent of English legislation.
1494. Poynings' law is passed (see note).

SUMMARIES.

IRELAND.—PART II. 1494—1801.

1534. Insurrection of the Kildares.
From this time a system of forfeiture and colonization was steadily carried out.
1536. Act of Supremacy passed by the Irish Parliament, repealed 1556, re-enacted with the Act of Uniformity 1560.
1542. Henry VIII. takes the title of King of Ireland instead of Lord of Ireland.
[1565. Insurrection of Shan O'Neill (Ulster) continues three years.]
[1577. Rebellion in Connaught.]
1579-80. Rebellion in Munster assisted by the Spaniards.
1595. Tyrone (O'Neal), assisted by Philip of Spain, rebels, and Sir John Norris is sent against him.
1598. Death of Sir John Norris in Ireland, and defeat of Bagnal by O'Neal.
1599. Essex is sent to Ireland against O'Neal. He fails, and returns to England.
1601. Spaniards land in Ireland and fortify Kinsale.
1602. O'Neal submits and is pardoned.
1611. Colonization of Ulster by natives of Great Britain begins.
1633. Wentworth governor in Ireland to 1640 (see 1633).
1641. Irish Rebellion.
1643. *Sept.* The Marquis of Ormond makes peace ("The Cessation") with the Irish and sends troops over to England.
1649. *Aug.* 15. Cromwell lands in Ireland.
Sack of Drogheda and of Wexford.
1652. Cromwellian Settlement (see note).
1661. Act of Settlement (see note).
1663. Irish ships excluded from the benefit of the Navigation laws.
1665. Importation of Irish live-stock or meat to England forbidden.
1689. Irish Catholics under Tyrconnel take part with James, besiege the Protestants in Londonderry and Enniskillen, and repeal the Act of Settlement.
1690. Battle of the Boyne.
1691. Battle of Aughrim and capitulation of Limerick.
Catholics forbidden to sit in Parliament.
1692. Severe laws passed against the Catholics in this year and during the reigns of William III. and Anne. They entered into every relation of life, and harassed the Catholics in the possession of their property, the education of their children, and the exercise of their religion.
1695. The Irish Parliament repeals all the Acts of James II.'s Parliament of 1691.
1699. Exportation of Irish manufactured wool prohibited.
1704 and 1713. Test Act and Schism Act extended to Ireland.
1719. Toleration Act passed by the Irish Parliament.
Statute passed to enable the English Parliament to legislate for Ireland.
1723. Great agitation against Wood's copper coinage. It is given up next year.
1727. Catholics forbidden to vote.
1779. Dissenters admitted to office in Ireland by an Act of the Irish Parliament.
1780. Irish volunteers demand legislative independence, and help the Parliament.

SUMMARIES.

1780. Free-trade granted to Ireland.
1781. The Permanent Mutiny Bill is passed.
1782. Grattan's Declaration of Right accepted by the Irish Parliament, and Statute 6 George I. and the Permanent Mutiny Bill repealed by the English, and other concessions made.
1783. Flood's motion for parliamentary reform rejected.
1785. Mr. Pitt proposes a wise and liberal measure, with a view of giving Ireland commercial freedom, but the jealousy and opposition of traders and others in the House of Commons forces him to abandon it.
1789. Irish Parliament ask the Prince of Wales to assume the Regency as his right.
1791. Formation of the United Irishmen.
1792-93. Catholic Relief Bills passed in the Irish Parliament.
1793. Franchise restored to Catholics.
1794. Lord Fitzwilliam becomes Viceroy of Ireland.
The United Irishmen apply to France and prepare for rebellion.
1795. Lord Camden succeeds Lord Fitzwilliam as Viceroy of Ireland.
First Orange lodges formed in Ireland, though Orangemen had existed before.
1796. The French expedition to Ireland is dispersed by a storm, and proves a complete failure.
1798. Irish Rebellion. Arrest of O'Connor, Lord Edward Fitzgerald, and others. Lord Cornwallis succeeds Lord Camden. Insurrection breaks out. General Lake defeats the rebels at Vinegar Hill, *June* 2. Humbert's expedition.
1800. Bill for the Union of England and Ireland passes the Irish Parliament.
Act for the Union of Great Britain and Ireland is passed.

IRELAND.—PART III. 1801—1882.

1803. Emmett and others are arrested, tried, and executed for insurrection at Dublin.
1823. Catholic Association formed.
1828. O'Connell is elected for the county of Clare, but cannot sit, being a Catholic.
1829. Complete repeal of the Catholic disabilities, and the qualification for county votes raised to £10.
O'Connell is re-elected for Clare. He agitates for repeal of the Union between England and Ireland in this and following years.
1831. Many outrages in Ireland this year, especially owing to the collection of tithes, which now becomes in many places impossible.
1833. The Church Temporalities (Ireland) Act, reducing and reforming the Irish Church, and appointing a commission, is carried.
A bill is passed on the subject of Irish tithes for collecting arrears of tithe, and giving the clergy £1,000,000 on loan in compensation for arrears.
March. A Coercion Bill for Ireland is passed.
1834. O'Connell's motion for repeal of the Union is thrown out by 523 to 38.
May 27. Ward moves that the Church Establishment in Ireland exceeds the wants of the population, and ought to be reduced.
June 2. Lord Althorp meets Ward's motion by

SUMMARIES.

announcing a special Commission (composed of laymen) on the revenues of the Irish Church.
1834. The Irish Coercion Bill is renewed.
The Irish Land-Tax Act, proposing a substitute for tithes, is thrown out by the Lords.
1835. Lord John Russell carries his motion involving the appropriation of the surplus revenues of the Irish Church to general, moral, and religious purposes. The Irish Tithe Bill, embodying the appropriation clauses, is passed by the Commons. In the Lords the appropriation clauses are rejected, and the bill accordingly abandoned.
1836. *June.* The Irish Municipal Bill having been carried in the Commons by 61, is altered by the Lords, and ultimately rejected by the Commons.
Aug. The Irish Tithe Bill having been carried in the Commons, its appropriation clause is rejected by the Lords, and the bill is abandoned.
1837. *May.* The Irish Tithe Bill (introduced for the fifth time) is afterwards dropped owing to the dissolution.
The Irish Municipal Bill is again defeated in the Lords.
1838. The Irish Poor Law is passed. The ministers announce the placing of the Irish tithe question on a new footing, which implies the abandonment of the appropriation clauses. The bill passed both Houses, and the tithes are allowed to be commuted.
1840. The Irish Municipal Act passes after six years' controversies and difficulties between the House of Commons and the House of Lords.
The agitation for the repeal of the Union is renewed.
1842. Young Ireland movement begins.
1843. A monster repeal meeting at Clontarf, near Dublin, is forbidden by a Government proclamation. O'Connell and other repeal leaders are arrested.
1844. Trial of O'Connell. He is sentenced to a year's imprisonment and a fine of £2000. This sentence is reversed on a technical error.
1845. Sir R. Peel's Maynooth Act is passed, augmenting and putting on a permanent basis the grant to Maynooth College.
Sir R. Peel founds the Queen's Colleges in Ireland for the improvement of undenominational education.
1846. On the Irish Coercion Bill the Government are defeated.
Potato famine in Ireland, followed by wholesale emigration (see note).
1847. The Government grant £10,000,000 for the relief of Ireland.
Coercion Bill passed for Ireland.
1848. Trial of O'Brien, Mitchel, and others in Ireland for treason felony.
July. Habeas Corpus Act suspended in Ireland.
Abortive rebellion under Smith O'Brien. Transportation of the leaders.
1849. Encumbered Estates Act (Ireland) passed to facilitate the sale of encumbered properties.
1850. Irish Tenant-Right League, including men of all sects, formed.
1852. Crawford's Tenant-Right Bill thrown out.
1856. Miall's motion in favour of Irish Church disestablishment is rejected by 70 votes.
1859. Phœnix conspirators arrested and tried. Their club, under O'Donovan Rossa, forms the nucleus of Fenianism.

SUMMARIES.

1860. Relations of landlord and tenant based on contract instead of tenure.
1865. Arrest of Fenian leaders.
1866. Habeas Corpus Act suspended.
Fenian insurrection.
1868. Mr. Gladstone moves resolutions advocating the disestablishment of the Irish Church.
1869. Irish Church disestablished and partially disendowed.
1870. Irish Land Act passed (see note).
Home Government Association formed.
1873. Home Rule League substituted for Home Government Association.
1877. Irish members begin to obstruct the proceedings of the House of Commons.
1879. Land League formed.
Great distress.
1880. Great agitation in connection with the land question.
1881. Protection of Life and Property and Peace Preservation Acts passed.
Gladstone's second Irish Land Act passed (see note).
1882. Murder of Lord F. Cavendish, Chief Secretary.
1885. A Land Purchase Bill (commonly called Lord Ashbourne's Act) passed.
1886. Home Rule accepted by Gladstone, but rejected by Parliament, and by the country.
1887. Criminal Law Amendment Act (Ireland) passed.

LAW COURTS.—1107—1881.

1107 The Curia Regis is organized and the Exchequer Court founded by Roger of Salisbury.
1154-89. By the Great Assize established during Henry II.'s reign recognition by jury in *civil* cases is allowed (as a substitute for trial by battle).
1166. The provincial administration of justice is rearranged. A jury of presentment is ordered in *criminal* cases (the *grand* jury).
1176. Instructions are given to itinerant justices, which are carried out by six detachments of justices sent on circuit.
1178. A selection of judges is made from the Curia Regis, out of which are afterwards developed the Courts of King's Bench and Common Pleas.
The highest appellate jurisdiction is reserved to the king in the Ordinary Council (see Summary: Council to 1641, p. 266).
1215. Trial by ordeal is abolished (and as a consequence trial by *petty* jury in *criminal* cases grows up).
Court of Common Pleas fixed at Westminster.
c. 1272. By the end of Henry III.'s reign the staff of Curia Regis is broken up into three distinct bodies for the Courts of Exchequer, King's Bench, and Common Pleas (see note.)
1300. The Chancery and King's Bench are still to follow the king: the Exchequer is to remain with the Common Pleas at Westminster.
1348. The separate jurisdiction of the Chancellor in the Court of Chancery is from this time definitely recognised.
1487. A new court is established, which becomes merged in the Star Chamber Court, and revives and extends the old criminal jurisdiction of the Ordinary Council.
1583. The High Commission Court is placed on a permanent footing.
1641. The Court of Star Chamber and the High Commission Court are abolished.

SUMMARIES.

1689. The late Court of Ecclesiastical Commission "and all other commissions and courts of like nature are illegal and pernicious" (Bill of Rights).
1701. "That . . . judges' commissions be made *quamdiu se bene gesserint* and their salaries ascertained and established; but upon the address of both Houses of Parliament it may be lawful to remove them" (*Act of Settlement*).
1825. A commission is appointed to inquire into the administration of the Court of Chancery (see note).
1852. In this and other years great improvements are effected in the procedure of the Courts both of Chancery and of Common Law.
1873. Supreme Court of Judicature Act, constituting one High Court of Justice (into which the Courts of Equity and Common Law are consolidated) and a Supreme Court of Appeal.

ARMY.—1073—1881.

[Up to the Conquest the defence of the country was confided to the fyrd or militia, but the Danish kings employed, besides, their bodyguard or huscarls. At the Conquest the practice of holding land by military tenure became general, and an additional force, the feudal levy, sprang up, and the sovereigns employed sometimes one, sometimes the other.]

1073. William I. employs an English army for the conquest of Maine.
1094. Flambard takes from the militia collected at Hastings to go to Normandy their journey-money.
1138. The militia is employed at the battle of Northallerton.
1159. The first regular scutage or payment, instead of feudal service, is collected.
1173. The militia is employed against the Scots.
1181. The militia is regulated by the Assize of Arms.
1213. The barons refuse to follow John to France, on the ground that their tenures forbid them.
1252. A writ is issued for enforcing the Assize of Arms.
1285. The Statute of Winchester re-enacts the Assize of Arms and regulates the militia.
[During the Hundred Years' War with France soldiers hired by the chief barons were employed by the sovereigns, who thus for the time being constituted a standing army; for defence against invasion, the militia of each county was organized by commissioners of array.]
1485. Henry VII. established the yeomen of the guard.
[When artillery was introduced, a few men skilled in its use were maintained in the chief fortresses, such as the Tower, Portsmouth, Berwick.]
[In the reign of Mary the militia of each county was placed under the command of a new officer, the Lord-Lieutenant.]
1642. The Commons request the king to place the charge of the fortified places and the command of the militia in their hands, but are refused.
1645. The new model army is organized, and continues as a standing army till 1660.
1660. The standing army is disbanded except two regiments, Monk's (the Coldstream) and one of horse.
1674 and 1677. The Commons oppose the increase of the numbers of the army; but it is increased both under Charles II. and James II.
1689. In the Bill of Rights a standing army without the consent of Parliament is declared illegal.
1689. In consequence of the mutiny of a Scottish regiment

SUMMARIES.

in England the first Mutiny Act is passed, and has been renewed annually down to the present time.

1689. [During the reigns of William III., Anne, George I., and George II. the Commons showed great jealousy of a standing army, and George II. had recourse to hiring Hessians and other foreigners.]

1704. The regiment of Royal Artillery, which had developed out of the skilled soldiers mentioned, was increased in numbers for the defence of Minorca, Gibraltar, and Annapolis, and gradually formed part of the regular army.

1757. The militia was reorganized under the direction of Pitt.

1803. In defence against the French the militia is embodied, yeomanry cavalry are raised, and volunteers are formed.

[1814. At the peace the volunteers were disbanded, but the yeomanry, with the militia, were retained, and called out occasionally for exercise.]

1847. Up to this time enlistment in the army had been for life; but this year short service of ten or twelve years was introduced, with the choice of joining for twenty-one years.

1859. A reserve force was created and organized by numerous subsequent statutes.

Volunteers are formed, and afterwards regulated by several statutes.

1870. Army Enlistment Act passed, instituting short service for six years.

By an Order in Council the commander-in-chief is placed under the control of the Secretary for War.

1871. The practice of purchasing commissions is abolished by Royal Warrant.

An Act is passed to provide for the resumption by the Crown of direct authority over the militia, yeomanry, and volunteers.

1875. Regimental Exchanges Act is passed.
1879. The Army Discipline and Regulation Act is passed.
1881. The Regulation of the Forces Act and the Army Act are passed.

SECTION B.

SUMMARIES WHICH BELONG TO SPECIAL PERIODS.

GRADUAL UNION OF ENGLAND INTO ONE KINGDOM.—449—827.

449. Kingdom of Kent is begun.
477. Kingdom of Sussex is begun.
495. Kingdom of Wessex is begun by Cerdic and Cynric.
547. Kingdom of Northumbria is begun.
(Kingdoms of East Anglia and Mercia, dates uncertain.)

617. *Supremacy of Northumbria.* Edwin, King of Northumbria, subdues all England except Kent.
633. Edwin is defeated and killed by Penda, King of Mercia, at the battle of Hatfield.
642. Oswald is defeated and killed by Penda, King of Mercia, at the battle of Maserfield.
655. Penda is defeated and killed by Oswy, King of Northumbria, at the battle of Winwidfield.
685. Egfrith, King of Northumbria, is defeated and killed by the Picts. *End of supremacy of Northumbria.*

757. Offa becomes King of Mercia.
Supremacy of Mercia.
774. Offa defeats the men of Kent at Otford.
777. Offa defeats the West Saxons at Bensington.

802. Egbert becomes King of the West Saxons.
825. Egbert defeats the Mercians at Ellandun.
Supremacy of Wessex.
826. The men of Kent, Sussex, Essex, and East Anglia submit to Egbert.
827. Egbert conquers the Mercians, and the Northumbrians submit to him.
[Egbert now is King of the English south of the Thames, and Overlord of all the English as far as the Forth.]

THE NORTHMEN IN ENGLAND.—787—897; 907—937 980—1017.

1. *Invasions and settlements of the Northmen.*
787. Northmen first invade England.
836. ,, are defeated by Egbert at Hengest's Down.
847. ,, are defeated at the mouth of the Parret.
851. ,, are defeated at Ockley by Ethelwulf.

SUMMARIES.

855. Northmen for first time remain over winter in Sheppey.
860. ,, sack Winchester.
865. ,, ravage Kent.
867. ,, take York.
868. ,, take Nottingham.
870. ,, defeat and kill Edmund, King of East Anglia.
871. ,, invade Wessex.
,, defeated at Englefield.
,, victorious at Reading.
,, defeated at Ashdown.
,, victorious at Basing.
,, victorious at Merton.
,, victorious at Wilton.
,, make peace with the West Saxons.
,, make peace with the Mercians.
,, ravage Northumbria.
,, apportion Northumbria.
877. ,, apportion Mercia.
878. ,, invade Wessex under Guthrum. [Alfred retreats to Athelney.]
,, defeated at Ethandun. *Peace of Wedmore.*
880. ,, apportion East Anglia.
893. ,, coming from France ravage England, assisted by the new settlers.
Much fighting all over England for four years.
897. ,, Alfred builds a new fleet and stops the invasions.

2. *Reconquest by the English of the Northmen's settlements in England.*

907. Ethelfleda fortifies Chester.
910. War with the Northmen renewed.
912. Edward recaptures London.
913. Edward fortifies Hereford and Witham.
Ethelfleda fortifies Tamworth and Stafford.
914. ,, fortifies Warwick.
917. ,, captures Derby.
918. ,, captures Leicester. Makes a treaty with the men of York.
919. Edward captures Bedford.
921. ,, compels East Anglia and Essex to submit.
922. ,, captures Stamford.
,, compels the district south of the Humber to submit.
923. ,, captures Manchester.
924. ,, fortifies Nottingham. The Northmen of Northumbria choose Edward for father and lord.
937. Northmen from Ireland with others defeated at Brunanburh by Athelstan.

3. *Political conquest of England by the Danes.*

980. The invasions of the Danish Northmen (now separated from the Swedes and Norwegians) begin.
991. Danes victorious at Maldon. First payment of Danegeld by the English. The Danes are bought off four times in the next twenty-one years.
994. Sweyn, King of the Danes, and Anlaf, King of the Norwegians, attack London and winter at Southampton.
1002. Massacre of the Danes on St. Brice's Day.
1003. Sweyn in revenge invades England again.
1013. Sweyn harries England. Ethelred flies to Normandy, and Sweyn is acknowledged as king.

1014. Sweyn dies. The Danes choose his son Canute, the English Ethelred, for king. Ethelred drives out Canute.
1015. Canute forces Wessex to submit.
1016. Canute marches through Mercia to York. Great struggle between Edmund and Canute for the kingdom. Edmund defeats the Danes at Pen Selwood, at Shirestone, and at Brentford. Edmund is defeated by Canute at Assandun. *Partition of England.* Edmund has Wessex, Essex, and East Anglia; Canute, Mercia and Northumbria.
1017. On the death of Edmund, Canute is chosen King of all England.

THE UNION OF NORMANDY AND ENGLAND.—1002—1071.

1002. Ethelred marries Emma, daughter of Richard I. of Normandy.
1017. Canute marries Emma.
1035. *William becomes Duke of Normandy.*
1036. Edward and Alfred, sons of Ethelred and Emma, come over from Normandy to Wessex. Alfred is blinded, and dies; Edward returns.
1041. Hardicanute sends to Normandy for his half-brother Edward.
1042. Edward the Confessor is chosen king.
1044. Robert of Jumièges appointed Bishop of London; first Norman bishop in England.
1051. Robert of Jumièges made Archbishop of Canterbury. Eustace of Boulogne quarrels with the men of Dover. William, Duke of Normandy, visits Edward.
1052. Godwin and his family return, and the foreigners are outlawed.
1066. Harold crowned king at Westminster. William sends to claim the crown and is refused. Harold collects an army and fortifies the southern coast; is forced to go north to repel Tostig and Harold Hardrada.
Sept. 28. William lands at Pevensey.
Battle of Hastings. Oct. 14. Edgar Etheling chosen king by the Witan. William marches to Berkhampstead. Edgar Etheling, Edwin and Morcar, and the men of London submit.
Dec. 25. William is crowned at Westminster.
1067. William visits Normandy. Rebellions in Kent and Hereford.
1068. William subdues Exeter. The people of Northumberland rebel, and call in Edgar Etheling from Scotland, but are subdued.
Harold's sons ravage Bristol.
1069. Great rising of the north, with the assistance of Danes and Edgar Etheling. William retakes York, and ravages the country between Humber and Tees.
1071. Rising of Edwin and Morcar. Edwin killed. Morcar joins Hereward, who is defeated by William. *Last struggle for independence. Norman conquest of England completed.*

SUMMARIES.

STRUGGLE BETWEEN THE KINGS AND THE FEUDAL NOBILITY.—1074—1174.

1074. Conspiracy of the Norman earls Ralf Guader and Roger of Breteuil.
1082. Odo, Bishop of Bayeux, Earl of Kent, apprehended, and his possessions seized by William I.
1088. Rebellion of Normans, headed by Odo of Bayeux, and Roger, Earl of Shrewsbury, against William II., who appeals to the English, and suppresses it.
1095. The rebellion of Robert Mowbray, Earl of Northumberland, and the Norman earls is crushed.
1102. Robert of Belesme rebels, and is expelled from England.
1135-54. The barons get the better of the Crown.
1155. Henry II. resumes the royal demesnes, and destroys many of the newly-built castles.
1173. General league against Henry by his son, the Kings of France and Scotland, the Earl of Flanders, and the Norman barons.
R. de Lucy and W. Mandeville defeat the insurgent barons in England.
1174. The insurgent barons of Norfolk are put down.
Last struggle of Norman barons against the king.

LAWS, CODES, AND CHARTERS UP TO THE TIME OF THE GREAT CHARTER.—c. 600—1215.

c. 600. Laws of Ethelbert.
690. Laws of Ine.
c. 890. Alfred's Laws.
959-975. Edgar's Ordinance of the Hundred.
1016-35. Canute's Laws.
1043-66. English laws, probably of Edward the Confessor (recorded under William the Conqueror, 1070).
1100. Charter of Henry I.
1136. Charter of Stephen.
1154. Charter of Henry II.
1164. Constitutions of Clarendon.
1166 and 1176. Assizes of Clarendon and Northampton.
1181. Assize of Arms.
1184. Assize of the Forest.
1215. *The Great Charter.*

THE HUNDRED YEARS' WAR BETWEEN ENGLAND AND FRANCE.—1338—1453.

1328. Death of Charles IV., succeeded by Philip VI. of Valois.
1329 and 1331. Edward does homage for his lands in France.
1337. The French promise to help the Scots. Edward takes the title of the King of France.

1338. *Beginning of the war.* The French attack Portsmouth and Southampton.
Edward embarks for Flanders.

SUMMARIES.

- 1338. [Edward is in alliance with the states on the northeast of France.]
- 1339. Edward invades France unsuccessfully.
- 1340. Edward defeats the French fleet off Sluys.
- 1341. Edward supports the claim of John de Montfort to Brittany.
- 1346. *July.* Edward invades Normandy, and advances to Paris. He crosses the Seine and retreats towards Calais.
  Aug. 26. Victory of Crecy.
- 1347. Surrender of Calais.
- 1350. Philip VI. dies, and is succeeded by John II.
- 1356. The Black Prince marches from Bordeaux to Berri.
  Sept. 19. Victory of Poitiers, and capture of John II.
- 1360. Edward besieges Paris. Peace of Bretigny.
- 1364. John II. dies at the Savoy.
- 1367. Expedition of the Black Prince to help Pedro of Castile.
- 1369. The Black Prince is summoned to Paris on account of his heavy taxation of the Gascons.
  Renewal of the war.
- 1370. Invasion of Gascony by the French. Massacre of Limoges.
- 1373. John of Gaunt's disastrous expedition from Calais to Bordeaux.
- 1374. *Loss of all French possessions except Calais, Bordeaux, and Bayonne.*
- 1377. The French ravage the south coast.
- 1385. Scotland receives help from France.
- 1396. Richard marries Isabella of France at Calais, and a truce for twenty-five years is made.
- 1404. France supports Glendower.
- 1407. Murder of the Duke of Orleans.
- 1411. Henry sends troops to assist the Burgundians.
- 1412. *May.* Henry allies with the Orleanists.
  English invade Normandy and Guienne.
- 1415. *Aug.* Henry invades Normandy.
  Sept. Captures Harfleur.
  Marches on Calais.
  Oct. 25. Battle of Agincourt.
- 1416. Henry allies with John, Duke of Burgundy.
- 1417. Henry again invades France.
- 1420. Treaty of Troyes.
- 1421. English defeated at Beaugé.
- 1422. Death of Charles VI., succeeded by Charles VII.
- 1423. Bedford marries Anne of Burgundy.
  Battle of Crevant.
- 1424. Battle of Verneuil.
  Gloucester tries to gain the lands of Jacqueline of Hainault, whom he had married in 1423.
- 1429. Siege of Orleans. Joan of Arc.
  Charles VII. crowned at Rheims.
- 1430. Joan captured at Compiégne.
- 1435. Congress of Arras.
  Death of Bedford.
- 1435-44. *Gradual loss of Normandy and Guienne.*
- 1444. Truce for two years.
- 1445. Marriage of Henry to Margaret of Anjou.
  Surrender of Anjou and Maine to Réné.
- 1449. War renewed.
  Loss of Rouen.
- 1453. Defeat and death of Talbot at Chatillon. *Final loss of France except Calais.*

263

SUMMARIES.

YORK AND LANCASTER.—1385—1563.

1385. Roger Mortimer, Earl of March, is declared heir to the throne.
1399. Henry of Lancaster is declared king as Henry IV.
1405. Conspiracy of Mowbray and Archbishop Scrope in favour of the Earl of March. They are both captured and executed.
1415. Conspiracy to place Edmund Mortimer, Earl of March, on the throne discovered.
The Earl of Cambridge, father of Richard (afterwards Duke of York), executed with others.
1435. Bedford dies, succeeded by Richard, Duke of York, as Regent of France.
1444. John Beaufort dies, leaving a daughter, Margaret (mother of Henry VII.).
1447. Gloucester arrested and charged with high treason; he is found dead, *Feb.* 23. This leaves York heir-apparent.
1450. The Duke of York returns from Ireland to England.
1451. A proposal is made in the House of Commons to declare York heir to the throne.
1452. York collects an army and demands the dismissal of Somerset.
Somerset and the king force York to swear allegiance.
1453. Henry falls ill and becomes unable to govern.
Birth of Prince Edward.
Somerset is imprisoned.
1454. York is appointed by the Lords to a limited protectorate of the realm without prejudice to the rights of the Prince of Wales. He puts his own friends in office.
1455. Henry recovers. York is dismissed. Somerset is released, and with his friends returns to power.
The Duke of York, Salisbury, and his son Warwick take up arms to protect the king, really against Somerset.
First battle of St. Albans. Death of Somerset.
Capture of Henry.
1458. Reconciliation between the two parties at St. Paul's.
1459. The queen's attempt to arrest the Earl of Salisbury brings on the battle of Bloreheath. Yorkists victorious.
Panic of Ludlow. Flight of the Yorkists.
1460. *July.* Battle of Northampton won by the three earls, March, Salisbury, and Warwick.
York claims the throne, and is made heir to Henry by Parliament.
The queen raises forces.
Dec. Battle of Wakefield. Lancastrians victorious and York killed. Salisbury is executed at Pomfret.
1461. *Feb.* 3. Edward, Earl of March, fights against Pembroke at Mortimer's Cross. Yorkists victorious.
Feb. 17. The queen fights against Warwick at the second battle of St. Albans. Lancastrians victorious.
Edward comes back to London and is declared king.
Edward advances to the north. Battles of Ferrybridge and Towton. Yorkists victorious with very great slaughter.
Margaret escapes with Henry and her son to Scotland.
June. Edward is crowned at Westminster.
1464. Battle of Hedgely Moor. Margaret defeated.
Battle of Hexham. Margaret again defeated

SUMMARIES.

1464. *Sept.* Edward's marriage with Elizabeth Woodville is announced.
1465. Henry, the late king, is captured and imprisoned in the Tower.
1469. Clarence, who has drawn off from his brother the king to Warwick, marries Warwick's daughter, Isabella Neville.
Battle of Edgecote. Rebels victorious. Warwick and Clarence take advantage of this to imprison the king.
The king is released and a reconciliation effected.
A new rebellion is defeated by Edward at Losecoat Field.
Warwick and Clarence, finding that Edward has proofs of their treachery, fly to France and unite with Margaret, the late queen.
Sept. Warwick lands at Dartmouth. Edward flies to Flanders, his queen taking refuge at Westminster, and Henry VI. is restored.
1471. Edward, by the assistance of the Duke of Burgundy, his brother-in-law, lands at Ravenspur, is joined by Clarence, and advances to London.
April 14. Battle of Barnet. Yorkists victorious and Warwick killed.
April 14. Margaret lands at Weymouth.
May 4. Battle of Tewkesbury.
Margaret is defeated and her son killed.
May 21. Death of Henry VI. in the Tower.
1478. Clarence, distrusted by his brother, is executed.
1483. Accession of Edward V.
Usurpation of Richard III.
Abortive conspiracy of Buckingham, the Earl of Richmond, Morton, and the Woodvilles.
1484. Death of Richard's son, Edward, Prince of Wales.
1485. Death of the queen. Richard proposes to marry his niece, the Lady Elizabeth.
Aug. 7. Henry, Earl of Richmond, having sailed from Harfleur, lands at Milford Haven.
Aug. 22. Battle of Bosworth. Richard is defeated and killed.
Edward Plantagenet, Earl of Warwick, son of Clarence, is imprisoned in the Tower.
1486. Henry VII. marries Elizabeth of York.
1487. Lambert Simnel (calling himself Earl of Warwick) lands in Ireland, and then in Lancashire. He is defeated at Stoke, with Lincoln (Richard III.'s nephew and heir), who is killed.
1492. Perkin Warbeck (calling himself Richard, Duke of York, son of Edward IV.) lands in Ireland, and is afterwards invited to the court of France.
1493. Warbeck goes to Flanders, where Margaret, Duchess of Burgundy, receives him as her nephew.
1497. Warbeck, coming from Ireland, lands in Cornwall, fails to revive the insurrection, and is captured.
1499. Warbeck, having escaped and been recaptured, is executed with the Earl of Warwick.
1506. The Archduke Philip, wrecked in England, has to agree to deliver up the Earl of Suffolk, nephew of Edward IV.
1513. Suffolk is executed after seven years' imprisonment.
1538. The Countess of Salisbury, mother of Cardinal Pole, is imprisoned.
1539. The Marquis of Exeter and others are executed for treason.
1541. The Countess of Salisbury is executed.
1563. Edmund and Arthur Pole (the last of the Yorkists) are convicted of treason and imprisoned till their deaths.

SUMMARIES.

THE COUNCIL TO 1641.

1107. The Curia Regis is organized by Roger of Salisbury.
1178. The highest appellate jurisdiction is reserved to the king in his Ordinary Council.
c. 1216. The permanent continual Council (whence arose later the Privy Council) attending on and advising the king dates its importance from the beginning of Henry III.'s reign.
1348. The Chancellor's Court of Chancery is definitely recognised as separate from the Council.
1351. In this year begin a series of petitions against the usurped jurisdiction of the Privy Council.
1386. The first records of the Privy Council appear in this year.
1389. The Commons pray that the Chancellor and the Council may not after the close of Parliament make any ordinance contrary to the common law.
1404. Henry IV., at the special request of the Commons, names six bishops, nine lords, and seven commoners to be his "great and continual Council." In 1406 and 1410 a similar request is made.
1422. Humphrey of Gloucester, uncle of the king, in Bedford's absence, made president of the Council. [This Council is not only the Ordinary or Privy Council, but also a real Council of Regency nominated by regular Act of Parliament.]
1437. The king begins to nominate his own Council absolutely. [From this time the Privy Council loses connection with the Parliament, and becomes an instrument in the hands of the king or the court.]
1487. A new court is established for the trial of powerful offenders (which afterwards is merged into the Star Chamber Court, and revives and extends the old criminal jurisdiction of the Ordinary Council).
1537. The "Council of the North" is instituted to keep order after the Pilgrimage of Grace and other insurrections.
1591. Eleven judges remonstrate against illegal commitments by the Privy Council. [There are in succeeding years frequent complaints against Star Chamber, the Council of the North, etc.]
1641. *July.* The king's Council is deprived of the power of arbitrary imprisonment and jurisdiction. Court of Star Chamber abolished (therewith the Council of the North and the Court of Wales).

AMERICAN WAR OF INDEPENDENCE.—1764—1783.

1764. Grenville passes an Act imposing customs and duties on the American colonies, and gives notice of the Stamp Act.
1765. The Stamp Act is passed, notwithstanding the protests of six colonies.
1766. Repeal of the American Stamp Act by Lord Rockingham's ministry, supported by Pitt.
1767. Charles Townshend, Chancellor of the Exchequer, passes an Act for taxing American imports by various small customs duties [the total produce of which was estimated at not more than £40,000].
1770. *March.* All the American import duties are removed except the tax on tea.

SUMMARIES.

1770. Disturbances at Boston.
1773. The people of Boston board the ships and throw the tea overboard.
1774. The petition of Massachusetts for the removal of its governor is rejected by the Privy Council, and Franklin is insulted.
The Boston Port Bill passed, closing the port of Boston.
By a conciliatory policy, and the legal establishment of the Catholic religion, the loyalty of Canada is secured.
June. The Assembly of Massachusetts meets (under the English Crown) for the last time. It recommends a Congress of the different colonies, and is dissolved by Gage, the governor.
The Congress meets at Philadelphia, and denies the right of Parliament to tax the colonies.
1775. Chatham and Burke both propose schemes of conciliation towards America, which are rejected.
Battle of Lexington, indecisive.
Ticonderoga and Crown Point, which command the valley of the Hudson, are taken by the colonists.
George Washington (of Virginia) is chosen Commander-in-Chief by the Americans.
English win the battle of Bunker's Hill.
1776. The English under Sir William Howe are forced to evacuate Boston. They drive the Americans from Long Island and take New York, *July* 15.
July 4. Declaration of Independence. Congress declares the thirteen united colonies free and independent states.
1777. English win the battle of Brandywine and take Philadelphia.
General Burgoyne marches down the Hudson from Canada to join Clinton from New York, but is forced to surrender at Saratoga.
The French send help to the Americans.
1778. France recognises the independence of the States, and makes a treaty with them.
The Duke of Richmond's motion to recognise the independence of the United States is opposed by Chatham in his last speech.
English evacuate Philadelphia.
1779. Spain declares war against England, joining the United States.
1780. French army lands in Rhode Island.
English under Lord Cornwallis defeat the colonists at Camden, and gain various successes in the Southern States.
Major André, who had been captured while negotiating the defection of Benedict Arnold, hung as a spy.
1781. The English under Lord Cornwallis win the battle of Guilford, but are forced to surrender at Yorktown.
1783. Peace is signed between England and the United States. The independence of the United States is acknowledged.

JACOBITES.—1691—1807.

1691. Preston's plot discovered.
1692. Louis and James collect a great fleet at Brest and an army on the coast of Normandy to invade England.
James issues a declaration which excepts great

SUMMARIES.

numbers of Englishmen from pardon in case he is successful.
1692. Mary (William being abroad) causes this declaration to be published with notes.
May. The French fleet is utterly defeated by Russell off La Hogue.
1696. *Feb.* A plot (arranged by Sir George Barclay) to murder William, and a design to invade England, managed by the Duke of Berwick, are discovered.
1701. James II. dies and Louis XIV. recognises the Pretender.
1708. The French fleet is delayed by the illness of the Pretender, who has the measles, and on sailing to the Firth of Forth to support the Jacobites, is put to flight by Byng.
1713. Oxford and St. John intrigue to secure the succession of the Pretender.
1715. The Earl of Mar in Scotland, Forster and Derwentwater in England, raise rebellions. *Nov.* Forster is defeated and taken at Preston, and Mar fights the indecisive battle of Sheriff Muir against Argyle. The Pretender comes over, but soon withdraws (1716) with Mar. Derwentwater and others are executed. Forster escapes from prison.
1719. The Spaniards invade Scotland, and are joined by some Highlanders, but are defeated at Glenshiels.
1722. A Jacobite conspiracy is discovered, and Atterbury, Bishop of Rochester, is sent to the Tower.
1744. The French fleet which was prepared to support an expedition of Charles Edward to England is so much damaged by a storm that the attempt is abandoned.
1745. Landing of Charles Edward Stuart in the Highlands. He outwits Cope; is proclaimed at Edinburgh. Defeats Cope at Prestonpans, *Sept.* 21; takes Carlisle, *Nov.* 15; reaches Derby, *Dec.* 4, and retreats; reaches Glasgow, *Dec.* 25.
1746. Charles Edward defeats General Hawley at Falkirk, *Jan.* 17, but is defeated at Culloden, *April* 16.
Execution of Kilmarnock, Balmerino, Lovat (1747), Derwentwater (or Charles Radcliffe) (1747), and Dr. Cameron (1753).
[1788. Death of Prince Charles Edward.]
[1807. Death of Cardinal Henry of York, the last of the Stuarts.]

FRENCH WAR.—1793—1815.

1793. War declared by England against France, *Feb.* 11.
Troops are sent to Holland and to the south of France.
Toulon occupied and abandoned.
1794. Lord Howe gains a great victory over the French fleet, *June* 1.
The Duke of York is defeated at Bois-le-Duc.
1795. Return of the British from Holland.
Fruitless expedition to Quiberon Bay.
1796. The French expedition to Ireland is dispersed by a storm, and proves a complete failure.
1797. Sir John Jervis and Nelson defeat the French and Spaniards off Cape St. Vincent, *Feb.* 14.
Admiral Duncan defeats the Dutch fleet off Camperdown, *Oct.* 11.
1798. *Aug.* 1. Nelson utterly defeats the fleet which had conveyed Napoleon and his army to Egypt in the battle of the Nile.

SUMMARIES.

1799. Sir Sidney Smith helps the Turks to hold Acre against Napoleon.
The Duke of York takes command of the English expedition to Holland, and is defeated at Bergen.
1800. Lord Grenville rejects Buonaparte's proposals of peace.
Lord Keith in conjunction with the Austrians besieges Genoa.
Malta is captured from the French.
The Armed Neutrality between Russia, Sweden, Denmark, and Prussia is revived.
1801. Abercrombie defeats the French at Alexandria, but is killed.
Nelson destroys the Danish fleet off Copenhagen, and the Armed Neutrality is broken up.
1802. Treaty of Amiens signed.
1803. Declaration of war.
Napoleon prepares for invasion. Large bodies of volunteers formed.
1805. Napoleon attempts, by decoying Nelson away to the West Indies, to gain command of the Channel, but fails.
July 22. Sir Robert Calder fights the French and Spanish fleets off Ferrol.
Napoleon breaks up his camp at Boulogne, and gives up his expedition against England.
Oct. 21. The French and Spanish fleets are defeated off Cape Trafalgar, but Nelson is killed.
1806. Fox opens negotiations with Napoleon, but fails.
General Stuart lands in Calabria, and defeats the French at Maida.
Napoleon issues his Berlin Decrees against English commerce.
1807. The Orders in Council are issued in reply to the Berlin Decrees.
General Whitelocke is defeated in an expedition against Buenos Ayres, and is dismissed from the service.
An expedition against Copenhagen bombards the city and forces the surrender of the fleet. Heligoland is taken.
1808. The Spaniards rise against the French and demand help from England. Sir Arthur Wellesley is sent to Portugal, and the war in the Peninsula begins.
Aug. Sir Arthur Wellesley defeats the French at Roriça and Vimiero.
Portugal is evacuated in accordance with the Convention of Cintra.
Sir John Moore having taken the command of the English in Portugal, advances into Spain towards Burgos to relieve the Spaniards.
1809. He retires to Corunna and defeats the French, but is killed in the action, *Jan.* 16.
Sir Arthur Wellesley defeats Soult at Oporto and Victor at Talavera, but being unsupported by the Spaniards is obliged to retreat.
A great expedition is sent to Walcheren under Lord Chatham, and proves a complete failure.
1810. Lord Wellington defeats Masséna at Busaco (*Sept.*), and retires behind the lines at Torres Vedras, which Masséna cannot penetrate, and is forced to retreat (*Nov.*).
1811. Sir Thomas Graham defeats Victor at Barossa, and Masséna retires towards Ciudad Rodrigo.
May. Wellington defeats Masséna at Fuentes d'Onoro and takes Almeida.
May. Beresford defeats Soult at Albuera, but fails to take Badajos.
1812. *Jan.* Wellington storms Ciudad Rodrigo

SUMMARIES.

1812. *April.* Wellington storms Badajos.
July. Wellington defeats Marmont in the battle of Salamanca, and advances to Madrid. He fails to take Burgos, and is forced to retreat.
1813. *June.* Wellington defeats Joseph at the battle of Vittoria. Beats Soult at the battle of the Pyrenees (*July*). Storms St. Sebastian (*Sept.*). Pampeluna surrenders (*Oct.*).
English forces join the Prussians in Holland, but fail before Bergen-op-Zoom.
1814. Wellington invades France and wins the battle of Orthez (*Feb.*), and defeats Soult at Toulouse (*April*), after an armistice had been signed between the French and the allies at Paris.
First Peace of Paris.
1815. Napoleon escapes from Elba and lands in France (*March*). Wellington and Blucher take the command of the allied forces in Belgium.
June 16. Napoleon defeats the Prussians at Ligny, and Wellington defeats Ney at Quatre Bras.
June 18. Wellington and Blucher completely defeat Napoleon at Waterloo.
July. Napoleon surrenders himself to the English at Rochefort, and is conveyed to St. Helena.
Nov. Second Peace of Paris.

CATHOLIC RELIEF.—1778—1829.*

[For Catholic Disabilities see 1562, 1678, 1700, etc., and Summary, Ireland, p. 253.]

1778. Sir G. Savile passes his measure for the relief of Roman Catholics.
1801. Pitt proposes to pass a measure for the relief of the Catholics. The king opposes it, and Pitt with his friends resigns. Addington forms a ministry, but the illness of the king delays the proceedings.
1804. Pitt forms a new administration, and agrees not to bring up the Catholic question.
1805. Lord Grenville's motion to consider the Catholic disabilities rejected by 178 to 49, and a similar motion by Fox in the Commons rejected by 236 to 124.
1810. Grattan's motion in favour of the Catholics is defeated by 213 to 109; in 1811 by 146 to 83; and in 1812 by 300 to 215. Similar motions in the Lords by Lord Donoughmore rejected by 154 to 68; in 1811 by 121 to 62; in 1812 by 174 to 102.
1812. *July.* Canning carries a motion for the consideration of the laws affecting Catholics early in the following session by 235 to 106. A similar motion by the Marquis Wellesley lost in the House of Lords by 126 to 125.
1813. *Feb.* Grattan introduces a bill for Catholic relief which passes the second reading by 245 to 203, but in Committee the clause admitting Catholics to sit in Parliament is rejected by 251 to 247, and the bill is abandoned. (The Speaker, Abbot, headed the opposition to the bill.)
1815. Sir H. Parnell's motion for a committee to consider Catholic claims rejected by 228 to 147, and a similar motion by Lord Donoughmore rejected by 86 to 60.

In this Summary the details differ considerably from the general outline, and there are various additions with a view of making the progress of the movement clearer.

1816. Grattan's motion to consider the Catholic claims rejected by 172 to 141, and in 1817 by 245 to 221. Similar motion by Lord Donoughmore rejected by 73 to 69, and in 1817 by 142 to 90.
1817. The Military and Naval Officers' Oath Bill passed, opening all ranks in the army and navy to Catholics.
1819. Grattan's motion for committee to consider the Catholic claims rejected by 245 to 221, and Lord Donoughmore's (in the Lords) by 147 to 106.
1820. Death of Grattan.
1821. Plunket carries a motion to go into Committee upon the Catholic claims by 227 to 221: he then introduces a bill, which passes the second reading by 254 to 243, and the third reading by 216 to 197, but is thrown out in the Lords by 159 to 120.
1822. Canning's bill to admit Catholic Peers to sit and vote in the House of Lords passes the Commons (leave given by 249 to 244; second reading passed by 235 to 223), but it is rejected in the Lords by 171 to 129.
1823. Plunket again introduces the Catholic claims, but on his motion to go into Committee to consider them, the adjournment of the House is carried by 313 to 111. Burdett, Hume, Hobhouse, and many leading Whigs leave the House, and refuse to follow Plunket's lead on account of his having joined the Government. Violent quarrel between Canning and Brougham during the debate.

Lord Nugent's bills for admitting English Catholics to the franchise, and for making them eligible for certain offices, pass the Commons: the first is rejected in the Lords by 80 to 73, and the second dropped. The bills are reintroduced in the Lords in 1824 by Lansdowne, and rejected by 139 to 101, and 143 to 109.

The Catholic Association in Ireland is formed.
1825. The Catholic Association is suppressed by a bill in Parliament limited to three years.

Burdett carries a motion to go into Committee to consider the Catholic claims by 247 to 234, and then introduces a bill which passes the second reading by 268 to 241, and the third reading by 248 to 227. It is thrown out in the Lords on the second reading by 178 to 130.
1827. Burdett's motion for consideration of the Catholic claims rejected by 276 to 272.
1828. Revival of the Catholic Association.

Burdett's resolution to consider the Catholic claims is carried by 272 to 266, but the Lords refuse to concur by 181 to 137.

O'Connell is elected M.P. for Clare County against Vesey Fitzgerald (who had stood for re-election on accepting office as President of the Board of Trade) by 2057 to 983.
1829. The ministry determine to grant Emancipation.

Peel resigns his seat for Oxford University, and is defeated by Sir R. Inglis (755 to 609). He is then returned for Westbury.

An Act passed suppressing the Catholic Association.

March. The Catholic Relief Bill carried through the Commons (leave given by 348 to 160; second reading passed by 353 to 173; third reading by 320 to 142).

April. The bill passes the Lords (second reading by 217 to 112; third reading by 213 to 109).

SUMMARIES.

CORN LAWS.—1815—1846.*

[For history of the Corn Laws up to 1815 see note (d), p. 190.]

1815. Corn Law Act passed prohibiting importation when the price is below 80s. per quarter (carried in the Lords by 245 to 77, and in the Commons by 128 to 21.)

1822. Amendment of the Act of 1815. Foreign corn admitted at 70s. with a duty of 12s., to be reduced to 5s. when the price is 80s., and to 1s. when the price is 85s.

1823. Whitmore's motion to reduce the importation price by 2s. annually till it reaches 60s. rejected by 78 to 25.

1824. Whitmore's motion to admit importation at 55s. rejected by 187 to 47. A similar motion in 1826 rejected by 215 to 81.

1827. Canning's Corn Bill, introducing a sliding scale (20s. duty when the price is at 60s., decreasing to 1s. at 70s., and increasing by 2s. for every 1s. decrease in price), passes the Commons but is lost in the Lords through an amendment of Wellington (carried by 78 to 74, and confirmed on the report by 133 to 122) that foreign corn should not be taken out of bond till the price reaches 66s.

(In the Commons an amendment to impose the 20s. duty at 64s. rejected by 229 to 160, and one by Whitmore to impose the 20s. duty at 50s. rejected by 335 to 50.)

1828. Wellington's sliding scale passed (duty of 36s. 8d. at 50s., decreasing to 16s. 8d. at 68s., and 1s. at 73s., and increasing as the price falls). Amendment by Hume for a fixed duty of 15s., to be reduced to 10s. in 1834, rejected by 139 to 27.

1829. Hume's motion for a committee to consider the Corn Laws with a view to their repeal rejected by 154 to 12. Similar motion in 1831 rejected by 194 to 6.

1833. Whitmore (in the Commons) and Lord Fitzwilliam (in the Lords) introduce resolutions condemnatory of the Corn Laws, which are rejected, the former by 305 to 206, and the latter without division.

Fryer's bill for the repeal of the Corn Laws rejected by 73 to 47.

1834. Hume's motion on the Corn Laws is defeated by 157 (312 to 155).

1837. *May.* Clay's motion for a fixed duty of 10s., to be reduced to 5s. in 1839 (seconded by Villiers), rejected by 223 to 89.

1838. *March.* Villiers' motion to consider the Corn Laws is thrown out by 300 to 95.

Sept. Anti-Corn Law League formed.

1839. *Feb.* Villiers' motion to hear counsel in support of a petition against the Corn Laws rejected by 361 to 172.

March. Villiers' motion for a committee on the Corn Laws rejected by 342 to 195, and in 1840 by 300 to 177.

Lord Fitzwilliam's resolutions in the Lords condemnatory of the Corn Laws rejected by 224 to 24 (Brougham, Durham, Minto, Hatherton, and Holland in the minority), and in 1840 by 194 to 42.

[In the debate in the Lords, March 14, 1839, the Premier, Melbourne, said, "To leave the whole agricultural interest without protection, I declare before God that I think it the wildest and mad-

---

* In this Summary the details differ considerably from the general outline, and there are various additions with a view of making the progress of the movement clearer.

SUMMARIES.

dest scheme that has ever entered into the imagination of man to conceive."]

1841. The ministers propose a fixed duty of 8s., but no measure is brought in owing to the dissolution.
1842. *Feb.* Anti-Corn Law League bazaar at Manchester.
Peel's sliding scale (20s. duty at 51s., decreasing to 12s. at 60s. and 1s. at 73s.; duty not to exceed 20s. when the price falls below 51s.) is carried.
Amendments in favour of a fixed duty proposed by Russell and Melbourne rejected by 349 to 226 in the Commons, and 207 to 71 in the Lords.
Amendments in favour of total repeal proposed by Villiers and Brougham rejected by 393 to 90, and 109 to 5.
Second reading in the Lords carried against the protectionists by 119 to 17.
1843. Motions by Russell and Monteagle to inquire into the effects of Peel's sliding scale rejected by 244 to 145, and 200 to 78.
Villiers' motion for total repeal rejected by 381 to 125; in 1844 by 328 to 124, and in 1845 by 254 to 122.
1844. Cobden's motion for committee to inquire into the effects of protection duties rejected by 224 to 133, and in 1845 by 213 to 121.
1845. Sir R. Peel (proposing to his colleagues to repeal the Corn Laws, on the dissent especially of Lord Stanley) resigns.
Great meeting of the Anti-Corn Law League at Manchester, £60,000 subscribed in an hour and a half.
1846. Sir R. Peel proposes (and carries the introduction of) complete free-trade in corn and the gradual repeal of the Corn Laws (to take final effect after three years). He is opposed both by protectionists and by some free-traders. The bill is finally carried by 327 to 229. [10s. duty when the price is under 48s., decreasing by 1s. for every 1s. increase up to 53s.: to remain at 4s. when the price is 53s. and upwards. After *Feb.* 1, 1849, all corn to be admitted at 1s. duty.]
The bill is carried in the Lords by 47 (211 to 164).
[1869. The 1s. duty is abolished.]

INDIA.—1600—1881.

1600. The East India Company receives its first charter.
1639. Madras acquired. First English territory in India.
1662. England receives Bombay from Portugal.
1680. Death of Sivajee, the Mahratta.
1690. Calcutta is founded, and Fort William soon afterwards built.
1693. A new charter is granted to the East India Company.
1698. A charter is granted to another and new East India Company, called the "English" Company (established in 1691).
1707. Death of Aurungzebe, the Moghul.
1708. The old and new East India Companies are united. (A partial union had been effected in 1702.)
1746. Madras is surrendered to the French.
1748. Madras is restored by the Treaty of Aix-la-Chapelle.
1751. Capture and defence of Arcot by Robert Clive, and surrender of Trichinopoly by the French (1752).
1756. Calcutta is captured by Surajah Dowlah. Tragedy of the Black Hole.
1757. Calcutta retaken. Battle of Plassy, *June* 23, secures Bengal for England.
1760. Victory of Wandewash secures Madras, and completes the downfall of French power in India.

SUMMARIES.

1761. Capture of Pondicherry by Coote (restored 1763).
1764. The defeat of the Nabob of Oudh at Buxar by Munro makes England the leading power in India.
1773. Lord North's Act for the regulation of India.
1774. The governor of Bengal, Warren Hastings, is made first Governor-General (see note 1773).
1780. Hyder Ali invades the Carnatic.
Hyder Ali defeated by Sir Eyre Coote at Porto Novo.
1782. Hyder Ali dies, succeeded by Tippoo Sahib.
1784. *May.* Pitt's India bill is passed (see note).
1785. Warren Hastings leaves India.
1786. Lord Cornwallis, Governor-General of India (to 1793).
1792. Submission of Tippoo Sahib.
1793. Pondicherry taken from the French.
Sir John Shore, Governor-General (to 1798).
1798. Lord Mornington (Marquis Wellesley), Governor-General (to 1805).
1799. Capture of Seringapatam. Death of Tippoo.
1802. Treaty of Bassein. The Peishwah transfers his suzerainty to the East India Company.
1803. Sir Arthur Wellesley gains the battle of Assaye over the Mahrattas.
General Lake wins the battle of Laswaree.
1805. Lord Cornwallis, Governor-General *(July-Oct.)*, succeeded by Sir G. Barlow (to 1807).
1806. Mutiny of the Sepoys at Vellore suppressed.
1807. Lord Minto, Governor-General (to 1813), succeeded by Lord Moira (Hastings) (to 1823).
1813. Trade with India made free to all by Parliament.
Nepaul war this and next year.
1818. Suppression of the Pindaries. Extinction of the Peishwahs.
1819. Singapore occupied by the English.
1823. Lord Amherst, Governor-General (to 1828).
1824. War with Burmah. Rangoon is taken.
1826. Storming of Bhurtpore.
1828. Lord William Bentinck, Governor-General (to 1835).
1833. The East India Company's charter is renewed (see note).
1836. Lord Auckland, Governor-General (to 1842).
1838. Dost Mahommed receives a Russian mission at Cabul. Declaration of war with the Afghans.
1839. Capture of Candahar.
1841. Insurrection at Cabul. Murder of Burnes.
1842. *Jan.* Evacuation of Cabul. Massacre of the army in the Khyber. *Sept.* Cabul reoccupied.
Lord Ellenborough, Governor-General (to 1844).
1843. Annexation of Scinde.
1844. Sir H. (afterwards Lord) Hardinge, Governor-General (to 1848).
1845. *Nov.* War declared against the Sikhs.
Dec. Battles of Moodkee and Ferozeshah.
1846. *Jan. and Feb.* Battles of Aliwal and Sobraon. Treaty of Lahore and end of first Sikh war.
1848. Lord Dalhousie, Governor-General (to 1856).
1849. Capture of Mooltan.
Battles of Chillianwallah and Goojerat.
Annexation of the Punjab. End of second Sikh war.
1852. Second war in Burmah. Annexation of Pegu.
1853. Last charter of the East India Company granted.
1856. Annexation of Oudh.
Lord Canning, Governor-General (Viceroy 1858) (to 1862).
1857. Indian mutiny. Outbreaks at Meerut, Delhi, Lucknow, and Cawnpore.
Nana Sahib is crowned as Peishwah.
July. Death of Sir Henry Lawrence at Lucknow.

SUMMARIES.

1857. Massacre at Cawnpore.
   Sept. Capture of Delhi.
   Relief of Lucknow by Havelock and Outram, who, joining the garrison, await further relief.
   Nov. Final relief of Lucknow under Sir Colin Campbell, commander-in-chief. Death of Havelock.
1858. *March.* Lucknow finally occupied by Outram. Final suppression of rebels. Campaign of Sir H. Rose in Central India.
   Nov. The government of India is transferred from the Company to the Crown. The Governor-General becomes Viceroy.
1862. Lord Elgin, Viceroy (to 1863).
1863. Sir John Lawrence, Viceroy (to 1869).
1869. Lord Mayo, Viceroy (to 1872).
1872. Lord Northbrook, Viceroy (to 1876).
1873. Abortive negotiations for a defensive alliance with Afghanistan.
1876. Lord Lytton, Viceroy (to 1880).
1877. The Queen is proclaimed Empress of India.
1878. The Ameer having received a Russian envoy, and refusing to receive an English envoy, Afghanistan is invaded and Cabul taken (see 1878).
1879. By the Treaty of Gundamak (*May*) the Ameer Yakoob Khan agrees to receive an English envoy, who is murdered (*Sept.*), and Afghanistan again invaded.
1880. Marquis of Ripon, Viceroy.
   A new Ameer, Abdurrahman, is set up, and his rival, Ayub Khan, after defeating the English at Maiwand, is defeated near Candahar.
1881. Evacuation of Candahar.

REFORM.—1745—1881.*

1745. *Oct.* Sir F. Dashwood moves an amendment to the address, advocating the reform of Parliament.
1776. Wilkes' motion for parliamentary reform is lost in the Commons without a division.
1780. The Duke of Richmond brings in a motion for reform, which is rejected without a division.
1782. Pitt's motion to consider the state of the representation negatived by 161 to 141.
1783. Pitt's resolution in favour of parliamentary reform thrown out by a majority of 144 (293 to 149).
1785. Pitt's motion for reform, in which he proposed to disfranchise thirty-six rotten boroughs (returning 72 members), to compensate their owners, and to give the members to the counties and to London, is thrown out by a majority of 74 (248 to 174).
1790. Flood's motion for parliamentary reform is withdrawn without discussion.
1792. The Society of the Friends of the People is formed to promote parliamentary reform.
   Mr. Grey's motion for reform lost by a large majority.
1793. Mr. Grey's motion for parliamentary reform is opposed by Burke and Pitt, and thrown out by a large majority (282 to 41) this year, and again in 1797 by 256 to 91.
1809. Sir Francis Burdett brings in his motion for reform, which is lost by 74 to 15.
1810. Brand's motion for a committee to consider parliamentary reform lost by 234 to 115, and in 1812 by 215 to 88.

* In this Summary the details differ considerably from the general outline, and there are various additions with a view of making the progress of the movement clearer.

SUMMARIES.

1817. Sir F. Burdett's motion for reform lost by 265 to 77.
1818. Burdett introduces a motion for universal suffrage, electoral districts, the ballot, and annual Parliaments, which is rejected by 206 to 0 (Lord Cochrane teller with Burdett).
1819. *July* 1. Burdett's motion that the House will consider the question of reform in the following session rejected by 153 to 58.
Aug. Manchester reform meeting in St. Peter's Fields. Attack of yeomanry. Arrest of Hunt and others.
Dec. 14. Lord J. Russell proposes resolutions in favour of reform, which are withdrawn.
1820. Lord J. Russell's bill for withholding writs for the new Parliament from Grampound, Penryn, Camelford, and Barnstaple passes the Commons and is thrown out in the Lords.
1821. *April.* Lambton's motion for household suffrage and triennial Parliaments rejected by 55 to 43.
May. Lord J. Russell's resolutions in favour of reform rejected by 155 to 124.
Lord J. Russell's bill for the disfranchisement of Grampound is carried, but his proposal to give the vacant seats to Leeds is rejected by the Lords, who substitute two additional members for Yorkshire.
1822. Lord J. Russell's motion that the present state of representation requires serious consideration is rejected by 105 (269 to 164).
1823. Seventeen thousand freeholders of Yorkshire petition for reform.
Lord J. Russell's motion for a committee to inquire into the number of voters in each constituency defeated by 128 to 90.
Lord J. Russell's motion for reform rejected by 280 to 169, and in 1826 by 247 to 123.
1827. Tennyson's bill for transferring the representation of East Retford to Birmingham abandoned.
Lord J. Russell's bill for disfranchising Penryn passes the Commons, and is then dropped; reintroduced in 1828, and thrown out in the Lords.
1829. Marquis of Blandford's motion for reform (seconded by O'Connell) rejected by 114 to 70.
1830. *Feb.* Blandford moves an amendment to the address in favour of reform, which is rejected by 96 to 11; he afterwards moves for a bill to restore the constitutional influence of the House of Commons, which is defeated by 160 to 57.
Lord J. Russell's proposal to enfranchise Leeds, Birmingham, and Manchester is rejected by 188 to 140.
Calvert introduces a bill for transferring the representation of East Retford to Birmingham, which is defeated by an amendment extending the right of voting for East Retford to the hundred of Bassetlaw. On the third reading O'Connell proposes to introduce the ballot, which is rejected, only 21 members (including Althorp, Hobhouse, Burdett, and Hume) voting with him.
May. O'Connell's motion for triennial Parliaments, the ballot, and universal suffrage rejected by 319 to 13, and an amendment by Lord J. Russell "that it is expedient to extend the basis of the representation of the people" by 213 to 117.
Lord Grey becomes Prime Minister. He at once stipulates that reform shall be a Cabinet measure
1831. *March* 1. The Reform Bill is introduced by Lord J. Russell. After a debate of seven nights, 71 speakers having spoken leave is given to bring in the bill.

SUMMARIES.

1831. *March* 21. The bill is carried at the second reading by a majority of 1 (302 to 301).
April. General Gascoyne's amendment in committee, that the number of members of Parliament for England and Wales ought not to be diminished, is carried by 8 (299 to 291).
April 22. Parliament is suddenly dissolved by the king in person, with a view of preventing Lord Wharncliffe's address in the Lords against the dissolution being carried.
June. The new Parliament meets. Reformers in a great majority.
The Reform Bill is carried (second reading) by a majority of 136 (367 to 231).
Aug. The Marquis of Chandos carries a clause (by a majority of 84) conferring the county franchise on £50 tenants-at-will.
Sept. 22. After many weeks of discussion the Reform Bill passes the Commons by 345 to 236, but is rejected (*Oct.* 8) in the Lords by 41 (199 to 158).
Dec. Parliament meets. A third Reform Bill is brought in, and is carried (second reading) by 162 (324 to 162).
1832. *Jan.* Parliament resumes work.
March. The Reform Bill passes the Commons by 355 to 239.
April 14. In the Lords the second reading is carried by 9 (184 to 175).
May 7. A motion in committee adverse to the bill (postponing the disfranchisement till after the consideration of the enfranchisement clauses) is carried in the Lords by 35 (151 to 116).
The king refusing to make new peers, ministers resign.
Lord Ebrington's motion regretting the resignation of the ministry carried by 288 to 208.
The Duke of Wellington fails to make a ministry.
Ministers again propose to the king to create new peers. The king consents, and intimates his intention to do this if necessary to the Opposition peers.
June. The Reform Bill passes the Lords by 106 to 22.
Reform Bills passed for Scotland and Ireland.
1833. Grote's motion for the Ballot rejected by 211 to 106; in 1835 by 317 to 144; in 1836 by 139 to 88; in 1838 by 315 to 198; and in 1839 by 333 to 216.
Tennyson's motion for repeal of the Septennial Act rejected by 213 to 164; in 1834 by 235 to 185; in 1837 by 96 to 87. Similar motion by Crawford in 1843 rejected by 46 to 23.
1839. Sir Hesketh Fleetwood's motion to reduce the county franchise to £10 rejected by 207 to 81.
1842. Ward's motion for the Ballot rejected by 290 to 157.
Great Chartist petition. Duncombe's motion to allow counsel to be heard in support of the petition rejected by 287 to 49.
1844. Sudbury disfranchised for bribery.
1848. Hume's motion for a Radical Reform Bill rejected by 351 to 84; in 1849 by 268 to 82; in 1850 by 242 to 96; in 1852 by 244 to 89. [Hume advocated household suffrage, triennial Parliaments, electoral districts, and the Ballot.]
1850. Irish Parliamentary Voters Bill reduces county franchise to £12, borough franchise to £8.
1851. *Feb.* 20. Locke King's motion for assimilating county to borough franchise is supported by some Liberals, and carried against the Government by 100 to 52. His bill is rejected on the second reading by 299 to 83.

SUMMARIES.

1851. Lord John Russell pledges himself to bring in a Reform Bill next session.
1852. *Feb.* Lord John Russell introduces a Reform Bill, which is afterwards abandoned. [£20 rating franchise in counties, £5 rating in boroughs; small boroughs to be grouped together; taxpayers to the amount of 40s. per annum to have the franchise in both boroughs and counties.]
Disfranchisement of St. Albans for bribery.
1854. *March.* A Reform Bill is introduced by Lord J. Russell, but withdrawn.
1857. Locke King's County Franchise Bill rejected by 192 to 179, and Property Qualification Abolition Bill by 204 to 145.
1858. Locke King's County Franchise Bill passes the second reading by 226 to 168, but is withdrawn.
Abolition of the property qualification.
1859. Disraeli announces the proposals of the Government on the reform of the franchise. (Walpole and Henley had retired on account of these proposals.)
March. Defeat of the ministry on the second reading of their Reform Bill by 39 votes.
1860. *March.* A Government Reform Bill is introduced by Lord J. Russell, but withdrawn later.
1861. The Government make no mention of reform in the royal speech.
Locke King's and Baines' motions for the reduction of the county and borough franchise are respectively negatived by 248 to 229, and 245 to 193.
The four seats vacant by disfranchisement of Sudbury and St. Albans assigned, two to the West Riding of Yorkshire, and one each to Birkenhead and South Lancashire.
1864. Locke King's County Franchise Bill and Baines' Borough Franchise Bill are thrown out by 254 to 227, and 272 to 216.
1865. Baines' Borough Franchise Bill rejected by 288 to 214.
1866. *March.* The Government Reform Bill introduced by Gladstone. After many evenings' debate it is carried by 5 votes only (the division being 283 Conservatives and 32 Liberals against 318 Liberals and 2 Conservatives, including tellers), the small majority being chiefly owing to the seceding Liberal "Adullamites," led by Lowe.
June. The Government is defeated by 11 (315 to 304) on Lord Dunkellin's amendment to the Reform Bill. The ministry resign.
1867. *Feb.* The new Government Reform Bill is brought forward by Disraeli.
March. Gladstone indicates various changes in the Government measure which would be necessary to make it a sound measure. Most of these were ultimately adopted.
July. The Reform Bill is read a third time without opposition.
Aug. The Reform Bill (England) passes the Lords.
1868. Reform Bills for Ireland and Scotland passed.
July 31. End of the last Parliament elected under the Reform Bill of 1832.
1877. *June.* Trevelyan's motion for extending county franchise is rejected by 274 to 218. The motion had been rejected in 1872 by 148 to 70; in 1873 it was talked out; in 1874 it was rejected by 287 to 173; in 1875 by 268 to 166; and in 1876 by 264 to 165.
[In 1878 it was rejected by 271 to 219, in 1879 by 291 to 226.]

SUMMARIES.

1884, 1885. Household Franchise extended to the counties, and a considerable redistribution of seats effected. (See Appendix III.)

NATIONAL EDUCATION.

[This summary is somewhat expanded from the outline given in the text.]
1805. Foundation of British and Foreign School Society.
1811. Foundation of National Society.
1833. First Parliamentary Grant in aid of Education (£20,000) on motion of Lord Althorpe.
1839. Formation of Committee of Council on Education. Letter of Lord John Russell to Lord Lansdowne, Lord President, containing principles of constitution of the new Committee.
1846. Publication of Minutes of Council laying foundation of English public elementary school system :—
  (1) Grants to be made to training colleges ; (2) building grants towards erection of new schools ; (3) annual grants for maintenance of schools.
1862. Introduction of Revised Code, by Robert Lowe, Vice-President.
1870. Elementary Education Act, introduced and passed by Forster.
1871. Introduction of New Code (Forster, Vice-President).
1876. Elementary Education Act introduced and passed by Lord Sandon.
1880. Elementary Education Act introduced and passed by Mundella.
1882. Introduction of New Code (Mundella, Vice-President).
1886. Royal Commission on Elementary Education Acts appointed.

APPENDIX I.

LIST of some of the CHIEF OFFICIALS in CHURCH and STATE to the beginning of Anne's reign.

A.—ARCHBISHOPS OF CANTERBURY FROM AUGUSTINE TO TILLOTSON.
(From Stubbs' "Registrum Sacrum Anglicanum.")

Name	Accession	Name	Accession
Augustine	597	Hubert Fitzwalter	1193
Laurentius	604	Stephen Langton	1207
Mellitus	619	Richard Grant	1229
Justus	624	Edmund Rich	1234
Honorius	627	Boniface	1245
Deusdedit	655	Robert Kilwardby	1273
Theodore	668	John Peckham	1279
Brihtwald	693	Robert Winchelsey	1294
Tatwin	731	Walter Reynolds	1313
Nothelm	735	Simon Mepeham	1328
Cuthbert	741	John Stratford	1333
Bregwin	759	Thomas Bradwardine	1349
Jaenbert	766	Simon Islip	1349
Ethelhard	793	Simon Langham	1366
Wulfred	805	William Whittlesey	1368
Feologild	832	Simon Sudbury	1375
Ceolnoth	833	William Courtenay	1381
Ethelred	870	Thomas Arundel	1397
Plegmund	890	Roger Walden	1398
Athelm	914	Thomas Arundel	1399
Wulfhelm	923	Henry Chichele	1414
Odo	942	John Stafford	1443
Dunstan	960	John Kemp	1452
Ethelgar	988	Thomas Bouchier	1454
Siric	990	John Morton	1486
Elfric	995	Henry Dean	1501
Elphege	1005	William Warham	1503
Living	1013	Thomas Cranmer	1533
Ethelnoth	1020	Reginald Pole	1556
Eadsige	1038	Matthew Parker	1559
Robert	1051	Edmund Grindal	1576
Stigand	1052	John Whitgift	1583
Lanfranc	1070	Richard Bancroft	1604
Anselm	1093	George Abbot	1611
Ralph d'Escures	1114	William Laud	1633
William de Corbeuil	1123	William Juxon	1660
Theobald	1139	Gilbert Sheldon	1663
Thomas Becket	1162	William Sancroft	1678
Richard	1174	John Tillotson	1691
Baldwin	1185		

APPENDIX.

B.—LEADING MINISTERS OF STATE

[The leading Justiciars and Chancellors before the reign of

	Lord Chancellors and Lord Keepers.	Secretaries of State.
Henry VIII., 1509.	1515. Wolsey. 1529. Sir T. More. 1532. (K.) } Audley. 1533. (C.) } 1544. Wriothesley.	....
Edward VI., 1547.	1547. (K.) St. John (created Earl of Wiltshire 1550). 1547. Rich. 1551. Goodrich, Bishop of Ely.	[In Edward VI.'s reign Petre, Paget, Sir T. Smith, Wotton, Cecil, and Cheke.]
Mary, 1553.	1553. Gardiner, Bishop of Winchester. 1556. Heath, Archbishop of York.	[In Mary's reign Petre, Bourne, and Boxall.
Elizabeth, 1558.	1558. (K.) Sir N. Bacon. 1579. Bromley. 1587. Hatton. 1592. (K.) Puckering. 1596. (K.) Egerton (created Lord Ellesmere 1603).	[In Elizabeth's reign William Cecil, Sir T. Smith, Walsingham, Wilson, Davison, Robert Cecil, Sir John Herbert.]
James I., 1603.	1603. (C.) Ellesmere (created Viscount Buckley 1616). 1617. (K.) } Bacon. 1618. (C.) } 1621. (K.) Williams, afterwards Bishop of Lincoln.	1616. Winwood and Sir Thomas Lake. 1618. Lake and Sir Robert Naunton. 1619. Naunton and Sir George Calvert. 1623. Calvert and Sir Edward (afterwards Lord) Conway. 1624. Conway and Sir Albert Morton.
Charles I., 1625.	1625. (K.) Coventry. 1640. (K.) Sir John Finch. 1641. (K.) Lyttelton. 1645. (K.) Lane.	1625. Conway and Sir John Coke. 1629. Coke and Lord Dorchester. 1632. Coke and Sir Francis Windebank. 1640. Windebank and Sir Henry Vane, senior. 1641. Vane and Sir Edward Nicholas. 1642. Nicholas and Lord Falkland. 1643. Nicholas and Lord Digby.
[Commonwealth 1649-1660.]		

APPENDIX.

FROM HENRY VIII. TO ANNE.

Henry VIII. have been mentioned in the General Outline.]

LORD HIGH TREASURERS.	DEPUTIES OF IRELAND.
[From 1501.] Surrey (created Duke of Norfolk 1514). 1522. Surrey (succeeded to the dukedom of Norfolk 1524). Son of the preceding.	1513. Kildare. 1522. Ossory. 1524. Kildare. 1526. Delvin. 1528. Ossory. 1530. Sir William Skeffington. 1532. Kildare. 1535. Lord Leonard Grey. 1540. Sir Antony St. Leger.
1547. Hertford (created Duke of Somerset the same year). 1550. Wiltshire (created Marquis of Winchester 1551).	1551. Sir James Croft.
....	1553. Sir Antony St. Leger. 1556. Earl of Sussex (Lord-Lieutenant).
1572. Burleigh. 1599. Buckhurst (created Earl of Dorset 1603).	1565. Sir Henry Sydney. 1571. Sir William Fitzwilliam (Lord Justice). 1575. Sir Henry Sydney. 1578. Sir William Drury (Lord Justice). 1579. Sir William Pelham. 1580. Lord Grey de Wilton. 1584. Sir John Perrot. 1588. Sir William Fitzwilliam. 1594. Sir William Russell. 1597. Lord Burgh (died the same year). Sir John Norris (died the same year). Earl of Ormond (Lord Justice). 1599. Earl of Essex (Lord-Lieutenant). 1600. Lord Mountjoy.
1609. Salisbury. 1612. (In commission.) 1614. Suffolk. 1618. (In commission.) 1620. Sir Henry Montagu (created Viscount Mandeville 1620). 1621. Cranfield (created Earl of Middlesex 1622.) 1624. Ley (created Earl of Marlborough 1626).	1603. Sir George Cary. 1604. Sir Arthur Chichester. 1616. Sir Oliver St. John. 1622. Lord Falkland.
1628. Weston. 1635. (In commission.) 1636. Juxon. 1641. (In commission.) 1643. Cottington.	1633. Lord Wentworth (Earl of Strafford 1640). 1640. Sir Christopher Wandesford. 1641. Earl of Leicester. 1644. Marquis of Ormond. 1647. (Under the Parliament) Lord Lisle.
....	[1649. Oliver Cromwell (Lord-Lieutenant); 1650, Henry Ireton; 1652, John Lambert; 1654, Charles Fleetwood; 1656, Henry Cromwell.]

APPENDIX.

B.—LEADING MINISTERS OF STATE

	Lord Chancellors and Lord Keepers.	Secretaries of State.
Charles II., 1660.	1660. Hyde (created Earl of Clarendon 1661). 1667. (K.) Bridgman. 1672. Shaftesbury. 1673. (K.) ⎫ Sir Heneage Finch (created Lord Finch 1674, and Earl of Nottingham 1681). 1675. (C.) ⎭ 1682. (K.) North (created Lord Guilford 1683).	1660. Nicholas and Sir William Morice. 1662. Morice and Sir Henry Bennet (created Lord Arlington 1664). 1668. Arlington and Sir John Trevor. 1672. Arlington and Henry Coventry. 1674. Coventry and Sir Joseph Williamson. 1679. *Feb.* Coventry and Sunderland. 1680. Sunderland and Sir Leoline Jenkins. 1681. Jenkins and Conway. 1683. Jenkins and Sunderland. 1684. *April.* Sunderland and Godolphin. *Aug.* Sunderland and Middleton.
James II., 1685.	1685. Jeffreys.	1688. Middleton and Preston.
William and Mary, 1689.	1689. (In commission.) 1693. (K.) ⎫ Somers. 1697. (C.) ⎭ 1700. (K.) Sir Nathan Wright.	1689. Shrewsbury and Nottingham. 1690. Nottingham and Sydney. 1692. Nottingham and Trenchard. 1694. Shrewsbury and Trenchard. 1695. Shrewsbury and Trumbull. 1697. Shrewsbury and Vernon. 1699. Jersey and Vernon. 1700. Vernon and Hedges. 1701. Vernon and Manchester.

OTHER OFFICIALS IN THE

Chancellors of the Exchequer.	Presidents of the Council.	First Lords of the Admiralty.
1689. Lord Delamere. 1690. Hampden. 1694. Godolphin. 1695. Montagu. 1699. Smith. 1701. Boyle.	1689. Carmarthen (made Duke of Leeds 1694). 1699. Pembroke. 1702. *Jan.* Somerset.	1689. Admiral Herbert (created Earl of Torrington). 1690. Pembroke. 1692. Cornwallis. 1693. Falkland. 1694. Admiral Russell. 1699. Bridgwater. 1701. Pembroke (Lord High Admiral).

[From the reign of Anne the

APPENDIX.

FROM HENRY VIII. TO ANNE—continued.

Lord High Treasurers.	Deputies of Ireland.
1660. Southampton. 1667. (In commission.) 1672. Clifford. 1673. Latimer (created Earl of Danby 1674). 1679. *March.* Essex (First Lord of the Treasury). *Nov.* Laurence Hyde (First Lord) (created Earl of Rochester, 1682). 1684. Godolphin (First Lord).	1660. Lord Robartes. 1661. Duke of Ormond (Lord-Lieutenant). 1669. Lord Robartes ,, 1670. Lord Berkeley of Stratton (Lord-Lieutenant). 1672. Earl of Essex ,, 1677. Duke of Ormond ,,
1685. Rochester (Lord High Treasurer). 1687. Belasyse (First Lord). 1689. Monmouth (formerly Mordaunt, afterwards Peterborough) (First Lord). 1690. *March.* Sir John Lowther (First Lord). *Nov.* Godolphin ,, 1697. Montagu ,, 1699. Tankerville ,, 1700. Godolphin ,, 1701. Carlisle ,,	1685. Earl of Clarendon ,, 1687. Earl of Tyrconnel ,, 1692-1693. Lord Sydney ,, 1695-1696. Lord Capel (died 1696) ,, 1700. Earl of Rochester ,,

REIGN OF WILLIAM III.

Treasurers of the Navy.	Master-Generals of the Ordnance.	Household Offices.	
1689. Russell. 1699. Sir Thomas Littleton.	1689, 1690. Schomberg. 1692. Sydney (afterwards Earl Romney).	Devonshire, Lord Steward Wharton, Comptroller Overkirk, Master of the Horse Portland (formerly Bentinck), Groom of the Stole till 1700, succeeded by Romney. Dorset, Lord Chamberlain, 1689-1697. Sunderland, ,, 1697. Shrewsbury, ,, 1699. Jersey, ,, 1700.	through- out the reign.

Ministries are given in the Notes.]

APPENDIX.

APPENDIX II.

The HOUSE OF LORDS, its Members and their Numbers at different times from 1295 to the present day.

	Dukes.	Marquises.	Earls.	Viscounts.	Barons.	Representing Scotland.	Representing Ireland.	Total Lay Peers.	Archbishops and Bishops.	Abbots and Priors.	Masters of Orders.	Total Spiritual Peers.	GRAND TOTAL.
1295	..	..	8	..	41	..	..	49	20	67	3	90	139
1st year of Edward II.	..	..	9	..	71	..	..	80	19	55	2	76	156
„ Edward III.	..	..	6	..	80	..	..	86	21	23	1	45	131
„ Richard II.	1	..	12	..	47	..	..	60	21	25	..	46	106
„ Henry IV.	5	1	10	..	34	..	..	50	20	26	1	47	97
„ Henry V.	..	..	6	..	32	..	..	38	20	26	1	47	85
2nd Parliament	2	..	9	..	29	..	..	40	21	26	1	48	88
1st year of Henry VI.	2	..	5	..	16	..	..	23	21	25	..	46	69
31st year of Henry VI.	5	..	12	3	36	..	..	56	21	26	1	48	104
1st year of Edward IV.	1	..	4	1	31	..	..	37	21	26	1	48	85
6th year of Edward IV.	3	..	9	..	34	..	..	46	21	26	1	48	94
1st year of Richard III.	3	..	7	2	26	..	..	38	21	26	1	48	86
„ Henry VII.	2	..	9	2	16	..	..	29	21	26	1	48	77
„ Henry VIII.	1	1	8	..	26	..	..	36	21	26	1	48	84
„ Edward VI.	1	2	12	..	32	..	..	47	27	..	..	27	74
„ Mary	1	1	14	1	32	..	..	49	26	..	..	26	75
„ Elizabeth	1	1	12	2	27	..	..	43	26	..	..	26	69
„ James I.	..	..	25	2	54	..	..	81	26	..	..	26	107
„ Charles I.	1	1	37	11	47	..	..	97	26	..	..	26	123
Long Parliament .	..	1	59	5	54	..	..	119	26	..	..	26	145
Restoration Parliament	4	4	56	8	68	..	..	140	26	..	..	26	166
1st year of James II.	14	3	66	8	67	..	..	158	26	..	..	26	184
„ William III.	13	4	71	9	69	..	..	166	26	..	..	26	192
„ Anne	21	1	65	9	66	..	..	162	26	..	..	26	188
„ George I.	23	2	74	11	67	16	..	193	26	..	..	26	219
„ George II.	31	1	71	15	62	16	..	196	26	..	..	26	222
„ George III.	25	1	81	12	63	16	..	198	26	..	..	26	224
„ George IV.	25	17	100	22	134	16	28	342	30	..	..	30	372
„ William IV.	23	18	103	22	160	16	28	370	30	..	..	30	400
„ Victoria	24	19	111	19	192	16	28	409	30	..	..	30	439
1881 August . .	26	19	117	25	254	16	28	485	26	..	..	26	511

APPENDIX.

APPENDIX III.

The HOUSE OF COMMONS, its Members, their Numbers and Distribution at different times from the reign of Edward I. to the present day.

In the reign of Edward I. thirty-seven counties returned two members each, the unrepresented counties being Durham, Cheshire, and Monmouthshire. The number of cities and boroughs that returned members is given as 166, so that the total number of members would be 406; but the towns varied, and the number of members elected in any particular Parliament would be considerably less than this. The names of 286 members are preserved for the Parliament of 1295, and the returns for the counties of Norfolk and Suffolk with their boroughs have been lost; the probable number of members in that year was 306. During succeeding reigns many boroughs ceased to return members, and the total number had fallen below 300 in Edward IV.'s reign. Every English city and borough previous to the Reform Bill of 1832 returned *two* members, except Monmouth (enfranchised by Henry VIII.), Abingdon, Banbury, and Higham Ferrers (enfranchised by Mary), and Bewdley (enfranchised by James I.), which returned one member each; and London, which from the time of Edward II. has sent four members. Elizabeth united the boroughs of Weymouth and Melcombe Regis, giving them a representation of four members conjointly instead of two each. The following is a table of the distribution of seats at various periods, beginning with the reign of Edward IV.:—

	County Members.	Borough Members.	University Members.	Total.
Reign of Edward IV.	74	222	..	296
End of reign of Henry VIII.	90	253	..	343
,, ,, Edward VI.	90	293	..	383
,, ,, Mary	90	312	..	402
,, ,, Elizabeth	90	372	..	462
,, ,, James I.	90	395	4	489
,, ,, Charles I.	90	413	4	507
,, ,, Charles II.	92	417	4	513
The Union with Scotland (1707)	122	432	4	558
,, ,, Ireland (1801)	186	467	5	658
From 1826 to 1832	188	465	5	658
After the Reform Bill of 1832	253	399	6	658
1861-1868	256	396	6	658
After the Reform Bill of 1867-68	283	366	9	658
After the Reform Bill of 1885	377	284	9	670

The members have been thus distributed:—

	England.	Wales.	Scotland.	Ireland.
1707-1800	489	24	45	..
1801-1832	489	24	45	100
1832-1868	471	29	53	105
1868-1885	463	30	60	105
Since 1885	465	30	72	103

APPENDIX.

The following constituencies were enfranchised or restored in the reigns of—

HENRY VIII. { The twelve Welsh counties, and the boroughs of Beaumaris, Brecon, Carnarvon, Carmarthen, Cardigan, Denbigh, Flint, Cardiff, Montgomery, Pembroke, Haverford West, Radnor, and Monmouth, returning one member each. Monmouthshire, Cheshire, Chester, Buckingham, Lancaster, Preston, Orford, Newport in Cornwall, Thetford, Berwick, Calais, returning two members each.

EDWARD VI. { Saltash, Camelford, West Looe, Penryn, Grampound, Bossiney, St. Michael, Maidstone, Boston, Westminster, Peterborough, Brackley, St. Albans, Liverpool, Wigan, Petersfield, Lichfield, Thirsk, Hedon, Ripon—two members each.

MARY. { Abingdon, Higham Ferrers, Banbury—one member each. Aylesbury, St. Ives, Castle Rising, Morpeth, Knaresborough, Boroughbridge, Aldborough (in Yorkshire), Woodstock, Droitwich—two members each In this reign Calais ceases to return members.

ELIZABETH. { East Looe, Fowey, St. Germans, St. Mawes, Callington, Tregony, Beeralston, Corfe Castle, Cirencester, Yarmouth (Isle of Wight), Newport (Isle of Wight), Queenborough, Newton (Lancashire), Newtown (Isle of Wight), Clitheroe, Andover, East Retford, Bishop's Castle, Minehead, Stockbridge, Lymington, Christchurch, Whitchurch, Tamworth, Sudbury, Eye, Aldeburgh, Haslemere, Richmond, Beverley—two members each.

JAMES I. { Oxford and Cambridge Universities, Amersham, Marlow, Hertford, Wendover, Tiverton, Harwich, Tewkesbury, Ilchester, Bury St. Edmunds, Evesham, and Pontefract—two members each. Bewdley—one member.

CHARLES I. { Cockermouth, Ashburton, Honiton, Okehampton, Weobley, Milborne Port, Seaford, Malton, Northallerton—two members each.

CHARLES II. Durham, county and city, Newark—two members each.

CHANGES IN THE DISTRIBUTION OF SEATS BY THE REFORM ACTS OF 1832.

ENGLAND.

Disfranchisement.   *Seats.*

55 boroughs returning 2 members each, Higham Ferrers returning 1 member } totally disfranchised } 113
Weymouth and Melcombe Regis to return 2 members conjointly instead of 4
30 boroughs returning 2 members each deprived of one member . . 30
                                                                     — 143

Enfranchisement.

22 cities and boroughs to return 2 members each . . . } 63
19 boroughs to return 1 member each . . . }
26 counties divided, each division to return 2 members each
Yorkshire, instead of 4 members, to have three divisions, each returning 2 } 55
  members . . . . }
Isle of Wight made a county in itself, and to return 1 member
7 counties to return 3 each instead of 2 7
                                                         — 125

Leaving a net loss of 18 seats to England, which were assigned thus—
Wales.—3 counties, each an additional member } . . . 5
  2 new boroughs, 1 member each . }
Scotland.—Additional members to Edinburgh and Glasgow
  Perth, Aberdeen, and Dundee (previously grouped with other burghs) } 8
    to return a member each
  Paisley, the Leith burghs, and Greenock, to return 1 each
Ireland.—Additional members to Dublin University, Belfast, Limerick, Galway, and Waterford } 5
                                                         — 18

APPENDIX.

CHANGES BY REFORM ACTS OF 1867 AND 1868.

ENGLAND.

Disfranchisement. — Seats.

6 boroughs returning 2 members	} totally disfranchised	.	17	
5 ,, ,, 1 member				
35 ,, ,, 2 members, deprived of 1 member each	.	35		
				— 52

Enfranchisement.

London University to return 1 member	1
Salford to return 2 members instead of 1	1
Leeds, Liverpool, Birmingham, Manchester, 3 members instead of 2	4
Chelsea and Hackney to return 2 each	4
9 other new boroughs to return 1 each	9
	— 19
Yorkshire (West Riding) to be divided into three divisions instead of two, each returning 2 members	2
Lancashire to be divided into four divisions, each returning 2 members (instead of North 2 and South 3)	3
10 counties to be divided into three instead of two divisions, each returning 2 members	20
	— 25
	44

Net loss, 8 seats.

These 8 seats were apportioned thus:—

An additional member to Merthyr-Tydvil	1
2 new Scotch University constituencies, each 1 member . .	2
Additional members to Glasgow and Dundee . . .	2
3 counties (Aberdeen, Ayr, Lanark) divided into two divisions, returning 1 each	3
Peeblesshire and Selkirkshire to return 1 member conjointly, instead of 1 each	1
	— 2
A member for the "Border Burghs"	1
	— 8

CHANGES BY REFORM ACT OF 1885.

ENGLAND AND WALES.

Disfranchisement. — Seats.

13 boroughs returning 2 members merged in counties . .	26
66 ,, ,, 1 member ,, . .	66
36 ,, ,, 2 members, deprived of 1 member . .	36
Macclesfield and Sandwich each returning 2 members, disfranchised	4
	— 132

New Seats.

This, with six new seats allotted to England and Wales, gave 138 seats to be disposed of	138

Enfranchisement.

London, including Croydon, to return 62 members instead of 22 .	40
Additional members given to provincial boroughs . . .	26
New provincial boroughs created	6
Additional members allotted to counties	66
	— 138

SCOTLAND.

Disfranchisement. — Seats.

2 boroughs returning 1 member each merged in counties .	2

New Seats.

12 new seats were allotted to Scotland	12
	— 14

APPENDIX.

	Enfranchisement.	Seats.
7 seats allotted to counties,		7
7 ,, ,,	Aberdeen, Edinburgh, and Glasgow	7
		— 14
	IRELAND.	
	Disfranchisement.	
22 boroughs returning 1 member each,		22
3 ,, 2 members each lost 1		3
		— 25
	Enfranchisement.	
21 seats allotted to counties,		21
4 ,, Dublin and Belfast		4
		— 25

The following towns return more than one member each :—

ENGLAND—London 61
          Liverpool 9
          Birmingham 7
          Manchester 6
          Sheffield and Leeds 5
          Bristol 4
          Bradford, Hull, Nottingham, Salford, and Wolverhampton, . 3
          Bath, Blackburn, Bolton, Brighton, Davenport, Derby, Halifax, Ipswich, Leicester, Newcastle, Northampton, Norwich, Oldham, Plymouth, Preston, Southampton, Stockport, Sunderland, and York 2
IRELAND—Dublin and Belfast 4
        Cork 2
SCOTLAND—Glasgow 7
          Edinburgh 4
          Dundee 2
WALES—Merthyr Tydvil, ... 2

The rest return one member each.

INDEX.

ABBOT, GEORGE, ARCHBISHOP, 85.
Abdul Aziz, 216.
—— Hamid, 216.
Abdurralman Khan, 222, 224.
Abercorn, James Hamilton, Marquis, afterwards Duke of, 208, 214.
Abercromby, General Sir Ralph, 161.
Aberdare, Lord, 215 (see Bruce, H. A.).
Aberdeen, George Hamilton-Gordon, Earl of, 182, 188, 196, 197, 199.
—— Ministry, 196.
—— J. C. Hamilton-Gordon, Earl of, 232.
Abhorrers, 113.
Abjuration Bill, 121.
Abu Klea, battle of, 229.
Abyssinia, 203, 209.
Acre, 27, 159, 189.
Adam, William, 152.
—— W. P., 2:0, 222.
Adderley, Sir C. (Lord Norton), 214.
Addington, H., Prime Minister, 160, 161 (see Sidmouth).
Addington's Ministry, 160.
Addison J., 130.
Additional Forces Act, 161, 217.
—— Titles Act, 217.
Addled Parliament, 87.
Adela, 16
—— of Louvain, 21.
Adelaide, Queen, 177.
—— 184.
Aden, 186.
Adrian IV. Nicolas Breakspear), 22.
Adrianople 176.
Adullam, Cave of, 206, 207.
Advertisement Duty, 197.
Adwalton, battle of, 96.
Affirmation Bill, 227.
Afghanistan,186, 214, 220, 221, 222, 231.
Agincourt, battle of, 57.
Agricola, Julius, 3 ; forts of, 3.
Agricultural Distress, Committees on, 185, 195, 221.
Agricultural Holdings Act, 216.
Ahmed Khel, battle of, 222.
Aidan, St., 3.
Aids, 28, 30, 41
Aislabie, John 131.
Aix-la-Chapelle 136, 137, 168.
Akierman, treaty of, 174.
Alabama, 207, 15.
Albany, Duke of, 67.

Albemarle, Duke of, 109 (see Monk).
Alberoni, Cardinal, 130.
Albert, Prince, 187, 205, 213.
Albert Edward, Prince of Wales, 207, 216.
Albuera, battle of, 165.
Alcuin, 4.
Aldern, battle of, 98.
Alençon, Francis, Duke of, 83.
Alexander I., of Scotland, 18, 20.
—— II., ——, 18, 30, 32, 34.
—— III., ——, 18, 34, 38, 39.
—— III., Pope, 22, 25 ; IV., ——, 34, 35.
—— I., of Russia, 160, 172.
—— II., ——, 198, 224.
—— III., ——, 224.
—— of Battenburg, 230, 234.
Alexandra, Princess, 207.
Alexandria, battle of, 161.
—— Bombardment of, 226, 227.
Alfgar, 15.
Alford, battle of, 98.
Alfred, King, 4, 7.
—— son of Ethelred II., 13.
Algeria, 176.
Algiers, 169.
Alien Act, (1), 157.
—— (2), 169.
Ali Musjid, 220.
Aliwal, battle of, 192.
Alliance, Holy, 166, 167.
Allotments Act, 237.
Alma, battle of, 199.
Almanza, battle of, 127.
Almeida, 165.
Almenara, battle of, 129.
Alnwick, 25.
Alost, 21.
Alphege, St., 11.
Althorp, J. C. Spencer, Viscount, 174, 176, 181, 182, 183 (afterwards Earl Spencer).
Amboyna, massacre of, 86.
Ameer of Afghanistan, 214, 220, 222.
America, 70.
American Settlements begun, 82, 84.
Amherst, William Pitt, Earl, 166, 172.
Amiens, Peace of, 160, 161.
—— Mise of, 37.
Anabaptists, 74.
Andrassy Note, 216, 217.
André, Major, 149.
Anglesey, H. W. Paget, Marquis of, 174.
Anglia, East, 5, 7, 9, 13.

INDEX.

Angora, battle of, 52.
Angoulême, Isabella of, 29, 34.
—— Genealogy of Counts of, 22.
Anjou, 21, 22, 29, 61.
—— Francis, Duke of, 83.
—— Geoffrey of, 21, 22.
—— Henry of (I.), 21, 22, 23 (see Henry II.).
—— Henry of (II.), 81.
—— Louis of, 46.
—— Margaret of, 59, 61, 63, 65.
—— Rene of, 61.
Anlaf (I.), 9.
—— (II.), 10.
Annates, 35, 72, 73.
Anne of Denmark, 85.
Anne, Princess, 119, 124; Queen, 125, 129.
Anselm, 19, 21.
Anson, George, Lord, 135, 138
—— Major, Hon. A. H. A., 206.
Anti-Corn Law League, 189, 190, 191 (see Corn Law Summary, 288).
Antonio of Portugal, 83.
Antwerp, 127.
Appeals to Rome, 23, 73.
Appellant, Lords, 51, 53.
Appellate Jurisdiction Act, 219.
Appropriation of Supplies, 108, 109, 113.
Arabi, 224, 226, 227.
Aragon, 39.
—— Ferdinand of, 66, 70.
—— Katharine of, 71, 73, 75.
Archbishops of Canterbury, 297.
Arcola, battle of, 158.
Arcot, 136.
Argyll, John, Duke of (I.) 129, 131, 132.
—— George Douglas, Duke of, 196, 198, 202, 205, 210, 222.
—— Archibald, Marquess of (I.), 98, 100, 108.
—— Archibald, Marquess of (II.), 114.
Arlington, Henry Bennett, Earl of, 109, 111.
Armada, 83.
Army (see Summary), 273, 274.
—— Discipline and Regulations Act, 221.
—— Parliamentary, 99, 101.
—— Standing, 107, 119, 120, 273.
Arnold, Benedict, 149.
Arras, 59.
Arrears Act, 227.
Arrest, freedom from, 63, 84 (see Parliamentary Summary).
Arrow, lorcha, 200.
Arthur, 3.
—— of Brittany, 22, 29.
—— Prince of Wales, 71.
Articles, Six, 74, 75.
—— Thirty-nine, 81, 147.
—— of Perth, 86.
—— Lords of, 90.
Articuli super Cartas, 43.
Artisans' Dwellings Act, 217.
Arundel, Thomas, Archbishop, 52, 53, 55, 57.
—— Earldom of, 23.
—— Richard, Earl of, 51, 52, 53.
—— Pedigree of, 52.
Ascough, Bishop, 61.
Ashantee, 172, 215.

Ashbourne, E. Gibson, Lord, 230, 231, 236.
Ashburton Treaty, 186.
Ashdown, 7.
Ashley-Cooper, Antony, 1st Earl of Shaftesbury, 109, 111, 113, 115.
Ashley, Anthony, Lord, 7th Earl of Shaftesbury, 181.
Aspern, battle of, 162.
Assam, 174.
Assandun, battle of, 13.
Assaye, battle of, 160.
Assize of Arms, 27, 35.
—— Bloody, 117.
—— of Clarendon, 25.
—— of the Forest, 27.
—— Great, 27.
—— of Northampton, 27.
Associated Counties, 96, 97.
Association, Catholic, 173, 175, 177.
Athelney, 7.
Athelstan, 9.
Atherton Moor, battle of, 97.
Athlone, 120.
Attainder defined, 86, 87.
Atterbury, Bishop Francis, 132
Auckland, William Eden, Lord, 160.
—— George Eden, Earl of, 176, 182, 185, 192.
Audit of Accounts, 55.
Audley, Lord, 63.
Aughrim, battle of, 120.
Augsburg, 124.
—— Confession of, 72.
—— Diet of, 72.
—— League of, 116.
—— Peace of, 73.
Augustine, 3.
Augustus, Emperor, 3.
Aumale, William of, 33.
Aurungzebe, 126.
Austerlitz, battle of, 160.
Australia, 124, 142, 152, 194.
—— South, 184, 194.
—— West, 176.
Australian Colonies Bill, 194.
Austria, Charles of, 124, 128, 134
—— Don John of, 80.
—— Leopold of, 28.
Auxiliary Forces, 213.
Avalon, Hugh of, 29.
Avignon, 42, 48.
Aylesbury Election Trial, 126, 27.
Ayoub Khan, 222, 224.
Ayrton, A. S., 210.

Babington, Antony, 83.
Bacon, Sir F., Lord Verulam, Viscount St. Albans, 87.
Badajoz, 165.
Badbury, battle of, 3.
Baden, Louis of, 126.
Bagnal, Sir H., 83.
Baillie, General, 98.
Baines, Sir E., 205, 206.
Baker Pasha, Valentine, 226
Balaclava, battle of, 199.
Baldwin, Archbishop, 27.

INDEX.

Balfour, A. J., 230, 236, 237.
Balliol, Devorguilla, 40.
—— Edward, 46, 47.
—— John, 18, 40, 41.
Ballot Act, 185, 186, 213.
Balmerino, Lord, Arthur Elphinstone, 137.
Bancroft, Archbishop Richard, 85.
Bank of England, 122, 123, 159, 183, 190, 191.
Bank Charter Act, 181, 191, 201, 209.
—— —— Indemnity Act, 201.
Bankes, George, 192.
Bankruptcy, National, 111.
—— Act, 227.
Bannockburn, battle of, 45.
Baptists, 108.
Barbados, 84.
Barebone's Parliament, 102.
Barbarossa, Frederic, 22, 25.
Barcelona, 127.
Barclay, Sir George, 123.
Baring, Alexander (Lord Ashburton), 182.
—— Francis (Lord Northbrook), 186.
—— Sir Evelyn, 219.
Barlow, Sir G., 160.
Barnet, battle of, 65.
Baronets, 85.
Barons, struggles of, with the Crown, 278
Barré, Colonel Isaac, 142.
Barrier, Treaty, 126.
Barrington, William Wildman, Viscount, 142.
Barrosa, battle of, 165.
Barwell, R., 144.
Basing, battle of, 7.
Basque Roads, battle of, 139.
Bassein, Treaty of, 160.
Bastille, 152.
Bastwick, 91, 93.
Bates' case, 85.
Bath, 3.
—— bishopric of, 72.
Batoum, 220, 221, 234.
Battle, trial by, 27, 171.
Bautzen, battle of, 166.
Bavaria, 124.
Bayeux, 61.
—— Odo of, 17, 19.
Bayonne, 49, 63.
Baxter, Richard, 115.
—— W. E., 210.
Beach, Sir Michael Hicks, 214, 230, 231, 235, 236, 237.
Beachy Head, battle of, 121.
Beaconsfield, Earl of (see Disraeli), 214, 219, 221, 223, 225.
Beaugé, battle of, 57.
Beauforts, 51, 60.
—— Genealogy of, 51.
—— Cardinal Henry, 53, 55, 59, 60, 61.
—— Edmund (1.), 60, 61, 63.
—— Edmund (II.), 60.
—— Jane, 60.
—— John, 60, 61.
—— Margaret, 61.
—— Thomas, 55, 60.
Beaufoy's Motions, 153, 155.
Beaumont's Bill, 213.
Becket, Thomas, 23, 25.

Beckford, Alderman, 142.
Bedchamber Question, 187.
Bede, 35.
Bedford, 9.
—— John, Duke of, 44, 57, 59, 61.
—— John Russell, Duke of, 134, 138, 140.
—— Whigs, 142, 143.
Belfast Riots, 235.
Belgium, 167, 176.
—— Neutrality of, 213.
Bellême, Robert of, 17, 2L
Bellingham, John, 165.
Benares, Rajah of, 153.
Benbow, Admiral, 125.
Benedict, St., 2.
Benefit of Clergy, 74, 75.
Benevolences, 65, 67, 77.
Bengal, 138.
Bentinck family, genealogy of, 184.
—— Earl of Portland, 125.
—— Lord George, 174, 192, 193.
—— Lord William, 174.
Beresford, Marshal, 165.
—— W., 196.
Beresina River, 164.
Bergen, 159.
Bergen-op-Zoom, 137, 167.
Berkeley, James, Earl of, 132.
Berkhamstead, 17.
Berksted, Stephen, 37.
Berlin Decrees, 162, 163.
—— Note, 219.
—— Treaty of, 220, 221, 223.
Berri, 49.
Berwick, 33, 47, 67, 91.
—— Pacification of, 92.
—— Marshal, 120, 127.
Besika Bay, 219.
Bessarabia, 221.
Bethell, Sir R. (Lord Westbury), 198, 202.
Bexley, Nicholas Vansittart, Lord, 173, 176.
Bhurtpore, 174.
Bible, 75, 85.
Bigod, Hugh, 25.
—— Roger, 41.
Birinus, 3.
Birmingham, 155, 175, 177, 180, 181.
—— League, 211.
Bishops' Courts, 19.
—— Election of, 20, 21, 31, 72, 73.
—— Seven, 117.
Bishoprics at Conquest, 16.
—— at Reformation, 72.
Bishops' Exclusion Bills, 93, 95, 183.
Bismarck, Prince, 204.
Black Death, 49.
Blackheath, battle of, 71.
—— Meeting of, 219.
Black Hole of Calcutta, 138.
Black Prince, 47, 49.
Black Sea, 198, 199, 210.
Blackwater, battle of, 83.
Blake, Admiral Robert, 103.
Blanketeers, 169.
Blenheim, battle of, 127.
Blois, Stephen of, 21, 22.
Bloody Assize, 117.

INDEX.

Bloreheath, battle of, 63.
Blucher, Marshal, 167.
Boadicea, 3.
Boers, 190, 192, 222.
Bohemia, Anne of, 47, 49, 51.
Bohemian Election, 86, 87.
Bohun, Humphrey de, 41.
—— Mary de, 53.
Bois le duc, battle of, 157.
Boleyn, Anne, 71, 73, 75.
Bolingbroke, Viscount (see St. John), 129, 131, 133, 137.
Bolivar, 167.
Bolton, Charles, Duke of, 132.
Bombay, 109.
Boniface, St., 4.
—— VIII., Pope, 41, 42.
Bonn, 125.
Bonner, Bishop, 79.
Booth, Sir G., 107.
Bordeaux, 49, 63.
Borodino, battle of, 164.
Boroughbridge, battle of, 45.
Boston, 142, 144, 145, 147.
—— Port Bill, 145.
Bosworth, battle of, 69.
Botany Bay, 142.
Bothwell Brig, battle of, 112.
—— James Hepburn, Earl of, 80.
Bouchain, 129.
Boulogne, 69, 75, 77, 160, 161.
Bouchier, R., 47.
Bourke, R. (Lord Connemara), 214, 230.
Bouverie, E. P., 198.
Bouvines, battle of, 31.
Boyne, battle of, 121.
Braddock, General, 138.
Bradlaugh, C., 223, 225, 229, 233.
Bramham Moor, battle of, 55.
Brandon, Charles, 71.
Brand's Motion, 165.
Brandywine, battle of, 147.
Breakspear, Nicolas (Adrian IV.), 22.
Breaute, Falkes de, 31, 33.
Breda, Promises of, 106, 107.
Brentford, Skirmish at, 95.
Brenville, battle of, 21.
Breslau, Treaty of, 134.
Brest, Expedition to, 122, 123.
Breteuil, Roger of, 17.
Bretigny, Peace of, 48, 49.
Bretons, 25, 55.
Breton, Cape, Isle of, 137, 139.
Brian Boru, 10.
Bribery, 123.
—— Acts, 141, 197, 199.
Brice's, St., Day, 11.
Bright, John, 191, 201, 210, 215, 222, 227.
Brisbane, 202.
Bristol, 1745, 97, 99, 179.
—— Bishopric of, 72.
—— John Digby, Earl of, 89.
Britain, 3.
Brithric, 5.
Brighton, 103.
British North America Act, 208.
Brittany, Arthur of (I.), 29.

Brittany, Arthur of (II.), 46.
—— Anne of, 69.
—— Constance of, 29.
—— Guy of, 46.
—— Jeanne of, 46.
—— John of, 46.
—— Duchy of, 47, 59, 61, 69.
Briton, The North, 141.
"Broad-bottomed Ministry," 135.
Broadhurst, Henry, 232.
Broglie, F. M., Marshal, 139.
Brownists, 108 (see Independents).
Brougham, Henry, created Lord, 169, 171, 173, 176, 182, 187, 189.
Bruce, David, 46, 47, 48.
—— Edward, 44.
—— Robert (I.), 40.
—— Robert (II.), 40.
—— Robert (III.), 18, 40, 43-46.
—— H. A. (Lord Aberdare), 202, 210.
Brunanburgh, battle of, 9.
Brunswick, Ferdinand of, 139.
—— Caroline of, 157.
Brussels, 166.
Bryce, James, 232.
Buckingham, genealogy of the Stafford Dukes of, 66.
—— Henry Stafford, Duke of, 66, 67.
—— Edward Stafford, Duke of, 66, 71.
—— George Villiers (I.), Duke of, 87, 89.
—— George Villiers (II.), Duke of, 109, 111.
—— George Grenville, Duke of ('Farmers' Friend), 188, 189, 192.
—— Richard Grenville, Duke of, 208.
—— Richard Grenville, Marquis of, 170.
Buckinghamshire, Robert Hobart, Earl of, 164.
Buenos Ayres, 163.
Buller, Sir J. Y. (afterwards Lord Churston), 187.
—— Sir R., 235.
Bulgaria, 216, 218, 220, 230, 232, 234, 236.
Bull's Run, battle of, 204.
Bunker's Hill, battle of, 145.
Buonaparte, Joseph, 162, 167.
—— Louis Napoleon, 192, 196, 210, 215.
—— Napoleon, 158-166, 167, 170.
Burdett, Sir F., 165, 169, 173, 175.
Burford, 101.
—— Battle of, 4.
Burgh, Hubert de, 33, 35.
Burgos, 163, 167.
—— Battle of, 162.
Burgoyne, General, 147, 152.
Burgundy, genealogy of the Dukes of, 58.
—— Anne of, 59.
—— Charles, Duke of, 64, 65, 66.
—— John, Duke of, 54, 55, 56, 57.
—— Margaret, Duchess of, 59, 65, 69.
—— Mary of, 70.
—— Philip, Duke of (I.), 46, 54, 56, 57, 59, 61, 64.
—— Philip, Duke of (II.), 69, 71.
Burials Bill, 223.
Burke, Edmund, 142, 145, 147-149, 150, 153, 155, 157, 159.
—— T. H., 227.
Burley, Simon, 51.

INDEX.

Burmah, 172, 196, 230, 232.
Burnell, Robert, 39.
Burnes, Sir Alexander, 188.
Burton, Henry, 91, 93.
Bury St. Edmunds, 61.
Busaco, battle of, 165.
Bute, John Stuart, Earl of. 139. 140, 141.
Bute's Ministry, 140.
Butt, Isaac, 215.
Buxar, battle of, 140.
Bye Plot, 85.
Byng, Sir George, Admiral, 127. 131, 132 (Lord Torrington).
—— John, Admiral, 139.
Byron, G. G. Noel-Byron, Lord, 172.

CABAL, 109, 111.
Cabinet (see Council).
Cabot, John, 70.
Cabul, 186, 188, 220, 222.
Cade, Jack, 61, 63.
Cadiz, 83, 89, 105.
Cadogan, George Henry, Earl, 234.
Caen, 61.
Cæsar, Julius, 3.
Cairns, Hugh, Earl, 202, 208, 209, 214, 220.
Calabria, 163.
Calais, 37, 47, 49, 57, 61, 63, 66, 79.
Calcutta, 120, 138.
Calder, Sir R., 161.
Calendar Reformed, 137.
California, 194.
Calixtus II., 20.
Calvin, 74.
Cambridge, Richard, Earl of, 50. 57.
—— University, 117.
Cambuskenneth, battle of, 41.
Camden, battle of, 149.
—— Charles Pratt, Lord, then Earl, 141, 142, 148, 150, 156.
Camden, John Jeffreys Pratt, Earl, afterwards Marquis, 156, 158, 160, 164.
Cameron, Dr., 137.
Campaign, Plan of, 235, 236.
Campbell, Sir Colin, Lord Clyde, 201.
Campbell, John, Lord, 202, 203.
Campbell-Bannerman, H., 222. 232.
Campeggio, Cardinal, 73.
Camperdown, battle of, 159.
Campion, Edmund, 81, 83
Campo Formio, Peace of, 158.
Canada, 139, 141, 144, 147, 154, 155, 164, 180, 184, 186, 208, 210, 230.
Candahar, 186, 222, 224.
Canning Family, genealogy of, 164.
—— George, 156, 162, 165, 169, 170, 171, 173, 174, 175.
—— C. J., Viscount, afterwards Earl, 191, 192, 196, 198, 200, 202.
Canning's Ministry, 174.
"Canningites," the, 174.
Cannon, General, 118.
Canterbury, 16, 25.
—— Archbishops of, Appendix I., p. 297.
Cantilupe, Archbishop, 35.
Canton, 186, 200, 201.
Canute, 11, 12, 13.

Cape Colony, 159, 160, 166, 192, 198.
—— La Hogue, battle of, 121.
Capel, Arthur, Lord, 101.
Capet, Hugh, 20.
Capital Crimes, 186, 187 (see Mackintosh).
Caractacus, 3.
Cardwell, Edward, afterwards Viscount, 196, 198, 202, 206, 210.
Carical, 150.
Carleton, Henry Boyle, Lord, 132.
Carlingford, Lord (see Chichester Fortescue), 222.
Carlisle, 19, 43, 137.
—— George Howard, Earl of, 174, 198.
—— George William Howard, Earl of, 202.
—— Bishopric of, 72.
Carlists, 182, 216.
Carmarthen, Marquis of (see Danby and Leeds), 121, 123.
—— —— II., 147, 150.
Carnarvon, Henry Herbert, Earl of, 202, 208, 209, 214, 221, 230, 233.
Carnatic, 146.
Caroline of Anspach, 133, 135.
—— of Brunswick, 157, 171.
Carr, Robert, Viscount Rochester, Earl of Somerset, 87.
Carteret Family, genealogy of, 134.
—— John, Lord, 132, 133, 134, 135.
—— Sir George, 109.
Carthagena, 135.
—— Battle of, 139.
Cartwright, Thomas, Professor, 80, 81.
Carucage, 28, 29.
Cash Payments stopped, 159.
—— resumed, 173.
Castile, 27.
—— Blanche of, 52.
—— Eleanor of, 39, 41.
—— Isabella of, 66.
—— Joanna of, 70.
Castlereagh, Robert Stewart, Viscount, 156, 160, 162, 163, 164, 165, 167 (see Londonderry).
Catholic (see Roman Catholic).
—— Association, 173, 175, 177.
Cato Street Plot, 171.
Cavagnari, Colonel Sir P. L. N., 220.
Cave, S., 208.
Cavendish, Lord F., 222, 227.
—— Lord J., 142, 148, 150.
Cavour, 204.
Cawnpore, 201.
Cecil, Robert, Earl of Salisbury, 85.
—— Robert, Marquess of Salisbury (see Cranborne), 214, 219, 221, 230, 231, 233, 234, 235.
—— William, Lord Burleigh, 79, 83.
Censorship of the Press, 123.
Central Criminal Court, 183.
Cerdic, 3.
Cessation, the, 96.
Ceylon, 158, 160, 166.
Chalgrove Field, battle of, 97.
Chaluz, 29.
Chamberlain, Joseph, 222, 232, 233, 235.
Chambers, Alderman, 89, 93.

INDEX.

Champlain, Lake, 167.
Chancery, Court of, 42, 43, 47, 103, 105, 174, 175.
Chandos Clause, 180.
Chaplin, H., 230.
Charasiab, battle of, 220.
Charles I., 87 ; reign of, 87-101.
—— II., 103, 105 ; reign, 107-115.
—— the Great, 4, 5.
—— IV., Emperor, 48.
—— V., 71, 72, 76, 78 ; genealogy of, 70.
—— VI., 128, 133, 134.
—— IV., of France, 46.
—— V., —— 44, 46, 48.
—— VI., —— 46, 48, 58.
—— VII., —— 46, 58, 62.
—— VIII., —— 46, 66, 68, 69, 70.
—— IX., —— 80.
—— X., 172, 176.
—— the Bad, 46.
—— of Naples, 138.
—— XII., of Sweden, 122, 126, 130.
—— II., of Spain, 123.
Charles Edward Stuart, 135, 137.
—— the Bald, 6.
—— the Simple, 8.
Charlotte, Princess, 167, 169.
—— Queen, 139.
Charter, Great, 30, 31, 33, 35.
—— Henry I.'s, 18, 31.
—— People's, 186, 187.
Charters, Confirmation of, 40, 41, 43.
Chartists, 187, 193.
Chartres, treaty of, 43.
Chateau Cambrésis, treaty of, 80.
Chatham, William Pitt, Earl of, 142, 144, 147, 149.
—— John Pitt, 156, 160, 162, 164.
Chatham Whigs, 142.
Chatillon, battle of, 63.
Chelmsford, Frederick Thesiger, Lord, 202, 208.
Cherbourg, 61, 139.
Chester, 9, 10, 23.
Chester, battle of, 3.
—— Bishopric of, 72.
Chesterfield, Philip D. Stanhope, Earl of, 132, 134, 137.
Chichele, Archbishop, 57, 59.
Chichester, Bishopric of, 16, 72.
Childers, Hugh C. E., 202, 210, 215, 222, 232.
Chillianwallah, battle of, 194.
Chippenham, 7, 135.
China, Wars with, 166, 186, 201, 202.
—— Trade with, 180.
Christian IV. of Denmark, 88.
Christianity, introduction of, 3.
Christopher, R. A. (afterwards took the name of Nisbett), 192.
Church of England (see Ecclesiastical Summary, 255-262).
—— and Pope, 16, 24, 33, 49, 51, 73.
Church Rates, 202, 203, 205, 209.
—— —— Abolition Bill, 185.
—— —— Act, 209.
—— Property, Confiscation of, 55.
—— Temporalities Ireland Act, 184, 186.

Church, Irish, disestablished, 210, 211 (see also Irish Summary, Part III., 270).
Churches built by Parliament, 169.
Churchill, genealogy of (see 120).
—— Lord, 119 (see Marlborough).
—— Lord Randolph, 230, 233, 234, 235, 236.
Cinque Ports, 129.
Cintra Convention, 163.
Circuits, Judges, 26.
Cirencester, 3.
Cissa, 3.
Ciudad Rodrigo, 165.
Civil Jury, 27.
Civil List regulated, 149.
—— —— Motion on, 177.
Civil Service thrown open, 212.
Claim of Right (Scottish), 119.
Clare election, 175, 177.
Clarence, George, Duke of, 60, 65, 67.
—— Lionel, Duke of, 44, 48, 50.
—— Philippa, of, 50.
—— Thomas, Duke of, 44, 55.
—— William, Duke of (see William IV.).
Clarendon, Assize of, 25.
—— Council of, 23, 24.
—— Edward Hyde, Earl of, 107.
—— Henry Hyde, Earl of, 117.
—— George W. Villiers, Earl of, 192, 196, 198, 202, 206, 210-212.
—— Code, 109.
Clarke, Sir E., 236.
Clarkson, T., 162.
Claudius, Emperor, 3.
Claverhouse, John Graham of, Viscount Dundee, 118.
Clavering, Sir John, 144.
Clement V., 42.
—— VII., 48, 72.
—— Jacques, 82.
Clerkenwell Prison, 209.
Clericis Laicos, Bull of, 40, 41.
Cleves, Anne of, 71, 75, 84.
Clifford, Sir Thomas, 109, 111.
Clinton, General Sir Henry, 147.
Clive, Robert, Lord, 136, 145.
Clontarf, 191 ; battle of, 10.
Closure, 227, 235, 237.
Cloth of Gold, Field of, 71.
Coalition against France, (1st) 157 ; (2d) 158, 159 ; (3d) 160, 161.
—— Ministry, 151.
Coal Mines Regulation Act, 237.
Cobbett, William, 169, 179.
Cobden, Richard, 189, 191, 192, 193, 200, 204.
Cobham, Lord (Sir John Oldcastle), 55, 57.
—— Richard Temple, Viscount, 132.
Cochrane, A. J., Lord (Earl Dundonald), 169.
Cockburn, Sir A., 196, 198.
Coercion Act (Irish), 181, 183.
Coffee-Houses, 111.
Coinage, debasement of, 77.
—— Renewal of, 123.
Coke, Sir Edward, 87.
—— J. W. (afterwards Earl of Leicester), 150.
Colbert, 114.
Colborne, Sir John, afterwards Lord Seaton, 187.

INDEX.

Colchester, 101.
Colchester, Charles Abbot, Lord, 202.
Colepepper, William, 125.
Collings, Jesse, 232, 233.
Colonial Secretary, 160, 198, 199.
Colonies (see Canada, Australia, etc.), 237.
—— Loss of American (see Summary, 282).
Columbia, 172.
Columbus, 68.
Combermere, Stapleton Cotton, Viscount, 174.
Combinations of Workmen, 172, 173.
Commercial Treaties with France, 153, 204, 215.
—— Russia, 157.
Commissions of Array, 95.
—— on Housing of the Poor, 229.
Committees, Grand, 227.
Common Pleas, Court of, 26, 27, 30, 37, 43.
Commons Estate, 40, 45.
Commonwealth, 101-167 (see Parliamentary Summary, 249-255).
Commune, 27.
Commune (Paris), 212.
Compensation for Disturbance Clause, 222, 223.
Comprehension Bill, 109, 119.
Compton, Henry, Bishop, 117.
—— Sir Spencer (Lord Wilmington), 133.
Comyn, the Red, 18, 40-43.
Condé, Louis, Prince of, 100.
Confederate States, 204.
Confirmation of the Charters, 40, 41.
Congé d'élire, 72.
Connecticut, 96.
Conrad, Emperor, 13.
—— —— IV., 32.
Conradin, 36.
Conservatives, numbers of, 181, 182, 187, 189, 197, 201, 203, 207, 211, 215, 223, 231, 235.
Consort, Prince, 205.
Conspiracy to Murder Bill, 203.
Constance, Council of, 56.
Constantine, Emperor, 3.
—— King of Scots, 9.
Constantinople, 61, 163, 216, 221.
Contract, the Great, 85.
Contractors, 149.
Conventicle Act, 109, 110, 167.
Convention, Parliaments, 107, 119.
Convention, National, 154.
Convicts, 152, 186.
Convocation, 40, 60, 61, 73, 93, 109, 131, 195.
Conway, General, Henry Seymour, 142, 149.
Conyngham, Francis Nathaniel, Marquis,182.
Cook, Captain, 142.
Coote, Sir Eyre, 138, 148.
Cope, Sir J., 137.
Copenhagen, battles of, 161, 163.
Corbiesdale, battle of, 102.
Corn Laws (see Summary, 272), up to 1815, 190; repealed, 193, 211.
Cornish men, 9, 71.
Cornish Rebellion (i.) 71, (ii.) 77.
Cornwall, Richard, Earl of, 24.
Cornwallis, Charles, Marquis, 149, 152, 158, 160.

Corporation Act, 109, 133, 153, 175.
—— Municipal Act (England), 185.
—— (Ireland), 185, 189.
—— of Towns, 26; remodelled, 115.
Correro, 90.
Corresponding Societies Act, 158, 159.
Corrupt Practices Acts, 199.
Corry, H. T. L., 208.
Corsica, 142.
Cornnna, battle of, 163.
Cottenham, C. C. Pepys, Earl of, 184, 192.
Cotton, Sir John Hynde, 132, 134.
Council, ordinary. 69 ; Great, 56, 57, 93; Privy, 55, 59, 61, 67 (see p. 278); cf the North, 75, 93 ; of State, 101 ; of Wales, 93.
Councils, Provincial, 39.
Council of Eleven, 51.
Council, Orders in, 162, 163, 165.
Counties, Associated, 96, 97.
County Franchise, 195, 215, 218.
Coup d'Etat, 196.
Courtenays, genealogy of, 64.
Courtenay, Edward, Marquis of Exeter, 46.
—— Henry, 64, 74.
Courtney, Leonard, 222.
Courts, Law, 256.
—— Spiritual, 73.
—— of High Commission, 82, 83, 93.
—— Star Chamber, 69, 93.
Coutance, Walter, Bishop of, 27, 29.
Covenant, Scotch (i.) 78, (ii.) 90.
—— Solemn League and, 97.
Covenanters, 90, 100.
Covent Garden Theatre, 191.
Coventry, 63.
—— Sir John, 111.
—— Sir Thomas, Lord, 91.
Cowell's "Interpreter," 84, 85.
Cowley, Henry Richard Wellesley, Lord, 203.
Cowper-Temple Clause, 211.
Cowper, William, Earl, 127.
—— F. T. de Grey, Earl, 222, 225.
Cranborne (see Salisbury, Marquis of (II.), 208, 209.
Cranbrook, Viscount (see Gathorne Hardy), 221, 230, 234.
Cranmer, Thomas, Archbishop, 73, 79.
Cranworth, R. M. Rolfe, Lord, 196, 198, 206.
Crawford, Sharman, 194, 197.
Crecy, battle of, 47.
Crediton, Bishopric of, 16.
Credit, Votes of, 221, 231.
Cressingham, 40.
Crevant, battle of, 59.
Crimean War, 199.
Criminal Law Amendment Act, 231.
—— (Ireland), 236, 237.
Criminous Clerks, 23, 24.
Crofters Act, 232.
Cromwell's Family, 106.
Cromwell, Henry, 106.
—— Oliver, 97, 98, 101, 103, 105-107.
—— Richard, 107.
—— Thomas, 75.
Cropredy Bridge, battle of, 97.
Cross, Richard Assheton, Viscount, 214, 217, 223, 230, 236.

295

INDEX.

Crown Point, 138, 145.
Crusades, 18, 19, 23, 32, 34, 36.
—— List of, 26.
Culloden, battle of, 157.
Culpepper (or Colepepper), John, 95.
Cumberland, 9, 11, 17, 19.
—— William, Duke of, 139, 143.
—— Ernest Augustus, Duke of, 176, 185.
Curia Regis, 21, 27, 37.
Custozza, battle of, 206.
Cuthbert, 5.
Cuthred, 5.
Cymric, 3.
Cyprus, 27, 221.

DAGSASTAN (Dawston), battle of, 3.
Dalhousie, James A. Ramsay, Earl, 192, 194.
—— John W. Ramsay, Earl, 232.
Damme, battle of, 31.
Dampier, 124.
Danby, Thomas Osborne, Earl of, 111, 113, 116, 117, 118 (see Carmarthen and Leeds).
Danegeld, 11, 17, 23, 28.
Danes, 10, 11, 13, 17 (see Summary, 275).
Danish Kings of England, genealogy of, 12.
—— War, 207.
Dangerteld, Thomas, 115.
Danton, G. J., 156.
Danubian Principalities, 170.
Darc, Jeanne, 59.
Darien Scheme, 123.
Darnley (Henry Stuart), commonly called Lord, 80; genealogy of, 80.
Darrein Presentment, 30.
Dartmouth, 65.
Dashwood, Sir Francis, 137, 140.
Davey, Sir Horace, 232.
David I. King of Scots, 18, 20-23.
—— II. —— 42, 46, 47, 48.
—— of Wales, 39.
Davitt, M., 221.
De Breauté, Falkes, 33.
De Burgh, Hubert, 33.
Debates, publication of, 133, 145 (see Parliamentary Summary, 254).
Debts, Henry VIII.'s, 75.
Debtors, 166, 167, 205.
Declaration of Indulgence (i.) 111, (ii.) 117, (iii.) 117.
—— of Right (English), 119; (Irish), 148.
Declaratory Act, 143.
De Donis Conditionalibus Clause, 30.
De Grey, John, Bishop, 29.
De Heretico Comburendo, 53, 79.
Delhi, 201.
Denison, J. E., Viscount Ossington, 161, 163, 174.
Denmark, 13, 161, 163, 206.
—— George, Prince of, 124, 125.
Deorham, or Dyrham, battle of, 3.
Derby, 8, 9, 137.
—— Earldom of, 24.
—— Henry Bolingbroke, Earl of, 51.
—— Edward Geoffrey Stanley, Earl of (see Stanley), 195, 196, 197, 199, 202, 209.
—— Edward Henry Stanley, Earl of (see Stanley, II.), 214, 219, 221.

Derby's Ministry, (1st) 196; (2nd) 202; (3rd) 208.
Derbyshire Insurrection, 169.
Dermot, 24.
Dervish Pasha, 226.
Derwentwater, James Radcliffe, Earl of, 131.
Desborough, General John, 197.
Desmond, 80.
Despenser, Hugh (father), 45.
—— Hugh (son), 45.
De Tallagio non Concedendo, 40.
Dettingen, battle of, 135.
De Vere, Robert, Earl of Oxford (Duke of Ireland), 51.
Devizes, 97.
Devon, Earldom of, 23.
—— Insurrection in, 77.
Devon William Reginald Courtenay, Lord, 208.
Devonshire, William, Duke of (I.) 117, 119, 124.
—— (II.) 135, 138, 139, 140, 142.
—— Ministry of, 138.
De Witt, 110.
Dey of Algiers, 167.
Digges, Sir Dudley, 89.
Dilke, Sir C., 222.
Dillon, J., 225, 237.
Directorate, 156, 159.
Disraeli, Benjamin, 191, 192, 193, 195, 196, 197, 202, 203, 208, 209, 215 (see Beaconsfield).
—— Ministry, (1st) 208; (2nd) 214, 215.
Dissenting Ministers' Relief Bill, 145.
Dissenters, Subscription of, 146.
Distribution of Seats Bills, 207.
Division Lists published, 185.
Dixon's Bill, 219.
Dodington, Bubb, 132, 134.
Dodson, J. G. (Lord Monk-Bretton), 210, 222.
Dominican Friars 32.
Don Carlos, 182.
Donald Bane, of Scotland, 16.
Donoughmore, R. J. Hely-Hutchinson, Earl of, 202.
Doomsday Book, 18.
Dorchester, Bishopric of, 16.
Dorset, Lionel Sackville, Duke of, 134.
Dorsetshire, 116.
Dost Mahomed, 186.
Douay, 129.
Doudal's case, 42.
Douglas, Earl of (I.), 51.
—— (II.), 55.
Doulton, Frederick, 206.
Dowdeswell, William, 142.
Dover, 33, 107.
—— Battle off, 103.
—— Treaty of, 110, 111.
Drake, Sir F., 83.
"Drapier's Letters," 132.
Dresden, battle of, 166.
—— Treaty of, 136.
Drogheda, 103.
Druids, 3.
Dreux, 57.
Dublin, Parliament, 118, 122.

INDEX.

Dubois, Cardinal, 130.
Duckworth, Sir J., 163.
Dudley family, genealogy of, 76.
—— Edmund, 71.
—— John (see Lisle, Warwick, and Northumberland), 75, 76, 77, 79.
—— Lord, 174, 175.
—— Lord Guildford, 76, 79.
—— Lord Robert (see Leicester).
Dudley Conspiracy, 79.
Duff, Mountstuart E. Grant, 210, 222.
Dufferin, F. Temple-Blackwood, Earl of, 206, 210, 228.
Duffy, Sir Charles Gavan, 192, 194.
Dulcigno, 222.
Dunbar, 1st battle of, 41 ; 2nd battle of, 103.
Duncan I., of Scotland, 18.
—— II., —— 18.
—— Admiral (Viscount Camperdown), 159.
Duncannon, John William Brabazon, Lord (afterwards Earl of Bessborough), 182, 184.
Dundalk, battle of, 44.
Dundas, Henry (Lord Melville I.), 150, 155, 156, 157, 160.
—— Robert, 162 (Lord Melville II.).
Dundee, Viscount (John Graham of Claverhouse), 118.
Dunes, battle of, 107.
Dunkellin, Ulick Canning de Burgh, Lord, 206, 209.
Dunkirk, 107, 109.
Dunning, William (Lord Ashburton), 142, 148.
Dunning's motion, 149, 173.
Dunstan, Archbishop, 9, 10.
Dunwich, Bishopric of, 16.
Duplin, battle of, 45.
Duquesne Fort, 138.
Durham, 16.
—— J. G. Lambton, Earl of, 176, 187.
Dutch Guards, 125.
Dyke, Sir W. Hart, 230, 233, 236.
Dyrham, battle of, 3.

EALSTAN, Bishop, 5.
Earnot, 9.
East Anglia, 4, 5, 7, 9, 13.
East India Bill, Fox's, 150, 151.
—— Company, Old, 82, 122, 126, 166, 180, 197, 199, 203 (see Summary, 289-291).
—— New, 120, 122, 126.
East India Press, 220.
East Retford, 175.
Ebrington, Hugh Fortescue, Viscount, 170, 186.
Ecclesiastical Commission (James II.'s), 117, 119.
—— —— 179, 183, 185.
—— Titles Bill, 195.
Economical reform, 147, 149.
Edgar, 4, 9, 11.
—— Atheling, 4, 16, 17, 18.
—— of Scotland, 18, 20.
Edgecote, battle of, 65.
Edgehill, battle of, 95.
Edict of Nantes, 82, 114.

Edinburgh, 66, 103.
—— Convention, 118.
Edington, or Ethandun, battle of, 7.
Edith, or Edgith, 12, 14.
Edmund, 4, 7, 9.
—— Ironside, 4, 13.
Edred, 4, 9.
Edric, Streona, 11, 13.
Education Grant, 187, 201.
—— Act, 180, 181, 189 (see Summary, 295).
Edward the Elder, 4, 7.
—— the Martyr, 4, 10.
—— the Confessor, 4, 12, 13, 15, 17 ; reign of, 15.
—— I., 34, 37 ; reign of, 39, 43.
—— II., 34, 41, 42, 46, 47 ; reign of, 43-45.
—— III., 44, 45 ; reign of, 45-49.
—— IV., 50, 63 ; reign of, 64-67.
—— V., reign of, 50, 67.
—— VI., 75, 77 ; reign of, 77.
—— son of Henry VI., 63, 69.
—— Black Prince, 34, 44, 49.
Edwin, King, 3, 17.
—— Earl, 15, 17.
Edwy, 4, 9, 11.
Effingham, Thomas Howard, Earl of, 152.
Egbert, 4, 5.
Egfrith, 5.
Eglinton, Archibald W. Montgomerie, Earl of, 202.
Egmont, John Perceval, Earl of, 140.
Egremont, Charles Wyndham, Earl of, 140, 141, 142.
Egypt, 158, 224, 226, 227, 229
Eikon Basiliké, 101.
Elba, 166, 167.
Elcho, David Wemyss, Lord, 96.
—— Francis Wemyss, afterwards Earl of Wemyss, 206.
Eleanor of England, 34, 35.
Election of Bishops, 23, 30, 81.
Elections, Parliamentary, 55, 59.
—— Control over, 84.
—— Petitions, 134, 145, 209.
Elementary Education Act, 211, 212.
—— Commission on, 233.
Eldon, John Scott, Earl of, 160, 162, 164, 174-176.
Elgin, James Bruce, Earl of, 202, 204, 206.
Elgiva, 4.
Eliot, Sir John, 87, 89, 90.
—— Edward G., Lord, afterwards Earl of St. Germans, 174, 178.
Eliott, General G. A., afterwards Lord Heathfield, 151.
Elizabeth, Lady, of York, 69, 73.
—— Queen, 79 ; reign of, 79-85.
—— Stuart, Princess, 85
Ella, 3.
Ellandun, battle of, 5.
Ellenborough, Edward Law, Lord (I.), 160, 169.
—— —— (II.) Earl of, 188, 190, 192, 202, 209.
Elmham, Bishopric of, 16.
Ellice, Edward, 176, 182.
Elliot, Sir Gilbert, 152 (see Earl of Minto).
—— Sir Henry George, 219.

297

INDEX.

Ely, Bishopric, 72
—— Bishop of, 23.
Emma, 4, 11, 13, 14.
Emmett, R., 161.
Employers' Liability Act, 223.
Empress of India, title taken, 218.
Empson, Richard, 71.
Encumbered Estates Court, 195.
Endowed Schools Act, 211, 215.
Englefield, battle of, 7.
English race, settlement of, 3.
—— Language restored in the Law Courts, 49.
Enniskillen, 118.
Episcopacy, Scottish, 84, 154.
Eric, 13.
Erskine, Thomas, Lord, 155, 157, 160.
Escourt, T. H. Sotheron, 202.
Espinosa, battle of, 162.
Escuage (Scutage), 23, 30.
Essex, kingdom of, 5, 9, 13 ; shire, 51.
—— Earldom of, 24.
—— Robert Devereux, Earl of, 83.
—— Robert Devereux, Earl of (son of former), 94. 95, 97, 99.
—— Arthur Capel, Earl of, 115.
Estates General, French, 48, 86, 152.
Etaples, Treaty of, 69.
Ethandun, battle of, 7.
Ethelbald, of Mercia, 5.
—— of Wessex, 4, 5, 7.
Ethelbert of Kent, 3.
—— of Wessex, 4, 7.
Ethelfleda, 9.
Ethelfrith, 3.
Ethelmer, Bishop, 35.
Ethelred I., 4, 7, 10.
—— II., 11.
Ethelwald, 7.
Ethelwulf, 4, 5, 7.
Eugene, Prince, 126, 127.
Eugenius III., 22.
Eustace, of Boulogne, 15.
—— son of Stephen, 23.
Evans, Colonel de Lacy, 182.
Evesham, battle of, 37.
Exchequer Court, 21, 26, 37, 43.
Excise, 107 ; Scheme, 132, 133.
Exclusion Bill, 110, 113, 115.
Exeter, 16, 17, 119.
—— Bishopric of, 72.
—— Henry Courtenay, Marquis of, 75.
Exhibition, Great, 195.
Exmouth, Edward Pellew, Viscount, 169.
Explanation, Act of, 108, 118.
Eylau, battle of, 162.
Eyre, Governor, 207.

FACTORY ACTS, 180, 193 ; Fielden's, 193.
Fairfax, Ferdinand, Lord, 97.
—— Sir Thomas, 97, 99, 101, 103, 107.
Falaise, treaty of, 25, 27, 31.
Falkirk, first battle of, 41 ; second battle of, 137.
Falkland, Lucius Cary, Viscount, 95, 97.
Family Compact, 138.
Fawcett, Henry, 215, 222.

Fécamp, 103.
Fees, clerical, 73.
Felton, John, 89.
Female Suffrage, 209.
Fenians, 204, 209, 210.
Fenwick, Sir John, 123.
Ferdinand of Aragon, 66, 70.
—— I., Emperor, 78.
Fergusson, Sir James, 236.
Ferozeshah, battle of, 190.
Ferrol, battle off, 161.
Ferry Bridge, battle of, 65.
Feudal Dues, 18, 23, 30, 106, 107.
Feudalism, 30, 107.
Fielden's Act, 193.
Fiji, 216.
Finch, Sir John, Lord-Keeper, 93.
Finisterre, Cape, battle off, 137.
Finlay, George, 195.
Fire of London, 109.
First-fruits, 43.
Fisher, John, Bishop, 73, 75.
Fitz-Gerald, Lord Edward, 159.
—— Maurice, 24.
Fitz-Gilbert, Richard, 24.
Fitzherbert, Mrs., 153.
Fitz-Osbert, W., 17, 29.
Fitz-Patrick, Richard, 152.
Fitz-Peter, G., 29, 31.
Fitz-Stephen, Robert, 24.
Fitzwilliam, William, Earl, 156.
Five Boroughs, 8.
Five Mile Act, 109.
Flambard, Ranulf, 19.
Flanders, 21, 39, 41, 47, 65, 69.
—— Count of, 25.
—— Robert of, 21.
Fleetwood, Charles, 107.
Flemings, 21.
Fleury, Cardinal, 132.
Flodden, battle of, 71.
Flood, Henry, 155.
Fontainebleau, Treaty of, 141.
Fontenoy, battle of, 137.
Forbach, battle of, 210.
Forest, Charter of, 33 ; reclamation of, 91, 93.
Fornovo, battle of, 68.
Forster, T., 131.
—— W. F., 206, 210, 211, 212, 222, 225.
Fortescue, Chichester, 206, 210 (see Carlingford).
Forth, Firth of, 103, 127.
Forty Shilling Freeholders (English), 59, 180 ; (Irish), 177.
Fongères, 61.
Fowler, H. H., 232.
Fox, Family of, 136.
—— Henry (Lord Holland), 137, 138, 139, 140, 141 (see Holland).
—— Charles James, 142, 144, 145 ; joins North, 148, 149, 150, 151, 153, 155, 157, 159, 160, 161, 163, 176.
—— George, 108.
France, Isabella of, 21, 49, 51.
—— Henrietta of, 87.
—— Katharine of, 55, 57, 61.

INDEX.

France, Treaties with, 49, 57, 67, 69, 71, 73, 77, 81, 91, 105, 111, 123, 129, 137, 141, 151, 161, 167 (see Commercial Treaties).
—— War begun with, 17, 19, 21, 25, 29, 31, 33, 35, 41, 47 (see Summary, 278), 51, 57, 67, 69, 71, 75, 79, 89, 121, 125, 135, 139, 147, 157 (see Summary, 284-286), 161.
—— and Scotland, 40, 57, 71, 76, 78, 80, 127, 135.
—— and Ireland, 159.
Franchise Bills, 197 (see Summary, 291-295).
Francis I., 70, 72, 76.
—— II., 78, 80.
—— I., Emperor, 136.
—— Sir Philip, 144.
Franciscan Friars, 32.
Frankfort League, 134.
Franking letters, 153.
Franklin, Benjamin, 145, 146.
Frederick II., Emperor, 30, 34.
—— Elector, 85, 86, 90.
—— I., of Prussia, 124.
—— II., Prince of Wales, 133, 135, 137.
—— the Great, of Prussia, 134, 138, 140.
Free Church of Scotland, 191.
Free Trade Agitation, 89 (see Summary, 288).
Fremantle, William, 170.
French help the American Colonists, 146.
—— Kings, genealogies of, 20, 46, 80.
—— Revolution, Reflections on (Burke's), 155.
Friedland, battle of, 162.
Friends of the People, 155, 157.
—— Society of, 108.
Frost, J., 187.
Fuentes d'Onoro, battle of, 165.
Fulford, battle of, 15.
Fyrd, 27 (see Summary, 273).

Gage, Governor, 144.
Gainsborough, battle of, 97.
Galway, Henry de Ruvigny, Earl of, 127.
Gama, Vasco da, 70.
Gambetta, 224, 226.
Gardiner, Stephen, Bishop, 77,
Garfield, President, 224.
Garibaldi, 203.
Gascony, 22, 33, 35, 39, 41, 45, 47, 49.
Gascoigne, Isaac, General, 179.
Gatton, 145.
Gaveston, Piers, 43.
Gaunt, John of, 34, 44, 49, 51, 53.
General warrant, 140, 141, 143.
Genoa, 74, 159.
Geoffrey of Anjou, 21.
—— of England, 22, 24, 25, 27.
—— of York, 27.
George I., Act 6th of, 148, 151.
—— reign, 129-133.
—— II., 129; reign of, 133-139.
—— III., reign of, 139-171.
—— madness of, 141, 151, 153, 165.
—— IV., 151, 153; reign of, 171-177.
Georgia, 132.
Gerard's Plot, 105.
Gerberoi, 17.
Germaine, Lord George Sackville-, 147.

Germany, 72.
German Emperor, title taken, 212.
Gertrudenberg, Conference at, 128, 129.
Gettysburg, battle of, 206.
Ghent, 46.
—— Treaty of, 167.
Gibraltar, 127, 133, 147, 151.
Gibson, Thomas Milner, 192, 197, 201, 202, 203, 206.
Gilbert's Act, 150, 151.
Ginkel, G. de (Earl of Athlone), 120.
Gironde, 154, 156.
Gladstone, W. E., 182, 188, 191, 192, 193, 196, 197, 198, 199, 202, 204, 205, 206, 207, 215, 217, 221, 225, 229, 231, 232, 233, 237.
—— 1st Ministry, 210; (2nd) 222; (3rd) 232.
Glanville, R. de, 27.
Glasgow, 133, 137; Assembly of, 90.
Glenbeigh, 235.
Glencoe, Massacre of, 120.
Glendower, Owen, 53, 55.
Glenelg (see Charles Grant), Lord, 184.
Glenshiel, battle of, 131.
Gloucester, city of, 3, 23, 33, 97.
—— Bishopric of, 72.
—— Gilbert, Earl of, 37.
—— Hadwisa of, 29.
—— Humphrey, Duke of, 44, 57, 58, 59, 61.
—— Richard of, 37.
—— Richard, Duke of, 67.
—— Robert, Earl of, 21, 23.
—— Thomas of, 51, 53.
—— William, Duke of, 125.
Goderich, F. J. Robinson, Viscount, afterwards Earl of Ripon, 174, 175, 176.
Goderich's Ministry, 174.
Godwin, Earl, 12, 13, 14.
Godolphin, Sidney, Earl of, 115, 118, 121, 123, 125; genealogy of, 120.
"Golden Bull," 48.
Goodwin's case (see 84).
Goojerat, battle of, 194.
Gordon, Lord G., 149.
—— C. G., General, 227, 229.
Goring, Charles, General, 99.
Gorst, J. E., 230, 236.
Gortschakoff Circular, 210.
Goschen, G. J., 206, 210, 223, 233, 235, 236.
Goulburn, Henry, 174, 182, 188.
Gower, Granville Leveson Gower, Earl, afterwards Marquis of Stafford, 138, 140, 142, 150.
—— Sir John Leveson, 124.
Grace, Acts of, 121, 131.
Grafton, A. H. Fitzroy, Duke of, 124, 140, 142, 143, 146, 148, 150.
Grafton's Ministry, 142.
Graham, Sir James, 176, 183, 188, 189, 190, 199.
—— John, Viscount Dundee, 118.
—— Sir Thomas, 165.
—— Sir Gerald, General, 229.
Grampound, 171.
Granada, 68.
Granby, John Manners, Marquis, 140, 142.
—— Charles Cecil (Duke of Rutland), 192.
Grand Remonstrance, 95.

INDEX.

Grant, Charles (Lord Glenelg) 174, 175, 176.
Grant, General U. S., 206.
Grantham, Thomas Robinson (Lord), 150.
Granville, Earl (see Carteret), 137, 138, 140.
—— George, 196, 197, 198, 202, 203, 205, 210, 219, 222, 223, 226, 229, 232.
Granville's Despatch, 149, 226.
Grasse, Count de, 149.
Grattan, Henry (I.), 148.
—— Henry (II.), 165, 167, 169, 176.
Gravelines, battle of, 71, 79.
Great Intercourse, 69.
Greece, 170, 172, 175, 176, 195, 222, 232.
Gregory the Great, 2.
Gregory VII., Hildebrand, 16.
—— IX., 32, 33.
—— XI., 48.
Gregory, Serjeant, 113.
Grenville, family, genealogy of, 144.
—— George, Prime Minister, 138, 140, 141.
—— Ministry, 140.
—— James, 142, 143, 144.
—— William Wyndham, Lord, 152, 155, 156, 157, 159, 161, 163, 164, 165, 170.
—— Ministry, 160; followers of, 171.
—— Thomas, 163, 170.
—— Whigs, 142.
Grey, John de, Bishop, 29.
Grey family, genealogy of, 76.
—— Lady Jane, 77, 79.
—— Lady Katharine, 76.
—— Charles (Lord Howick, and Earl Grey), 157, 160, 164, 165, 176, 177, 180, 183.
—— Ministry, 176.
—— Henry George, Earl, son of above, 192, 193.
—— Sir George, 182, 186, 192, 198, 202, 206.
—— Sir John of Groby, Lord Ferrers (died Lord Grey of Groby), 65.
—— Sir Richard, 67.
—— Earl de (I.), 182, 188.
—— (II.), see Ripon.
Griffith, 15.
Grindal, Edmund, Archbishop, 81.
Grosseteste, Robert, Bishop of Lincoln, 35.
Ground Game Act, 223.
Grosvenor, Robert, 1st Marquis of Westminster, 150.
—— Earl (1st Duke of Westminster), 206.
—— Lord R., 206.
Grote, George, 185.
Guadaloupe, 139.
Guiana, 166.
Guienne, 22, 29, 42, 61; lost, 63.
—— Eleanor of, 23, 25, 27, 29.
Guildford, battle of, 149.
Guinegaste, or the Spurs, battle of, 71.
Guiscard, 129.
Guise, Mary of, 80, 81.
Guise family, genealogy of, 78.
—— Mary of, 74.
—— Duke of, 79.
Gundamuk, treaty of, 220.
Gunpowder Plot, 85.
Gustavus Adolphus, 90.
Gutenberg, 60.
Guthrum, 7.

HABEAS CORPUS ACT, 112, 113, 123, 141, 157, 168, 169, 195, 207.
Haddington, Thomas Baillie-Hamilton. Earl of, 182, 192.
Hadrian's, Emperor, walls, 3.
—— IV. (Nicolas Breakspear), 22.
Hadwisa, of Gloucester, 29.
Haguenau, battle of, 126.
Hainault, Jacqueline of, 58.
—— Philippa of, 45 47.
Hales, Sir E., 117.
Halfdene, 7.
Halidon Hill, battle of, 47.
Halifax, Charles Montague, Earl of, 125.
—— George Montague, Earl of, 138, 140, 141, 142.
—— George Savile, Marquis of, 113, 115, 117, 118, 121.
—— Viscount (Sir C. Wood), 210.
Halsbury, Hardinge Giffard, Lord, 230, 234.
Hamilton, James, Duke of, 100, 101.
—— William Gerard, "Single Speech," 142.
—— Lord George, 214, 230, 236.
—— Lord Claude, 220.
Hampden, Edward, 89.
—— John, 91, 95, 97.
Hampton Court, 101.
—— Conference, 85.
Hanover, 135, 185.
—— Genealogy of the House of, 158.
—— Treaty of, 133
Hanoverian troops, 135.
Hansard, 188.
Harcourt, Sir W. V., 222, 232, 235.
Hardicanute, 12, 13, 15.
Hardinge, Sir H., Viscount, 182, 188, 190.
Hardwicke, Philip Yorke, Earl of, (I.), 134 136, 137, 138.
—— (II.), 196, 202.
Hardy, T., 157.
—— Gathorne, 202, 208, 214 (Viscount Cranbrook).
Harfleur, 57.
Harley, Robert, 127, 129 (see Oxford).
—— Ministry, 128
Harold I., 12.
—— II., 12, 13, 15, 17.
—— Hardrada, 15.
Harrington, William Stanhope, Earl of, 134.
Harrowby, Dudley Ryder, 1st Earl, 160, 164, 174.
—— (II.), 2nd Earl, 198.
—— Dudley Francis Stuart Ryder, 3rd Earl, 230.
Hartington, Marquis of (I.), 134.
—— (II.), Spencer Compton Cavendish, Marquis of, 206, 210, 217, 221, 222, 223, 233, 235.
Hastenbach, battle of, 139.
Hastings, 19.
—— Battle of, 17.
—— William de, Lord, 67.
—— Warren, 144, 152, 153, 155, 159.
Hatfield, battle of, 3.
Hatherley, William Page Wood, Lord, 210.
Havannah, 141.
Havelock, Sir Henry, General, 201.

INDEX.

Havre, 57, 139.
Hawke, Edward, Lord, Admiral, 142.
Hawkesbury, Lord (Charles Jenkinson), 156 (created 1st Earl of Liverpool).
—— Robert Bankes Jenkinson, 160, 162 (see Liverpool).
Hawley, General, 137.
Haxey's case, 50, 51.
Hazelrig, Sir Arthur, 95.
Healy, Timothy, 227.
Hedgeley Moor, battle of, 65.
Hedges, Sir Charles, 124.
Heligoland, 163.
Heneage, Edward, 232, 233.
Hengist's Down, battle of, 5.
Henley, Robert, Lord (see Northington), 140.
Henley, Joseph Warner, 192, 196, 202, 203.
Henrietta Maria, 87, 95, 99.
Henry I., 4, 16, 18; reign of, 19-21.
—— II, 16, 21; reign of, 22-27.
—— III., 22, 82; reign of, 33-37.
—— IV., 34, 44, 53; reign of, 53-55.
—— V., 44; reign of, 55-57.
—— VI., 44; reign of, 57-65.
—— VII., 67; reign of, 69-71.
—— VIII, reign of, 71-77.
—— Stuart, Prince of Wales, 87.
—— I., of France, 20.
—— II. —— 76, 80.
—— III., —— 80.
—— IV. —— 82, 84; genealogy, 80.
—— III., Emperor, 16.
—— V. —— 20, 21.
—— VI. —— 26, 27.
—— of Blois, Bishop of Winchester, 23.
—— the Lion, 25.
—— son of Henry II., 22, 25, 27.
Herbert, Arthur, Admiral (see Torrington).
Herbert, Henry, 198.
—— Sidney, 182, 188, 192, 196, 198, 199, 202.
Hereditary Peerage Decree (France), 178.
Hereford, 16, 17.
Hereford, Roger, of Breteuil, Earl of, 17.
Hereward, 17.
Herries, John Charles, 174, 182, 196.
Herrings, battle of, 59.
Herschell, Farrer, Lord, 232, 235.
Hertford, 9.
—— Earl of, 24, 75, 77 (see Somerset).
—— Francis Seymour Conway, Earl, afterwards Marquis, 142.
Hervey, Augustus, Earl of Bristol, 142.
Herzegovina, 216.
Hessian troops, 135, 139.
Hexham, battle of, 16, 65.
Heytesbury, William A'.-Court, Lord, 182.
Hibbert, J. T., 232.
Hicks Pasha, 226.
Hidage, 28.
High Commission, Court of, 82, 83, 85, 91, 93.
—— Court of Justice, 217 (see Summary. 273).
Highlanders disarmed, 137.
—— Rowland, 187.
Hillsborough (Wills Hill), Earl of (Marquis of Downshire), 142.

Hispaniola, 68.
Hobart, Robert, Lord, afterwards of Earl Buckinghamshire, 160, 198.
Hobart Town, 160.
Hobhouse, Sir J. C. (Lord Broughton), 192.
Hochkirchen, battle of, 138.
Hochstädt, battle of, 124.
Hogue, La, battle of, 121.
Hohenlinden, battle of, 158.
Holderness, Robert D'Arcy, Earl of, 138.
Holland, 84, 95, 103, 105, 109, 111, 131, 149, 152, 159, 167 (see Dutch).
—— Henry Rich, Earl of, 91, 101.
—— Henry R. Vassall-Fox, Lord, 140, 176. (see Fox, Henry).
—— Sir Henry (Lord Knutsford), 230, 236.
—— Sir T., 34.
Holles, Denzil, 90, 95.
Holmby House, 101.
Holstein, 206.
Holy Alliance, 166, 167.
—— League, 71.
—— Roman Empire, 160.
Home Rule, 212, 231.
—— —— Bill, 232, 233, 235.
Home Rulers, strength of, 223.
Homildon Hill, battle of, 53.
Hone, W., 169.
Honfleur, 61.
Hongkong, 188.
Honorius III., 3.
Hooper, John, Bishop of Worcester, 79.
Horsman, Edward, 198, 206
Hospitallers, Knights, 75.
Hotham, Sir J., 95, 99.
Hounslow Heath, 117.
House Tax, 175.
Howard family, genealogy of, 52, 76.
—— Henry, Earl of Surrey, 77.
—— John, Lord, created Duke of Norfolk, 76.
—— Lady K., 71, 75.
—— Charles, Lord, of Effingham, 83.
—— Thomas, Duke of Norfolk (I.), 81.
—— Thomas, Duke of Norfolk (II.), 81.
Howards, The, 79.
Howe, Richard, Earl, Admiral, 142. 157.
—— Jack, 124.
—— Sir W., 147.
Howick, Lord (I.), 163 (see Grey and Earl Grey).
—— (II.), 184, 189 (Earl Grey)
Hubertsburg, Treaty of, 140.
Hugh of Avalon, 29.
Huguenot, 81, 88
Hull, 95, 97, 99.
Humber, 17.
Humbert, General, 158.
Humble Petition and Advice, 104. 105.
Hume, J., 180, 186.
Hungarian Insurrection, 194.
Hungerford, 119.
Hunt, John (Orator), 171.
—— Ward, 208, 214.
Huntingdon, David, Earl of, 18, 40.
—— Earldom of, 23.
—— Henry, Earl of, 18.
—— Thomas Holland, Earl of, 53.

INDEX.

Husklsson, William, 156, 162, 164, 174, 175, 177.
Huss, John, 56.
Hyde, Anne, 115.
—— Edward (see Clarendon), 95.
—— Park Riots, 209.
Hyder Ali, 146, 148.
Hyderabad, battle of, 188.

IDDESLEIGH, STAFFORD N., EARL OF, 230, 234.
Impeachment, 49, 86, 87.
Impey, Sir Elijah, 144.
Impositions, 85.
Income Tax, 95, 159, 189, 191, 193, 201, 207.
Indemnity, Acts of, 107, 121; Bill, 169.
—— —— for Nonconformists, 133.
Independence of United States, 146.
Independents, 99, 101, 103, 108.
India (see East India and Summary, 273, 274, 275).
—— Act, Pitt's, 150, 151, 152, 153.
—— Bill, Fox's, 150, 151.
—— Bill, Derby's, 202, 203.
—— Empress of, title assumed, 217.
—— Trade, 180.
Indian Mutiny, 201.
Indulgence Declaration (I.) 109; (II.) 117; (III.) 117.
Ine, 5.
Inglis, Sir R., 177, 192.
Inkerman, battle of, 199.
Innocent III., 31, 32.
—— IV., 34.
Inspector of Schools, 186, 187.
Instrument of Government, 103, 104.
Interdict, 31.
Interpreter, The. 84, 85.
Inverlochy, battle of, 98.
Iona, 3.
Ionian Islands, 202, 207.
Ireland, Summary of history of, to 1494, 268; under the Tudors, 269; under the Stuarts, 269; under the Hanoverians, 269, 270; since the Union, 270, 271, 272.
—— English Parliament to legislate for, 131.
—— Population of, 192, 193.
—— French in, 158, 159.
—— Spanish in, 80.
Ireton, Henry, 103.
Irish Church, 22, 180, 181, 183, 185, 209.
—— —— Act, 210, 211.
—— —— Disestablished, 211.
—— Famine, 134.
—— Land Acts, 203, 205, 211, 212, 224, 225.
—— Municipal Bill, 185, 188, 189.
—— Trade, 108, 110, 122, 146.
—— Free-holders disenfranchised, 177.
—— University Act, 220, 221.
Isabella, of England, 34.
Isandhlwana, battle of, 220.
Ismail, storming of, 154.
Italy, 68, 204, 236.
Ivry, battle of, 82.

JACKSON, GENERAL ("Stonewall"), 204.
——. W. L., 236.
Jacobites (see Summary, 283, 284).
Jacquerie, 48.

Jamaica, 104, 206.
—— Bill, 186, 187.
James I., reign of, 85-87.
—— II., 109, 111, 113, 121, 125; reign of, 115-119.
—— I. (Scotland), 42, 54, 55, 58, 59, 60.
—— II., —— 42, 60, 62.
—— III., —— 42, 62, 67, 68.
—— IV., —— 42, 68, 69, 70, 71.
—— V., —— 70, 75.
—— VI., —— 80, 83 (see James I., of England).
James Town, 84.
Jemappes, battle of, 154.
Jena, battle of, 162.
Jenkinson, Charles, 142 (see Hawkesbury).
Jersey, Edmund Villiers, Earl of, 124.
Jerusalem, 18, 26.
Jervis, Sir J., 159 (see St. Vincent).
Jesuits, 74, 81.
Jews, 27, 39, 105, 139.
Jewish Relief Bill, 181, 195, 197, 203.
John, 22, 27, 29, 34; reign of, 29-33.
Joan of England, 32.
John, of Gaunt, 49, 51, 53.
John I., of France, 46.
—— II., —— 46, 48, 49.
—— XXII., 45.
Johnson, Reverdy, 211.
Jones, General, 101.
Joyce, Cornet, 101.
Jubilee, the Queen's, 237.
Judicature, Supreme Court of, 215 (see Summary, 273).
Judith, 6.
Juliers, 84.
July, Revolution of, 176.
Juniéges, Robert of, 15.
June 1, battle of, 157.
"Junius," letters of, 143, 145.
Junot, Marshal, 163.
Jurors, 18.
Jury, Civil, 27.
—— Grand, 25.
—— Petty, 30.
Justice, High Court of, 101.
Justices, Itinerant, 25, 26.
—— Lords, English, 129.

KAFFIR WARS, 182, 196.
Kaffraria, 196.
Kars, 201, 218, 221.
Katharine Grey, 76.
—— Howard, 71, 75.
—— of Aragon, 70, 71, 73.
—— of France, 57.
—— Parr, 75.
—— of Portugal, 107, 109.
Kay-Shuttleworth, Sir Ughtred J., 232.
Keble, John, 180.
Kelly, Sir F., 202.
Keith, George Keith Elphinstone (Lord, then Viscount), 159.
Kenilworth, 45.
—— Dictum of, 37.
Kenneth, of Scotland (I.), 4.
—— (II.), 11.

INDEX.

Kennington Common, 193.
Kent, County of, 51, 69, 101.
—— Edmund, Earl of, 34, 47.
—— Thomas Holland, Earl of, 53.
—— Edward, Duke of, 158.
—— Joan of, 34, 51.
—— Kingdom of, 3, 5, 7.
—— Nun of, 73.
Kentish Petition, 124.
Keogh, Judge, 193.
Keppel, Augustus, Viscount, 142, 147, 148, 149, 150.
Ket, Robert, 77.
Khartoum, 228, 229, 231.
Khyber Pass, 188.
Kildares, insurrection of the, 72.
Kilkenny, Statute of, 49
Killiecrankie, battle of, 118.
Kilmarnock, William Boyd, Lord, 137.
Kilsyth, battle of, 98.
Kimberley, John Wodehouse, Lord, then Earl of, 210, 212, 222, 232.
Kimbolton, Edward Montagu, Lord, 95 (see Manchester).
King's Bench, 26, 27, 37, 43.
King *de facto*, 69.
Kingston, Evelyn Pierrepoint, Duke of, 132.
Kinsale, 83.
Kissingen, battle of, 206.
Kirke, Colonel, 117, 118.
Klosterseven, 139.
Knatchbull, Sir E., 188.
—— Hugessen, E. H. K., afterwards Lord Brabourne, 210.
Knighthood, distraint of, 35, 39, 91, 93.
Knights of the shire, 37, 47.
Knights Templars, 43.
Knox, John, 80.
Königgratz, battle of, 206.
Kossuth, 193.
Kunersdorf, battle of, 138.

LABOUCHERE, HENRY (Lord Taunton), 156.
Labourers, Statutes of, 48, 49.
Laing, Samuel, 222, 226.
Laing's Nek, battle of, 224.
Lagos, battle off, 139.
Lahore, treaty of, 192.
Lake Gerard, Viscount, General, 158, 160.
Lamb, William, 174, 175 (see Melbourne).
Lambert, John, General, 105, 107, 109.
Lambeth, 33.
Lancashire, Presbyterianism in, 99.
—— Cotton famine, 205.
Lancaster, Blanche of, 34.
—— Duke of (see John of Gaunt)
—— Duke of (see Henry IV.), 34.
—— Edmund, Earl of, 34, 35.
—— Henry, Earl of, 34, 47.
—— Thomas, Earl of, 34, 43, 45.
Land Bank, 123.
—— Acts (Irish), 205, 211, 225, 237.
—— League, Irish, 221, 223.
—— Act (Lord Ashbourne's Irish), 231.
—— Purchase Bill (Gladstone's Irish), 233, 234.
—— Tax, 122, 123.

Land Tax, Irish, 183.
—— Transfer Act, 217.
Landen, battle of, 123.
Lansdowne, 2nd Marquis of (see Shelburne).
—— Henry Petty Fitzmaurice, 3rd Marquis 174, 176, 192, 198.
—— Henry Charles Keith, 4th Marquis, 210.
Lanfranc, Archbishop, 17, 19.
Langensalza, battle of, 206.
Langport, battle of, 99.
Langside, battle of, 81.
Langton, Stephen, Archbishop, 31.
Laswaree, battle of, 160.
Lateran Council, 30.
Latimer, Hugh, Bishop, 79.
—— Thomas, Lord, 49.
Latin, use of, 133.
Laud, William, Archbishop, 89, 90, 91, 93, 99.
Laudabiliter Bull, 22.
Lauderdale, John Maitland, Earl (afterwards Duke), 109.
Lauffeld, battle of,
La Vendée, 156.
Lawrence, J., 42.
—— Sir H., 201.
—— Sir J. (Lord), 206.
Lawson, Sir W., 223.
Layard, Austen Henry, 210.
Laybach, treaty of, 170.
League, Catholic (France), 80.
—— National, 233, 237.
Lee, General, Robert, 206.
Leeds, Duke of (see Danby), 123.
—— (II.) (see Carmarthen, II.), 155.
—— (Kent), 45.
—— (Yorkshire), 170, 177, 180.
Lefevre, George James Shaw, 210, 222.
Legates, Papal, 32, 33.
Legge, Henry Bilston, 138.
Legions withdrawn, 3.
Legislation, Commons' share in, 40, 45, 51. 53, 55, 57.
Legislative Assembly (French), 154.
Leicester, 8, 9, 16, 23, 73.
—— Earl of (see Montfort).
—— Robert Dudley, Earl of, 81, 82, 83.
—— House Party, 132.
Leighton, Dr. Alexander, 90.
Leipzig, battle of, 166.
Leith, 53.
Lens, battle of, 100.
Lenthal, William, 93.
Leofric, 13, 15.
Leopold, Prince, of Saxe-Coburg, 167 176, 178.
Lepanto, battle of, 80.
Leslie, Alexander (Earl of Leven), 97, 102.
—— David, 98, 102.
Leuthen, battle of, 138.
Levellers, 101.
Lewes, battle of, 37.
—— Mise of, 37.
Lewis Frankland, 74.
—— Sir G. C., 198, 202.
Lexington, battle of, 145.
Libel, law of, 145, 155.

INDEX.

Liberals, or Whigs, numbers of, 181, 183, 187, 189, 197, 201, 203, 207, 211, 215, 223, 231, 235.
Licensing Act, 122, 123.
—— —— (Liquors), 215.
Lichfield, 5, 16.
—— Lord, 206.
Liège, 125.
Liegnitz, battle of, 34.
Life Peers, 201, 211.
Ligny, battle of, 167.
Lille, 127.
Limerick, 120.
Limoges, 49.
Limousin, 22.
Lincoln, 8.
—— Abraham, 206.
—— Battle of (i.), 23.
—— —— (ii.), 33.
—— Bishopric of, 72.
—— Bishop of, 23.
—— John de la Pole, Earl of, 69.
—— Henry Pelham-Clinton, Earl of, afterwards Duke of Newcastle, 191.
Lincolnshire, 96, 97.
Lindisfarne, 3, 16.
Lindesey, 16.
Linlithgow, 42.
Lisle (John Dudley), Lord (afterwards Warwick and Northumberland), 75.
Littleton, 182.
Liturgy (Scottish), 90.
Liverpool, R. B. Jenkinson, Earl of, 171, 175 (see Hawkesbury (ii.), 164, 165).
—— Bishopric of, 72.
—— Earl of, Ministry, 164.
Llewelyn, 39.
Loans, forced, 73, 89.
—— Lord North's, 149.
Local Government Board, 213.
—— Option, 223.
Locke, J., 123.
Locke-King, P. J., 195, 205, 207.
Lodi, battle of, 158.
Lollards, 51, 55.
Lombardy, 202.
London, 9, 11, 13-17, 23, 27, 29, 63, 65, 91, 93, 97, 107, 151, 184, 189.
—— Plague of, 109.
—— Treaty of, 175.
Londonderry, 118.
—— G. H. Vane-Tempest, Marquis of, 236.
—— Robert Stewart, Marquis of (see Castlereagh), 173.
Long, W. H., 236.
Longchamp, William, 27.
Long Island, 174.
Lord-Lieutenant, 95, 117.
Lord-Lieutenancies forfeited, 140, 141, 147.
Lords, House of, 47; abolished, 101 (see Parliamentary Summary, 249, and Appendix ii., p. 302).
Lords Ordainers, 43.
Lorraine, Duke of, 114.
Losecoat Field, battle of, 65.
Lostwithiel, battle of, 97.
Lothian, 10, 13, 25.

Lothian, Schomberg H. Kerr, Marquis of, 236.
Loughborough, Lord A. Wedderburn, 156, 157 (afterwards Earl of Rosslyn).
Louis vi., 20.
—— vii., 20, 23, 25, 26.
—— viii., 20, 31, 32, 33.
—— ix., 20, 32, 36, 37.
—— x., 44.
—— xi., 46, 62, 65, 66, 67.
—— xii., 70, 71.
—— xiii., 84, 86, 96.
—— xiv., 96, 109, 113, 115, 116, 118, 121, 127, 130.
—— —— Marriage treaty, 106.
—— xv., 130, 132, 144.
—— xvi., 144, 156.
—— xviii., 166, 172.
—— Philippe, 177, 192.
Louisbourg, 137, 139
Louvain, Adela of, 21.
Lowe, Robert (Viscount Sherbrooke), 196, 198, 202, 206, 210, 211, 213, 215.
Lowther, James, 214.
Lovat, Simon Fraser, Lord, 137.
Lovel, Francis, Viscount, 69.
Lowestoft, battle off, 109.
Lucknow, 201, 203.
Lucy, R. de, 25, 27.
Luddites, 165.
Ludlow, 63, 67, 103.
Lumley, Richard, Viscount (afterwards Earl of Scarborough), 117.
Lunéville, treaty of, 158.
Luther, Martin, 70, 76.
Lutter, battle of, 88.
Luttrell, Henry Lawes, Colonel, 143 (Earl of Carhampton).
Lützen, battle of (i.), 90.
—— —— (ii.), 166.
Luxembourg, Jacquetta of, 59.
Lyndhurst, John Singleton Copley, Lord, 174, 179, 182, 188.
Lyons, Council of, 34, 35.
Lyttleton, George, Lord, 132, 142.
Lytton, Sir E. Bulwer, Lord, 202.
—— Robert, Lord, afterwards Earl of, 216, 217.

Macaulay, Zachary, 162.
—— T. B. (Lord), 176, 186, 192.
Macbeth, 15.
Mackay, Hugh, General, 118.
M'Clellan, General, 204.
Macclesfield, Thomas Parker, Earl, 132.
Mackintosh, Sir J., 171.
Macmahon, Marshal, 210.
Madoc, 41.
Madras, 90, 136, 138.
Madrid, 162, 166.
Magdala, 209.
Magdalen College, 118, 119.
Magenta, battle of, 202.
Magna Charta, Great Charter, 30.
Mahdi, 229, 231.
Mahrattas, 160.
Maida, battle of, 163.
Maidstone, 101.

INDEX.

Main Plot, 85.
—— River, 135.
Maine, 17, 22, 29, 61.
Mainwaring, Dr. Roger, 89.
Maiwand, battle of, 222.
Major-Generals, 105.
Majuba Hill, battle of, 224.
Malcolm I., 9.
—— II., 13, 16, 17.
—— III., Canmore, 14, 18, 19.
—— IV., 18, 21, 22, 24.
Maldon, battle of, 10.
Malmesbury, James Howard Harris, Earl of, 192, 196, 202, 208, 214.
Malplaquet, battle of, 127.
Malt Tax (Scottish), 132.
—— (British), 181, 195, 223.
Malta, 159, 160, 166.
—— Indian Troops at, 221.
Manchester, 9, 177, 189.
—— Bishopric of, 72.
—— Earl of (see Kimbolton), 97, 99.
"Manchester Massacre," 171.
Mandeville, William, 25.
Manilla, 141.
Manners, Lord J., afterwards Duke of Rutland, 192, 196, 202, 208, 214, 229, 230, 236.
Mantes, 19.
Mar, John Erskine, Earl of, 131.
March, Edmund, Earl of, 50.
—— Edward, Earl of, 63 (Edward IV.
—— Roger, Earl of, 51.
—— Lord (Duke of Richmond), 202.
Marche, Hugh, Count de la, 29, 34.
Mare, Peter de la, 49.
Marengo, battle of, 158.
Margaret, of England (I.), 4, 16.
—— —— (II.), 34.
—— of Anjou, 61, 63, 65.
—— of France (I.), 20.
—— —— (II.), 39.
—— of Norway, 18, 40.
—— of Scotland (I.), 40.
—— —— (II.), 42.
—— Tudor, 71.
Maria Theresa, of Austria, 133, 134, 137.
—— —— of Spain, 124.
Marlborough, Sarah, Duchess of, 129.
—— George, Duke of, 140.
—— John, —— 122, 123, 125, 127, 129, 132 (see Churchill).
—— John Winston —— 208, 214.
—— Statute of, 37.
Marprelate Tracts, 83.
Marriage Act, Royal, 144, 145.
—— (Hardwicke's), 136, 137.
Marshall, Richard, 33, 35.
—— William, Earl of Pembroke (I.), 29, 33.
—— —— (II.), 34, 35.
Marston Moor, battle of, 97.
Martin v., Pope, 56, 57.
Mary I., of England, 71, 73, 79.
—— II., —— 113 ; reign of, 119-123.
—— of Modena, 115.
—— Queen of Scots, 74, 75, 76, 78, 80, 81, 83.
—— Tudor, 71.
Maserfield, battle of, 3.

Mason, 205.
Massachusetts, 88, 96, 114, 144, 145.
Massena, Marshal, 165.
Massey, John, Dean of Christ Church, 117.
Match Tax, 213.
Matilda, Lady of the English, 16, 21, 23.
—— wife of Henry I., 4, 16, 21.
—— wife of Stephen, 22.
—— wife of William the Conqueror, 17.
Matthews, Henry, 234.
Maule, Fox, 192 (Lord Panmure).
Mauritius, 164, 166.
Maximilian, 70.
May, quoted, 152, 158, 162, 168, 174, 178, 182, 186, 192.
Maynooth, Grant, 191.
Mayo, R. S. Bourke, Earl of, 208, 212 (see Naas).
Mazarin, Cardinal, 106.
Mazzini, 191.
Meagher, T. F., 192, 193.
Meaux, 57.
Medway, 109.
Mecanee, battle of, 188.
Meerut, 201.
Melbourne, 194.
—— Viscount (see Lamb), 176, 182, 183, 184, 185, 189.
Melbourne's First Ministry, 182.
—— Second Ministry, 184, 186.
Melcombe Regis, 180.
Melville, Viscount (Henry Dundas) 160, 161.
—— Robert, ——, 164.
Merchants, 30 ; forbidden to make grants, 49.
—— Shipping Bill, 217.
Merchandise Marks Act, 237.
Mercia, 5, 7, 13.
Merton, battle of, 7.
—— Walter de 39.
Merv, 228.
Messina, 27.
Methodists, 133.
Methuen, Treaty, 124, 125.
Metz, 210.
Miall, E., 201, 213.
Middlesex, county of, 147.
—— Election, 143, 145, 149.
—— Lord, 87.
Midlothian Tour, 221.
Milford Haven, 69.
Mile Act, 108.
Miles, Sir William, 192.
Military and Naval Officers' Oaths Bill, 169.
Militia, 139, 197 (see Summary, 273).
—— Ballot suspended, 177.
—— Bill, 95.
Mill, J. S., 209.
Millenary Petition, 84, 85.
Mills, Arthur, 204 ; quoted, 199.
Minden, battle of, 139.
Ministers, appointment of, 35, 46, 51.
Minorca, 127, 149.
Minto, Earl of, 160, 162 (see Sir G. Elliot).
—— Sir Gilbert Elliot, 192.
Mirabeau, Count de, 154.
Mise of Amiens, 36, 37.

INDEX.

Mise of Lewes, 36, 37.
Missive, Letter, 72.
Mitchel, John, 192, 193, 217.
Mitford's Bill, 155.
Modena, Mary of, 115.
Mohammed, 2.
Mohacs, battle of, 72.
Moira, Francis Rawdon, Earl of, 160, 166 (see Marquis of Hastings).
Molesworth, Sir W., 197.
Moleyns, Adam, Bishop, 61.
Molwitz, battle of, 134.
Mompesson, Sir G., 87.
Monasteries, 73, 75.
Money Grants, 55.
Mongols, 34.
Monk, George, General, Duke of Albemarle, 103, 107.
Monmouth, James Fitzroy Scott, Duke of, 115, 116.
Monopolies, 83, 91.
Mons, 127.
Monsell, William Edward (Lord Emly), 206, 210.
Monson, Colonel, 144.
Montague, Charles, 121, 123 (see Earl of Halifax).
—— Dr. Richard, 87.
Montenotte, battle of, 158.
Montfort, Simon de, 34, 35, 37.
Montgomery, Roger of, 19.
Montrose, James Graham, Marquis of, 96, 98, 102.
—— Duke of (I.), 160.
—— (II.), 208.
Moodkee, battle of, 190.
Mooltan, 193.
Moore, Sir J., 163.
Moore, Captain Stephen, 217.
Moravians, 181.
Morcar, 15, 17.
Mordaunt, Charles (see Earl of Peterborough).
More, Sir Thomas, 73, 75.
Moreau, General, 158.
Morgan, G. Osborne, 222, 232.
Morley, John, 232, 235.
Morning sittings, 181.
Mornington (Richard Colley Wellesley), Earl of, 158 (see Wellesley).
Mort d'ancestor, 30.
Morpeth, George William Frederick, Lord, 184, 192 (Earl of Carlisle).
Mortimer, Edmund, Earl of March (I.), 50.
—— Edmund (II.), 50, 55, 57.
—— Edward, Earl of March (Edward IV.), 63.
—— Roger, Earl of March, 45, 47.
—— Roger, Lord, 50, 51.
Mortimers, 55 (for genealogy see p. 50)
Mortimer's Cross, battle of, 63.
Mortmain, statutes of, 38, 39, 51, 73.
Morton, John, Cardinal, 67.
Moscow, 164.
Mowbray, Robert, Earl of Northumberland, 19.
—— Thomas, Earl of Nottingham (father), 51, 53 (see Norfolk).

Mowbray, Thomas, Earl of Nottingham (son), 55.
Muir, T., 157.
Muhlburg, battle of, 76.
Mulgrave, Henry Phipps, Lord, afterwards Earl of, 160, 162, 164.
—— Constantine Henry Phipps, Earl of, 184 (Normanby, Marquis of).
Mundella, A. J., 222, 232.
Municipal Reform Act, 185.
Munro, Major Hector, 140.
Murdoch, Duke of Albany, 42.
Murad, 216.
Mutiny Act, 118, 119.
—— —— Perpetual, 148, 149, 150, 151.
—— Indian, 201, 203.
—— of the Fleet, 159.

Naas, Richard Southwell Bourke, Lord, 196, 202, 208 (afterwards Earl of Mayo).
Namur, 123, 127.
Nancy, 66.
Nankin, treaty of, 188.
Nantes, Edict of, 82, 114.
Napier, family, 198.
—— Sir C. (I.), 194.
—— —— (II.), 198, 199.
Napoleon I., 163, 164, 166, 170.
—— III., 196, 210.
Naseby, battle of, 99.
Natal, 180, 190.
Nation, The, 192.
National Union, 180.
National Assembly (French), 152.
—— Debt, 121, 137.
Navarino, battle of, 175.
Navarre, 27.
—— Berengaria of, 27.
—— Joan, Queen of (I.), 46.
—— —— (II.) 53.
Navigation Acts, 103, 172, 173, 195.
Necker, 146.
Nelson, Horatio, Viscount, 159, 160, 161.
Nepaul, 166.
Netherlands, 80, 81, 83, 84, 125.
Neutrality, Armed, 146, 150, 161.
Neville, Alexander, Archbishop, 51.
—— John, Lord, 49.
—— Isabella, 65.
—— Anne, 67.
Nevill's Cross, battle of, 47.
New Model Army, 99.
New Orleans, 167.
New South Wales, 142, 152, 186, 194.
New Style, 136, 137.
New York, 108, 147.
New Zealand, 186, 198, 196, 216.
Newark, 33.
Newburn, battle of, 93.
Newbury, first battle of, 97.
—— Second battle of, 99.
Newcastle, 67.
—— Thomas Pelham, Duke of (I.), 132, 133, 134, 138, 139, 140, 141, 142.
—— 1st Ministry, 138; 2nd Ministry, 138.
—— Henry Pelham-Clinton, Duke of, 174, 176.

306

INDEX.

Newcastle, Henry Pelham-Clinton, Duke of (see Lincoln), 196, 198, 202.
—— William Cavendish, Earl of, 97.
Newdegate, C. N., 192.
Newhaven (U. S.), 96.
Newman, J. H., Cardinal, 191.
Newmarket, 95, 101.
Newport, in Isle of Wight, 101.
—— in Wales, 187.
Newspaper Stamp Duty, 129, 185, 199.
Newton, Sir Isaac, 123.
Newtown Butler, battle of. 118.
Ney, Marshal, 167.
Nice, 202.
Nicolas, Czar, 172, 198.
Nicopolis, battle of, 50.
Nilo, battle of, 150.
Nimwegen (Nimeguen), treaty of, 112.
No-Rent manifesto, 225.
Nobles (see Barons, Lords, House of).
Nonconformists (see Summary, 259 to 262, column B).
—— Marriages of, 185.
Nonjurors, 118, 119.
Non-residence Act, 187.
Nootka Sound, 155.
Nore, Mutiny at, 150.
Norfolk, county of, 25, 77.
—— Earldom of, 24.
—— Island, 192.
—— Hugh Bigod, Earl of, 25.
—— Ralf Guader, Earl of, 17.
—— Roger Bigod, Earl of, 41.
—— Thomas Howard, Duke of (I.), Earl of Surrey, 76, 77.
—— —— (II.), 76, 81.
—— Thomas Mowbray, Duke of, 52, 53. (For genealogy of the Howard family, see p. 76.)
Norham, 41.
Normanby, John Sheffield, Marquis of, afterwards Duke of Buckingham, 124.
—— (see Mulgrave), 186.
Normandy, 6, 19, 21, 22, 25, 27, 29, 47, 57, 61, 63.
—— Emma of, 11, 13.
—— Robert of, 16, 17, 18, 19, 21.
Norris, Sir J., 83.
North Briton, 141.
North, Frederick, Lord, afterwards Earl of Guilford, 142, 143, 145, 149, 150, 152.
North's, Lord, Ministry, 142.
North, Revolt of the, 81.
Northallerton (Battle of the Standard), 21.
Northampton, Assize of, 27.
—— Battle of, 63.
—— Council of, 25.
—— Earldom of, 24.
—— Treaty of, 47.
Northbrook, Thomas George Baring, Lord, afterwards Earl of, 210, 212, 217, 222.
Northcote, Sir S., 202, 208, 214, 219 (Earl of Iddesleigh), 230, 234, 236.
——'s Procedure Resolutions, 219, 221.
Northington, Earl of (see Henley), 142.
Northmen, 5, 6, 8, 9, 10 (see Danes).
Northumberland, 17, 20, 45.

Northumberland, Duke of (see Lisle and Warwick), 77, 79.
—— Robert Mowbray, Earl of, 19.
—— Henry, Earl of (I.), 53, 55.
—— Thomas Percy, Earl of, 81.
—— Duke of, 196, 214.
Northumbria, Kingdom of, 3, 5, 7, 9, 15.
Norton, Lord (see Adderley).
Norway, 10, 12, 146.
—— Maid of, 38, 41.
Norwich, 16.
—— Bishopric of, 72.
Notables, French, 152.
Nottingham, 7, 8, 9, 13, 95, 178.
—— Thomas Mowbray, Earl of, 51.
—— Daniel Finch, Earl of, 118, 121, 125, 126.
Novel disseisin, 30.
Noy, 90.
Nugent, Sir C., 170.
Nun of Kent, 73.

OATES, TITUS, 113, 115.
O'Brien, Smith, 192, 193, 194.
—— William, 235.
Obstruction, 219, 221, 227.
Occasional Conformity Act, 128, 129, 131.
Ockley, battle of, 5.
O'Connell, Daniel, 175, 177, 183, 191.
O'Connor, A., 158.
—— Feargus, 191.
Octennial Act, Ireland, 142.
Œcumenical Council, 210.
Odo, of Bayeux, 17.
Offa, 5.
Offa's Dyke, 5.
O'Kelly, J. J., 225.
Oldcastle, Sir J., 55, 57.
Oltenitza, battle of, 196.
O'Neal, Hugh (or O'Neil), Earl of Tyrone, 83, 85.
Oporto, battle of, 165.
Orange, Prince of, genealogy, 82.
—— William the Silent, Prince of, 82.
—— —— 110 (see William III.).
—— House of, 152.
—— Free State, 192.
Orangemen, 156.
Ordainers, Lords, 42, 43.
Ordeal, 30.
Orders in Council, 162, 165.
Orford, Lord (I.), (see Russell, Edward), 125.
—— (II.), (see Walpole), 135.
Orleans, 59.
—— Louis, Duke of (I.), 46.
—— —— (II.), 54, 55.
—— Charles, Duke of, 57, 61.
—— Philip, Duke of, Regent, 130.
Orleanists, 56.
Orleton, Adam, Bishop, 45.
Ormond, James Butler, Earl, Marquis, and Duke of (I.), 86, 101.
—— Duke of (II.), 128, 129, 131.
Ormsby, Justiciar of Scotland, 40.
Orsini, 201, 203.
Orthez, battle of, 167.
Osborne (see Danby and Leeds).
Osric, 5.

INDEX.

Oswald, 3.
Oswy, 3.
Otford, battle of, 5.
Otho, Legate, 35.
—— of Greece, 178.
Otterburn, battle of, 51.
Otto the Great, Emperor, 10.
—— II. —— 10.
—— IV. —— 31.
Oudh, 200.
—— Nabob of, 140.
Oudenarde, battle of, 127.
Outram, Sir James, General, 201, 203.
Overbury, Sir T., 87.
Oxford, 23, 31, 87, 95, 97, 99, 115.
—— Bishopric of, 72.
—— Corporation of, 142.
—— Earl of (Harley), 129, 131.
—— Earldom of, 24.
—— Provisions, 36, 37.
—— University of, 115, 117.

PACIFICO, DON, 195.
Paine, T., 157.
Pains and Penalties, Bill of, 171.
Pakington, Sir J. (Lord Hampton), 196, 202, 208.
Palatine, Elector, 85, 86, 87, 90.
Palæologus, Manuel, 53.
Palmer, T. F., 157.
Palmerston, Henry John Temple, Viscount, 164, 174, 175, 176, 182, 184, 192, 193, 195, 196, 197, 198, 201, 202, 207.
—— 1st Ministry, 198 ; 2nd, 202.
—— Memorandum to, 194.
Pampeluna, 167.
Pandulf, 31, 33.
Panics, Commercial, 175, 209.
Panmure, Lord (see Fox Maule), 198.
Papal Bulls, 81.
—— Infallibility, 210.
—— Nuncio, 117.
—— Power, 73 (see Pope and also Ecclesiastical Summary, pp. 255-258).
Paper Duty Bill, 205.
Paris, 47, 61, 210, 212.
—— Treaties of (I.), 141 ; (II.), 166 ; (III.), 166, 167 ; (IV.), 201 ; (V.), 213.
Parke, Sir J. (Lord Wensleydale), 200.
Parker, Matthew, Archbishop, 81.
Parliament (see Summary, Part I., to 1295, p. 249 ; Part II., 1295-1430, p. 249 ; Part III., 1430-1689, p. 251 ; Part IV., 1689-1832, p. 253 ; Part V., 1832-1888, p. 254).
—— Duration of, 71.
—— Meeting of, 153.
—— (Special), The Mad, 37.
—— The Model, 41.
—— The Good, 49.
—— The Merciless, 51.
—— of Shrewsbury, 53.
—— The Seven Years, 73.
—— The Addled, 87.
—— The Short, 93.
—— The Long, 93, 107.
—— of Oxford (Charles I.), 97.
—— Barebones', 102.

Parliament, Convention (i.), 107.
—— of Oxford (Charles II.), 115.
—— Convention (ii.), 119.
Parliamentary Reform (see Summary, p. 291).
Parnell, C. S., 219, 223, 225, 235.
—— Sir H., afterwards Lord Congleton, 177.
Parr, Katharine, 71, 75.
Parret, River, 5.
Parsons, Robert, 81.
Party Government, 123, 125.
Partition Treaties, 124, 125.
Passaro, Cape, battle off, 131.
Passau, Peace of, 76.
Patent Laws Bill, .
Patrick, Saint, 2.
Patten, J. Wilson (Lord Winmarleigh), 208.
Patronage Acts (Scotland), 129, 191, 215.
Paullinus, 3.
Pavia, battle of, 72.
Peace Preservation Acts, 212, 217, 223.
Peasant revolt, 51.
—— War, 72.
Pecquigny, treaty of, 67.
Pedro the Cruel, 49.
Peel, Sir Robert (I.), 164, 171, 174, 175, 182, 183, 185, 187, 188, 189, 191, 192, 193, 195.
—— 1st Ministry, 182 ; 2nd, 188, 192.
—— Frederick, 202.
—— General Jonathan, 202, 208.
—— Sir R. (II.), 202.
Peelites, 198, 199.
Peerage Bill, 130, 131.
—— Irish, 158.
—— Scottish, 126.
Peers, creation of, 129.
—— Pitt's, 160.
Pegu, 196.
Peishwah, 160, 168.
Peiwar Heights, battle of, 220.
Pekin, 203.
Pelham, Henry, 133, 134, 135, 139.
—— Ministry, 134.
—— Thomas (see Newcastle).
—— Thomas, Lord (afterwards Earl of Chichester), 160.
Peltier, 161.
Pembroke, county of, 21 ; town of, 101.
—— Earldom of, 24.
—— Henry Herbert, tenth Earl of, 147.
—— Jasper Tudor, Earl of, 63.
—— Thomas Herbert, eighth Earl of, 124
—— William Marshall, Earl of, 33.
Penda, 3.
Penjdeh, battle of, 231.
Penn, W., 105.
Penruddock, Colonel John, 105.
Penryn, 175.
Pen Selwood, battle of, 13.
Pensions, 149.
Pepys, Sir C. C. (Earl of Cottenham), 184.
Perceval's Ministry, 164.
—— Spencer, 161, 162, 163, 164, 165.
Percies, 53.
Percy, Henry, Earl of Northumberland (I.), 55.
—— Henry (Hotspur), 50.
Perpetuation Bill, 103.
Perrers, Alice, 49.

308

INDEX.

Persia, 200.
Perth, 42, 96.
—— Articles of, 86.
Peterborough, Bishopric of, 72.
—— Charles Mordaunt, Earl of, 127.
Peter des Roches, 31, 33, 35.
—— the Great, 118, 122, 132.
Petition and Advice, 105.
—— Great Yorkshire, 147.
—— of Right, 88, 89.
—— the Millenary, 84, 85.
"Petitioners," 113.
Petre, Edward, 119.
Petty Jury, 30.
—— Lord H., 160.
Pevensey, 16.
Philadelphia, 144, 147.
Philip Augustus of France, 20, 26, 27, 29, 31.
—— of Burgundy (I.), 56, 58, 59, 64.
—— of Burgundy (II.), 69, 74.
—— I. of France, 14, 19, 20, 46, 47.
—— III. —— 20, 38, 46.
—— IV. —— 20, 38, 41, 44.
—— V. —— 44, 46.
—— VI. —— 46, 48.
—— II. of Spain, 78, 79, 82.
—— III. —— 82, 86.
—— IV. —— 86.
—— of France, v. of Spain, 124.
—— of Orleans, 130.
Philiphaugh, battle of, 98.
Phillimore, Dr. Joseph, 170.
Philippa, Queen, 49.
Philip, Archduke, 71.
Philipot, John, 49.
Phœnix Park Murders, 226.
—— Club, 204.
Picts, 4, 5.
Pilgrimage of Grace, 75.
Pillory, 187.
Pindaries, 168.
Pinkie, battle of, 77.
Pir Paimal, battle of, 222.
Piræus, 195.
Pisa, Council of, 54.
Pitt family, genealogy of, 144.
—— William (father), 137, 138, 139, 141, 143 (see Chatham).
—— William (son), 149, 150, 151, 153, 157, 159, 161.
—— 1st Ministry, 150, 156; 2nd Ministry, 160.
Pittsburg, 138.
Pius V., 81.
Place Bill, 135.
Placemen Act, 127.
—— dismissed for votes in Parliament, 141.
Plague, Great, 109.
Plantagenet, Edward, Earl of Warwick, 69.
Plassey, battle of, 138.
Playfair, Sir L., 232.
Plays, stage, 95.
Plevna, 218.
Plimsoll, Samuel, 217.
Plunket, W. C., afterwards Lord, 170, 176.
—— D., 230, 236.
Pluralities, 73.

Plymouth, 67.
—— (U. S.), 86, 96.
Poitevins, 33, 35.
Poitiers, battle of, 49.
Poitou, 22, 29, 31, 33, 35.
Poland, First Partition of, 144; second partition, 156; third partition, 156.
Poles, De la, genealogy of, 68, 74.
Pole, Arthur, 81.
—— Edmund, 81.
—— Edmund de la, Earl of Suffolk, 50.
—— John de la, Earl of Suffolk, 50.
—— John de la, Earl of Lincoln, 50, 69.
—— Michael, de la, Earl of Suffolk, 51.
—— Reginald, Cardinal, 79.
—— Richard de la, 50.
—— William de la, Duke of Suffolk, 61.
Polish Succession, War of, 132.
Political Register, 169.
Poll-tax, 49.
Pondicherry, 138, 141, 150, 156.
Pontefract, 45, 67.
Poor Law Board, 193.
Poor Laws, 84, 85, 182, 183.
—— Rate, 182; Housing of Poor, 229.
Poor Law Union Chargeability Bill, 207.
Pope, 16, 31, 33, 35, 37, 43, 71, 72, 73; power abolished, 73 (see Summary, pp. 255-258).
Popish Plot, 113.
Porteous Riots, 133.
Portland, William Henry Cavendish-Bentinck, Duke of, 150, 151, 156, 157, 163, 165.
—— 1st Ministry of, 150; 2nd, 162.
—— (II.), 174.
Porto Bello, 135.
—— Novo, battle of, 148.
Portsmouth, 47, 61, 89, 161.
Portugal, 163, 174.
Post Office, Reformed, 153.
—— Letters opened at, 191.
Potato Crop, failure of, 191, 193.
"Pouch, Captain," 85.
Poundage, 48, 49, 86, 89.
Poynings Act, 68, 69.
Praed, 182.
Præmunientes clause, 40.
Præmunire, Statute of, 48, 49, 51, 59, 73.
Pragmatic Sanction, 133.
Prague, battle of, 86.
Pratt, Charles 141 (see Camden).
Prayer Book, first of Edward VI., 77; second, 77; of Elizabeth, 79; Charles II.'s, 109.
—— Scottish, 90.
Presbyterians (English), 99, 101, 108, 109.
—— (Scottish), 82.
Press, freedom of, 123.
Preston, battle of, first, 101; second, 101.
—— Richard Graham, Viscount, 121.
Prestonpans, battle of, 137.
Pretender (Old), 117, 119, 125, 127.
—— (Young), 137.
Prevention of Crimes Bill, 227.
Pride, Thomas, Colonel, 101.
Priestly, Dr., 155.
Priories, Foreign, 57.
Private grants forbidden, 49.

INDEX.

Privilege of Parliament, 84, 85, 86, 87 (see Summary, 250, 252, 254, 255).
Privy Council, 33, 37, 49, 59, 61, 83, 89.
Procedure Resolutions, 227, 235, 237.
Proclamations of Henry VIII., 75, 77.
Property Qualification Act, 129, 202.
Prophesyings, 81.
Propositions of Parliament to Charles I., 94, 95.
Protection of Life and Property Act, 225.
Protectorate, 103, 107.
Protestants, advanced, 81.
Provençals, 35.
Provence, Eleanor of, 33, 35.
Provisions of Oxford, 36, 37.
Provisors, 43, 48, 49, 51, 57, 59.
Proxies, Lords', 209.
Prussia, subsidy to, 139.
—— Frederick of, 134, 138, 140.
—— William of, 204, 212.
Pruth, river, 196, 218.
Prynne, William, 91, 93.
Public Advertiser, 143.
Publication of debates, 133, 145.
Public Prosecutor, 221.
—— Worship Regulation Act, 215.
Pulteney, William, afterwards Earl of Bath, 131, 132, 133, 134, 135.
Pultowa, battle of, 126.
Punjab, 194.
Purchase in the Army abolished, 213.
Puritans, 81, 83, 93.
Purse, control over the (see Parliament Summary, 249, 250, 252).
Purveyance, 107.
Pusey, E. B., 191.
Pym, John, 87, 93, 95, 97.
Pyrenees, Treaty of, 106.
—— Battle of, 167.

QUADRUPLE ALLIANCE, 131.
Quakers, 108, 181.
Quatre Bras, battle of, 167.
Quebec, 139.
Queen Anne's Bounty, 126, 127.
Queen's Colleges (Irish), 191.
Queensland, 202.
Quia Emptores, 39.
Quiberon Bay, battle off, 139.
—— Expedition to, 159.
Quo Warranto, writ of, 39, 115.

RADCOT BRIDGE, battle of, 51.
Radicals, 171.
Raglan, Fitzroy Somerset, Lord, 199.
Raikes, H. C., 236.
Railways opened, 177.
Raleigh, Sir W., 82, 85, 87.
Ralf Guader, 17.
Ramillies, battle of, 127.
Ramsbury, Bishopric of, 16.
Rangoon, 172.
Ratcliff, Charles, titular Earl of Derwentwater, 137.
Rates, book of, 85.
Rathmines, battle of, 101.
Ravaillac, 84.

Ravenspur, 53, 65.
Read, C. S., 214.
Reading, battle of, 7.
Reciprocity of Duties Bill, 173.
Red River Expedition, 210.
Redesdale, Robert of, 65.
—— John Mitford, Lord, 174.
Regimental Exchanges Act, 217.
Reform Bills (1832), 178, 179, 180, 304 ; (1867), 208, 210, 211, 305 ; (1884-5), 229, 230, 305.
—— Parliamentary (see Summary, p. 291).
Reformers (Scottish), 81.
Regency Bill, first, 141 ; second, 152, 153 ; third, 165.
Regent (George IV.), 165, 169.
Regicides, 107, 121.
Reginald, the Sub-prior, 29.
Regulating Act (Indian), 144, 145.
Regulation of the Forces Act, 225.
Relief defined (see Feudal dues).
Relief of Distress Acts (Ireland), 223.
Religious Tests Abolition Bill (Oxford and Cambridge), 212, 213 ; Dublin, 215.
Remonstrance, Grand, 94, 95.
Repeal of the Union, 177, 183, 189.
Republic, French, 154.
Retainers, 55.
Revenue Officers, 148.
Revolution (English), 119.
—— (French), first, 152 ; second, 176 ; third, 192 ; fourth, 210.
Rhé, Isle of, 89.
Rheims, 58.
Rhodes, Island of, 70, 146, 147.
Rich, Edmund, Archbishop, 35.
Richard I., 22, 25, 27, 29.
—— II., 34, 44, 49, 53, 63.
—— III., 50, 67, 69.
—— King of the Romans, 22, 34, 35, 36, 37.
Richelieu, Cardinal, 86.
Richmond, Charles Lennox, third Duke of, 142, 147, 148, 149, 150.
—— Charles Gordon-Lennox, fifth Duke of, 176, 183, 192.
—— Charles Gordon-Lennox, sixth Duke of (see March), 208, 213, 214, 230.
—— Henry of, 69 (see Henry VII.).
—— (United States), 206.
Richmont, Arthur of, 59.
Ridley, Nicolas, Bishop of London, 79.
Ridolphi Plot, 81.
Rigby, Richard, 142.
Right, Claim of, 118.
—— Declaration of, 119.
—— —— (Irish), 148.
Rights, Bill of, 120, 121.
Riot Act, 130, 131.
Riots, 169, 171, 175.
Ripon, Bishopric of, 72.
—— (see Goderich), 183.
—— De Grey and, G. F. S. Robinson, Earl, 202, 206.
—— Marquis of (see above), 210, 223, 232.
Ritchie, C. T., 230, 236.
Rivers, navigation of, 30.
—— Anthony Woodville Lord, 67 (see p. 64).
Rizzio, David, 80.

INDEX.

Robert, Duke of Normandy, 16. 17, 18, 19, 21.
— of Bellême, 17.
— of France, 20.
— of Jumiéges, 5.
— Mowbray, 17, 19.
— I., of Scotland, 42.
— II., — 42, 50.
— III., — 42, 50, 54.
Roberts, General Sir F., 222.
Robespierre, 156.
Robinson, Sir T., 138 (afterwards Lord Grantham).
— (Goderich, see Robinson and Ripon), 164, 173.
Rochefort, 167.
Rochelle, battle off, 49.
— siege of, 87, 88.
Roches, Peter des, 31, 33, 35.
Rochester, 16, 119.
— Lawrence Hyde, Earl of, 115, 117, 125.
Rochford, William Henry Nassau, Earl, 142.
Rockingham, Charles Watson-Wentworth, Marquis of, 140, 142, 143, 148, 149, 150.
— — 1st Ministry, 142.
— — 2nd Ministry, 148.
— Forest, 90.
— Whigs, 142.
Rodney, George Brydges, Lord, 147, 149.
Roebuck, John Arthur, 195.
Roger, of Breteuil, 17.
— of Shrewsbury, 19.
— of York, 25.
Rollo, 6, 8, 14.
Roman Catholics, 81, 83, 85; excluded from the House of Lords, 112, 113; from Irish Parliament, 120; disabilities, 123, 125, 146, 147 (see Summary, 286).
— (Irish), disfranchised, 132; enfranchised, 156.
— (Scottish), 157.
— Clergy, Endowment of, 173.
— Bishops, 195.
Romans, 3.
Rome, 72, 194, 210.
Romilly, Sir S., 169, 186.
Rooke, Sir George, 127.
Root and Branch Bill, 93.
Rorica, battle of, 163.
Rosbrach, battle of, 138.
Rose, Sir H. (Lord Strathnairn), 203.
Rosebery, Archibald Philip Primrose, Earl of, 222, 232.
Roses, Wars of, begun, 63 (see Summary, 280, 281).
Rossa, O'Donovan, 204, 211.
Rothschild, Lionel Nathan de, 193, 195.
Rouen, 57.
Roundaway Down, battle of, 97.
Rowton Heath, battle of, 99.
Roxburgh, 42.
Royal Marriage Act, 145.
— Warrant (Purchase), 213.
Rumbold, 115.
Rump Parliament, 107.
Runnymede, 31.

Rupert, Prince, 97, 99, 109.
Russell, Edward, 117, 121; Admiral, 123 (Orford).
— Lord, 77.
— Lord John (Earl), 171, 173, 175, 176, 179, 182, 184, 185, 186, 189, 192, 193, 195, 196, 197, 198, 199, 200, 202, 205, 207, 211, 221.
— 1st Ministry, 192.
— 2nd Ministry, 206.
— William, Lord, 115.
— Sir Charles, 232.
Russells, genealogy of, 114.
Russia, 146, 155, 186, 198, 199, 201, 210, 216, 218, 220, 224, 228, 231, 234.
— Katharine of, 146.
Rutland, Edward, Earl of, 53.
— John, Duke of, 138, 142.
— John Henry, — 192.
— John — (see Manners).
Ryder, see Harrowby, 164.
Rye-House Plot, 115.
Ryswick, Peace of, 122, 123.

SACHEVERELL, DR. HENRY, 128, 129.
Sackville, Lord George, afterwards Germain, and Viscount Sackville, 147
Sadleir, 194.
Sadowa, battle of, 206.
Saintonge, 22.
St. Albans, 31.
— Battle of (i.), 63 ; (ii.), 63.
— Bishopric of, 72.
St. Arnaud, Marshal, 198.
St. Bartholomew, Massacre of, 80.
St. Bernard, 22.
St. Eustatia, island of, 149.
St. Germain, treaty of, 80.
St. German's, Edward Granville Eliot, Earl of, 188, 192, 196, 198.
St. Giles' Fields, 53.
St. Helena, island of, 167.
St. John, Henry, 127, 129 (see Bolingbroke).
St. Juan, arbitration, 212.
St. Leonard's, Edward B. Sugden, Lord, 196.
St. Lucia, 166.
St. Paul's, reconciliation at, 63.
St. Peter's Field, meeting, 171.
St. Pol, Count of, 59.
St. Quentin, battle of, 79.
St. Ruth, General, 120.
St. Sebastian, 167.
St. Vincent, battle of, first, 147 ; second, 159.
— Cape, 123.
— Sir John Jervis, Earl, 160.
Saintes, battle of, 35.
Saladin Tithe, 27.
Salamanca, battle of, 166.
Salaries, official, 153.
Sale of Seats, 142.
Salisbury, 16, 72.
— Bishopric of, 19, 21, 41, 67, 105.
— Earldom of, 24.
— Margaret Pole, Countess of, 75.
— Richard Neville, Earl of (I.), 59.
— — (II.), 63.
— Robert Cecil, Earl of, 85.

311

INDEX.

Salisbury, Robert Cecil, Earl of, 111.
—— —— Marquis of (I.), 196, 202.
—— —— (II.), 214, 219, 221, 231, 235, 236.
—— —— 1st Ministry, 230.
—— —— 2nd Ministry, 234.
—— Roger, Bishop of, 21, 22.
—— William, Earl of, 31.
—— Oath, 18.
Sancroft, William, Archbishop, 117.
San Domingo, 105.
San Stephano, treaty of, 220.
Sandon, Viscount, 214, 215 (see Harrowby).
Sandwich, battle off, 33.
—— John Montagu, Earl of, 140, 141.
Sandys, Samuel (afterwards Lord), 132, 134, 135, 140.
Saracens, 26.
Saragossa, battle of, 129.
Saratoga, surrender of, 147.
Sardinia, 198, 202.
Savile, George, Marquis of Halifax (see Halifax).
—— Sir George, 142.
Savoy, Conference, 109.
—— Boniface of, Archbishop, 35.
—— Duke of, 105.
—— Peter of, 35.
Sawtre, W., 53.
Saxe-Coburg, Albert of, 187, 205, 213.
Say, James Fiennes, Lord, 61, 63.
Scarborough, 79.
Schism Act, 129, 131.
—— Great, 48, 54, 56, 57.
Sclater Booth, 214.
Schleswig, 206.
Schmalkald, League of, 72.
Schools (see Education).
—— National (Irish), 179.
Scinde, 188.
Scotland (see Summary, Part I., to 1290, p. 263; Part II., 1290-1603, p. 264; Part III., 1603-1707, p. 266; Part IV., 1707-1888, p. 268.
—— Allies with France, 40, 47, 57, 71.
—— Charles I. and, 90, 92.
—— Charles II. in, 100, 102, 103.
—— Connection with England, 9, 11, 19, 23, 25, 27, 41, 85, 127.
—— Elizabeth and, 81.
—— Episcopacy in, 84, 90, 108.
—— Homage done by kings of, 9, 13, 17, 19, 23, 31, 33.
—— Invaded by English, 41, 43, 45, 51, 53, 67, 75, 77.
—— Kings of, captured, 25, 47.
—— Reformation in, 80.
—— Revolution in, 118.
—— Succession, question of, 41.
—— Union with, 127.
Scots invade England, 19, 21, 25, 47, 51, 53, 69, 71, 93; help the Parliament, 97, 99.
Scottish Education Bill, 211.
Scrope, Richard, Archbishop, 55.
Scutage, 23, 30, 51.
Search, right of, 134, 135.
Seats, Parliamentary, sale of, 145.
Sebastopol, siege of, 199, 200.

Secession (Free Church of Scotland), 190, 191.
—— from Parliament, 79, 147, 159.
Secret Service Money, 141.
Secretary (for War), 160, 198, 212.
—— (at War), 157.
Security, Act of, 126.
Sedan, battle of, 210.
Sedgemoor, battle of, 117.
Seditious Meetings Acts, 159, 171.
Selborne (Roundell Palmer), Lord, afterwards Earl, 210, 222.
Selden, John, 87.
Self-denying Ordinance, 99.
Selsey, Bishopric of, 17.
Senlac, or Hastings, battle of, 17.
Separatists, 181.
Sepoys, 201.
Septennial Act, 131.
Seringapatam, 158.
Servian War, 216.
Settlement, Act of (English), 125.
—— (Irish), Cromwellian, 102; Charles II., 108, 118.
Seven Bishops, 117.
Seven Years' War begins, 138, 140.
Severus, 3.
Seville, peace of, 133.
Seymour, Lady J., 71, 75.
—— Edward, 113
—— Sir M., 200.
—— Thomas, Lord, of Sudeley, 77.
—— William, 85.
Shaftesbury, Antony Ashley-Cooper, first Earl, 109, 111, 115.
—— Antony, Lord Ashley, seventh Earl, 181.
Sharp, William, Archbishop, 112.
Shaw, William, 219.
Shelburne, Earl of, 142, 147, 148 (see Lansdowne), 150.
—— Ministry, 150.
Sherburne, Bishopric of, 16.
Shore Ali, 220.
Sheridan, T. B., 150, 152, 160.
Sheriffmuir, battle of, 131.
Ship Money, 91, 93.
Shire, knights of, 35.
Shirestone, battle of, 13.
Shirley's Case, 84, 85.
Shore, Sir John (afterwards Lord Teignmouth), 156.
Shovel, Sir C., 127.
Shrewsbury, 39, 95.
—— Battle of, 55.
—— Charles Talbot, Earl, then Duke of, 117, 118, 121, 129.
—— John Talbot, Earl of, 63.
—— Parliament of, 53.
Sibthorpe, Dr. Robert, 89.
—— Colonel Charles de L. W., 192.
Sicily, 27, 35, 39.
Sidmouth, Henry Addington, Viscount, 160, 161, 164, 165, 168, 171, 176.
—— Circular, 169.
Sidneys or Sydneys, genealogy of, 76.
Sidney, Algernon, 115, 117.
—— Henry, 117.
—— Sir Philip, 83

312

INDEX.

Sierra Leone, 152.
Sigebert, 5.
Sigismund, 50, 57.
Sikhs, 190.
Silesia, 134.
Silistria, siege of, 198.
Silk Duty, 163.
Simnel, Lambert, 69.
Simpson, General Sir J., 199.
Singapore, 168.
Sinking Fund, 152, 153.
Sinope, 196.
Sivajee the Mahratta, 112.
Siward, 5, 17.
Six Acts, 170, 171.
Sixtus v., 83.
Slave Trade, abolition of, 153, 155, 162, 163.
—— Circular, 217.
—— Ships, 153.
Slavery, abolition of, 181.
Slidell, 205.
Sliding Scale, Peel's, 189.
Sluys, battle of, 47.
Smith, Sir Sidney, 159.
—— Vernon, afterwards Lord Lyveden, 198.
—— W. H., 214, 230, 233, 234, 235, 236.
Smuggling, 151.
Smyrna Fleet, 123.
Smythe, George A., Viscount Strangford, 191.
Sobieski, John, 114.
Sobraon, battle of, 192.
Sodor and Man, Bishopric of, 72.
Solemn League and Covenant, 97, 108.
Solferino, battle of, 202.
Solway Moss, panic of, 75.
Somers, John, Lord, 123, 125, 127.
Somerset, Duke of, 129.
—— Beaufort Dukes (see genealogy of, p. 60).
—— Edmund Beaufort, Duke of, (I.), 61, 63.
—— Edmund Beaufort, Duke of, (II.), 60.
—— John Beaufort, Duke of, 61.
—— Edward Seymour, Duke of, 77.
—— Edward Adolphus Seymour, Duke of, 202, 206.
Sommerset's Case, 145.
Sophia of Hanover, 126, 128.
Soudan, 228, 229.
Soult, Marshal, 165, 167.
South Africa Bill, 219.
South American Republics, 173.
South Sea Scheme, 129, 131.
Southampton, 47.
Southwold Bay, battle of, 111.
Spa Field Riots, 169.
Spain, Treaties with, 85, 98.
—— Wars with, 83, 87, 105, 141, 147, 159, 161.
—— Revolution in, 170; French invasion of, 172.
Spanish Marriages, 192.
—— Succession (genealogy), 123.
Spencer, George John, Earl, 160.
—— John Poyntz, Earl, 210, 222, 226, 232.
—— Earl (see Althorp), 183.
—— Lord Charles, 150.
Spitalfield weavers, 173.
Spithead, mutiny at, 159.
Spooner, Richard, 192.

Spring Rice, 176, 182, 188.
Spurs, battle of, 71.
Stafford, 9.
—— Conspiracy, 79.
—— Edward, Duke of Buckingham, 66, 71.
—— Family, genealogy of, 66.
—— Henry, Duke of Buckingham, 66, 67.
—— William, Viscount, 76, 115.
Stamford, 8, 9, 43.
—— Bridge, battle of, 15.
Stamp Act, 140, 141, 143.
—— Duty on newspapers, 129, 185, 199.
Stanhope, James, General, 127, 130, 131.
—— Edward, 214, 230, 234, 236.
—— Philip Henry, Earl, 192.
Stanley Edward Geoffrey (Mr. and Lord), 174, 176, 183, 188, 189, 191, 192, 193, 195, 198 (see Derby, I.)
—— Edward Henry, Lord, 196, 202, 203, 208 (see Derby, II.).
—— Frederick (Lord Stanley, of Preston), 214, 221, 230, 236.
—— Edward J., Lord of Alderley, 202, 206.
—— Sir W., 69.
Stansfeld, James, 206, 232.
Star Chamber, 69, 91, 93.
States-General (French), 86, 152.
Statutes, Form of, 65, 236.
Steinkirk, battle of, 121.
Stephen of Blois, 16; reign of, 21-23.
Stephens, James, 204.
Stewart, Sir Herbert, 229.
Stigand, Archbishop, 15, 17.
Stirling, 42, 102.
Stockdale's, John, Trial, 155.
—— John Joseph, case, 189.
Stoke, battle of, 69.
Stoney-Stratford, 67.
Strafford, Thomas, Earl of (Wentworth), 89, 90, 91, 92, 93.
Strasbourg, 114.
Stratford, John, Archbishop, 47.
—— Robert, 47.
Strathclyde, 3, 9.
Straw, Jack, 56.
Strickland's case, 81.
Strode, William, 95.
Stuart, Arabella, 85.
—— Family, genealogy of, 42, 80, 116.
—— Henry, Lord Darnley, 80.
—— Sir John, General, 163.
—— Walter, 42.
Sturges-Bourne, William, 174.
Subsidy defined, 86.
Succession Act (i.), 75; (ii.), 124.
Sudbury, Simon of, Archbishop, 51.
Suetonius Paullinus, 3.
Suez Canal, 210, 217.
Suffolk, 45.
—— Charles Brandon, Duke of, 76.
—— De la Pole, Dukes of, genealogy of, 68.
—— Greys, Dukes of, genealogy of, 76.
—— Henry Grey, Duke of, 76, 79.
Sugar Duty Bill, 189.
Sullivan, T. D., 239.

INDEX.

Sunderland, Robert Spencer, Earl of, 113, 115, 117, 118.
—— Charles Spencer, Earl of, 127, 130, 131.
—— Family, genealogy of, 122.
Supremacy, Act of, 74, 75, 78, 81.
—— Royal, defined, 80.
Supreme Court of Judicature Act, 214, 215 (see Summary, 273).
Surajah Dowlah, 138.
Surrey (Howards), genealogy of, 76.
—— Henry Howard, Earl of, 76, 77.
—— Bernard Howard, Earl of, 150.
—— Thomas Howard, Earl of, 76.
Sussex, Kingdom of, 3, 5.
Suwarrow, Marshal, 154.
Sweden, 10, 109, 146.
Sweyn (I.), 11, 12; (II.), 13.
Swynford, Katharine, 51.
Sydenham, Charles Powlett-Thomson, Lord, 182.
Sydney, 152.
—— Thomas Townshend, Viscount, 150, 155.
Sydneys, or Sidneys, genealogy of, 76.

Taous, 175.
Taillebourg, battle of, 35.
Talavera, battle of, 165.
Talbot, Sir J., 59, 63 (Earl of Shrewsbury).
Talents, Ministry of, 161.
Tallage, 28, 47.
Tallard, Marshal, 127.
Talmash, Thomas, General, 123.
Tamworth, 9.
—— Manifesto, 183.
Tariff, Peel's reduction of, 191.
Taunton, 117.
Taxation, 41, 48, 49, 53, 55, 95.
—— Control of, 46 (see Parliamentary Summary, 249-251).
Taylor, Thomas Edward, Colonel, 208.
Tea Tax (American), 143.
—— (English), 205, 207.
Tees, River, 17.
Teignmouth, 121.
Tel-el-Kebir, battle of, 227.
Templars, Knights, 43.
Temple, Richard, Earl (I.), 138, 142, 143.
—— —— (II.), 150, 151, 160.
—— Sir W., 113.
Temple's, Sir W., Scheme, 112.
Tenants' Right Bill, Crawford's, 194.
Test Act, 111, 117, 121, 126, 133, 153, 175.
Tewkesbury battle of, 55.
Thame, 95.
Thelwall, John, 157.
Theodore, Archbishop, 5.
—— King, 209.
Thessaly, 222.
Thetford, Bishopric of, 16.
Thirty Years' War, 84, 100.
Thistlewood, Arthur, 171.
Thorpe, Speaker, 63.
Three-cornered Constituencies, 209.
Thurkill, 13.
Thurlow, Edward, Lord, 147, 148, 150, 155.
Ticonderoga, 138, 145.
Tient-Tsin, treaty of, 203.

Tierney, George, 163, 174.
Tilly, General, 88.
Tilsit, treaty of, 162.
Times, The, 237.
Timour, 52.
Tipperary, Election, 211.
Tippermuir, battle of, 96.
Tippoo Sahib, 148, 154, 158.
Tithes Commutation Act, 184, 185.
—— (Irish), 179, 181.
Tobago, 166.
Toleration Act, 119.
—— Irish, 130.
Tonnage and Poundage, 48, 49, 86, 87, 93, 95, 107, 127.
Tooke, Horne, 157.
Torbay, 119.
Torgau, battle of, 138.
Tories, 113 (see Conservatives).
Torres Vedras, 165.
Torrington, Earl of (Herbert), 126.
Torture, use, 65.
Tostig, 15.
Toulon, 157.
—— battle off, 135.
Toulouse, 23.
—— battle of, 167.
Touraine, 22, 27.
Towns, 28.
Townsend, Alderman, 142.
Townshend, Charles (I.), 138, 142, 143.
—— —— (II.), 150.
—— Thomas, 150 (Viscount Sydney).
—— Charles second Viscount, 130, 131, 132, 133.
—— George, fourth Viscount, 150.
Towton, battle of, 65.
Tractarians, 180, 181.
Trades Unions, 183.
—— Unionism at Sheffield, 209.
Trafalgar, battle of, 161.
—— Square Riots, 233, 239.
Traitorous Correspondence Act, 157.
Transvaal, 204, 222; annexed, 218; surrendered, 224; 228.
Treason Acts, 48, 49, 77.
—— Trials, 77, 122, 123.
Treasonable Practices Act, 159.
Treason-Felony Act, 193.
Trent, Council of, 76.
Trent, Affair of the, 205.
Trevelyan, Sir G., 215, 219, 222, 226, 232, 233, 235.
Trichinopoly, 136.
Triennial Act (i.), 92, 93. 108, 109; (ii.), 123.
Triers, Board of, 105.
Trincomalee, 150.
Trinidad, 160.
Triple Alliance (i.), 108. 109; (ii.), 131.
Triplow Heath, 101.
Troyes, treaty of, 57.
Tromp, Van, 103.
Troppau, Congress of, 170.
Truro, Bishopric of, 72.
Tudela, battle of, 162.
Tudors, genealogy of, 70.
Tudor, Jasper, Earl of Pembroke. 63.

INDEX.

Tudor, Henry (Henry VII.), 67.
—— Margaret, 71.
—— Mary (I.), 71.
—— Mary (II.), see Mary, Queen.
Tuilleries, 154.
Tunis, 224.
Turin, battle of, 126.
Turks, Ottoman, 61, 70.
Turnham Green, 95.
Tutbury, 81.
Tyler, Wat, 51.
Tyrconnel, Richard Talbot, Earl of, 117, 118.
Tyrone, O'Neal, Earl of, 83.

ULM, 160.
Ulster, 84.
Ulundi, battle of, 220.
"Undertakers," 86.
Uniformity, Act of (i.), 77 ; (ii.), 81 ; (iii.), 108, 109.
Union of England and Wales, 39, 75.
—— Scotland, 85, 105, 125, 126, 127.
—— Ireland, 158, 159.
—— Repeal of, 177, 183, 189.
Unitarians, 167.
United Irishmen, 150, 156.
United Irishman, 192.
United States (see American Colonies), 146, 147.
—— War with, 164, 165, 167.
Universities, 73.
—— Tests Bill, 211, 213.
Urban VI., 48.
"Urgency" resolution, 225.
Ushant, battle off, (i.), 137 ; (ii.), 147.
Utrecht, treaty of, 128, 129.
Uxbridge, negotiations at, 98, 99.

VAGRANCY, 77.
Valence, William of (I.), 35.
—— William of (II.), 35, 37.
Valmy, battle of, 154.
Valois, Charles of, 20, 46.
—— Philip of, 46, 48.
—— Genealogy of house of, 46.
Van Arteveld, Jacques, 46.
Van Diemen's land, 194.
Vane, Sir Henry, 105, 109.
Vansittart, Nicolas, 164, 173 (afterwards Lord Bexley).
Van Tromp, 103.
Varennes, 154.
Varna, 174, 199.
Vasco da Gama, 70.
Vaudois, 105, 114.
Vellore, mutiny, at, 160.
Venables, General Richard, 105.
Vendôme, Marshal, 127.
Venner's Plot, 107.
Verneuil, battle of, 59.
Verona, Congress of, 170.
Versailles, treaty of, 150, 151.
Vervins, treaty of, 82.
Vicksburg (U. S.), 206.
Victor IV., 22.
—— Emmanuel, 203.

Victor, Marshal, 165.
Victoria, 169, 187, 195.
—— (Colony), 194.
Vienna, 114.
—— Treaty of (i.), 133 ; (ii.), 133.
—— Congress of, 167.
—— Conference, 196, 197, 198.
Vigo Bay, battle of, 125.
Villafranca, treaty of, 202.
Villars, Marshal, 127.
Villeins, 23.
Villenage, 51.
Villeneuve, Admiral, 160.
Villeroi, Marshal, 127.
Villiers, George, Duke of Buckingham (I.), 87, 89.
—— George, Duke of Buckingham (II.), 109.
—— Charles Pelham, 187, 189, 202, 06.
Viniero, battle of, 113.
Vinegar Hill, battle of, 158.
Virginia, 84.
Visitation, Ecclesiastical, of Edward VI., 77.
Vittoria, battle of, 167.
Volunteers (English), 161, 203.
—— (Irish), 146.
Vowell's Plot, 105.

WAGRAM, battle of, 162.
Wakefield, battle of, 63.
Walcheren, island of, 165.
Waleran, Count, 21.
Wales, Prince of (see Llewelyn).
—— 17, 19, 23, 25, 31, 35, 45, 55, 75, 93, 101.
—— Statute of, 39.
—— Union with England, 75.
Wallace, W., 40, 41, 43.
Wallenstein, 90.
Waller, Sir W., 97, 99.
—— Sir Edmund, 97.
Wallingford, 23.
Walpole, Sir Robert, 127, 129, 130, 131 132 133, 135 (afterwards Earl of Orford).
Walpole's Ministry, 132.
—— S. H., 196, 202, 203, 208.
Walsingham, Sir Francis, 83.
Walter, Hubert, Archbishop, 29.
Waltheof, 17, 18, 23.
Walworth, William, 49.
Wandewash, battle of, 138.
War, Secretary for, 157, 160, 198, 212.
Warbeck, Perkin, 69, 71.
Ward, 183.
Wareunne, John, Earl of, 40.
—— Genealogy of, 52.
Warren, Sir Charles, 228.
Warrington, battle of, 101.
Warwick, Grey, Earl of, 43.
—— Thomas Beauchamp, Earl of, 51, 53.
—— Richard Neville, Earl of, 63, 65.
—— Edward Plantagenet, Earl of, 71.
—— Earldom of, 24.
Washington, 167.
—— Treaty of (Ashburton's), 188.
—— (Alabama), 213.
—— George, 144.
Watch and Ward, 35.
Waterford, 121.

Y

INDEX.

Waterloo, 127.
—— Battle of, 167.
Waterworks (London) Bill, 223.
Watling Street, 7.
Webster, Sir R., 230, 236.
Wedderburn, Alexander, 145, 157 (Loughborough).
Wedmore, treaty of, 6.
Wellesley, Sir Arthur, 160, 162, 165 (see Wellington).
—— Richard Colley Wellesley, Marquis of (Mornington), 158, 164, 165, 171, 182.
Wellington, Viscount and Duke of, 165, 167, 174, 175, 177, 181, 182, 183, 188, 197.
—— Ministry, 174.
Wells, Bishopric of, 16.
Welsh, 3, 9, 15, 33, 39.
Wenceslas, 52.
Wensleydale, Baron, James Parke, 201.
Wentworth, Sir T., 89, 90, 91 (Strafford).
—— Paul, 81.
—— Peter, 83.
Wesley, Charles, 133.
—— John, 133, 135.
Wessex, 3, 5, 7, 13, 15.
West Indies, 109.
Westbury, Richard Bethel, Lord, 207.
Western Counties, revolt of, 77.
Westminster, 15, 65.
—— Assembly, 98, 99.
—— Bishopric of, 72.
—— Courts fixed at, 30, 43.
—— Election, 153.
—— Provisions of, 36, 37.
—— Statute of, 38, 39.
Westmoreland, Charles Neville, Earl of, 81.
—— John Fane, Earl of, 160, 162.
Weston, Richard, Lord (afterwards Earl of Portland), 90.
Westphalia, peace of, 100.
Wexford, 103.
Weymouth, 65, 180.
—— Thomas Thynne, Viscount (afterwards Marquis of Bath), 142.
Wharncliffe, James Archibald Stuart-Wortley, Lord, 179, 182, 188.
Wharton, Philip, Lord, 111.
—— Thomas, Lord (afterwards Marquis), 123.
Whigs (see Liberals), 113.
Whitby, 5.
Whitfield, George, 133.
Whitelocke, John, General, 163.
Whitgift, John, Archbishop, 83, 85.
Whithern, Bishopric of, 16.
Wickliffe, or Wycliffe, John, 49, 51.
Wigan, battle of, 101.
Wight, Isle of, 101.
Wilberforce, William, 154, 161, 162.
Wilderness (U. S.), battle of, 206.
Wilfrid, Bishop, 5.
Wilkes, J., 141, 143, 145, 147.
—— Captain, 205.
William I., 12, 14, 15, 16, 17-19 : genealogy of, 14.
—— II., 16, 19.
—— III., 110, 113, 116, 117, 119-125 (see p. 82).

William IV., 174, 175-185.
—— I., of Prussia, 204.
—— Clito, 21.
—— Fitz-Osbern, 17.
—— of Valence (I.), 35.
—— of Valence (II.), 35, 37.
—— Son of Henry I., 16, 21.
—— the Lion, 18, 24, 25, 27, 30, 40.
—— Fort, 120.
Williams, General Sir W. F., 201.
—— John, Archbishop, 91.
Wilmington, Sir Spencer Compton, Earl of, 135.
—— Ministry, 134.
Wilson, Sir Charles, 231.
Wilton, battle of, 7.
Winceby, battle of, 27.
Winchelsea, Archbishop, 41, 43.
Winchelsea and Nottingham, Daniel Finch, Earl of, 134, 142.
—— —— George William Finch-Hatton, Earl of, 176.
Winchester, 7, 16, 23, 33.
—— Statute of, 39.
Windham, 152, 156, 157, 160.
Window Tax, 195.
Windsor, 99.
Winterbotham, Henry Selfe Page, 210.
Winwidfield, battle of, 3.
Wishart, George, 43.
Witenagemot, 5, 13, 17 (see Parliamentary Summary, 249).
Witham, 9.
Wittenberg, 70.
Wodehouse, John (see Earl of Kimberley), 202, 206.
Woodvilles, genealogy of, 64 (see Rivers, 67).
—— Elizabeth, 65.
Wolfe, General James, 139.
Wolseley, Colonel, 118.
—— Garnet Joseph, Viscount, 227.
Wolsey, Thomas, Cardinal, 71, 73.
Wolverton, G. G. Glynn, Lord, 222, 232.
Wood, Sir C., afterwards Viscount Halifax, 192, 196, 198, 202, 206.
Wood's Halfpence, 132.
Wool, 41, 49.
Worcester, 95, 97.
—— Battle of, 103.
—— Bishopric of, 16.
Workmen's Combinations, 172, 173.
Worms, Baron Henry de, 236.
—— Concordat of, 20.
—— Treaty of, 134.
Wörth, battle of, 210.
Wulfhere, 4.
Wyatt, Sir T., 79.
Wykeham, William of, 49.
Wynn, Charles, 170, 176.
—— Sir Watkin, 170.

Yakoob Khan, 220.
York, 7, 9, 16, 17, 81, 95, 97.
—— Genealogy of the House of, 50.
—— Edmund, Duke of, 44, 50.
—— Edward, Duke of (Rutland), 50, 57.
—— Elizabeth of, 50, 69, 71.

316

INDEX.

York, Frederick, Duke of, 157, 158, 163, 173, 175.
—— New, 108, 147.
—— Richard, Duke of (I.), 50, 57, 60, 61, 63.
—— Richard, Duke of (II.), 50, 67.
Yorke, Charles (I.), 143.
—— —— (II.), 160.
Yorkshire, 81, 97, 170, 173.
—— Petition, 147.

Yorktown, surrender at, 149.
"Young England" Party, 191.
"Young Ireland" Party, 192.
Young, G. F., 192.
—— Sir J., afterwards Lord Lisgar, 198.

ZOLLVEREIN, 180.
Zorndorf, battle of, 138.
Zulu War, 220.
Zutphen, battle of, 83.

SUPPLEMENTARY INDEX FROM 1888-1890.

AFRICA, 229a.
Ashbourne Act, 229.

BALFOUR, A. J., 229b.
Bayard, 227l.
Bismarck, 229a.
Boulanger, General, 229a.
Brazil, 229a.

CHAMBERLAIN, J., 227l.
Channel Tunnel, 227m.
Chief Constables, 227m, 228.
Children, Protection of, Act, 229b.
County Councils, 227m, 228, 229.

DELAGOA BAY, 228.
Dillon, J., 229b.
Dock Labourers, Strike of, 229b.
Drainage Act (Ireland), 229.

EDUCATION CODE, 229b.
Evictions, 227m.

FREDERICK III. of Germany, 227l.

GEFCKEN, 228.
Germany, 227b.
Gladstone, W. E., 229, 229b.
Goschen, 227m, 229b.
Grenfell, General, 229a.

HARRISON, General, 228.
Heligoland, 229a.
Housing of Working Classes Amendment Act, 229b.

LABOUCHERE, H., 229.
Land Purchase Bill, Irish, 227l, 229, 229b, 229d.
Lansdowne, Marquess of, 227l.
Licensing Clauses, 227m.
Light Railways Act (Ireland), 229, 229b.

Local Government (England and Wales) Act, 227m, 228.
Local Government Act (Scottish), 229.
Local Taxation, 229b.
Loughrea, 227m.

M'CARTHY, Justin, 229d.
Morley, J., 229.

NATIONAL DEBT, 227m, 229.
Naval Defence Bill, 229.
New Guinea, 228.
New South Wales, 227l.

O'BRIEN, W., 227m, 229b.
Onslow, Earl of, 227l.

PARNELL, 227m, 229b, 229d.
Pigott, Richard, 229.
Police Act, 229b.
Procedure, Parliamentary, 227m.

ROYAL GRANTS, 229.

SMITH, W. H., 227m.
South African Company (British), 229b.
Suakim, 228.
Sugar Bounties, 227l.

Times Newspaper, 229.
Tithes Bill, 229b.
Tupper, Sir C., 227l.

UNITED STATES, 227l.

WAD-EL-NJUMI, battle of, 229a.
Wales, Prince of, 229.
West Australia, 229a.
Wexford, 227m.
William I. of Germany, 227l.
William II. of Germany, 227l.
Worms, Baron de, 227l.

317

www.ingramcontent.com/pod-product-compliance
Lightning Source LLC
Chambersburg PA
CBHW031432230426
43668CB00007B/500